Encyclopedia of Social Work with Groups

What do you have to know today to be an effective group worker, and what are the different group work approaches? With 109 entries, this book provides a comprehensive overview of social work with groups, from its initial development to its astounding range of diverse practice today with many populations in different places.

The articles have been written by social workers trained in the group approach from the United States, Canada, the United Kingdom, Australia, Spain, and Japan, and all involved are well known group workers, acknowledged as experts in the area. The book covers all aspects of social work with groups, including its history, values, major models, approaches and methods, education, research, journals, phases of development, working with specific populations and ages, plus many more. Each article includes references which can be a major resource for future exploration in the particular subject area.

Both editors have many years of productive work in group work practice and other areas, and are board members of The Association for the Advancement of Social Work with Groups. The *Encyclopedia of Social Work with Groups* will be of interest to students, practitioners, social work faculty, and novice and experienced group workers.

Alex Gitterman is the Zachs Professor of Social Work and Director of the Doctoral Program at the University of Connecticut School of Social Work, USA.

Robert Salmon is a Professor at Hunter College School of Social Work, USA.

Encyclopedia of Social Work with Groups

Edited by
Alex Gitterman
and
Robert Salmon

 Routledge
Taylor & Francis Group
NEW YORK AND LONDON

First published 2009
by Routledge
711 Third Ave, New York, NY 10017

Simultaneously published in the UK
by Routledge
2 Park Square, Milton Park, Abingdon, Oxon OX14 4RN

Routledge is an imprint of the Taylor & Francis Group, an informa business

Transferred to Digital Printing 2009

Typeset in Baskerville by
Book Now Ltd, London

Library of Congress Cataloging-in-Publication Data
Encyclopedia of social work with groups/edited by Alex Gitterman and
Robert Salmon.
    p. cm.
1. Social group work—Encyclopedias. I. Gitterman, Alex, 1938–
II. Salmon, Robert, 1930–
HV45.E53 2009
361.403—dc22   2008019157

ISBN10: 0–7890–3636–3 (hbk)
ISBN10: 0–7890–3637–1 (pbk)

ISBN13: 978–0–7890–3636–0 (hbk)
ISBN13: 978–0–7890–3637–7 (pbk)

Contents

Group Work Values

Group Work Major Models

Group Work Approaches and Methods

Group Stages of Development

Group Work Phases of Helping

Group Work Education

Group Work Research

Group Work with Specific Populations

Group Work Over the Life Course

Group Work and Community Context

Group Work and Organizational Context

Group Work Leadership

Group Work and Technology

Preface

Bill Cohen, the publisher of Haworth Press, invited the Association for the Advancement of Social Work with Groups (AASWG) to edit an encyclopedia. The Executive Committee and the Board of Directors of AASWG periodically discussed the concept of an *Encyclopedia of Social Work with Groups* over a time period that extended into years. This would be a new kind of endeavor—a first— and it would require a significant commitment of time and effort for the editor or editors who agreed to take on the task. A substantial publishing history also was seen as an important requirement for the editor(s). Recruitment was difficult. In fact, the last four Association presidents, Alex Gitterman, Toby Berman-Rossi, Nancy Sullivan, and Paul Abels were unable to recruit editors. Professors Salmon and Gitterman were invited on numerous occasions, but they declined. However, about 2 years ago, Bob Salmon proclaimed that he would be willing to serve as editor, but only if Alex Gitterman also agreed to serve in the same capacity. For Alex, a long-time friend of Bob's, this was an invitation too difficult to refuse. So the journey began!

Our first task was to develop a clear understanding of functions and roles with the Association's Executive Committee and Board of Directors. We reached an agreement that while the *Encyclopedia* would represent collaboration between the Association and the editors, as editors we would have total independence and autonomy over the project. During the time of the project, one of us would serve as an ex officio Board member to keep members informed of our progress. This arrangement has worked extremely well. We thank Board and Executive Committee members for their generous support.

Our next task was to recruit an internationally prestigious editorial board. We knew those we invited would have very busy schedules, and were unsure about their responses. To our great pleasure, our invitations were met with enthusiasm rather than hesitation. The editorial board members provided us with thoughtful advice throughout the life of this project. We express our appreciation to Paul Abels, Mark Doel, Maeda Galinsky, Charles Garvin, Lorraine Gutiérrez, Timothy Kelly, Carolyn Knight, Mark Macgowan, Andrew Malekoff, Ellen Sue Mesbur, Lawrence Shulman, Dominique Moyse Steinberg, Ronald Toseland, Peter Vaughn, and Phyllis Ivory Vroom.

With an editorial board in place, we turned our attention to the process of obtaining entries for the *Encyclopedia*. In the long-established group work tradition of membership participation, we decided that social workers working with groups should have the opportunity to contribute rather than have us select the contributors. To this end, we placed a call for abstracts on numerous list serves and newsletters, and sent emails to numerous institutions. We sought to encourage practitioners and administrators to publish, as well as colleagues outside the borders of the United States. We are pleased that more than 35 practitioners and administrators contributed to the *Encyclopedia*. We are also extremely pleased that we have three contributors from Australia, six from Canada, six from the United Kingdom, one from Japan and two from Spain. Most of the 109 entries are approximately 1,000 words, but a few historical and specialized entries are longer (about 2,500 words). We express our deep appreciation to the contributors—for their willingness to rewrite their entries, and for their responsiveness to our follow-up queries, and for their investment in, and commitment to, this project.

Editing the entries and "chasing" the contributors was a daunting task. On a few occasions we wondered what we had got ourselves into. However, time passed, we continued to edit and "chase," and to our amazement the day arrived when all remaining entries were submitted. The final task was to organize the entries. Since encyclopedias usually are presented in alphabetical order, we began with the simple logic of arranging by alphabet. We were unhappy with this format and sought feedback from the editorial board. Members encouraged us to emphasize substance over order, and common sense over precedence. Consequently, we arranged our entries in the following manner: Group Work History: Past, Present and Future; Group Work Values; Group Work Major Models; Group Work Approaches and Methods; Group Work Stages of Development; Group Work Phases of Helping; Group Work Education; Group Work Research; Group Work Journals; Group Work in Fields of Practice; Group Work with Specific Populations; Group Work Over the Life Course; Group Work and Community Context; Group Work and Organizational Context; Group Work Leadership; and Group Work and Technology.

Retrospectively, editing the *Encyclopedia* was extremely time consuming. So, we would like to thank each other. For both of us, this project was a labor of love. Our practice, supervisory, administrative, consultative and educational careers have been enriched by our exposure to the group work modality. The *Encyclopedia* provides us with the opportunity to demonstrate our appreciation to our historical mentors, our teachers, our colleagues, and our students. We hope the *Encyclopedia* enhances the practice of social work with groups as the torch is passed on to our younger colleagues.

A. G.
B. S.

Introduction

This volume, the first *Encyclopedia of Social Work with Groups*, includes entries that describe the extraordinary complexity, diversity and particular usefulness of social group work theory, practice, and research within historical, philosophical, and societal contexts. The implicit foundation for all of the work presented in this volume is that social group work, throughout its history, practice, and structure, has been an optimistic and positive way of working with people. Group work affirms people's strengths and emphasizes, "the contribution that each person can make to others' lives ... in today's troubled world effective group work is needed more than ever" (Kurland & Salmon, 1998, p. 1).

Throughout the 1970s, and continuing to the present, schools of social work in the United States have been required to prepare students for generalist practice in the foundation year. With the shift in educational emphasis, most MSW students appeared to be graduating without an adequate understanding of group work practice. Many graduate students did not have an opportunity to take group work courses or gain experience in working with groups. The knowledge and teaching of effective group work practice was on the wane. In 1963, 76% of graduate schools had a group work concentration, but, by 2000, less than 5% of the graduate schools offered a one (Birnbaum & Wayne, 2000). Similarly, while in early the 1990s only 19% of graduate schools required a group work course, less than half of the graduate schools offered a group work elective, and only 15 % of the students registered for a group work elective (Birnbaum & Auerbach, 1994). These survey findings also demonstrated students' lack of familiarity with basic group work concepts about group formation, mutual aid, and stages of group development.

The concern about the diminution of group work in the curriculum, and the quality of group work practice in the field led to two crucial events in the late 1970s. The first was the creation in 1978 of the journal, *Social Work with Groups*, which provided a forum for those interested in group work to share, discuss, and develop their experience, findings, and ideas. The second was the 1979 creation of the Association for the Advancement of Social Work with Groups (AASWG), an organization committed to furthering group work within the profession.

The initial activity of AASWG was the sponsorship of a 1979 symposium on group work in Cleveland, Ohio. It was a great success and testimony to the ongoing professional interest of those social workers from around the world to explore group work's past, present, and future. Since then, a symposium has been held each year in sites in the United States, Canada and Germany.

The publication of this encyclopedia demonstrates the viability of group work practice. Robert Salmon and Alex Gitterman agreed to be its editors and a call for entries were sent to all AASWG members. The response was beyond all expectations. Proposals were submitted and accepted from group workers in the United States, Canada, the United Kingdom, Australia, Japan, and Spain. The completed entries arrived quickly and they are presented in this volume. They are written with clarity and passion, and the range is astonishing. Group workers seem to be everywhere, doing important, useful and creative work. While there are, inevitably, some gaps in this first encyclopedia, we are sure that the comprehensiveness, scholarliness, and passion of the authors for their group work practice will be of enormous use to the readers and to the profession.

References

Birnbaum, M. L., & Auerbach, C. (1994). Group work in graduate social work education: The price of neglect. *Journal of Social Work Education, 30*(3), 325–335.

Birnbaum, M. L., & Wayne, J. (2000). Group work in foundation generalist education: The necessity for curriculum change. *Journal of Social Work Education, 36*(2), 347–356.

Kurland, R., & Salmon, R. (1998). Teaching a methods course in social work with groups. Alexandria, VA: Council on Social Work Education.

Group Work History

Past, Present, and Future

Canada

Nancy E. Sullivan, Ellen Sue Mesbur, and Norma C. Lang

The establishment of agencies and the evolution of social group work, while not synonymous, grew up entwined with one another. The origins of group work in Canada lie in two social phenomena of the late 19th and early 20th centuries: the Social Gospel movement and the settlement movement.

The *Social Gospel movement*, with strong roots in the Canadian Prairie Provinces, brought together religious and social ideals to form a collectivist approach to understanding the causes of social problems and an embracing of social justice through social action. Based on Social Gospel philosophy and purposes, the *settlement movement*, which began in the United Kingdom in the 1870s as a response to the dramatic and dire effects of the Industrial Revolution, spread to Canada by the early 1900s. It provided personal and community assistance to people in need, and as a vehicle for social action to address the new realities of industrialization: migration to cities, harsh and dangerous working conditions, health-threatening community environments, poverty, and fractured family and community life. Settlement house workers participated alongside fellow community members, in contrast to the top-down approach of conventional charity (James, 2001).

Rooted in religious beliefs and practices, but established under both religious and secular auspices, settlement houses began appearing in Canadian cities. The first of these, Evangelia House in Toronto in 1902, was an undertaking between Sara Libby Carson and Mary Lawson Bell and the Dominion Council of the YWCA. In 1907, All People's Mission was established in Winnipeg by J. S. Woodsworth. In 1911, the Presbyterian Church set up a chain of settlement houses under the supervision of Sara Libby Carson, co-founder of Georgina House. These included St. Christopher House in Toronto in 1912, Chalmers House in Montreal in 1912, Robertson Memorial House in Winnipeg in 1913, St. Columba House in Point St. Charles in Montreal in 1917, Vancouver Community House in Vancouver in 1918, and Neighbourhood House in Hamilton in 1922.

The Roman Catholic Church had been active in social service provision prior to the settlement movement. In Toronto, its focus on social issues was formally affirmed in 1913 by Archbishop Neil McNeil, who, in 1922, commissioned a survey of social welfare to be conducted by Dr. John Lapp from the National Catholic Welfare Council, Washington, DC. The resulting report placed special emphasis on the existence of poverty and its prevention using group activities, in particular those targeting families and children (Lapp, 1922). Lapp strongly suggested that Catholic Charities establish organizations and group activities to keep children and adolescents from "delinquency". In response, Catholic Charities expanded its commitment to group work activities, especially in the areas of family and children's services. The Roman Catholic legacy of social group work exists in the present day in the work done by Catholic Family Services, established in 1922.

Some settlement houses, which were established as secular organizations, considered social advocacy to be central to their mission. Two major Toronto examples are the University Settlement House (USH), established by the University of Toronto, and Central Neighbourhood House (CNH), both established in 1911. These and other secular organizations introduced social activism into the work of the settlement movement, which acknowledged people as members of social groups differentiated according to social, economic, and/or political conditions, largely responsible for determining their quality of life. It followed that the means of intervention and social change would be a group work modality, in the belief that those affected should be involved together in the reform efforts (Breton, 1990). In fact, a central tenet of Canada's early settlement houses was to provide a democratic meeting place and social centre for their respective neighbourhoods (CNH; USH). Case conferences on relief services, held at various settlement houses in Toronto, led in 1913 to the organization of the Neighbourhood Workers' Association (now the Family Services Association), an early social work agency. Through camps, clubs, language classes, lessons in cooking and sewing, as well as workshops on citizenship and the democratic method, attendees had opportunities to develop morally, socially, and economically through group participation (CNH; USH; StC; Georgina). This movement thereby laid a strong foundation for social group work practice into the 1930s.

In Nova Scotia, the Halifax Explosion of 1917 (when the city of Halifax was devasted by the huge detonation of a French cargo ship) provided the impetus for the emerging profession of social work. The massive importation of relief workers offered social workers from across North America an opportunity to establish social work services based upon new ideas of society. The work of the Rehabilitation Committee included group services, notably in the area of children's services (Boyd, 2007).

In response to the stream of immigrants from Eastern Europe toward the end of and following World War I, the Federation of Jewish Philanthropies (FJP) was founded in Toronto in 1917. Its first annual report lists several group work organizations, including the Jewish Orphan's Home, Jewish Girl's Club, the Jr. Council of Jewish Women, the Big Brother Movement, and a Maternity and Sewing Circle (FJP, 1918). Samuel B. Kaufman, an experienced social worker from Indianapolis, was imported to be the organization's head in 1921, as part of the organization's deliberate attempt to replace its predominantly volunteer base with trained and professional social workers (Speisman, 1979).

In 1938, the United Jewish Welfare Fund (UJWF) replaced the FJP, with a scope broadened to encompass aid for immigrant and refugee families fleeing Europe. In 1948 the United Jewish Appeal, was created coinciding with increased professionalization of Jewish social services. Throughout its history, Jewish social work in Canada has included many group-focused services, with special emphasis on aid for immigrant families.

The period between the 1930s and the 1950s reflected settlement movement concepts in social group work services in a myriad of settings: community centres, Jewish Community Centres, Girls' and Boys' Clubs, YW and YMCAs, Hebrew Associations Girl Guides and Boy Scouts, church youth groups, and in the camping movement, the co-op movement, *animation sociale* in Québec, and in community development work. Democratic group forms and democratic processes, that is, a social goals approach (Papell & Rothman, 1966), were regarded as essential to individual fulfilment and vital to a participatory citizenry. Impacted greatly by the Great Depression of the 1930s and later by World War II (1939–1945), the Canadian social welfare system developed national responses to socioeconomic problems. With the view of social services as a necessity, much social work shifted from mainly voluntary, private, and charity-based to government-financed services. Private not-for-profit agencies continued to offer services, many therapeutically based, and group work services within these settings focused on remedial and "treatment"-oriented group work (influenced heavily by Freudian psychology), while the community-based group work agencies tended to maintain the social goals approach.

By the 1960s federal and provincial funding of the social welfare system had expanded. Concurrently, grassroots political unrest fuelled by the anti-poverty, student, labour, and peace movements, saw the rise of grassroots advocacy and social action activities. Social group work services reflected the political and social realities, with efforts focusing on outreach and innovative services, many, in particular, to youth. Services focused on the enhancement of individual growth through democratic participation and social responsibility and reflected the early tradition of social group work to carry forward its social action dimension.

Two group work organizations, had been formed toward mid-century, the American Association of Group Workers (AAGW) and the American Association for the Study of Group Work (AASGW), both of which were made up of members from Canada and the USA. In the late 1970s, the international Association for the Advancement of Social Work with Groups (AASWG) was formed for the purpose of preserving the strength of group work as a viable and essential human service modality. Canada has hosted four of AASWG's annual symposia, attended by academics and practitioners from around the globe: Toronto (1982), Montreal (1989), Québec City (1997), and Toronto (2000).

Since the 1970s, Canada has experienced numerous fiscal crises, giving rise to greater conservatism in politics and in social policies. Cutbacks in health, education, and welfare programs, a trend in the contracting out of services, a greater focus on law and order, and privatization of universal programs have impacted the nature and availability of social group work services. Short-term groups with a focus on special populations and problems, self-help groups, consciousness-raising groups, and personal growth groups have proliferated, often emerging and disappearing with changing priorities of funding bodies, both public and private.

By the second decade of the 20th century, social work had moved toward recognition as a profession, accomplished largely through its incorporation into university programs across the country. As part of this momentum, social group work education in Canada evolved in tandem with its development in the United States, with practice influences flowing in both directions. Although most schools of social work in Canada offered courses in social group work, many were established in the 1960s and 1970s. This history focuses on the earliest established schools reflecting the origins of group work education.

From 1918 to 1920, Robert M. MacIver served as Dean of the School of Social Work, University of Toronto, the first school of social work in Canada. Later, MacIver served as advisor to Grace Coyle's doctoral dissertation (1930), as professor of sociology at Columbia University. At the University of Toronto, group work practice elements appeared in courses offered between 1914 and 1917: "Settlement Work", "Playground Work", and "Play and Games"; and in 1918–1919: "Recreation and Playground Work", and "Settlement Methods". In the 1920s, courses on group work with boys were added: "Society and the Boy" in 1921–1922; and "Boy Behavior and Methods of Boys' Work" and "Work with Adolescent Boys", both in 1926-1927. The first course in "group work" per se, appeared in 1931–1932 under the title "Principles of Group Work". The School also initiated field work placements at local organizations engaged in group work activities, many of which were also the source of the department's early faculty, such as the Department of Health, Toronto General Hospital, the Presbyterian Church, and the various settlement houses in the area (University of Toronto Archives, 1915–1920). From the 1930s, the group work method was taught at most of Canada's earliest social work faculties.

Early group work instructors at the University of Toronto included: Donald Grey McCullagh (1940–1943), who worked part time at University Settlement House, Mark Tarail (1943–1946), who later became Executive Director of the Jewish Community Center in Brockton, MA; and Bert Gold (1946–1947) who later joined the Jewish Community Center in Newark, N. J. Opal "Poppy" Boynton, from thewestern United States, joined the faculty in 1947, and Alan F. Klein taught there from 1948 to 1959. Reginald W. Bundy, John Farina and Jack Byles succeeded Klein, and in the early 1960s, Ben Zion Shapiro, Norma Lang and, in 1970, Margot Breton became University of Toronto faculty members. Klein, Shapiro, Lang and Breton made significant contributions to teaching and the development of group work theory. Charles E. "Chick" Hendry was a significant influence on group work both in Canada and the USA, was the first editor of the journal *The Group* (published 1939–1955), the first chair of AASGW, and served as Dean of the University of Toronto School of Social Work from 1951 to

1969. Ralph Garber, a Canadian, obtained his doctorate from the University of Pennsylvania, and was Director of the School of Social Work at Rutgers and at St. Louis, and Dean of the University of Toronto Faculty of Social Work from 1977 to 1990.

The early group work programs at Western Reserve University School of Applied Social Science in Cleveland with Grace Coyle, and at the University of Pittsburgh with Gertrude Wilson and Gladys Ryland, served as the source of early theoretical development and the loci of group work training. Numerous Canadians studied in the social group work program at the University of Pittsburgh in the 1940s, including Jacqueline Edelson, Molly Donaldson, Cuthbert Gifford, and Simone Paré.

Simone Paré established group work at L'École de Service Social, L'Université Laval Québec City, where early courses included a seminar on group work ("service social collectif"). Many of the early professors were drawn from social work organizations in the region, namely, local hospitals and family service agencies. Paré received her MSW from the University of Pittsburgh in 1948, and her PhD in 1961 from Columbia University, where Gisela Konopka was her classmate. She translated the group work theory into French for her students, and throughout her career, also translated important journal articles on group work annually for students. In addition to Laval, Paré lectured at McGill University and L'Université de Montréal. Her book, *Groupes et Service Social*, was published in 1956 and re-edited in 1971.

McGill University opened its School for Social Workers in 1918, in 1933 becoming the Montreal School of Social Work. Group work was a component of the program from its inception, with professors drawn from local group work agencies. From the late 1930s until the late 1940s, group work was taught by Harvey Golden, Executive Director of the YMHA, Catherine S. Vance, a graduate of the New York School of Social Work (NYSSW) and General Secretary of the YMCA, and Charles H. Young, another NYSSW graduate. In 1948, Anne B. Zaloha from the University of Chicago was made Assistant Professor of Group Work and Supervisor of Field Work in Group Work. Cuthbert Gifford and Arthur Rotman, a Western Reserve graduate, taught group work from the late 1950s to the late 1960s, continuing the group work specialization begun in the early years. McGill was one of the schools that continued a major in group work until the 1980s.

In the early 1900s, Winnipeg, Manitoba received over 30,000 European and Russian immigrants per year, their poverty, lack of language, and traumatized families setting the stage for the development of the social welfare system in Manitoba. While a training program in social welfare was established in 1914 at the University of Manitoba it was short-lived and the social work program was officially established in 1943. Cuthbert Gifford became Director in 1968. Courses and a specialization in social group work have been offered over the years, with greatest emphasis from the late 1950s to the early 1970s.

The University of British Columbia also delivered courses in group work early in its existence. Pioneering faculty members included Dorothy Brown from the University of Washington, Florence Ray Stein, who had studied at the University of Pittsburgh, Louis Zimmerman, Henry Maier, and Lawrence Shulman.

In all respects, the authors, teachers, and practitioners of group work knowledge in the early period spanned Canada and the United States: group work no border.

In current Canadian social work education and practice, the spirit of the settlement and Social Gospel movements and early social group work can be seen in the ideological underpinnings and content themes of empowerment, anti-oppression, social action, mutual aid, and social justice, even though much group practice and education is problem-focused and specific to particular vulnerable and marginalized populations, often time-limited and structured in format. The settlement movement's enduring mission to provide a collective means for personal growth and development and social change toward a just society is evident in the growing phenomenon of groups that are focused on diversity and personal and community capacity-building.

References

Boyd, M. H. (2007). *Enriched by catastrophe: Social work and social conflict after the Halifax explosion*. Halifax Nova Scotia: Fernwood Publishing.

Breton, M. (1990). Learning from social group work traditions. *Social Work with Groups*, 13(3), 21–34.

Central Neighbourhood House (CNH). City of Toronto Archives: Central Neighbourhood House Fonds, 1005 (SC5), *Mission Statement*, 1911; Annual Reports & Subject Files 1911–1977.

Coyle, G. L. (1930). *Social process in organized groups*. New York: Richard R. Smith.

Federation of Jewish–Philanthropies. Ontario Jewish Archives: Annual Reports of the Federation of Jewish Philanthropies, 1917–1938. *Annual Report*, 1918.

Georgina House. City of Toronto Archives: Georgina House Fonds, 1009(SC9), *Annual Reports*, 1912–1942.

James, C. (2001). Reforming reform: Toronto's Settlement House Movement, 1900–1920. *The Canadian Historical Review*, 82(1), 55.

Lapp, J. (1922). *Social work survey of the Archdiocese of Toronto*. Washington, DC: National Catholic Welfare Council.

Papell, C., & Rothman, B. (1966). Social group work models: Possession and heritage. *Journal of Education for Social Work*, 2(2), 66–77.

Speisman, S. (1979). The Jews of Toronto. Toronto: McClelland & Stewart.

St. Christopher House (Stc). City of Toronto Archives: Saint Christopher House Fonds, 1484(SC484), *Annual Reports*, 1916–1922.

United Jewish Welfare Fund. Ontario Jewish Archives: *Annual Reports of the United Jewish Welfare Fund*, 1938–1996.

University Settlement House (USH). City of Toronto Archives: University Settlement House Fonds, 1024(SC24), *Mission Statement*, 1911; Annual Reports 1911–1916.

University of Toronto Archives: *Course Calendars of the University of Toronto*, 1915–1920.

United States

Albert S. Alissi

Social group work origins can be traced to the mutual aid and philanthropic initiatives that were organized to improve people's lives and social conditions brought about by the Industrial Revolution in England, initiatives that spread and picked up momentum in America. Mutual aid was a natural product of the times, evidenced in the "clubbing institution," that permeated 19th-century London social life. Left to fend for themselves in a laissez faire climate, people turned to each other to form social clubs, societies and cooperatives to meet the need for companionship, and to share resources for mutual health, accident and death benefits. Similarly, neighbors joined together in the "spirit of association" that Tocqueville found so influential in early America, which served to advance their common welfare by creating self-help networks that were then expanded by millions of immigrants and minorities well into the 20th century.

Motivated primarily by religious and personal convictions, and endowed with a spirit of activism and experimentation, the early volunteers and workers directly engaged the impoverished, the vulnerable, the young and needy in groups to achieve varied missions. And, as these philanthropic missions grew and developed, the quality of the group experience itself became recognized as central to the helping process. Although social group work was yet to be formulated, traces of its early underlying traditions—voluntarism, mutual aid, democratic group participation, group self-government, participatory democracy, program activities, advocacy and social action—found expression in the character-building, leisure time youth serving agencies and social settlements. The face-to-face group became the natural medium adopted by the expansive network of organizations, such as the YMCA, YWCA, the Boys and Girls Clubs, Boys and Girls Scouts, the YM and YW Hebrew Associations, Catholic Youth Organizations, 4-H Clubs and organized camp programs. These, along with the social settlements, neighborhood and Jewish community centers, as well as adult informal education and recreation programs, came to be known as "group work" agencies.

The settlement house movement was particularly influential. The aim of the first settlement, Toynbee Hall (est. 1884) in London, was to bridge the gulf between the social classes, as university men became "settler" residents in slum neighborhoods, forming friendships and group relationships, promoting free association between individuals and groups to serve as outposts for education and culture. America's first settlement, the Neighborhood Guild (est.1886) in New York was organized around close-knit self-governing club experiences that became the common denominator in most settlements (Woods & Kennedy, 1922). Small group participation was considered an essential democratic building block for influencing social conditions. Interest in social problems developed naturally within club relationships where living conditions—housing, health, safety, labor, wages, and politics—were no longer "remote" but were shared as important personal issues instead (Wald, 1915).

Group work's identity with advocacy, social reform and action was evidenced throughout the Progressive Era in the activities and programs initiated by prominent settlement leaders such as Jane Addams, (Chicago Hull House, est. 1889), Robert Woods, (Andover House, Boston, est. 1891), Lillian Wald (New York's Henry Street Settlement, est. 1893), and Graham Taylor (Chicago Commons, est. 1894). The settlements' influence was far reaching: they started educational experiments in childcare, kindergarten programs and vocation training; they helped establish public playgrounds, summer camps and "Fresh Air" programs; they established "social centers" club house programs in public schools; they supported labor and worked to unionize women, and eliminate child labor; and they sought legislative reforms in housing, health, sanitation, immigration, and political practices.

During the period from the late 1920s to the late 1930s agencies embracing recreational, educational, character-building, and community-organized group activities flourished. Social reform and activism declined after the Progressive Era, and became suspect during the Red Scare, after World War I. The commitment to advance social goals remained strong as agencies established and maintained long-standing relationships with individuals, groups, and families in their communities, providing community-based social, informal educational, and recreational services throughout the war and depression years. An American Association of Social Work (AASW) job analysis conducted by Williamson (1929) of over 40 group work positions in group work agencies found that although there was no clearly unified "field" of practice in what she called a "group work movement" there was a growing awareness of common professional philosophies, similar practices and training techniques.

The first course on group work, "Group Services," was introduced at the School of Applied Social Sciences, Western Reserve University in Cleveland in 1923, and by 1927 the first 2-year group work sequence was established there under the direction of Wilbur Newstetter. Grace Coyle joined the faculty in 1934 and became a leading national figure in establishing group work as a social work method. Faculty members such as Clara Keiser and Gertrude Wilson advanced group work education in other schools of social work as well. Keiser joined the faculty of the New York School of Social Work in 1935 and helped develop its group work program. In 1938, Wilson along with Newstetter, moved to the University of Pittsburgh School of Social Work and introduced a group work sequence the following year (Maloney, 1963). By 1937, there were 13 educational institutions offering group work courses, 10 within schools of social work.

Newstetter and Coyle, both sociologists, were among the first to advance the social scientific knowledge of small group processes that became an essential part of group work training. The Wawokiye Camp Research Project, conducted by Newstetter and his associates, was one of the earliest "experimental sociology" efforts to use objective sociometric measures of small face-to-face group interaction to assess social adjustments through group association. For Newstetter, it was only the "combined and consistent pursuit" of both individual and social goals that qualified as group work process (Newstetter, Feldstein & Newcomb, 1938, p. 111). Coyle's *Social Process in Organized Groups* (1930) became a classic group work resource for categorizing universal processes found in small face-to-face groups— significant processes that influence both individual and group behavior. Her Pugsley Prize–winning paper, "Group Work and Social Change," presented at the 1935 National Conference of Social Work in Montreal stressed group work's social responsibilities for providing essential collective living experiences to strengthen democratic values and effect social change.

The Ligonier (PA) Conference of Group Work held in 1933 brought together group work educators and leaders in what became an organized effort to nationalize group work interests. It contributed to the establishment of a group work section at the National Conference of Social Work in 1935. This development marked a turning point as group work's alignment with social work began to overshadow recreation and informal education. It also led to the founding of the American Association for the Study of Group Work (AASGW) in 1936 which in turn began publication (from 1939 to 1955) of an influential national bulletin, *The Group—in Education, Recreation, Social Work* (the sub-title emphasizes the major interests—and conflicts—of its members).

The progressive education ideas of John Dewey, the play and recreation theories of Neva Boyd, the political philosophy of Mary Follett, and the social philosophy of Eduard Lindeman dominated group work thinking. Their influences shaped a consensus effort to define group work as an educational process, based on voluntary democratic participation, required skilled group leadership and creative program activities to enhance normal personality development, social skills, and citizenship responsibilities. There was less agreement, however, regarding group work's purposes and functions. Moved by group work's uniqueness, there were those who believed that group work had no boundaries: it belonged to all professions. Many continued to emphasize recreation and educational aspects in developing individual personalities; while others focused on social responsibility and citizen participation. Some began to see group work as a means for improving individual adjustment and solving personal problems—functions that called for better-trained workers. And still others insisted group work was just another name for social action (Alissi, 1980).

The 1940s and 50s was a period of synthesis and consolidation as group work was introduced to new settings and formally established as a social work method. Group workers came together with caseworkers and took on new roles by assisting in relief and reconstruction efforts during the depression and New Deal era, and by providing special services related to the war effort. The threat of totalitarians during the war years and the emergence of the Cold War generated new interest in democratic principles, although McCarthyism stymied social action. The 1950s witnessed group work's expansion into general and psychiatric hospitals and clinics; into institutions for children, the aged, mentally ill, and physically handicapped; into public schools, public welfare and correctional agencies; and into neighborhood outreach programs—all of which hastened group work's alignment with social work.

The 1940s brought about a rapid increase in group work literature. Three readers appeared that helped consolidate ideas that shaped group work thinking: Joshua Lieberman's (1938), edited in collaboration with NASGW, contained articles dealing with social/education and philosophical influences; Dorathea Sullivan's (1952) included articles highlighting the growing interest in social and behavioral sciences; and Harleigh Trecker's (1955), a collection of articles exploring theoretical foundations and developing practices published in *The Group* throughout its history from 1939 to 1955. Influential texts appeared by Coyle (1947, 1948), Konopka (1949, 1954), Phillips (1951), Klein(1953), and Trecker (1955, 1956). Wilson and Ryland's

Social Group Work Practice (1949) (affectionately referred to by group work students as the "green bible") provided the most complete comprehensive textbook on practice methods, program media and group work recording, and included chapters on supervision and administration processes as well.

In 1946, members of the AASGW voted to change from a study to a professional organization, forming the American Association of Group Workers (AAGW). In 1949, the AAGW officially defined group work as a method that enables various groups to function in ways that advance both group interaction and program activities that contribute to individual growth and desirable social goals. AAGW entered deliberations with other associations to move toward the development of a single new professional social work association. Although views differed on how group work traditions and priorities would fare, AAGW members decided to join with six other social work professional organizations in 1955 to form the National Association of Social Workers (NASW), with group work as one of its constituent sections.

Group work's entrance into therapeutic settings brought changes that have profoundly influenced group work's development. Although some isolated recreational group work methods were introduced in a Chicago hospital and a training school for girls as early as 1918 (Boyd, 1935), the trend started with Giesela Konopka's group work at Pittsburgh Guidance Center in 1938 and Fritz Redl's Detroit Group project in 1942, which trained group workers to use groups for diagnostic and treatment purposes for emotionally disturbed children. The use of groups in treatment expanded as hospitals, clinics and rehabilitation centers created new demands for trained group workers with therapeutic skills. The lack of trained group workers to meet the demand led to what Robert Vinter (1959) referred to as a "near crises situation" that called for group work to redirect its resources to deal exclusively with personal and social adjustment problems.

The economic deprivation, racial tension, urban unrest, and violence that characterized the 1960s brought about renewed interest in social change, as federally sponsored programs in the War on Poverty introduced programs to redress differential opportunities, at times, challenging the "relevancy" of traditional social work practices.

The newly formed NASW Group Work Section's Committee on Practice, conducted a major membership study that provided a "frame of reference" that reaffirmed group work's multiple functions adaptable to changing service needs and demands. Five critical areas were identified: restoration or remedial; prevention of personal social breakdown; normal growth and development; personal enhancement, and citizen responsibility and participation (Hartford, 1964). Other efforts to develop social group work practice theory and knowledge were interrupted by a NASW decision in 1962 to eliminate its practice sections and redirect resources to address broader professional matters. The 1960s also saw a shift in social work education policies that stressed generic practices that contributed to social group work's decline as a discrete social work method.

While early efforts focused on distinguishing group work as a social work method different from recreation and informal education, after NASW was organized, group work's identity within the social work profession became the focus of attention. And the model building that occurred in the late 1950s and 1960s produced multiple perspectives regarding that identity.

Three major models were central to the process. The *social goals model*, drawn from the work of early theorists, characterized the worker as agent of the agency, an "enabler," who enhances individual growth and development through democratic participation in the pursuit of desirable social goals. The *reciprocal model* (also identified as mediating, interactionist, mutual aid) developed by Schwartz (1961, 1971) saw the worker as a "mediator" who, drawing from social system and field theory, establishes reciprocal relationships developing mutual aid to meet common goals. And the *remedial model* (also preventative and rehabilitative) formalized by Vinter (1967), saw the worker as a "change agent" who intervenes with members, groups and social systems to alter or reinforce individual behavior (Papell & Rothman, 1966). Variations on these models followed. Roberts and Northen (1976) edited a collection of 10 theoretical orientations variously labeled as generic, psychosocial, functional, organizational, mediating, developmental, task-centered, socialization, crisis-intervention, and problem-solving. Particular attention was given to developmental models, to normal growth and development processes (Tropp, 1977), and to an influential "Boston School" model (Garland, Jones, & Kolodny, 1976) of group development stages that inspired additional versions such as Schiller's (1995) "relational" model applicable to women's groups. Renewed attention was also given to conceptualizing and utilizing program processes broadly conceived as a "non-verbal method" (Middleman, 1968).

As model building progressed, group work scholars integrated dominant group work ideas and practice into a "central identity" model called mainstream practice (Gitterman, 1979; Gitterman & Germain, 1976). Democratic participation, the pursuit of social goals, recognizing the values inherent in program content, utilizing the power inherent in group processes, and disciplined intervention of a group worker—all were essential in mainstream thinking (Papell & Rothman, 1980).

By the 1980s social work education policies that stressed generic practices had reduced attention devoted to group work content and training and had contributed to the declining numbers of trained group workers entering practice. The waning interest led to attempts to re-energize group work. The *Journal of Social Work with Groups— A Journal of Community and Clinical Practices* began publication in 1978 to fill a void in group work professional communication that had existed since The *Group* ceased publication in 1955. An informal gathering of group work educators attending the 1979 Council on Social Work Education (CSWE) Annual Program Meeting in Boston led to the formation of the Association for the Advancement of Social Work with Groups (AASWG) that expanded into an international organization with affiliated local Chapters. It has sponsored annual symposia ever since 1979 when its first Annual Symposium was held in Cleveland. It has also established a liaison with CSWE to promote group work content and training (Middleman, 2000). As a result, certain CSWE publications have been devoted to group work education, including a full text on teaching a social group work methods course (Kurland & Salmon, 1998).

By the end of the century, group work knowledge continued to be updated and articulated in textbooks (Gitterman & Shulman, 2005; Shulman, 2006; Toseland & Rivas, 2009); and group work's presence in a wide range of areas was fully portrayed in a comprehensive *Handbook* (Garvin, Gutiérrez Galinsky, 2004). Yet, group work as a discrete method continued to decline in the wake of reduced professional training and major shortages of trained group workers sufficiently dedicated to achieve traditional group work functions.

Of historical significance was the shift from agency-based group work practices to individualized professional practices, evidenced in the abandonment of the group work host agency that sustained group work efforts into the mid-1950s. Unlike their early counterparts, today's group workers are less likely to be working in agencies where decisions regarding agency practice and resources are made by group workers, and are coordinated to facilitate programs that insure long-standing relationships with self-governing groups and clubs, families, and volunteers. Instead, today's group workers are more isolated and challenged in settings where key decisions are made by other disciplines, and where agency resources are not necessarily devoted to group work ideals—voluntarism, mutual aid, democratic group participation, group self-government, creative program activities, advocacy, and social action—that throughout history inspired group work practice.

References

Alissi, A. S. (Ed.) (1980). Social group work: Commitments and perspectives. *Perspectives on social group work practice: A book of readings* (pp. 5–35). New York: The Free Press.

Boyd, N. L. (1935). Group work experiments in state institutions in Illinois. *Proceedings of the National Conference on Social Work* (pp. 339–345). Chicago: University of Chicago Press.

Coyle, G. (1930). *Social process in organized groups*. New York: Richard R. Smith.

Coyle, G. (1935). Group work and social change. *Proceedings of the National Conference of Social Work* (pp. 393–405). Chicago: University of Chicago Press.

Coyle, G. (1947). *Group experience and democratic values*. New York: The Woman's Press.

Coyle, G. (1948). *Group work with American youth*. New York: Harper Row.

Garland, J. A., Jones, H. E., & Kolodny, R. L. (1976). A model for stages of development in social work groups. In S. Bernstein (Ed.), *Explorations in group practice* (pp. 12–53). Boston: Boston University of Social Work.

Garvin, G. D., Gutiérrez, L. M., & Galinsky, M. J. (Eds.). (2004). *Handbook of social work with groups*. New York: Guilford Press.

Gitterman, A. (1979). Specialized group content in an integrated method curriculum. In S. Abels & P. Abels (Eds.), *Social work with groups* (pp. 66–81). Louisville, KY: Committee for Advancement of Social Work with Groups.

Gitterman, A., & Germain, C. B. (1976). Social work practice: A Life Model. *Social Service Review, 50*(December), 601–610.

Gitterman, A., & Shulman, L. (2005). *Mutual aid groups, vulnerable and resilient populations and the life cycle* (3rd ed.). New York: Columbia University Press.

Hartford, M. (Ed.). (1964). Social group work 1930 to 1960: The search for a definition. *Working paper: Toward a frame of reference for social group work* (pp. 62–76). New York: National Association of Social Workers.

Klein, A. (1953). *Society, democracy and the group*. New York: Whiteside.

Konopka, G. (1949). *Therapeutic group work with children*. Minneapolis: University of Minnesota.

Konopka, G. (1954). *Group work in the institution*. New York: Association Press.

Kurland, R., & Salmon, R. (1998). *Teaching a methods course in social work with groups*. Alexandria, VA: Council on Social Work Education.

Lieberman, J. (Ed.). (1938). *New trends in group work.* New York: Association Press.

Maloney, S. (1963). *The development of group work education in schools of social work in the United States.* Unpublished doctoral dissertation, School of Applied of Social Sciences, Western Reserve University.

Middleman, R. R. (1968). *The non-verbal method in working with groups.* New York: Association Press.

Middleman, R. R. (2000). A brief history of AASWG. *Social Work with Groups Newsletter, 16*(1), 16–17.

Newstetter, W., Feldstein, M. J., & Newcomb, T. M. (1938). *Group adjustment: A study in experimental sociology.* School of Applied Social Sciences, Western Reserve University.

Papell, C., & Rothman, B. (1966). Social group work models: Possession and heritage. *Education for Social Work, 2,* 66–77.

Papell, C., & Rothman, B. (1980). Relating the mainstream model of social work with groups-to-group psychotherapy and the structured group approach. *Social Work with Groups, 3,* 5–23.

Phillips, H. (1951). *Essential of social group work skill.* New York: Association Press.

Roberts, R. W., & Northen, H. (Eds.). (1976). *Theories of social work with groups.* New York: Columbia University Press.

Schiller, L. Y. (1995). Stages of development in women's groups: A relational model. In R. Kurland & R. Salmon (Eds.), *Group work practice in a troubled society* (pp. 117–138). Binghamton, NY: Haworth Press.

Schwartz, W. (1961). The social worker in the group. *Social Welfare Forum* (pp.146–177). New York: Columbia University Press.

Schwartz, W. (1971). Social group work: The interactionist approach. In R. Morris (Ed.-in-Chief), *Encyclopedia of social work* (16th ed., vol. 2, pp. 1252–1263). New York: National Association of Social Workers.

Shulman, L. (2009). *The skills of helping individuals, families, groups and communities* (6th ed.). Belmont, CA: Thomson/Wadsworth.

Sullivan, D. (1952). *Reading in group work.* New York: Association Press.

Toseland, R. W., & Rivas, R. F. (2005) *An introduction to group work practice* (5th ed.). Boston: Allyn Bacon.

Trecker, H. B. (Ed.). (1955). *Group work: foundations & frontiers.* New York: Whiteside.

Trecker, H. B. (1956). *Group work in the psychiatric setting.* New York: Whiteside, William Morrow.

Tropp, E. (1977). Social group work: The developmental approach. In R. Morris (Ed.-in-Chief), *Encyclopedia of social work* (16th ed., vol. 2, pp. 1246–1252). New York: National Association of Social Workers.

Vinter, R. D. (1959). Group work: perspectives and prospects. In *Social work with groups.* New York: National Association of Social Workers.

Vinter, R. D. (Ed.). (1967). *Readings in group work practice.* Ann Arbor, MI: Campus Publication.

Wald, L. D. (1915). *The house on Henry Street.* New York: Henry Hold & Co.

Williamson, M. (1929). *The social worker in group work.* New York: Harper & Brothers.

Wilson, G., & Ryland, G. (1949). *Social group work practice: The creative use of social process.* Boston: Houghton Mifflin.

Woods, R. A., & Kennedy, A. J. (1922). *The settlement horizon: A national estimate.* New York: Russell Sage Foundation.

Jane Addams

Judith A. B. Lee

Jane Addams (1860–1935) was the founder of Chicago's Hull House and the eloquent spokeswoman for the settlement house movement from which social group work takes its proud heritage. From Hull House, where she lived and worked until her death in

1935, she developed a model of reciprocal helping relationships, and ventured forth to lead in major, and often unpopular (to those in power) reform efforts. These included being a co-founder of the National Association for the Advancement of Colored People in 1909, major international efforts for world peace during World War I, formidable advocacy for children's and women's labor laws and trade unions, and tireless efforts for human equality. She was an intellectual activist, a sensitive humanist, and a tireless worker for justice. A prolific writer and challenging speaker, she wrote 11 books and numerous articles, including *Democracy and Social Ethics*, her Hull House books and *Peace and Bread in Times of War*. Her vivid stories of people struggling with poverty and despair prodded America to respond to the terrible conditions that accompanied industrial development. Her pacifism and anti-war leadership branded her "the most dangerous woman in America" by the "super patriots" of the time. Yet, she was recognized in 1931 as one of the first two Americans and the first American woman to win the Nobel Peace Prize. She remained president of the Women's International League for Peace and Freedom until she died. Posthumously, in 1973, she was inducted into the National Women's Hall of Fame.

Addams was born in Cedarville, Illinois on September 6, 1860, exactly two months before Abraham Lincoln was elected President of the United States. Her lifetime takes her through the country's conflict over slavery, the Civil War, a series of Depressions, World War I, the Suffragist Movement and women finally getting the vote, the Great Depression, and the New Deal of Franklin D. Roosevelt. Certainly the times she lived in influenced this frail young girl from a wealthy household whose mother died before she was three. She was among the first generation of women to go to college, graduating from Rockford College in 1882, a time when women could not respectably live alone or unmarried, or enter professions. She battled depression after her father died in 1881, a loss compounded by a series of severe medical problems. Yet her devotion to her father and his Quaker views and a natural compassion and keen intellect also shaped the woman of courage and strength she would become. Believing one could change the thinking that shapes our times, she influenced the times as much as she lived them and left an indelible and distinctive mark on American history and the history of the social work profession.

Along with her friend Ellen Starr, Jane Addams visited the university settlement, Toynbee Hall in the East End of London in 1888. She was intrigued and excited by the reform history of this settlement that brought thinkers of the day and college students together with poor people. In 1889 Addams and Starr rented an old mansion on Chicago's impoverished West Side between the stockyards and shipyards, an area teeming with new immigrants. They called it Hull House. They moved in and invited both famous people and neighborhood residents to programs and to dialogue. They were aided by financial contributions, including that of the young Chicago heiress Mary Rozet Smith who also helped in the music school and nursery. Her lovely portrait hangs near Jane's smaller portrait, both commissioned by Jane, above the marble mantlepiece in the Hull House Museum. Scholars generally agree that Addams and Smith were partners/companions in life who owned a home in Maine, traveled as a pair and spent more than 30 years in a loving committed relationship. Mary Rozet Smith died in 1934 and Jane followed a year later in 1935.

Soon the residents of Hull House formed an impressive group: Julia Lathrop, Dr. Alice Hamilton, Florence Kelley, who, with a radical flair, researched and exposed sweat shop conditions that led to the passing of the Illinois Factory Act, Edith and Grace Abbott, and Sophonisba Breckinridge among them. Mary Kenney and Alzina Stevens working-class labor leaders educated the "middle-class" residents in workers' issues and the college-educated women influenced them in turn. Hull House was alive with thinking and activism. John Dewey and Frederick Douglass were among the speakers invited to the Discussion Groups. Addams considered racism and discrimination as "the gravest situation in American life" (Addams, 1930, p. 401).

Yet it was the expressed and observed needs of neighborhood residents that shaped the many programs, from day care and kindergarten to the Discussion Clubs, children's activity groups, a library, an art gallery, music and art classes, a theater, and an employment bureau. The Jane Club, a cooperative residence for women was a prototype for services for working women. It was Addams' clear purpose not to plan *for* but *with* and *in dialogue* with the neighborhood residents. Her philosophy was to encourage the abilities of the residents without dominating it; her way was to promote the work of others. This early forerunner of the empowerment perspective in social work and group work methodology modeled reciprocity and the community of equals as practice principles.

Kathleen Pottick (1988) points out that Jane Addams' practice model represented a departure from the social thought of her times that glorified philanthropic giving. She thought that such giving perpetuated social stagnation and undermined self-determination thereby undermining democracy itself. She felt that social stagnation as reflected in the "giver–receiver" relationship could be reduced as reciprocal independence was "fostered, nurtured and maintained" (Pottick, 1988). For this thinking and for her leadership in legislative and economic programs, her anti-War, bread and peace leadership, women's and children's rights, and anti-racism and discrimination activities, Jane Addams was hailed in a Congressional speech by Thomas Bayard of Delaware in 1926. He saw her as a radical and a teacher of radicals, "a social—worker-who has often been painted by magazine and newspaper writers as a sort of modern Saint of the Slums— that both she and Hull House can campaign for the most radical movements, with hardly a breath of public suspicion" (www.spartacus.schoolnet.co.uk/USAaddams.htm). It was precisely her radicalism and her practice model that prompted Judith Lee (1987) to plea in a plenary speech at the Sixth Annual Symposium of for the Advancement of Social Work with Groups in Chicago in 1984: "Jane Addams Won't You Please Come Home?"

When Jane Addams died in May of 1935 Louise Bowen wrote [excerpted]:

She "lay in state" in Bowen Hall at Hull House. Thousands of neighborhood people and others waited all day to file by the coffin and kneel and say a prayer. The Hull House Women's Club formed a guard of Honor and stood on either side of the Hall while members of the children's clubs dressed in white and acted as ushers. The coffin and the courtyard were surrounded in flowers and the Hull House Music School furnished the music. It was a most touching and democratic gathering. Strong men and women with children in their arms all stood weeping for the friend they had lost.

(Spartacus.schoolnet.co.uk, p. 14)

The people had spoken loud and clear that day testifying to who Jane Addams was and what she did for them in her role as designer and "mother" of our group work heritage. We are privileged to claim her as our own.

References

Addams, J. (1910). *Twenty years at Hull House*. Rpt. New York: Macmillan, 1961.

Addams, J. (1930). *The second twenty years at Hull House*. New York: Macmillan.

Jane Addams. Retrieved March 2, 2007 from http://www.spartacus.schoolnet.co.uk/USAaddams.htm: 1–14.

Lee, J. A. B. (1987). Social work with oppressed populations: Jane Addams won't you please come home. In J. Lassner, K. Powell, & E. Finnegan (Eds.), Social group work: Competence, and values in practice (pp. 1–16). Binghamton, NY: Haworth Press.

Lee, J. A. B. (1988). Introduction: Return to our roots. In J. A. B. Lee (Ed.), *Group work with the poor and oppressed* (pp. 5–9). Binghamton, NY: Haworth Press.

Lee, J. A. B. (1992). Jane Addams in Boston: Intersecting time and space. In J. Garland (Ed.), *A group work reaching out: People, places and power* (pp. 7–21). Binghamton, NY: Haworth Press.

Lee, J. A. B. (2001). *The empowerment approach to social work practice: Building the beloved community*. New York: Columbia University Press.

Pottick, K. (1988). Jane Addams revisited: Practice theory and social economics. In J. A. B. Lee (Ed.), *Group work with the poor and oppressed* (pp. 11–26). Binghamton, NY: Haworth Press.

Schoenberg, N. *Hull-House Museum poses the question "Was Jane Addams a lesbian?" Chicago Tribune*. Posted on February 14, 2007, pp. 1–3. http://www.myrtlebeachonline.con/mld/myrtlebeachonline/news/national

Grace Longwell Coyle

David S. Crampton

Grace Longwell Coyle (1892–1962), a pioneer in the development of social group work, was born in North Adams, Massachusetts, to John Patterson and Mary Cushman Coyle. Her father was a Congregational minister. Her brother, David Cushman Coyle (1887–1969) was a well-known author of popular books about economics and public policy, and a member of Franklin Roosevelt's "Brain Trust." As a young girl, she read the works of Jane Addams, which inspired her to enter social work. Coyle graduated from Drury High School in North Adams in 1910 and received her AB degree from Wellesley College in 1914 where she was elected Phi Beta Kappa. While in college, she volunteered at a Boston settlement house. She subsequently received a scholarship from the College Settlement Association to study social work at the New York School of Philanthropy, while living at the College Settlement and using her work there for field credit. She graduated with a Diploma in Social Work in 1915.

Coyle was first employed as a settlement house worker in the coal region of northeast Pennsylvania (1915–1917), where she learned about the needs of new immigrants and factory workers. She then became a field worker for the Young Women's Christian Association (YWCA) in Pittsburgh (1917–1918) and industrial secretary for the YWCA national board in New York City (1918–1926). In that position she developed adult education and recreation programs for women industrial workers throughout the country and this experience led her to want to learn more about economics. She earned an MA in economics (1928) and a doctorate in sociology (1931), both from Columbia University. From 1930 to 1934 she directed research for the YWCA as head of their national laboratory division. Through her work in the adult education and progressive education movements, she became interested in the functioning of small groups. Her study of group theory became her dissertation, *Social Process in Organized Groups*, which was published as a book in 1930 and became a well-read text in both social work and sociology. She joined the faculty of the School of Applied Social Sciences of Western Reserve University in 1934. She regularly invited students to her home to meet prominent public figures and teachers and to discuss current events. Part of the memorial resolution passed by the faculty of the School of Applied Social Sciences spoke of her influence as a teacher:

> Grace Coyle came to this faculty in 1934. Throughout the years of her career of teaching she has contributed to the professional development of many students at this School who are now in positions of strategic leadership within this country and throughout the world. Her capacity to involve students in their own learning, the impact of her personality and mind, the basic respect and real affection which students felt for her will continue to dominate their memory.
>
> (Cited by Kasius, 1962)

In the latter years of her life, her writings focused on the use of social science theory in social work. For almost three decades until her death in 1962, she taught, did research on, and wrote about human behavior in small groups. She also pioneered the method of group work as a way of shaping human behavior. Coyle was a former president of three of the country's leading social work organizations: the National Conference of Social Work in 1940, the American Association of Social Workers (1942–44), and the Council on Social Work Education (1958–1960).

A bibliography of Grace Coyle's work lists 74 articles, books and speeches published between 1922 and 1962 (Shapiro, 1965). Her prominent works include: *Social Process in Organized Groups* (1930); *Studies in Group Behavior* (1937) which describes group case studies written by students in the School of Applied Social

Sciences; *Group Experience and Democratic Values* (1947) a collection of some of her major speeches and essays; *Group Work with American Youth* (1948) a practice-oriented book for leaders of leisure groups for youth; and *Social Science in the Professional Education of Social Workers* (1958), which was based on a study funded by the Russell Sage Foundation. Her PhD thesis, "Social Process in Organized Groups," provided her with a foundation of life's work. Harold Laski, John Dewey, and Robert MacIver (her thesis advisor) intellectually influenced her. She also followed in the footsteps of Edward Lindeman and his tradition of community-based work. Dr. Coyle believed that social work was overly dependent on psychodynamic theory as its knowledge base, so she promoted the idea that people are a product of their socialization and that their behavior is shaped as much by their reference groups as by their developmental stages.

Among her many colleagues, perhaps Mary Louise Summers, Raymond Fisher, Wilbur Newstetter, and Margaret Hartford are most eminent. Summers taught at the University of Chicago for many years. Fisher, Newstetter, and Hartford developed their careers under Coyle's leadership at Western Reserve University and helped develop the University's reputation among schools of social work. Hartford's book, *Groups in Social Work* (1971), reflects the legacy of Coyle's lifelong work.

Her historical contributions are well known and include: authorship of the first entry on group work in the *Social Work Year Book*, her leadership in developing the group work curriculum at the School of Applied Social Sciences, her presidency of the Council on Social Work Education, and her lifelong commitment to using social science to inform social work practice, especially social work practice with groups.

Her major intellectual contributions to the field of group work include: ensuring that group work training became part of social work rather than adult education or recreation; developing the democratic approach to groups which grew into methods of community organizing; using small group theory to inform our understanding of group process; and pioneering the systematic approach to studying groups. Many of these points are highlighted in the definition of social group work, which she developed.

Due to her work in the YWCA, Grace Coyle was familiar with the use of groups in adult education and recreation, but as she stresses in the definition above, she was interested in the use of groups in promoting social goals and, hence, thought group work should be part of social work training and professional work. She believed that working in groups was not something that people know instinctively; rather they must learn to do it through group work activities. She further believed that group work would help people personally but would also improve community life and democratic governance. Thus she taught group workers to help their groups develop a "constitution" including rules for voting. Through her dissertation and ongoing work, she showed how small group theory can inform group work. She also developed a method of studying and evaluating groups to improve group work practice.

This brief entry provides a mere introduction to the many contributions made by Grace Coyle as pioneer, scholar, teacher and leader in group work practice and education.

References

Coyle, G. L. (1930). *Social process in organized groups.* New York: Richard R. Smith.

Coyle, G. L. (1937a). Social group work. In *Social work year book, 1937* (pp. 461–464). New York: Russell Sage.

Coyle, G. L. (Ed.). (1937b). *Studies in group behavior.* New York: Harper and Brothers.

Coyle, G. L. (1947). *Group experience and democratic values.* New York: Women's Press.

Coyle, G. L. (1948). *Group work with American youth: A guide to the practice of leadership.* New York: Harper and Brothers.

Coyle, G. L. (1958). *Social science in the professional education of social workers.* New York: Council on Social Work Education.

Hartford, M. E. (1963). Grace Longwell Coyle (1892–1962). *American Sociological Review, 28*(1), 136.

Hartford, M. E. (1971). *Groups in social work.* New York: Columbia University Press.

Kasius, C. (1962). Editorial notes: Grace Longwell Coyle—1893–1962. *Social Casework, 43,* 376.

Shapiro, B. Z. (1965). *Grace Longwell Coyle: Contributions to the philosophy and practice of social work.* Cleveland, OH: Western Reserve University.

The Association for the Advancement of Social Work with Groups, Inc., An International Professional Organization (AASWG)

John H. Ramey

Ruth Middleman recounted:

> In March 1979 at a CSWE [Council on Social Work Education] Annual Program Meeting in Boston, four of us in the hotel lobby looked at the program and were aghast at the disappearance of sessions on work with groups. We had come into social work with a background in group work and expected to find more about groups in our national meetings. We put up a little sign by the elevators, "If You're Interested in Group Work, Come to Room 22xx at 6:30 Today!
>
> Over 60 persons crowded into the small bedroom. They decided to gather in November in Cleveland "to honor Grace Coyle and the first masters level class there in 1923.
>
> (*Social Work with Groups Newsletter*, 2000, p.17)

Paul Abels arranged for the Symposium to meet at Case Western Reserve University School of Applied Social Science, interest expanded and hotel arrangements had to be made. Over 450 people attended. After the Symposium, an ad hoc committee convened by Abels met in a room near the back of the auditorium. It was decided to hold a second Symposium at the University of Texas Arlington. Various responsibilities were distributed among those present.

During the second year, since it was decided to hold the Symposia annually, the Committee for the Advancement of Social Work with Groups (CASWG) was incorporated as a not-for-profit corporation in the State of New York, with Middleman as the first Chair. CASWG then was set up as a mutual aid organization with the members voluntarily carrying out the various functions as their professional and social responsibilities. Beulah Rothman, Catherine "Katy" P. Papell, and Ruth R. Middleman are recognized as AASWG's "Founders."

The Third Symposium was in Hartford, Connecticut. Albert S. Alissi, the Symposium Chair, earlier had agreed to do a survey of the participants of previous Symposia about the form of organization they would prefer. On the basis of the report, Hartford attendees decided to develop the organization as a worldwide individual membership association with Local Chapters. Officers and the Board were elected. A bylaws committee was formed. It was deemed that sufficient operational competence was built into the membership to function without an executive staff. AASWG, Inc., added "An International Professional Organization" to its name to assert its worldwide interest and operations. And, inasmuch as group workers are specialists in organizing, the operational strategy became to spread responsibility and work among the members.

AASWG's formally adopted membership statement conveys the spirit of the Association.

> Group work is a precious commodity. Membership in AASWG is viewed as a contribution and commitment to its preservation and further development within the profession of social work ... [it] augments and does not substitute for other professional affiliations .... It exists and functions through the voluntary efforts of its members as a communications network, an arena for the enhancements of practice and education, and an instrument for advocacy for group work ....
>
> (Middleman, 2000)

AASWG seeks to unite group work workers in all kinds of settings and with all client groups and needs, spanning the range from community and educational to clinical practices. During the mid-2000s institutional membership was developed and many organizations have joined.

Although a majority of members live in the USA, from the beginning participation and membership was worldwide, including group workers from Germany, Japan, Australia, France, Norway, South Africa, Israel, Hong Kong, and many other countries. The members are primarily practitioners with about one-third academicians, and one one-third of those are retired. Many members have moved from practice to academia during their membership years or are only part-time.

The Board and Committees meet twice a year, once at the Symposium and the other time in New York City. In addition to the officers, the Board includes one representative of each Chapter, nine at large members, the Editor of *Social Work with Groups*, life members, and appointed committee chairs. AASWG Chairpersons/ Presidents have been Ruth Middleman, Judith A. B. Lee, James A. Garland, Alex Gitterman, Toby Berman-Rossi, Paul A. Abels, and Nancy Sullivan.

Chapters and Affiliates are self-organized on the initiative of local members. Several have developed after their local areas have sponsored Symposia. Within the framework of AASWG purposes and procedures, Chapters and Affiliates carry on their own programs of meetings, workshops, advocacy, and communications (newsletters, etc.).

All members in Chapter areas are members of the Chapter and all Chapter members are required to be members of AASWG. In the development of a Chapter or Affiliate an "organizing unit" is first recognized while the necessary documentation and negotiations proceed. Several new Chapters are currently being developed.

Pre-existing local group work organizations in Toronto, Miami, and Virginia became Chapters along with other areas with concentrations of group workers. Germany had a large contingent of group workers with strong connections in the United States, stemming from the work of many group workers after World War II to develop democratic processes in post-war Germany. Heinz Kersting, who was honored at the Boston Symposium in 2003, was a leading figure in the development of the German Chapter. The Toronto Group Work Network, a pre-existing organization which maintains that name, became one of the first Chapters. Likewise, the Barry University Center for Group Work Studies became the Florida Chapter, and the group workers association in Virginia became the Virginia Chapter.

Current Chapters include Connecticut, Florida, Germany, Illinois, Kentucky, Long Island, Massachusetts, Michigan, Minnesota, New York City Red Apple, Northeast Ohio, North Texas, Southern California, and Toronto.

In addition to Chapters, an organizational category of "Affiliate" has been developed to provide for alliances with AASWG by units in countries off the North American continent where language, value or transfer of money, law or other political or cultural consideration make it difficult or impossible to form a Chapter as defined by AASWG. Current Affiliates are India and Ghana. The large India Affiliate (IAASWG) is centered in Nagpur. Dr. (Mrs.) Banmala and Manohar Golpelwar, the current President, were instrumental in organizing it. Golpelwar is the executive of the Indian Youth Welfare Association. In 2007 Ghana was recognized as an Affiliate (GAASWG). It has developed under the leadership of Simons Boamah, Executive Director of Safety for New Generation Network (SANGNET) in Accra. It is another large membership unit.

Chapters and Affiliates have the same organizational structure, purposes, and programs. Affiliates, as with Chapters outside the USA, are incorporated in their home countries. There are many other members scattered throughout world, many isolated from others with group work knowledge and skills. Some have developed smaller regular gatherings of members and others interested in group work.

In the early years communication with members was primarily through occasional letters, the annual Preliminary Program, and other announcements of forthcoming

Symposia. In 1974 the regular publication of *Social Work with Groups Newsletter* *(SWwGN)* was established, and in 1975 John H. Ramey and Ruby B. Pernell became the Co-editors. After a few years Pernell retired as Co-editor and Ramey became the Editor and continued through a total of 22 years. He retired in late 2007. Michael W. Wagner of the Children's Aid Society in New York City is now the Editor.

SWwGN publishes news about AASWG including the Symposia, Board, Committees, Chapters, and Affiliates. There are articles about the activities of its members, developments in group work education and services, about books and journals, lists of contributors and new members, articles about honorees, reports of the deaths of members, summaries of selected papers presented at Symposia, poetry and other creative pieces, and other news of interest to members. In its first decade *SWwGN* was distributed widely to all former participants in the Symposia, to all Schools of Social Work in the USA and Canada, many national and international organizations, and others who had inquired or showed interest in group work. More recently it has been distributed only to members and subscribers.

The annual "International Symposia on Social Work with Groups" are a core activity. Group workers gather to share experience, knowledge, and skills, and to participate in developing the strategies for the future of AASWG.

In addition to Cleveland (1979), Arlington (1980), and Hartford (1981, 1994), Symposia have been held in Toronto (1982, 2000), Detroit (1953, 2004), Chicago (1954, 2009), New Jersey (1985, 2007), Los Angeles (1986), Boston (1987, 2003), Baltimore (1988), Montreal (1989), Miami (1990, 1998), Akron (1991), Northeast Ohio (2001), Atlanta (1992), New York City (1993, 2002), San Diego (1995, 2006), Ann Arbor (1996), Québec City (1997), Denver (1999), Minneapolis (2005), and Cologne, Germany (2008). The Symposia have attracted group workers from throughout the world. In addition to professionals, it invites the membership, support, and participation of all who are interested in group work.

Included in the Proceedings of each Symposium are the Plenary and Invitational papers, and a representative selection of papers on other subjects presented there. The Symposium Committees or other publishers published early editions. For many years now they have been published by The Haworth Press, Inc.

The publication of *Standards for Social Work Practice with Groups* in 1999 was a major contribution to the field (AASWG, 2006a). For the first time the basic elements of practice were defined in a way against which the competence of all group workers could be measured. The Practice Committee wrote them over a period of several years and after many hearings. Carolyn Knight edited the first edition. In 2006 AASWG published the greatly expanded second edition. The Committee Chairs for the second edition were Paul A. Abels and Charles D. Garvin, 2003. John H. Ramey did final design, production, and initial distribution for both editions. In 2006 *Standards* was translated by Andrés Arial Astray of Madrid and published in Spanish as *Estaandares para la Practica del Trabajo con Groupos* (AASWG, 2006).

A statement of standards is one of the major criteria for recognition of a profession. Other criteria include: an organized association of practitioners, public recognition including possible; licensure, a body of literature, and education for a defined set of skills. *Standards* are useful and/or necessary for numerous purposes: adjudication in court or by regulatory bodies, including licensure boards; recognition by insurance companies of basic competence; recognition by prospective employers for selecting personnel for employment for positions requiring social work with groups; recognition by current employers relating to assignment, promotion, and compensation; provision of a commons basis for teaching work with groups; and provision of assurance to the public and clients that the worker is prepared to give competent service. *Standards* sets forth the minimum set of core knowledge, values, tasks, skills, and actions necessary for competent practice (Ramey, 2006).

A statement of standards is always a work in progress. New technologies develop, cultural and legal/political changes occur, new knowledge becomes available, new professional terms come into usage, areas of practice develop and change, etc. Thus, one can expect hearings and revised statements to occur at intervals in future years. *Standards* may be purchased from AASWG or downloaded from the Web site, www.aaswg.org.

The Commission on Group Work in Social Work Education was established in the mid-1990s to develop policies and to take action to improve the presence and quality of group work education. At first, under the leadership of Lawrence Shulman, the emphasis was on the USA. In more recent years, with the addition of Ellen Sue Mesbur as Co-chair, similar consideration in relation to Canada has been developed. Carolyn Knight has also provided leadership. Studies of group work courses and curricula in schools of social work in the USA by Birnbaum and Auerbach (1994) and Birnbaum and Wayne (2000) revealed that there was little being taught at the graduate level and that, with a few exceptions, even this was minimal. Group work was more often being taught at the undergraduate level. Realizing that more and more social work services were being provided in group settings made emphasis on teaching of group work skills more imperative.

The Commission initiated discussion with CSWE about specifying group work as such in their educational policy standards and the accreditation criteria. Chapters also worked with local schools on development of course and curricula. The Commission realized the importance of developing texts for teaching group work. A series of books entitled "Strengthening Group Work Education" was commissioned in the mid-1990s to be co-published with CSWE. Two books have been published: *Teaching a Methods Course in Social Work with Groups* (Roselle Kuirland and Robert Salmon, 1997) and *Group Work Education in the Field* (Julianne L. Wayne and Carol S. Cohen, 2001). The third volume, on teaching group work in an integrated practice course, is yet to be completed. Toby Berman-Rossi was preparing it at the time of her death.

Among those tasks distributed at the end of the first Symposium was development of the mailing list by John H. Ramey of the University of Akron. The position of General Secretary grew out of this activity. It had been developed to be a voluntary, transparent, behind-the-scenes support activity until the late 1990s.

Ramey worked at it for over 23 years. The General Secretary position had expanded to provide support for the officers, committees, chapters and general membership. During the last 10 years Carol Ramey managed the membership services and many other supporting functions. The generous support of the University of Akron School of Social Work through the use of its equipment and services and as AASWG's mailing address for many years made it possible. Ramey retired from this position in 2002. After several years of a replacement General Secretary, Raymie Wayne, and other arrangements for handling membership and other selected central functions, AASWG members Suzanne Palombo and Kathleen Sweeney of Rahway, New Jersey, now operate the Administrative Support Team.

As a self-help organization AASWG operates on a fairly modest budget, purchasing only those goods and services not available within the organization. Symposia budgets are separate and vary according to attendance and location. Operating income is primarily from annual dues but also includes contributions, income from the Endowment Fund, miscellaneous sales of training videos, etc. Funds are solicited for an Annual Fund, which provides for special projects, and for the John H. and Carol E. Ramey Endowment Fund, income from which helps pay for the work of the General Secretary or Administrative Support Team. Chapters and Affiliates have their own budgets. Chapters receive program support from the operating budget.

Two years before the first Symposium Beulah Rothman and Catherine P. "Katy" Papell founded *Social Work with Groups: Journal of Community and Clinical Practice (SWwGJ)* at The Haworth Press (now a part of Taylor & Francis). They had noted that there was a paucity of group work articles available for publication. Few were being written because there had been nowhere to publish them and even with the new journal not many were yet being submitted. Beginning with the first Symposium and for many years the papers were submitted to *SWwGJ* if they were not published in the Symposium *Proceedings*. After Rothman died, Papell continued for a few years. Then Roselle Kurland and Andrew Malekoff were appointed Co-editors. Since Kurland's untimely death, Malekoff continues as the Editor.

AASWG endeavors to develop and maintain formal and informal working relationships with other social work organizations on the national and international levels. A formal agreement with the National Association of Social Workers (NASW) in the USA provides for linkages through Web sites and work on joint projects. Formal liaison has been established with CSWE and the Canadian Association of Schools of Social Work. *SWwG Newsletter* carries conference listings, calls for papers, etc., for related organizations, and similar news releases are shared with the staffs of these organizations.

The AASWG logo, by artist John Morrell of Rochester, New York, was adopted at the first Symposium in Cleveland. It is titled "Life Is Sharing the Same Park Bench." The original may be seen as a wall mural on the building on the northeast corner of East Ninth Street and Rockwell Avenue in downtown Cleveland, Ohio. It recognizes and celebrates AASWG's commitment to diversity and its work to bring diverse peoples together through group work.

Entering the modern age of communications, in the mid-2000s the AASWG Web site, www.aaswg.org, was created by Timothy B. Kelly, then at Barry

University in Miami and now at Glasgow Caledonian University, as the Webmaster. Andrew Cicchetti is now the Webmaster.

The AASWG archives are housed with the Social Welfare History Archives at the University of Minnesota in Minneapolis. Chapters and members are encouraged to send their papers to the Archives.

AASWG is now in its fourth decade as the organization representing group work and working for its improvement and wider recognition as a major mode of social work practice.

References

Association for the Advancement of Social Work with Groups. (2006a). *Standards for social work practice with groups* (2nd ed.). Rahway, NJ: Author.

Association for the Advancement of Social Work with Groups. (2006b). *Estaandares para la Practica del Trabajo con Groups*, (Andrés Arial Astray, Trans.). Rahway, NJ: Author.

Birnbaum, M. L., & Auerbach, C. (1994). Group work in graduate social work education: The price of neglect. *Journal of Social Work Education, 30*(3), 325–335.

Birnbaum, M. L., & Wayne, J. (2000). Group work in foundation generalist education: The necessity for curriculum change. *Journal of Social Work Education, 36*(2), 347–356.

Kurland, R., & Salmon, R. (1997). *Teaching a methods course in social work with groups: Strengthening group work education*. Alexandria, VA: Council on Social Work Education.

Middleman, R. R. (2000). Brief history of AASWG. *Social Work with Groups Newsletter, 16*(1), p.17.

Ramey, J. H. (2006). The understanding and use of *Standards for the practice of social work with groups*. Workshop presentations in San Diego Symposium, Northeast Ohio Chapter AASWG, Ohio Chapter NASW State Conference, and other locations.

Wayne, J. L., & Cohen, C. S. (2001). *Group work education in the field: Strengthening group work education*. Alexandria: VA: Council on Social Work Education.

Summer Camps

Meryl Nadel and Susan Scher

The intentional community of the residential summer camp invites creative interaction, psychosocial development, and opportunities for mutual aid in a strengths-based, group-focused environment. For many who have experienced residential camping, memories of enduring friendships, the natural environment, proud accomplishments, and a singular sense of freedom remain significant throughout life. The cabin group at such camps offers a near-ideal setting for the development of social group work theory, the study of group process, and the implementation of innovative group work practice. Reflecting these opportunities, many prominent group workers (including William Schwartz, Wilber I. Newstetter, Fritz Redl, Gisela Konopka, Roselle Kurland, Charles Grosser, Harry Specht, George Brager, Ruth Middleman, Ronald A. Feldman, and the editors of this encyclopedia) formed productive affiliations with residential camps. Entries in all editions of the

Social Work Year Book (1929–1960) validate the significance of the camp setting as a vital field of practice serving a wide range of populations. This entry reviews the history and development of social group work in organizational (social agency) camps from its beginnings over 100 years ago to its current position.

Camping has been defined as "[s]ustained experience which provides a creative, recreational, and educational opportunity in group living in the out-of-doors. It utilizes trained leadership and the resources of natural surroundings to contribute to each camper's mental, physical, social, and spiritual growth" (American Camping Association [ACA], as cited by Eells, 1986, p. 3). Breton (1990) posits that social group work developed from three "fountainheads": the settlement movement, the recreation movement, and the progressive education movement. The residential camp setting exemplifies the merger of these three sources to produce the unique social group work milieu illustrated by the ACA definition.

Although the first camps, established late in the 19th century, were primarily private, social agencies soon entered the picture, beginning with fresh air and "Y" activities. The fresh air movement, begun in the 1850s by church groups and charity organizations, was an attempt to help poor children and mothers regain health lost from living in the congested, industrialized cities. Fresh air programs included day trips to the ocean or mountains, visits with country families, and colonies or camps in the country with larger numbers of children or families on sites developed for them (Carpenter, 1995). Early in the 20th century, settlement houses and charity organizations with professional orientations developed such fresh air camp programs (Ingram, 1907; Sharp, 1930). Influenced by the private camping movement, YMCA staff members, beginning in 1885, took children on camping trips during the newly expanded summer vacations. This practice, featuring 2-week stays at settled locations, developed quickly (Eells, 1986). Social agency camps unable to afford a large outlay for infrastructure were assisted by public/private entities such as the Palisades Interstate Park Commission (PIPC) in New York and New Jersey. In 1913, PIPC began leasing developed campsites equipped with the facilities needed to operate a camp. Non-profit organizations just needed to bring campers and staff (Brown, 1918). The model, which continues to this day, allowed more than 500 organizations to operate non-profit camps in Harriman State Park, NY (Binnewies, 2001).

By the 1920s, "organized camping," that is, a structured program of activities, had begun to replace the more casual trips to the country (Collins, 2003; Sharp, 1930). In 1930, the White House Conference on Child Health and Protection estimated that camping programs served 3 million youth annually (*Social Work Year Book*, 1933). Summer camps were shifting their emphasis from recreation to education, particularly "character" education (Dimock & Hendry, 1929). In a 1948 publication, Blumenthal describes how camping soon "embraced the group-work method" (p. 9), with its focus on small groups, democratic process, individualization, and trained leadership.

As the residential camping movement grew, it served as a key setting for the development of group work theory and concepts, as evidenced by a rich literature. In 1926, Western Reserve University's Wilber I. Newstetter, the first director of the first social group work specialization in the country, established and directed a camp serving boy clients from the Cleveland Child Guidance Clinic. Many camp staff were group work students and graduates. The camp program incorporated a research project that focused on observing and improving group interaction (Newstetter, 1930; Newstetter, Feldstein, & Newcomb, 1938). Group workers leading other camps also implemented research projects (see, for example, Dimock & Hendry, 1929) or conceptualized the benefits of consciously utilizing group work principles in their camps. The latter emphasis is exemplified by Louis Blumenthal's book, *Grop Work in Camping* (1937). Although the terminology has changed, his descriptions of camp as an ecosystem, leadership and group process, the importance of relationship and interaction, the strengths perspective, social control, group composition, and the opportunity for campers to try out new roles paint a picture of camps as ideal settings for group work.

As group work became more therapeutically oriented, Fritz Redl, Gisela Konopka, and others brought their expertise to the camp world. Redl established a camp for boys referred by courts and child guidance clinics as part of the Detroit Group Project and published an article that more generally suggested proactive approaches to deal with potential problems facing first-time campers (1966).

William Schwartz identified characteristics of the group experience in camp. Focusing on stages of group development, the demand for intimacy, the opportunity to try out new behaviors, and the need for belongingness, Schwartz (1994) discussed their implications for structure and program. In the post-World War II period, this growing integration of group work theory and the organizational camp experience produced sophisticated social group work practice in camps such as those operated by agencies in Chicago, New York City, and Mt. Vernon, NY ("Children's Camps," 1949; Goldberg, 1956).

Camps Willoway, Wagon Road, Minisink, Surprise Lake, Chi, and Vacation Camp for the Blind exemplify camps in which social group workers took active roles as counselors, program directors, camp directors, trainers, board members, and clinicians (Stein, 1943). Wel-Met, one of the largest social work camps in the United States (Eichel, 1965), served as a major source for group work recruitment and training. In these camps, interactional processes in small groups and the appreciation of nature were emphasized. The cabin/bunk was the central focus within which groups decided on activities and processed daily issues. Group focus began at camp registration, which included group intakes as a means of orienting the children to group dialogue. Group supervision of staff was developed to enhance practice skills (Getzel, Goldberg, & Salmon, 1971). Recruitment programs associated with the Social Work Recruiting Center of Greater New York motivated staff considering social work careers (Eichel, 1965; G. Getzel, personal communication, 2007; R. Steinberg, personal communication, 2007).

From their early days to the present, organizational camps have sought to meet the needs of impoverished children, children/youth, families, elders, children with physical disabilities and medical concerns, and others. Although some mainstream camps have continued to employ social workers (Root, 2005; J. Matthews, personal communication, 2006), over the past 30 years the profession has had its greatest impact with camps for populations-at-risk, encompassing three types. In the first type professional group workers serve as administrators in camps offering respite for inner city children (Fresh Air Fund, inner city "Y" camps, settlement house camps) (Collins, 2006).

"Therapeutic camps" focus on benefiting youth by providing a unique treatment setting (Kelk, 1994). Such programs include wilderness/adventure camping and other programs for children with behavioral issues (Davis-Berman & Berman, 1989; Marx, 1988; Middleman & Seever, 1963) as well as camps for children with learning disabilities and psychosocial problems (Michalski, Mishna, Worthington, & Cummings, 2003; Mishna, 2005; Mishna, Michalski, & Cummings, 2001); Family camping has also been utilized for therapeutic purposes (Vassil, 1978).

Another group of camps seek to enhance resiliency by using their strengths-based approach to impart protective factors for children and families. They include camps for HIV-infected and HIV-affected children and families (Langdon & Kelk, 1994; Taylor-Brown, 1999), children with cancer (Beder, 2000), burn-injured adolescents (Williams, Reeves, Cox, & Call, 2004), children who lost parents in the World Trade Center, lesbian, gay, bisexual and transgender (LGBT) youth, children with diabetes, children from conflict regions, and many other populations. Group workers play key roles in these camps as administrators, unit heads, group leaders, and consultants. These camps, as do others, seek to provide growth-enhancing experiences for their campers through group process.

Today's camps also present a rich milieu for service learning. Both undergraduate and graduate students can benefit from well-supervised opportunities to serve and learn in camp settings (Nadel, 2007; Williams, King, & Koob, 2002; Williams & Reeves, 2004). This entry has not dealt with day camps, some of which share a strong social group work orientation. In conclusion, group work's long and substantive connection with residential summer camps has been mutually beneficial. Camping, now serving 10 million youth annually, (American Camping Association, 2007) continues to provide strengths-based settings in which group work at its best is practiced.

References

American Camping Association. (May 22, 2007). *Camp trends: New changes occurring at camps.* Retrieved August 31, 2007 from http://www.acacamps.org/media_center/about_aca/tips070522.php

Beder, J. (2000). Training oncology camp volunteers. *Cancer Practice, 8*(3), 129–134.

Binnewies, R. (2001). *Palisades: 100,000 acres in 100 years.* New York: Fordham University Press.

Blumenthal, L. (1937). *Group work in camping.* New York: Association Press.

Blumenthal, L. (1948). Group work in camping—Yesterday, today and tomorrow. In C. E. Hendry (Ed.), *A decade of group work* (pp. 9–16). New York: Association Press.

Breton, M. (1990). Learning from social group work traditions. *Social Work with Groups, 13*(3), 21–34.

Brown, E. (1917). Public health and recreation encampments in the Palisades Interstate Park. *The American City, XVII*(1), 51–55.

Camping. In *Social work year book* (1930, 1933, 1935, 1937, 1939, 1941, 1943, 1945, 1947, 1949, 1951, 1954, 1957, 1960). New York: various publishers.

Carpenter, C. (1995). *The social production of fresh air charity work, 1870–1930.* Unpublished doctoral dissertation, Syracuse University.

Children's camps take on new look. (1949, July 6). *The New York Times*, p. 31.

Collins, L. (2003). The lost art of group work in camping. *Social Work with Groups, 26*(3), 21–41.

Collins, L. (2006). The meaning of camp and social group work principles. *Social Work with Groups, 29*(2/3), 133–148.

Davis-Berman, J., & Berman, D. S. (1989). The wilderness therapy program: An empirical study of its effects with adolescents in an outpatient setting. *Journal of Contemporary Psychotherapy, 19*(4), 271–281.

Dimock, H.S., & Hendry, C. E. (1929). *Camping and character.* New York: Association Press.

Eells, E. (1986). *History of organized camping: The first 100 years.* Martinsville, IN: American Camping Association.

Eiche, E. (1965). *It happened hereabouts: A glance backwards at thirty years of a community project.* New York: Wel-Met Inc.

Getzel, G. S., Goldberg, J. R., & Salmon, R. (1971). Supervising in groups as a model for today. *Social Casework, 52*(3), 154–163.

Goldberg, J. R. (1956). Myths and realities in camping. *Journal of Jewish Communal Service, 32*(4), 416–429.

Ingram, H. (1907). The value of the fresh air movement. In A. Johnson (Ed.), *Proceedings of the 34th Annual National Conference on Charities and Correction* (pp. 286–298). Indianapolis, IN: Press of Wm. B. Burford.

Kelk, N. (1994). Camping and outdoor activities as psychosocial interventions. *Australian Social Work, 47*(2), 37–42.

Langdon, P., & Kelk, N. (1994). The paediatric AIDS camp: Three years of good times. *Australian Social Work, 47*(3): 43–49.

Marx, J. D. (1988). An outdoor adventure counseling program for adolescents. *Social Work, 33*(6), 517–520.

Michalski, J., Mishna, F., Worthington, C., & Cummings, R. (2003). A multi-method impact evaluation of a therapeutic summer camp program. *Child and Adolescent Social Work Journal, 20*(1), 53–76.

Middleman, R., & Seever, F. (1963). Short-term camping for boys with behavior problems. *Social Work, 8*(2), 88–95.

Mishna, F. (2005). The application of self psychology to therapeutic camps. *Psychoanalytic Social Work, 12*(1), 51–71.

Mishna, F., Michalsti, J., & Cummings, R. (2001). Camps as social work interventions: Returning to our roots. *Social Work with Groups, 24*(3/4), 153–171.

Nadel, M. (2007). Populations-at-risk/immersion experience: Service learning at summer camp. In M. Nadel, V. Majewski, & M. Sullivan-Cosetti (Eds.), *Social work and service learning: Partnerships for social justice* (pp. 133–146). Lanham, MD: Rowman & Littlefield.

Newstetter, W. I. (1930). *Wawokiye Camp: A research project in group work.* Cleveland, OH: School of Applied Social Sciences, Western Reserve University.

Newstetter, W. I., Feldstein, M. J., & Newcomb, T. M. (1938). *Group adjustment: A study in experimental sociology.* Cleveland OH: School of Applied Social Sciences, Western Reserve University.

Redl, F. (1966). Psychopathological risks of camp life. In F. Redl, *When we deal with children: Selected writings* (pp. 440–451). New York: Free Press.

Root, V. B. (2005). Social work goes to summer camp. In L. M. Grobman (Ed.), *Days in the lives of social workers* (3rd ed., pp. 147–151). Harrisburg, PA: White Hat Communications.

Schwartz, W. (1994). Characteristics of the group experience in resident camping. In T. Berman-Rossi (Ed.), *Social work: The collected writings of William Schwartz* (pp. 427–433). Itasca, IL: F. E. Peacock.

Sharp, L. B. (1930). *Education and the summer camp: An experiment.* New York: Columbia University Press.

Stein, H. (1943). The caseworker in a children's camp. *The Family: Journal of Social Casework, XXIV*(3), 163–170.

Taylor-Brown, S. (1999). Family unity camping weekend: Dreams come true for HIV-affected families. *Reflections, 5*(1), 51–59.

Vassil, T. V. (1978). Residential family camping: Altering family patterns. *Social Casework, 59*(1), 605–613.

Williams, N. R., King, M., & Koob, J. J. (2002). Social work students go to camp: The effects of service learning on perceived self-efficacy. *Journal of Teaching in Social Work, 22*(3/4), 55–70.

Williams, N. R., & Reeves, P. M. (2004). MSW students go to burn camp: Exploring social work values through service-learning. *Social Work Education, 23*(4), 383–398.

Williams, N. R., Reeves, P. M., Cox, E. R., & Call, S. B. (2004). Creating a social work link to the burn community: A research team goes to burn camp. *Social Work in Health Care, 38*(3), 81–103.

Contemporary Landscape

Harriet Goodman

Over three decades, changes in human services delivery have reshaped the meaning and configuration of social group work. Contemporary developments have resulted in expanded privatization, fiscal austerity, increased demands for productivity (Braye & Preston-Shoot, 1999), loss of professional autonomy, and heightened emphasis on quantitative service outcome measures. In the face of this shifting terrain, group workers struggle to maintain the best values and traditions of the method.

Three trends that have profoundly influenced group work are the ascendancy of evidence-based practice, privatization of services and, already widely discussed in the group work literature (Birnbaum & Auerbach, 1994), changes in social work education. Some (Bransford, 2005) entreat social workers to use the authority vested in the values and principles of the profession to promote socially conscious practice. Many others accept these transformations as part of a fixed, new terrain and passively adapt to contemporary agency realities (Watt & Kallmann, 1998). When this occurs, group workers subjugate these forces to a status "beneath the surface." However, closer examination of the current landscape can illuminate how these developments potentially undermine the vibrancy of practice.

Evidence-based practice (EBP) is actively promoted among social workers, primarily through the synthesis of rigorous research studies, to determine whether or not interventions are effective. Social work optimism about EBP rests in concerns about the professional status of social work and the desire to make practice decisions on the basis of the best empirical evidence (Mcgowan, 2006; Pollio, 2002). Evidence-based practice is laudable for grounding practice in empirical studies, since demonstrable research underpinnings elevate professional standards. Nonetheless, evidence-based practice presents problems for social group workers, among them the paucity of research about social group work practices other than cognitive-behavioral groups. When researchers conduct studies to determine the effectiveness of a particular intervention, they must establish practices that can be replicated by other researchers and consistently put into practice by group workers. Under the rigorous standards established by organizations such as the Cochrane and Campbell Collaborations that review research on clinical interventions and establish criteria for studies included in their reviews, the randomized controlled trial is the gold standard for research.

These considerations lead to manuals with specific practice directives that operationalize an intervention. Once a practice is codified, other researchers can replicate it, and if deemed effective through the review process, the manualized version of the group intervention can be sanctioned. Of course few manualized groups are subject to rigorous evaluation, but those that are and hold up under the scrutiny of the review process are prized.

Cognitive-behavioral group work (CBGW) treatments often appear as evidence-based practices. Rose (2004) emphasizes the empirically based approach of CBGW, which has produced numerous techniques that have been evaluated using experimental research designs. However, he also recognizes few skilled group workers will conduct these groups using problem-solving and mutual aid strategies (Rose, 2004).

EBP has given credibility to specific group manuals, because their effectiveness has been empirically tested. However, manualized group practice has been disparaged in some quarters because the practitioner is no longer considered the best judge of practice. The expert authority of an educated group worker is not necessary, since the claim for authority is displaced to the empiricists. The group work screed against manualized groups might soften if group workers became actively involved in their development or viewed their practice as curriculum-based, rather than curriculum-driven (Galinsky, Terzian, & Frazer, 2006; Kurland & Malekoff, 1998). Manuals require skilled practitioners to bring the group to life within the context of a predetermined structure, a point underscored by Rose's (2004) call for skilled cognitive-behavioral group work practitioners. More active engagement in social group work research, perhaps in collaboration with academic researchers, could provide an emollient for the domination of CBGW groups in the EBP canon of group practice.

Since the 1980s, managed care organizations (MCOs) have dominated health and mental health services, reshaping the financing and structure of sectors. The MCO revolution transformed payment for health services through capitated schemes, and controlled spending by limiting services and designating preferred providers. The Tax Equity and Fiscal Responsibility Act of 1982 (TEFRA) contained Medicare costs through diagnostic-related groups for reimbursement, linking service costs to diagnostic categories. Later acts refined qualifications for beneficiaries and increased managed care choices for Medicare and Medicaid recipients.

Mental health services were initially untouched, but entrepreneurs ultimately entered the behavioral health market, which remained relatively unregulated. Large, for-profit chains specialized in treating psychiatric disorders and substance abuse (Geller, 1996). The introduction of privatization into what had previously been the purview of voluntary providers changed both the culture and the stakes of behavioral health care. Profits and care-giving are not necessarily incompatible, but stockholders demand profitable corporations, so that business plans and solutions are more likely to shape care for vulnerable clients.

Social group workers historically recognized the power of groups as vehicles for internal change and for community action to address problems. One of the dramatic features of increased privatization has been to dampen the role of advocacy in social work generally and for group workers in particular. A profit-driven environment, which attempts to suppress clients who wish to seek redress on their own behalf, makes it difficult for social workers to offer clients support in doing just that. Social group workers face a dilemma: should they embrace the thrust of group members to re-enforce each other and promote activism among members or yield to the need to remain employed?

Privatization can distort group work processes, particularly when group services are viewed as an efficient vehicle for profit-making organizations. Group purpose is dominated more by the need to serve as many people as possible and less with the shared needs of individual members. Just as evidence-based practices encourage the use of manualized groups, curricular adherence is a hallmark of privatized practice in behavioral health. Rigid compliance with a pre-determined work plan is an essential feature on the landscape of practice dominated by for-profit settings. Practice efficiency is dominant; worker autonomy is suppressed and authority shifts to bureaucrats (Munson, 1996).

Prepared manuals are useful to for-profit organizations. Employing established curricula justifies lack of training or supervision for group leaders. Organizations can hire less credentialed and cheaper staff members to conduct groups. Although this mechanistic approach to group practice severely undermines the potential of groups to promote mutual support among members, standardization trumps group purpose in this environment.

Professional social workers are likely to be supervisors or administrators rather than direct service providers in for-profit behavioral health organizations (Lawler, 2007). In these positions, group workers can develop manuals that promote curriculum-based, rather than curriculum-driven groups. They can also model group work principles in supervisory meetings and inject their practice expertise in planning and decision-making roles. These actions require strong identification with the principles and values of social group work and creative tactics to bring about high standards of practice.

References

Birnbaum, M. M., & Auerbach, C. (1994). Group work in graduate social work education: the price of neglect. *Journal of Social Work Education, 30*(3), 325–336.

Bransford, C. L. (2005). Conceptions of authority within contemporary social work practice in managed mental health care organizations. *American Journal of Orthopsychiatry, 75*(3), 409–420.

Braye, S., & Preston-Shoot, M. (1999). Accountability, administrative law and social work practice: Redressing or reinforcing the power imbalance? *Journal of Social Welfare & Family Law, 21*(3), 235.

Galinsky, M. J., Terzian, M. A., & Fraser, M. W. (2006). The art of group work practice with manualized curricula. *Social Work with Groups, 29*(1), 11–26.

Geller, J. L. (1996). Managed care, unmanaged care and mismanaged care. *Smith College Studies in Social Work, 66*(3), 223–237.

Kurland, R., & Malekoff, A. (1998). From the editors. *Social Work with Groups, 21*(1/2), 1–3.

Lawler, J. (2007). Leadership in social work: A case of *caveat emptor? British Journal of Social Work, 37*(1), 123–141.

Macgowan, M. J. (2006). Evidence-based group work: A framework for advancing best practice. *Journal of Evidence-Based Social Work, 3*(1), 1–21.

Munson, C. E. (1996). Autonomy and managed care in clinical social work practice. *Smith College Studies in Social Work, 66*(3), 24–260.

Pollio, D. E. (2002). The evidence-based group worker. *Social Work with Groups, 25*(4), 57–70.

Rose, S. D. (2004). Cognitive-behavioral group work. In C. D. Garvin, L. M. Gutiérrez, & M. J. Galinsky (Eds.), *Handbook of social work with groups* (pp. 111–135). New York: Guilford Press.

Watt, J. W., & Kallmann, G. L. (1998). Managing professional obligations under managed care: A social work perspective. *Family & Community Health, 21*(2), 40–49.

Struggle for Survival

Shirley R. Simon and Joyce A. Webster

Social group work, with its rich history as a method, practice, and philosophical orientation, is engaged in a struggle for survival. Throughout social work's history, social group work has been a mainstay of the profession (Andrews, 2001; Goodman & Munoz, 2004; Toseland & Rivas, 2005). With its democratic and strengths-based perspectives, mutual aid orientation, positive approach to conflict, and emphasis on empowerment and universalization, group work has proven to be a powerful and effective modality across the wide range of social work contexts (Drumm, 2006; Gitterman & Shulman, 2005; Toseland & Rivas, 2005). Its multi-dimensional, broad-based approach is as relevant today as it has been since social work's inception. Yet, this long-standing pillar of social work is in danger of collapsing.

As early as 1978, and evermore vociferously in recent decades, leaders in social group work have issued warnings about group work's diminished place in education and practice (Drumm, 2006; Goodman & Munoz, 2004; Kurland & Salmon, 2002; Middleman, 1990; Salmon & Steinberg, 2007; Tropp, 1978). Sweeping academic and economic changes have negatively impacted social group work's stature. Now, at the beginning of the 21st century, group work has a diminished place within the academic community, a decreased number of trained group work professionals, a devaluation and marginalization within the practice environment, an aging core of group work leaders, and a membership crisis in its professional association, the Association for the Advancement of Social Work with Groups (AASWG) (Bergart & Simon, 2005; Drumm, 2006; Goodman & Munoz, 2004; Simon, Webster, & Horn, 2007). What has led to the decline of this powerful social work methodology? What needs to happen if it is to survive?

The decision in 1969 by the Council on Social Work Education (CSWE) to collapse individual methodological approaches into one generalist perspective has frequently been cited as the beginning of the decline of group work within social work education (Birnbaum & Auerbach, 1994; Drumm, 2006; Goodman & Munoz, 2004; Kurland & Salmon, 2002; Salmon & Steinberg, 2007). Prior to this decision, social work curricula were typically organized around concentrations in casework, group work, and community organization (Birnbaum & Auerbach, 1994). As programs shifted from these method-specific approaches to a more integrative and generalist approach, the presence of social group work within schools of social work drastically diminished (Birnbaum & Auerbach, 1994; Goodman & Munoz, 2004; Middleman, 1990; Simon et al., 2007).

According to a study published by Birnbaum & Auerbach in 1994, the number of graduate programs offering a concentration in group work declined from 76% of the schools surveyed to a mere 7% percent from 1963 to 1991. By 1991 only 17 programs, less than 20% of the schools surveyed, required even one group work course for their students. Group work courses were offered only as electives at 46% of these schools and nearly two-thirds of all schools surveyed had no requirement for group work as part of the field experience. (Birnbaum & Auerbach, 1994). While this study has not been replicated, accounts from today's group work leaders and educators indicate the situation has only deteriorated further. Today's social work students are rarely, if ever, required to take a single course in group work and only three graduate programs offer a concentration in group work.

This generalist educational approach has also resulted in a diminished need for group work educators (Birnbaum & Auerbach, 1994). Without academic positions dedicated to social group work, there is little opportunity and incentive for those passionate about group work to teach and conduct research in this area of practice. In addition, faculty who teach integrative practice courses typically have little formal education in group work and are, therefore, frequently poorly prepared to incorporate it into their courses.

The number of trained professionals who feel comfortable with, and informed about, group work has been severely curtailed by the absence of a strong curricular focus. This diminished curricular attention, coupled with group work's long-standing heritage as casework's "step-sister," has created an environment of neglect that allows graduates to leave social work programs with the perception that group work is less valuable and significant than other methods of practice (Cohen, 1995; Drumm, 2006; Kurland & Salmon, 1992; Salmon & Steinberg, 2007). As a result, today's practitioners are not as likely to implement and advocate for group work as a method of choice (Birnbaum & Auerbach, 1994; Cohen, 1995). This is further complicated when the practitioner is also a supervisor (Bergart & Simon, 2005). Supervisors, lacking group work expertise, are naturally reluctant to encourage their students and staff to utilize group work methodology. Even when supervisees demonstrate an interest in group work, supervisors typically lack the skills necessary to foster such practice. This is particularly significant for students in field placements, where the absence of supervisory expertise inhibits not only the quality of current practice but, more importantly, the development of critical foundation-level group work skills (Birnbaum & Auerbach, 1994; Goodman & Munoz, 2004; Strozier, 1997). This contributes to an environment in which group work practice is readily marginalized and devalued (Cohen, 1995; Drumm, 2006).

Paradoxically, despite all of the factors that inhibit effective group work practice, the need for group workers has increased (Goodman & Munoz, 2004; Simon et al., 2007; Strozier, 1997). Managed care is requiring that agencies provide group work services regardless of orientation and level of group work expertise (Birnbaum & Auerbach, 1994). Group work is frequently mandated because it is perceived to be "cost effective," with little attention to the actual skills of the agency staff. With increasingly limited resources and a concurrent emphasis on productivity, agencies are typically unable to provide the continuing education and in-service training necessary to address these skill deficits (Bergart & Simon, 2005). The absence of adequately trained group workers, coupled with the demand for short-term, measurable treatment outcomes, has made the notion of structured, curriculum-driven groups attractive. Core social group work concepts such as mutual aid, time for the natural emergence of the stages of group development, the dynamic use of group process, and member empowerment are being supplanted by structured, curriculum-driven agendas. The magic of group process is at risk of being undermined by pre-determined curricular content (Goodman & Munoz, 2004).

Furthermore, those practitioners who do employ social group work methodology are frequently isolated and lonely (Goodman & Munoz, 2004; Kurland & Salmon, 2002). In previous decades, it was common to find a cadre of group work-oriented practitioners within the same social service agency (Bergart & Simon, 2005). Today, such supportive and collaborative environments for the practice of group work are increasingly rare. With budget cutbacks, increased workloads, decreased opportunities for in-service training, and a diminished voice for group work in academic and practice settings, group work practitioners often struggle to defend and legitimize their work in environments that neither understand nor appreciate their perspective (Bergart & Simon, 2005; Drumm, 2006). Thus, the effectiveness of current group work practice is, at best, open to question.

While leaders in group work have been vocal and clear in their call for action, the leadership ranks themselves have been shrinking. Whether through retirement, illness, or death, the voices of many spokespersons have been silenced. In recent years, group work has lost an inordinate number of eloquent champions—Janice Schopler, Gisela Konopka, Toby Berman-Rossi, Janice Andrews-Schenk, Ruth Middleman, Roselle Kurland, Helen Northen, and Albert Alissi. Their likes are not easily replaced, further contributing to group work's precarious position. Not only has group work lost many of its vital spokespersons, but it has yet to mentor a younger generation of advocates to assume the leadership mantle. The dearth of ready leaders to champion social group work's cause is of fundamental concern.

Given all of these confluent factors, the rich tradition and power of social group work is in serious danger of being lost. Group work, practiced by those not schooled in its methods, may soon become unrecognizable. If social group work is to survive as a skilled modality, issues such as the enhancement of group work's place within the academic community, the need for well-trained, motivated educators and practitioners, the appreciation and endorsement of group work within the practice environment, and the cultivation of new group work leaders all need to be vigorously and quickly addressed.

AASWG, a strong advocate for social group work for nearly three decades, is also struggling to survive (Simon et al., 2007). Like most professional associations, AASWG is currently confronting membership and volunteer crises (Putnam, 2000; Sullivan, 2006). At exactly the time when group workers are most in need of a supportive community of similarly minded peers, AASWG's membership has slipped, with only a small number of over-worked and dedicated members fostering its charge (Sullivan, 2006). Given group work's precarious position, this situation is of particular concern. Without a strong professional association, there can be no collective voice to articulate social group work's critical place within contemporary practice. Thus, the strengthening of AASWG is imperative. AASWG is the logical venue through which to advocate for social group work and partner with academic communities, accrediting bodies, and practice arenas to elevate group work to its rightful place. To be effective, AASWG needs to immediately strengthen its membership and leadership ranks. The next generation of leaders must be identified and mentored to replace group work's aging cadre of spokespersons. Because AASWG, like all professional associations, is dependent on an ongoing influx of new, dues-paying members and their concomitant energy and ideas, the recruitment and retention of students and new professionals needs to be a high priority (Simon et al., 2007).

It is evident that current AASWG leadership understands the critical importance of these goals and has taken a number of steps to strengthen the organization. The Association has greatly expanded its outreach to both students and new professionals. At the 29th Annual AASWG International Symposium in 2007, this topic was a prevalent theme. Students and new professionals presented numerous papers, participated heavily in town hall discussions, and were recognized by the AASWG Board of Directors for their many contributions. There was significant ongoing discussion regarding the attraction and retention of new members through a reduction in membership fees for recent graduates, the encouragement of student presentations at annual symposia, the appointment of students to the Board of Directors and its committees, the establishment of competitive Chapter awards for outstanding student papers, and the development of a wider array of educational programs for professionals. It was noted that several AASWG Chapters were offering continuing education workshops and further expansion of these efforts was strongly encouraged (Salmon & Steinberg, 2007). With its recent efforts to curtail expenses and increase the number of institutional and individual memberships, AASWG has considerably improved its financial situation (G. Tully, personal communication, June 29, 2007). As the Association gains strength, it will be in a better position to fulfill its mandate as the powerful advocate of social group work and facilitate the changes needed within academic and practice communities.

Partnering with the academic community, AASWG could advocate for the re-evaluation of curricular standards, increased exposure to group work within foundation-level practice courses, and enhanced curricular opportunities for students with a specific interest in this area (Birnbaum & Auerbach, 1994; Drumm, 2006). CSWE, as the accrediting body for social work programs, needs to be held accountable for the inclusion of substantial content on group work theory and practice (Drumm, 2006). AASWG could play a significant role in lobbying CSWE for these curricular changes (Birnbuam & Auerbach, 1994). Because a cadre of informed and passionate faculty is essential in order to foster group work's agenda in academia, attention should also be given to faculty development. It is imperative to find ways to encourage and promote the development of group work educators and researchers. Opportunities and support for faculty to write and do research in areas related to group work, and to disseminate this knowledge to both group work and broader-based audiences, needs to be fostered (Kurland & Salmon, 1992). Accumulating replicable research demonstrating the significance of the lack of group work education and training is critical in effectively articulating group work's case to the various influential constituent bodies (Kurland & Salmon, 1992).

Within practice arenas, the identification and development of field agencies and supervisors who can adequately train students in group work methodology is a critical component in ensuring group work's future (Birnbaum & Auerbach, 1994). Increasing the availability of continuing education and certificate programs in group work for both paraprofessionals and social work graduates is also crucial (Drumm, 2006; Salmon & Steinberg, 2007). This is particularly essential to enhance supervisors' and practitioners' comfort with group work as a modality of choice. Experienced group workers and local AASWG Chapters must become more widely involved in facilitating trainings and consultations for agencies (Kurland & Salmon, 1992; Salmon & Steinberg, 2007). The recently revised *Standards for Social Work Practice with Groups* (AASWG, 2006) should be widely disseminated to assist with the effective application of group work skills in agency settings. To decrease the prevalent isolation and loneliness of group work practitioners, more immediate opportunities for connection and support are essential (Bergart & Simon, 2005). While AASWG's symposia provide an annual opportunity for peer support, more on-line and face-to-face connections must be available on an ongoing basis (Bergart & Simon, 2005).

Social group work's importance has suffered from a downward spiral of concurrent, cyclical forces resulting in its struggle for survival. The crisis in group work is real; the time to act is now. Social group work's very identity as a competency-based practice modality is in jeopardy. Group workers in AAWSG, the academic community, and the practice arena need to come together to address this crisis and restore group work to its rightful place in social work education and practice.

References

Andrews, J. (2001). Group work's place in social work: A historical analysis. *Journal of Sociology and Social Welfare, 28*(4), 45–65.

Association for the Advancement of Social Work with Groups. (2006). *Standards for social work practice with groups* (2nd ed.). Rahway, NJ: Author.

Bergart, A., & Simon, S. (2005). Practicing what we preach: Creating groups for ourselves. *Social Work with Groups, 27*(4), 17–30.

Birnbaum, M., & Auerbach, C. (1994). Group work in graduate social work education: The price of neglect. *Journal of Social Work Education, 30*(3), 325–335.

Cohen, C. (1995). Making it happen: From great idea to successful support group. *Social Work with Groups, 18*(1), 67–80.

Drumm, K. (2006). The essential power of group work. *Social Work with Groups, 29*(23), 17–31.

Gitterman., A., & Shulman, L. (2005). *Mutual aid groups, vulnerable and resilient populations and the life cycle* (3rd ed.). New York: Columbia University Press.

Goodman, H., & Munoz, M. (2004). Developing social group work skills for contemporary agency practice. *Social Work with Groups, 27*(1), 17–33.

Kurland, R., & Salmon, R. (1992). *Making a joyful noise: Presenting, promoting and portraying group work to and for the profession*. Plenary presentation at the 14th Annual Symposium of the Association for the Advancement of Social Work with Groups, Atlanta, GA. Also in (1996) Stempler, B., & Glass, M. (Eds.), *Social group work today and tomorrow: Moving from theory to advanced training and practice* (pp. 19–32). Binghamton, NY: Haworth Press.

Kurland, R., & Salmon, R. (2002). *Caught in the doorway between education and practice: Group work's battle for survival*. Plenary Presentation at the 24th Annual Symposium of the Association for the Advancement of Social Work with Groups, Boston.

Middleman, R. (1990). Group work and the Heimlich maneuver: Unchoking social work education. In D. F. Fike & B. Rittner (Eds.), *Working from strengths: The essence of group work* (pp. 16–39). Miami, FL: Center for Group Work Studies.

Putnam, R. (2000). *Bowling alone: The collapse and revival of American community*. New York: Simon & Schuster.

Salmon, R., & Steinberg, D. M. (2007). *Re-visiting "… joyful noise": Gateways from the blues to the Hallelujah Chorus*. Plenary presentation at the 29th annual symposium of the Association for the Advancement of Social work with Groups, Jersey City.

Simon, S., Webster, J., & Horn, K. (2007). A critical call: Connecting students and professional associations. *Social Work with Groups, 30*(4), 5–19.

Strozier, A. (1997). Group work in social work education: What is being taught? *Social Work with Groups, 20*(1), 65–77.

Sullivan, N. (2006). From the President's pen: Why belong to AASWG? *Social Work with Groups Newsletter, 22*(59).

Toseland, R., & Rivas, R. (2005). *An introduction to group work practice* (5th ed.). Boston: Allyn & Bacon.

Tropp, E. (1978). What ever happened to group work? *Social Work with Groups, 1*(1), 85–94.

Group Work Values

Humanistic and Democratic Values

Urania Glassman

Group work's history has emphasized democracy, the rights of the members, freedom of expression, and social responsibility (Klein, 1953; Konopka, 1978; Lindeman, 1980). Group work's humanistic values and democratic norms are a foundation for developing members' skills in democratic participation. Along with these, the tenets in the *UN Declaration of Human Rights* (UN, 1948) highlight the universality of these values and norms. Experiences in totalitarian regimes (Glassman & Skolnik, 1984; Konopka, 1978; Theodorakis, 1973) emphasize the fragility of these values and norms, and the necessity for protecting them as rights in societies, and in groups.

Democratic norms are the humanistic values in action. They are the explicit and implicit standards developed in the members' transactions that guide their behavior. However, the enactment of humane and democratic norms is not guaranteed. The group worker functioning within professional values must foster the development of democratic group norms through the purposeful use of skill.

Humanistic Value 1

People have *inherent worth and capacities* regardless of race, class, status, age, gender, as well as physical and psychological condition. The democratic norm *of protecting each member's right to contribute to and receive from the group*, insures that people possessing more knowledge or experience do not invalidate others' contributions and needs in the group. The worker role emphasizes the value of each member to the life of the group, explicitly stating that each member's opinions and goals significantly contribute to determining the group's direction.

Humanistic Value 2

People are *responsible for and to one another* because social life is a natural and necessary human characteristic. The democratic norm that *members interact through caring and mutual aid rather than exploitive relations* highlights social responsibility and authenticity as central to group life. Members learn to respond to each other's feelings, concerns, and ambitions, while sharing their own resources toward one another's growth. The *worker role* emphasizes caring and connection and validates presenting a range of positive and negative expressions that establish communication, relationship, and safety. The norm for *building cooperative rather than competitive relations in the group* fosters members' collective abilities to create a caring and supportive milieu poised to facilitate member change. The worker role is to indicate competition among members and to highlight when they are not hearing or responding to others' needs.

Humanistic Value 3

People have *the right to belong,* and to be included. The democratic norm for *inclusion rather than exclusion* creates openness and permeability that permits membership to a range of different members rather than closed group boundaries. A related norm that the group *deals openly and rationally with prospective members* creates transparent criteria for adding members. The norm for developing ways of *permitting and maintaining membership to "difficult members,"* expands the group's abilities to relate to a range of personalities. The norm guiding the use of exclusion as a therapeutic tool permits members to apply sanctions for harmful behaviors. The worker role is to foster acceptance of one another's membership in the group, and to strengthen confidence in addressing a range of issues. Discussing membership and boundaries expands skills and vision of the group's sanctuary. Providing sanctions curtailing or dismissing a member for hurtful behaviors may be necessary.

Humanistic Value 4

People having emotional and intellectual voices that are essential to their existence, have *the right to take part and to be heard.* The norm provides for the *development of procedures that permit everyone to participate.* Mechanisms are needed for fostering participation, limiting the input of members, and providing space for the inclusion of quieter members. The worker role includes perceiving when others want to speak and if a speaker has been tuned out. Interrupting long-winded presentations, and redirecting discussion to include others, expands participation and self-regulation. Addressing participation inequalities, and inviting others to speak is required.

Humanistic Value 5

People have the right to *freedom of speech, and freedom of expression.* The norm fosters the development of an *open communication system without reliance on narrow ideology.* Members are free to present feelings and expressions that emanate from the affective domain of human interaction and far less from ideology. The task is to weave a flexible communication system encouraging a broad expression of feelings and ideas. The *open expression of feeling and tempering premature self-disclosure* promotes participation by regulating premature self-disclosures that may result in members' exiting the group. If not stopped, overly assertive members can become grandiose, subtly denigrating others. The worker role involves fostering open expression of feeling. When excessive personal information is presented early on, the worker stops the full story from unfolding, generalizing the issue to make it relevant to the group.

Humanistic Value 6

People have the right to be *valued for their differences*, which are seen as enriching the process. The norm is for members to *foster each other's diversity rather than to push for conformity*. A group that is unable to accept or tolerate individuals who are different in expression, feeling, or views, rigidifies its belief system, and runs the risk of becoming narrowly focused on ideology rather than on the value of differences and human interaction. The worker role begins with self-awareness regarding difference. Statements supporting difference and protecting different persons or opinions from becoming submerged, help solidify membership for a wide range of individuals and prevent member departures due to feeling closed out.

Humanistic Value 7

People have the *right to freedom of choice*. The norm for *fostering the equal distribution of power* in the group insures that influence, leadership, and control will be mutual, shared and not resting with a clique. The norm for *open decision-making processes* in the group promotes hearing minority opinions, empathizing with all viewpoints, developing skills in consensus and compromise, and reaching beyond simple voting. The worker role focuses on examining implicit decision making in order to make the process more explicit. Modeling empathy with dissident views, and highlighting when a decision is premature, redirects them toward consensus and compromise. The norm permitting members to *try out and take different roles* through opportunities, which include programming efforts, fosters experimenting with new roles and behaviors in the group. The worker role highlights a member's behavioral change, harnesses examination of the impact of behavioral change on the group, including when a member's change is unrecognized, and assists in program planning. The norm fostering *freedom to change versus coercion* protects the member's right to choose how and if personal change occurs. The task is to clarify that behavior change involves risk, and trust, and that the individual member decides which change to undertake. The worker protects the member's right by asking directly if this questioning or discussion is something the member wishes to pursue at present. The worker points out group pressure to conform to majority views.

   The norm governing how *member behavior outside of the group is shaped by the standards that guide behavior* in the group recognizes that although newly acquired behaviors will be carried over to the outside, the use of group cohesion to attain a rigid adherence to standards in and out of the group jeopardizes individual autonomy. This norm prevents the distorted use of the group's cohesion for the development of the group as a demagogue or cult whose norms are used to control every aspect of the members' lives. The worker role is to consider when a group is using cohesion to exert authoritarian control over member's lives in and out of the group, and to focus on flexibility in abiding by group rules without aggressive authoritarian control.

Humanistic Value 8

People have the *right to question and challenge those in authority* who have sanction to guide and direct their lives. The norm is for members to *develop direct ways of expressing reactions to the worker.* The group's open expression about the worker role helps members to understand their enactments and relationship to authority. This enables ownership of the group and more intimate and authentic relationships with each other. The worker role is to invite member expression of reaction to the participation of the worker. Recognizing that the group's expression about authority figures is a latent presentation of their own concerns about the worker, the worker addresses these concerns directly and asks members to share reactions to the worker.

The operationalization of humanistic values through democratic norms fostered by the worker role facilitates the creation of an egalitarian and trusting group that provides belonging and healing, and repairs the social and emotional hurts that result from oppressing and invalidating environments.

References

Glassman, U. (2008). *Group work: A humanistic and skills building approach.* Newbury Park, CA: Sage.

Glassman, U., & Kates, L. (1986). Developing the democratic humanistic norms of the social work group. In M. Parnes (Ed.), *Innovations in group work* (pp. 149–172). Binghamton, NY: Haworth Press.

Glassman, U., & Skolnik, L. (1984). The role of social group work in refugee resettlement. *Social Work with Groups, 7*(1), 45–62.

Klein, A. (1953). *Society, democracy, and the group.* New York: Women's Press and William Morrow.

Konopka, G. (1978). The significance of group work based on ethical values. *Social Work with Groups, 1*(2), 123–132.

Lindeman, E. (1980). Group work and democratic values. In H. Trecker (Ed.), *Group work foundations and frontiers* (Rev ed., pp. 13–25). Hebron, CT: Practitioner's Press.

Theodorakis, M. (1973). *Journal of resistance* (G. Webb, Trans.). New York: Coward, McCann & Geohegan.

United Nations. (1948). *UN Universal Declaration of Human Rights.* Adopted by General Assembly Resolution 217 A (III), December 10, 1948.

Social Context

Maura McIntyre and Lynne Mitchell

Social group work occurs in a social context or milieu. When people come together in groups, whether it is for self-help or mutual aid, current social values of how individuals in groups should operate impact our practice. The social world in which group work found its origins at the beginning of the last century was both practical and idealistic. The democratic process, inclusion, social participation, and social change were the core values that guided the development of group work as a method (Kurland & Salmon, 1998). Social group work values of the time were grounded in the assumption that serving the individual also meant serving a broader social good, and that these goals were mutual and intertwined. With individuals turned out toward a world that they could make a better place through participation in a group, a heady optimism permeated the advancement of social group work as a method. In a time before television, before computers, palm pilots, iPods and headphones people engaged with one another in groups for purposes of personal growth, learning, recreation, and community development.

Over the last several decades of the 20th century, the purposes of social group work and the populations served by the method have dramatically expanded. Groups for the very old and infirm, or for people living with dementia, cancer or HIV, or for children of parents who are undergoing "gender journeys," reflect the multitude of changes—from social and environmental to a longer lifespan itself—that is our changing world (Russell, 2007). Difference and diversity have expanded the horizons of group work practice, but how have social group work values responded to the realities of a changing world? How do group workers reconcile the individualistic values of a "me" generation obsessed with isolating technologies with the belief in human engagement so fundamental to group work? Can group work survive, or is it past its time with its historic values the weakest link? As Doel and Sawdon (1999) suggest:

> In the ebb and flow of professional fashions, it might be felt that groupwork is past its time ... [and] the collectivist ideal which group work embodies has been washed up on the post-modernist beach, stranded by the tide of privatized, atomized experiences in an environment which is no longer capable of supporting life forms like groupwork.
>
> (p.7)

The value base of the social context and milieu in which social group work operates in the 21st century is difficult to characterize and describe. Previous understandings about what human contact and connection look like have been overwhelmed and altered by the Internet and media. For example, different types of groups are currently popular in the genre of reality television; however, the values promoted in these programs are completely opposed to group work values. On shows such as *Survivor*, core group work values such as altruism and universality and core group work concepts such as the group as a mutual aid system are destroyed daily—and people (millions of them) seem to love to watch!

This clash of values has implications for the morale of the group worker and the practice of social group work. Contemporary society has been permeated with the values promulgated and idealized in reality television. Finding congruence between the values of the institutions where we do groups with the values guiding our practice, and then searching for confluence with the values of the surrounding social world can feel like a daunting task.

A practice illustration: The authors were facilitating a youth group that focused on violence and abuse prevention. Some members sporadically participated. An incident occurred in which these less committed members were accused by their peers of arriving only to partake of the pizza and bus tickets. Group members were adamant that these fringe members should be deprived of the pizza, and requested the facilitators to immediately remove them from the group. The authors believed that group members shared common values of altruism and universality with the facilitators and appealed to these values. In response, the group members became angry. They wanted no part of this group process and accused the authors of being too soft. Eventually, the targeted members left.

The authors had hoped that some group members would have come forward with an alternative view, thereby permitting a therapeutic process to unfold. Instead, group members voted the fringe members off the island. No therapeutic dynamics for these youth. No humanistic values of altruism, instillation of hope, and universality for these youth. No recognition of the power of the group to facilitate helpful connections between group members in a variety of ways for these youth (Northen in Malekoff, 2004; Shulman, 2006; Steinberg, 2002). No faith in group process, or faith in a group's capacity to process a failure of group process for these youth (Harrison & Ward, 2000).

The change in societal values represents a significant challenge to social work with groups in the 21st century. How do we encourage participants to believe that something good will arise from this process, a tangible, positive experience that will enable them to move forward in their lives. How do we have members buy into our notion of "lending a vision": our belief that by involvement with the group, things can improve; our vision of the essential goodness and power of people coming together and helping each other; our vision of communication, connection and community. Each one of us, each time we facilitate a group, we must emphasize group work values. In so doing, we renew our own commitment and expose our members to the collectivist ideal that continues to resonate in the culture of group work practice.

References

Doel, M., & Sawdon, C. (1999). *The essential groupworker: Teaching and learning creative groupwork.* London: Jessica Kingsley.

Harrison, M., & Ward, D. (2000). Values as context: Groupwork and social action. In O. Manor (Ed.), *Ripples: Groupwork in different settings* (pp. 165–180). London: Whitting and Birch.

Kurland, R., & Salmon, R. (1998). Purpose: A misunderstood and missed keystone of group work practice. *Social work with Groups, 21*(3), 5–17.

Malekoff, A. (2004). *Group work with adolescents: Principles and practice* (2nd ed.). New York: Guilford Press.

Russell, H. (September, 2007). *Group work with a minoritised, stigmatized population: Gender journeys: A psycho-educational group for anyone wondering about their gender identity.* Unpublished course paper. Ontario Institute for Studies in Education of The University of Toronto.

Shulman, L. (2006). *The skills of helping individuals, families, groups and communities* (5th ed.). Belmont, CA: Thomson/Wadsworth.

Steinberg, D. (2002). The magic of mutual aid. *Social Work with Groups, 25*(1/2), 31–39.

Group Work Major Models

Cognitive-Behavioral Model

Randy Magen

In the 1970s the first articles and books appeared, written by social workers, describing the application of behavioral theory to social work with groups (Rose, 1972; Sundel & Lawrence, 1970). Since that time, cognitive-behavioral theory has become one of the dominant perspectives guiding group work practice. The compatibility between evidence-based practice and cognitive-behaviorally based interventions assures the place of this theory at the forefront of group work.

Behavior theory starts in psychology with the work of Ivan Pavlov (Thomlison & Thomlison, 1996). Pavlov's experiments with salivating dogs are well known and lead to the principles of classical conditioning. Classical conditioning is a theory about learning and is sometimes referred to as respondent conditioning.

An example of classical conditioning in group work can be found in the behavior of clients attending a cancer support group. Group members had received chemotherapy at the cancer center where the group held weekly meetings. The chemotherapy drugs (Unconditioned Stimulus) induced severe nausea (Unconditioned Response). After several weeks of chemotherapy the clinic setting (e.g., personnel, smells, sights, etc.) induced the nausea before the chemotherapy drugs were administered. Thus, the clinic setting became a Conditioned Stimulus for nausea (Conditioned Response). Fortunately, the social worker whose group was disrupted by nauseated clients understood classical conditioning and introduced progressive relaxation training to assist the group members in extinguishing the link between the US (chemotherapy drugs) and the CS (Boynton & Thyer, 1994).

Operant conditioning (Skinner, 1953) explains many more behaviors and learning conditions than classical conditioning. The key aspect of operant conditioning is the consequence (C) that follows a behavior. Behaviors (B) are strengthened—they continue or increase—if they are reinforced and are weakened—they decrease or are extinguished—through punishment. Reinforcement and punishment can be either positive (doing something) or negative (taking away something).

In a group for men who batter their partners, operant conditioning was used to increase members' regular attendance. At the end of each group meeting, members who had arrived on time and attended the entire group session were refunded, in cash, $5.00 of the fee they had paid to attend the group. Attending the group on time (B) and staying for the entire group session (B) were positively reinforced (C) with the cash.

Social learning theory (Bandura, 1977a) extended the ideas of classical and operant conditioning by including people's perceptions and thoughts. Bandura's early experiments demonstrated that people imitate others, which led to the law of observational learning, the basis for the principle of modeling (see for example, Bandura, 1973). Further work lead to the development of the concept of self-efficacy—belief in the ability to carry out a behavior affects whether that behavior is enacted (Bandura, 1977b). Other aspects of social learning theory focus on perceptions and thoughts as the antecedents (A) that lead to or set-up behaviors, A–B–C. In this model, behaviors can be changed not only through consequences but also through different antecedents. Self-efficacy then is an antecedent to behavior (B).

These three sets of theory, classical conditioning, operant conditioning, and social learning, form the foundation of cognitive-behavioral theory. While some might credit other authors (e.g., Thorndike, Watson, Ellis, Beck) for the development of various aspects of cognitive-behavioral theory, the basic principles elucidated above are constant across variations of the theory.

In social work, cognitive-behavioral theory has been used as both a theory of intervention and a theory for group work practice. Most common in remedial model groups, the hallmarks of cognitive-behavioral interventions in groups are: (1) identifying specific target thoughts and behaviors; (2) setting precise, measurable goals to empirically evaluate change efforts; (3) intervening—changing antecedents, consequences or CS–US links; and (4) relapse prevention as well as generalization of the changes to other behaviors, thoughts, and settings.

In behavioral parent training, for example, parents are taught to "catch their child being good" (Becker, 1971). Theoretically, the idea is to increase a behavior incompatible with the troubling (e.g., fighting over toys) behavior (Magen & Rose, 1994). Parents are trained to positively reinforce acceptable behavior, which should result in an increase in desirable behavior and a decrease in unacceptable behavior. First, parents are asked to monitor and record the number of instances their child spontaneously shares a toy with a sibling. In a group setting the discussion with other parents can help to normalize children's fighting over toys. The parents then set a goal for how frequently they would like the sharing behavior to occur; in the group setting other members can help the parent set realistic goals. In the intervention phase, parents provide the child with verbal praise (positive reinforcement) when the child shares his or her toys. Parents would first practice the skill of verbal praise in the group and learn a variety of ways to provide positive reinforcement by observing other group members. In the final phase parents generalize their use of verbal praise to increase other behaviors and develop a plan for reminding themselves to "catch their child being good." The group might use a buddy system where parents call each other outside of the group to remind each other to continue to use verbal praise (Rose, 1989).

Sheldon Rose has contributed the most to the use of cognitive-behavioral theory as a theory of intervention in groups as well as a theory for group work practice. Rose's developmental approach to group work research resulted in the demonstration of the efficacy of a cognitive-behavioral group work approach to stress management (Tolman & Rose, 1989), assertiveness, pain management (Subramanian & Rose, 1988), anger management, children's social skills, parent training, and groups for men who batter. As a theory of group work practice, for example, Rose applied cognitive-behavioral principles to leader behavior: instructing leaders to use positive reinforcement verbally and through tokens, identifying how leaders can serve as models for group members, and how leaders can use data to monitor group conditions. Other applications of cognitive-behavioral theory to group work practice by Rose and his colleagues have focused on modeling and rehearsal in group sessions and the use of homework to aid in generalization of change (Rose, 1998).

References

Bandura, A. (1973). *Aggression: A social learning analysis*. Englewood Cliffs, NJ: Prentice-Hall.

Bandura, A. (1977a). *Social learning theory*. Englewood Cliffs, NJ: Prentice-Hall.

Bandura, A. (1977b). Self-efficacy: Toward a theory of behavior change. *Psychological review, 84*, 191–215.

Becker, W. C. (1971). *Parents are teachers: A child management program*. Champaign, IL: Research Press.

Boynton, K. E., & Thyer, B. A. (1994). Behavioral social work in the field of oncology. *Journal of Applied Social Sciences, 18*, 189–197.

Magen, R. H., & Rose, S. D. (1994). Parents in groups: problem solving versus behavioral skills training. *Research on social work practice, 4*, 172–191.

Rose, S. D. (1972). *Treating children in groups*. San Francisco: Jossey-Bass.

Rose, S. D. (1989). *Working with adults in groups*. San Francisco: Jossey-Bass.

Rose, S. D. (1998). *Group therapy with troubled youth: A cognitive-behavioral interactive approach*. Thousand Oaks, CA: Sage.

Skinner, B. F. (1953). *Science and human behavior*. New York: Macmillan.

Subramanian, K., & Rose, S. D. (1988). Group training for management of chronic pain in interpersonal situations. *Health and Social Work, 21*(3), 29–49.

Sundel, M., & Lawrence, M. (1970). Time-limited behavioral group treatment with adults. *Michigan Mental Health Research Bulletin, 4*, 37–40.

Thomlison, B., & Thomlison, R. (1996). Behavior theory and social work treatment. In F. J. Turner (Ed.), *Social work treatment: Interlocking theoretical approaches* (pp. 39–68). New York: The Free Press.

Tolman, R. M., & Rose, S. D. (1989). Teaching clients to manage stress: The effectiveness of structured group stress management training. *Journal of Social Service Research, 13*(2), 45–66.

Empowerment Model

Rhonda E. Hudson

The empowerment model of group work practice grew out of an assortment of political movements that included the feminist and black liberation movements, Paulo Freire's literacy campaigns, and the Civil Rights and Welfare Reform eras.

The empowerment model evolved in response to the plights of marginalized and oppressed individuals of our society. It advanced to support and advocate for social justice and equality for clients. Although there is no singular empowerment group approach, several social workers have tailored this methodology to advocate for their clients. Among them are Mary Bricker-Jenkins, an author and activist, who began a grassroots campaign to empower women on welfare. Two social workers, Lee and Gutiérrez, have led in advances to increase the knowledge and understanding of this group approach with their publications describing their work with the poor, underserved, oppressed, stigmatized, disenfranchised, and marginalized Guyanese homeless women in the Beloved Community (Johnson & Lee, 1994; Lee, 2001), and the racial, ethnic, sociocultural, sexual, and gender inequalities for women of color (Gutiérrez & Lewis, 1999).

The theoretical foundations of this approach to group work include: William Schwartz, who strongly believed in the client as being the agent of change in the helping relationship between client and worker, and that the worker mediates between the client and his or her environment (Schwartz, 1961, 1971). Paulo Freire, who described the oppressed as those who have "lost their humanization, or have it stolen away" (Freire, 1970, p. 30). The oppressed tend to "internalize the image of the oppressor, and adopt his guidelines" (Freire, 1970, p. 31), and only the oppressed has power to free him or herself and also free the oppressor. Alex Gitterman and Carel Germain (2008) wrote about the link between the eco-logical system and persons in their environment. Barbara Solomon, who focused on an empowerment theory that not only advocated for social justice, but also sought to increase clients' self-esteem and feelings of helplessness (Solomon, 1976). Jane Addams, who added the concept of the small groups with an empha-sis on mutual aid during the settlement movement, when she merged the divide between formal and informal systems of social welfare so that both worked together for social change (Addams, 1961).

The nature of the helping paradigm is grounded in the ecological perspective, an integrated framework designed for social work practice. This perspective allows the social worker to view the client as interconnected with the environment in a reciprocal, give-and-take relationship. The individual and the environment are in dynamic fluctuation with each other (Gitterman & Germain, 2008).

The function of the empowerment social worker is to act as mediator between the group and society. The worker and group act in a fluid, give-and-take man-ner, with both receiving fulfillment from the other (Schwartz, 1961, 1971). The worker envisions a sharing of the work, so that the social worker is not viewed as the "leader" in this symbiotic relationship. Rather, the worker is a "co-worker," "co-activist," "co-teacher," or "co-investigator."

The social worker applies the practice principles of direct and indirect power blocks, consciousness-raising and praxis, and development of confidence (Lee, 2001, 1997; Gutiérrez & Lewis, 1999). The empowerment group is interactionist in nature and supportive mutual aid is a hallmark of the group. Reciprocity between worker and clients is principal, and the worker is viewed as a co-teacher or co-leader, alongside clients. The worker recognizes that the group members are experts in their own right, and so shares knowledge without taking "center stage" (Lee, 2001, p. 295). The worker is not to be seen or thought of as the leader of the group. The worker cooperates with members by encouraging interactions and communication among members.

The empowerment model does not prescribe methods and skill. They represent a combination or blending of the interrelationships between the personal and the political, between the clinical and the personal, and between group members and the worker and members. The social worker uses a repertoire of skills simultaneously to promote mutual aid while working on the personal, interpersonal, and political levels. Skills include using the multi-focal lens to "tune in" to consider the struggles of the group members. Through a dialogical process of relationship and intercommunication between members, and between worker and members (Lee, 2001, p. 313), the worker develops the contract, asks for clarification, affirms, reframes, empathizes, validates feelings, personally shares, reaches for fears and feelings, and asks for the work to continue. The worker also challenges obstacles to the work, points out the common ground and directs members to speak directly to each other to promote mutual aid. The worker also gently confronts, challenges the position, waits for silences, and stays with the anger.

Specific skills include task-centered and political skills to assist members in beginning to use cognitive and reflective restructuring so that they will be able to begin to critically understand the struggle against the oppressor, and guiding praxis (making practical application or reflecting) after taking action (Gutiérrez & Lewis, 1999). The worker makes political statements, challenges false beliefs, provides information and access for help, and uses codifications (poems, music, pictures, or other items that have cultural familiarity appeal, but also contradict and remind members of the struggle against the oppressor) and decodifiers (critical questions that help members critically understand the meaning of a code) (Freire, 1970; Gutiérrez & Lewis, 2001; Lee, 1999). Workers also use humor and levity and spontaneity to empower the group.

The immediate and intermediate outcome is that the group develops a raised consciousness that includes an application of the knowledge gained to challenge the oppressor, whether personally, interpersonally, or politically. The empowerment model is relevant for any poor, oppressed, stigmatized, disenfranchised, and/ or marginalized group or community, as long as members are able and willing, and need each other to do the work.

References

Addams, J. (1961). *Twenty years at Hull House*. New York: Macmillan.

Freire, P. (1970). *Pedagogy of the oppressed* (M. B. Ramos, Trans.). New York: Herder and Herder.

Gitterman A., & Germain, C. (2008). *The Life Model of social work practice: Advances in theory and practice* (3rd ed.). New York: Columbia University Press.

Gutiérrez, L. M., & Lewis, E. A. (1999). *Empowering women of color*. New York: Columbia University Press.

Johnson, A., & Lee, J. A. B. (1994). Empowerment work with homeless women. In M. Mirkin (Ed.), *Women in context: Toward a feminist reconstruction of psychotherapy* (pp. 408–432). New York: Guilford Press.

Lee, J. A. B. (1997). The Empowerment group: The heart of the Empowerment Approach and an antidote to injustice. In J. K. Parry (Ed.), *From prevention to wellness through group work* (pp. 15–29). Binghamton, NY: Haworth Press.

Lee, J. A. B. (2001). *The empowerment approach to social work practice: Building the Beloved Community.* New York: Columbia University Press.

Schwartz, W. (1961). The social worker in the group. *Social Welfare Forum* (pp. 146–177). New York: Columbia University Press.

Schwartz, W. (1971). Social group work: The interactionist approach. In R. Morris (Ed.-in-Chief), *Encyclopedia of social work* (16th ed., vol. 2. pp. 1252–1263). New York: National Association of Social Workers.

Solomon, B. (1976). *Black empowerment: Social work in oppressed communities.* New York: Columbia University Press.

Mutual Aid Model

Dominique Moyse Steinberg

Mutual aid refers to a set of dynamics through which people help one another. Inherent in the concept as it applies to social work with groups are a few basic beliefs. One is that all people have strengths that can be harnessed to help themselves and to help others. (*Strengths* simply refers to ways of being and doing that help people negotiate the world.) In fact, this belief is central to all social work, and helping people to discover their strengths is a fundamental task of practice. Another is that people with common needs and goals have great potential to help one another. Yet another is that helping strengthens not only the recipient but the donor by providing the intrinsic rewards of altruistic behavior.

The concept of mutual aid has long been central to other fields, such as biology and sociology. For example, in 1908, social scientist Petr Kropotkin wrote:

> Beside the "law of Mutual Struggle" there is in Nature the "law of Mutual Aid" ... I obviously do not deny the struggle for existence, but I maintain that the progressive development of the animal kingdom, and especially of mankind, is favoured much more by mutual support than by mutual struggle.
>
> (p. x)

The term "mutual aid" was introduced to social work by William Schwartz in the 1960s (Schwartz, 1961). Long before that, however, social group workers understood the power inherent in bringing people in common cause. Settlement houses of the 19th and 20th centuries throughout the United States, for instance, relied on such a process to help immigrants acclimate to new ways of life with new rights and responsibilities.

Today, mutual aid is acknowledged as the hallmark of social work with groups and helps the method to meet some of the profession's most powerful mandates. With its inherent duality of focus on individuals as members and the group as collective, it meets the mandate for psychosocial practice. By inviting the totality of people's life experiences to the group rather than just the needy parts, it meets the mandate for a holistic approach to helping. By requiring a focus on strengths it meets the mandate that practice be strength-centered rather than problem-centered. Finally, by expecting groups to share authority over their affairs it meets the mandate for respecting people's right to self-determination.

Originally conceptualized as an intra-group process, the value and applicability of mutual aid to inter-group collaboration is now well established (Breton, 1990; Steinberg, 2003). In no other helping profession does mutual aid play such a pivotal role in working with groups.

First articulated by Lawrence Shulman (2006) the dynamics of mutual aid are understood as: (1) *data sharing*—sharing information, ideas, wisdom, experiences, etc.; (2) *dialectic process*—exploring, debating, and integrating various points of view; (3) *discussion of taboos*—talking about topics that are unwelcome in other venues; (4) *"all in the same boat" phenomenon-universality*—being with others who share important similarities; (5) *mutual support*—expressing sympathy or empathy; (6) *mutual demand*—asking for serious attention to task; (7) *individual problem solving*—using the group to address individual problems; (8) *rehearsal*—using the group to try new ways of being, thinking, and doing; and (9) *strength in numbers*—using the power of numbers to exercise force. Thus, to catalyze mutual aid means to help members learn about, understand the value of, engage in, and maintain as many of these dynamics as are relevant for as much of the time as possible. The degree to which, and the manner in which, groups develop into mutual aid systems depends on the worker's approach to practice, nature of setting and purpose, and the psychosocial needs, desires, and capacities of members. However, groups do not need to experience all dynamics at all times to be conceptualized as such. Mutual aid is expressed in different ways and at different levels of intensity both during the life of a group and across different groups (Gitterman & Shulman, 2005; Steinberg, 2002).

Opportunities for mutual aid exist in all groups from the school room to the board room but are catalyzed most readily when: (1) members perceive their self-interest to coincide; (2) they are free to communicate with one another if and as they deem relevant; (3) they use personal experience as the primary helping mechanism; and (4) group affairs are governed by democratic and humanistic norms. Perceptions that self-interest coincides helps members to be open to the possibility that they will be understood and that sharing experiences has value. Because people often have difficulty in identifying their self-interest with that of others, however, the more palpable the common ground, the more readily they develop a sense of community and become open to mutual aid. Helping a new group to develop its sense of community is referred to as *group building* (Hartford, 1978; Middleman & Wood, 1990; Papell & Rothman, 1980). The freedom of members to participate if and as they believe they have something to contribute rather than at the worker's discretion creates the venue for exchanging experiences and strengths in the moment. When members speak in turn, for example, or interact primarily with the worker, opportunities for mutual aid are lost, an approach that has been labeled as *aggregational therapy of individuals* (Hartford, 1978) or *casework in a group* (Kurland & Salmon, 1992). The style of communication that most readily lends itself to mutual aid is a *free-floating* one (Middleman & Wood, 1990), although members' developmental needs, stage of group development, content, and other factors may require variation.

The use of personal experience as a primary helping process creates a mechanism through which members develop insight, empathy, and innovation. In revisiting their histories they identify common ground and develop empathy, and in sharing stories they contribute a variety of perspectives for group review. Success stories are confirmed; opportunities to learn new skills are provided; in either case, mutual aid occurs. Finally, shared governance over group affairs helps to guarantee that efforts remain relevant, gives all of the group's voices an opportunity to integrally effect and affect process, and provides a way for members to exercise existing or develop new leadership skills. A central practice task, therefore, is to set and keep in motion norms that help members identify common ground, help them accept one another as viable sources of help, and foster the exchange of strength and shared leadership. The result is a climate that values freedom of expression balanced with respect for difference, mutuality balanced with appreciation for individuality, exploration balanced with real-world implications, and structure balanced with flexibility.

Skills for helping groups to develop into mutual aid systems fall into two general categories: those that build relationships among members and those that influence the nature and direction of those relationships (Coyle, 1949). Relationship-building skills are crucial because it is the multiplicity of relationships in a group that creates the potential for mutual aid. Skills to influence their nature and direction are crucial because groups can exert tremendous negative as well as positive pressure on members. These skill sets are useful for working with a wide array of group types that aim to maximize their collective human potential toward a common good and with goals that may range from task to recreation to political action (Steinberg, 2004, and others).

References

Breton, M. (1990). Learning from social group work traditions. *Social Work with Groups, 13*(1), 21–45.

Coyle, G. (1949). Definition of the function of the group worker. *The Group, 11*(3), 11–13.

Gitterman, A., & Shulman, L. (Eds.). (2005). *Mutual aid groups, vulnerable and resilient populations and the life cycle* (3rd ed.). New York: Columbia University Press.

Hartford, M. (1978). Groups in the human services: Some facts and fancies. *Social Work with Groups, 1*(1), 7–13.

Kropotkin, P. (1908). *Mutual aid: A factor of evolution.* (Reprinted 1989). Montreal, Canada: Black Rose Books.

Kurland, R., & Salmon, R. (1992). Group work vs. casework in a group: Principles and implications for teaching and practice. *Social Work with Groups, 15*(4), 3–14.

Middleman, R., & Wood, G. G. (1990). From social group work to social work with groups. *Social Work with Groups, 13*(3), 3–20.

Papell, C., & Rothman, B. (1980). Relating the mainstream model of social work with groups to group psychotherapy and the structured group approach. *Social Work with Groups, 3*(2), 5–23.

Schwartz, W. (1961). The social worker in the group. *The social welfare forum: Official proceedings from the National Conference on Social Welfare* (pp. 146–171). New York: Columbia University Press.

Shulman, L. (2006). *The skills of helping individuals, families, groups, and communities* (5th ed.). Belmont, CA: Thomson Brooks/Cole.

Steinberg, D. M. (2002). The magic of mutual aid. *Social Work with Groups, 25*(1), 31–38.

Steinberg, D. M. (2003). Social work with groups, mutual aid, and social justice. In N. Sullivan, D. Goodman, N. Lang, E. S. Mesbur, & L. Mitchell (Eds.), *Social justice through personal, community, and societal change* (pp. 91–102). Binghamton, NY: Haworth Press.

Steinberg, D. M. (2004). *The mutual-aid approach to working with groups: Helping people help one another* (2nd ed.). Binghamton, NY: Haworth Press.

Psychodynamic Model

Carol Tosone

The term *psychodynamic group work* has traditionally been associated with long-term, insight-oriented psychotherapy groups with fixed membership and a leader who focuses on the individual needs and goals of each member. With the advent of managed care and the demand for cost-effective, short-term treatment for homogeneous, problem-specific groups, the psychodynamic group work model has been modified to accommodate symptom-focused groups with narrower, more limited goals (Yalom & Leszcz, 2005). Correspondingly, psychodynamic group work practitioners are generally presumed to be psychoanalysts when, in fact, social workers (Konopka, 1949, 1954, 1983; Northen, 1969, 1976; Scheidlinger, 1982) and other mental health professionals (Tuttman, 1991) have transformed the model to meet the needs of the populations they serve.

Konopka (1949, 1954, 1983), Northen (1969, 1976), and Scheidlinger (1982) are perhaps the best known social work proponents of the psychodynamic group work model. Konopka (1983) viewed group therapy and social group work as interchangeable, especially when the latter "helps persons enhance their social functioning through purposeful group experiences and to cope more effectively with their personal, group, or community problems" (p. 26). She emphasized the purpose of the group as helping members improve their capacity to balance the demands of their inner motives with those of the social environment. Konopka (1983) highlighted the interactive nature of the group and individual dynamics, noting that the group process is expressed through the kind and quality of relations between its members. Conflict-solving and decision making are core individual skills acquired through the group, and the role of the group worker is to provide leadership which furthers individual development through group association.

Northen (1969, 1976) also emphasized the therapeutic value of interpersonal learning, as well as the interdependence of individual and group work. Her *psychosocial approach* highlights the "interrelationship between psychological and social forces and the interaction between the person, the small group of which he is a member, and the environment" (1976, pp. 116–117). She views the group leader as an interactive contributor to problem solving, a facilitator of member relationships, and as an influencer of individuals. Northen, like Konopka, draws heavily on strength-based social work and systems perspectives, both of which are compatible with psychoanalytically oriented ego psychology.

The psychodynamic group therapy models articulated by non-social work clinicians Yalom & Leszcz (2005) and Ormont (1992) share much in common with the approaches of Northen (1969), Konopka (1983), and Scheidlinger (1982) including: (1) using the group as a vehicle for individual goals; (2) attending to individual and member-to-member verbal and non-verbal communication; and (3) addressing the three levels of group observation—individual, interpersonal, and the group as a whole. The differences, however, are that these non-social work group practitioners, along with Schleidlinger, who was dually trained as a social worker and psychologist, draw more heavily on theoretical concepts derived from individual psychoanalysis, notably transference, countertransference, resistance, and working through.

To best understand the common denominator in psychodynamic group work, it is important to identify the therapeutic factors responsible for individual change. These change mechanisms, first enumerated by Yalom in 1970, are interdependent and operate in all groups, although the importance of each can vary from group to group, from different stages in the life of a particular group, and from different members within the same group. The eleven primary therapeutic factors are: (1) instillation of hope; (2) universality; (3) imparting of information; (4) altruism; (5) development of socializing techniques; (6) imitative behavior; (7) catharsis; (8) corrective recapitulation of the primary family group; (9) existential factors; (10) group cohesiveness, and (11) interpersonal learning. Together these curative factors help to answer the question as to what makes group treatment effective.

For the non-social work proponents of psychodynamic group work, notably Yalom and Leszcz (2005) and Ormont (1992), the emphasis is on interpersonal learning and the corrective emotional experience brought about by the recapitulation of the primary family group. A member may interact with the leader and other group members as if operating in the family of origin. Unresolved conflicts and patterns, such as sibling rivalry, alliance against the parent(s), and a struggle for dominance, may get repeated in the group. In his seminal work, *Group Psychology and the Analysis of the Ego*, Freud (1921) outlined his formulations about the influence of groups on human behavior, likening the group leader to an omnipotent father figure who reigns over his members and serves as their ego ideal, as can occur in the church or army (Frued, 2001). As such, members are prone to develop transference reactions to the leader and other members based on their early life experiences. The group leader uses his or her countertransference reactions, coupled with the members' transference reactions to help them work through unresolved childhood conflicts in vivo, by linking these repetitive patterns to current experiences in the group. When this occurs successfully, a corrective emotional experience has taken place that repairs the traumatic influence of the past.

The role of the leader, according to Yalom and Leszcz (2005) is to provide a safe and supportive atmosphere to allow this process to unfold, while also offering well-timed interpretations, honesty of expression, and reality testing. Member insight, a key feature of interpersonal learning, becomes the principal vehicle through which behavioral patterns inside and outside of the group can be altered. Yalom and Leszcz (2005) suggest four types of insight central to interpersonal learning: (1) an objective perspective on how one is perceived by other members of the group; (2) understanding one's intricate patterns of interaction with others; (3) motivational understanding as to why the individual interacts with others in a particular way; and (4) genetic insight into how current patterns of interaction are derived from early childhood experiences.

Interpersonal learning relies heavily on the "here and now" interactions of the members with the leader and with other members of the group, particularly in those groups in which members are able to express strong affect, both positive and negative. Practitioners of this approach, notably Yalom and Leszcz (2005) and Ormont (1992), draw a sharp distinction between the content and process of the group, stressing that when there is some affectively charged group process being ignored, members are not attentive to the content being discussed. At such times, the leader's role is to address the resistance to the group process, encouraging the members' self-disclosure and expression of affect. This approach leads to the major goals of psychodynamic group work: fostering the development of insight, ego strength, interpersonal skills and communication, and enhancing one's adaptive functioning in the larger environment.

References

Freud, S. (2001). *Group psychology and the analysis of the ego*. London: International Psychanalytic Press.
Konopka, G. (1949). *Therapeutic group work with children*. Minneapolis: University of Minnesota Press.
Konopka, G. (1954). *Group work in the institution: A modern challenge*. New York: William Morrow.
Konopka, G. (1983). *Social group work: A helping process* (3rd ed.). Englewood Cliffs, NJ: Prentice-Hall.
Northen, H. (1969). *Social work with groups*. New York: Columbia University Press.
Northen, H. (1976). Psychosocial practice in small groups. In R. W. Roberts, & H. Northen (Eds.), *Theories of social work with groups*. New York: Columbia University Press.
Ormont, L. R. (1992). *The group therapy experience: From theory to practice*. New York: St. Martin's Press.
Scheidlinger, S. (1982). *Focus on group psychotherapy: Clinical essays*. New York: International Universities Press.
Tuttman, S. (1991). *Psychoanalytic group theory and therapy: Essays in honor of Saul Scheidlinger*. Madison, CT: International Universities Press.
Yalom, I. (1970). *The theory and practice of group psychotherapy* (1st ed.). New York: Basic Books.
Yalom, I., & Leszcz, M. (2005). *The theory and practice of group psychotherapy* (5th ed.). New York: Basic Books.

Task-Centered Model

Charles D. Garvin

Task-centered practice (TC) is a generalist approach to social work practice that enables individuals, families, groups, and organizations to accomplish their purposes and attain their goals through defining and accomplishing tasks (Tolson, Reid, & Garvin, 2003). Task-centered group work, in particular, employs task-centered methods and concepts, in the context of the group, to help group members solve their problems by utilizing the many resources the group experience makes available.

TC was created in the early 1970s by Reid and Epstein (1972) who, in their book *Task-Centered Casework*, presented a model of social work to be employed in short-term services to social work clients. Shortly after this book appeared, Garvin (1974) published an article "Task-centered group work" in which he demonstrated that task-centered practice could be used in groups in ways that were consistent with the values and practice theories of social work with groups.

Task-centered group work (TCG), as with other models of group work practice, seeks to help the group become a system of mutual aid. Processes of mutual aid are drawn upon by the members to help one another to define goals and accomplish tasks to attain such goals. TCG also utilizes the other values of group work, such as democratic decision making, self-determination of members, and respect for persons. TCG can be utilized with both individual change and task groups although it has predominantly been used with the former and these will be the main focus of this article.

TCG draws upon the following characteristics of all task-centered applications:

- It is structured in that it utilizes specific procedures.
- It focuses on solving problems as members perceive them.
- It is time limited.
- It is theoretically open and thus can be used with many theoretical orientations.
- Change occurs through the use of tasks which are activities designed to ameliorate the identified problems.
- It is an empirical approach to practice.
- It is appropriate for use with culturally diverse clients.

(This list was adapted from Tolson et al., 2003, p. 4.)

Ramos and Garvin (2003) have identified several reasons why TCG is an appropriate approach for work with clients from many cultures. They discuss its compatibility with the values of many cultures. In addition they take note of several of its characteristics and how these correlate with different sets of cultural conditions, such as its use of a variety of intervention strategies, its focus on accomplishing tasks, its short-term nature, its respect for client-defined problems, its consideration of environmental contexts, and its focus on change of oppressive environments. They indicate, however, that some aspects of TCG may have to be modified for some cultures, such as its structured format, its use of time frames for each phase of practice, and how the concept of "problem" is defined.

The ways that TCG groups may develop and the actions practitioners may take to facilitate this process can be considered in terms of the beginning, middle, and ending phases of the group. These phases are suggested by our knowledge of group development and by the logic inherent in defining and carrying out member tasks (Tolson et al., 2003).

Prior to the *beginning* of the group, there are several activities in which practitioners engage. These include determining the type of problem(s) upon which the group will focus, based on the needs and wants of people that the agency serves or intends to serve. The practitioner should also consider the evidence as to whether any type of group service is an appropriate and effective means of addressing these types of problems. The practitioner also considers principles of group composition in inviting people to join the group (Garvin, 1997).

At the initial meeting of the group, practitioners, as with any group service, help members to initiate relationships with one another and the practitioner. In addition, members clarify the purposes of the group; this may necessitate making changes in the explanation of purposes that they may have received from the practitioner in initial pre-group interviews. The practitioner also explains the ideas behind TCG practice. Group norms are developed and the number of sessions (usually six) determined. Members begin to clarify with each other the problems they will seek to ameliorate in the group and the goals with relationship to these problems that will seek to attain in the group.

In the *middle* phase of the group, a process takes place referred to as "The task planning and implementation sequence." Through this, members help each other to define tasks and select those that they believe will help them reach their goals. The details for each task are specified, including incentives members may need to work on tasks. Some tasks may occur in group sessions and often take the form of simulations, such as role plays, that help the members carry out tasks between group sessions (Garvin, 1997, p. 311). Examples of tasks are filling out an employment application, completing a homework assignment, or arranging for a speaker.

Task-centered groups, as all groups, go through a *termination* process, in which members assess accomplishments, plan follow-up, evaluate the group experience, bid farewell to one another, and express their feelings about endings. In task-centered groups, in particular, members engage in a final problem review in which they help one another to determine changes in the problem situation since the initial phase. Group members will be especially helpful in this regard if they have had an opportunity to observe each other in situations outside of the group such as typically occurs in most school-based groups. Members of a task-centered group created to attain changes in the environment will determine whether the problem in the environment has been ameliorated and the environment change goals achieved.

Members will also help one another make future plans. This may include joining other task-centered groups, affiliating with a different kind of group, or seeking assistance through one-on-one or family forms of helping. Members may also assess whether their problem-solving skills, in general, have been enhanced through the task-centered group.

A number of evaluations of TCG have been published that attest to its effectiveness. Garvin, Reid and Epstein (1976) reported on two projects: one with patients in an outpatient psychiatric setting and the other with high school students. Newcome (1985) reports on an application in an adult day-treatment program. Toseland and Coppola (1985) reported an experience with elderly people. Pomeroy, Rubin, and Walker (1995) described an evaluation of TCG with family members of people with acquired immune deficiency syndrome (AIDS). Kilgore (1996) employed TCG with adult male sex offenders. Raushi (1994) developed a task-centered model for work with single-mother students in a community college setting. While all of these studies provide positive evidence regarding the feasibility and effectiveness of using TCG in a variety of settings, they do not provide as strong support for the effectiveness of TCG as may be desired. Some lack appropriate control groups, validation of instruments, and sample sizes that would provide this support. We hope that the future of TCG will include even more rigorous studies of this approach.

References

Garvin, C. (1974). Task-centered group work. *Social Service Review, 48*, 494–507.

Garvin, C. (1997). *Contemporary group work* (3rd ed.). Boston: Allyn & Bacon.

Garvin, C., Reid, W. J., & Epstein, L. (1976). A task-centered approach. In R. Roberts, & H. Northen (Eds.), *Theories of social work with groups* (pp. 238–267). New York: Columbia University Press.

Kilgore, D. K. (1996). Task-centered group treatment of sex offenders: A developmental study. *Dissertation on Abstracts International Section A: Humanities and Social Science, 57*(2A), 0865.

Newcome, K. (1985). Task-centered group work with the chronically mentally ill in day treatment. In A. E. Fortune (Ed.), *Task-centered practice with groups and families* (pp. 78–91). New York: Springer.

Pomeroy, E. C., Rubin, A., & Walker, R. J. (1995). Effectiveness of a psychoeducational and task-centered group intervention for family members of people with AIDS. *Social Work Research, 19*, 129–152.

Ramos, B., & Garvin, C. (2003). Task-centered work with culturally diverse clients. In E. R. Tolson, W. J. Reid, & C. D. Garvin (Eds.), *Generalist practice: A task-centered approach* (2nd ed., pp. 441–464). New York: Columbia University Press.

Raushi, T. M. (1994). *A task-centered model for group work with single mothers in the college setting*. PhD Dissertation, State University of New York at Albany.

Reid, W. J., & Epstein, L. (1972). *Task-centered casework*. New York: Columbia University Press.

Tolson, E. R., Reid, W. J., & Garvin, C. D. (2003). *Generalist practice: A task-centered approach* (2nd ed.). New York: Columbia University Press.

Toseland, R. W., & Coppola, M. (1985). A task-centered approach to group work with older persons. In A. E. Fortune (Ed.), *Task-centered practice with groups and families* (pp. 101–114). New York: Springer.

Group Work Approaches and Methods

Activity: History

Maxine Lynn and Danielle Nisivoccia

The planful use of activity and program are among the unique contributions of social group work to the social work profession and to the development of group work theory (Kurland & Salmon, 1998). Historically, its wide range of purposes influenced group work, particularly a focus on enjoyment, enhancing quality of life through cultural activities, and problem solving (Boyd, 1938; Schwartz, 1985; Toseland & Rivas, 2005). The history of program activity is rooted in recreation and education (Coyle, 1947).

The Industrial Revolution and movement of families and immigrants to urban centers created a need for innovative ways to help individuals and families make an adjustment to a new way of life. In 1885 public recreation was created, which brought people together in activity-focused groups. The first settlement houses were established between 1894 and 1900 (Coyle, 1947). Their purpose was to help people live together and to enrich social relationships, often through performing and creative arts. Recreational clubs were formed to help achieve these aims.

The early group workers coming from work experience in recreation, education, settlement houses, camping, and mental hygiene faced common dilemmas, but remained isolated (Coyle, 1947; Schwartz, 1985). As organizations developed, workers wanted a more effective way and the technology to become skilled leaders. After 1920, workers discovered that helping groups to participate in activities enhanced the confidence of members and fostered a sense of accomplishment. "Doing" provided personal satisfaction (Coyle, 1947). Boyd (1938) emphasized the importance of action-games and expressive play in strengthening relationships.

In 1935 a Group Work Section in the National Conference of Social Work was created (Coyle, 1947). Group workers from recreation and education backgrounds explored common problems. In 1936 the American Association of Group Workers was developed. In a report of the Curriculum Committee on Group Work to the American Association of Schools of Social Work a framework for the practice of group work was presented, which called for the inclusion of program and activity content and knowledge (Coyle, 1947; Schwartz, 1985).

Coyle (1947) fully separated group work from recreation and placed it in social work practice. The group worker uses group interactions and activities to contribute to the growth of the individual and achieve goals (Coyle, 1947; Middleman, 1968/1982).

Wilson and Ryland (1949) established program activity as an important part of group work in the book *Social Group Work Practice*. A major contribution was the use of program activities as tools to help individuals and groups achieve personal and social goals. The use of an activity was connected to a knowledge and value base. The importance of program activities was highlighted but the skills needed for delivering content were ignored (Middleman, 1968/1982). By the end of the 1940s program activities were accepted as a way of understanding individuals and provided experiences which contribute to their growth.

In the 1950s social workers were defining the profession. The major effort was in connecting group work theory and program content to the purpose of social work (Kurland & Salmon, 1998). Murphy (1959) notes in the curriculum study by the Council on Social Work Education that social group workers need to know: resources for program activities; criteria for the selection of an activity; and how to access program needs. The worker needs to have the ability to observe, facilitate, and interpret communication through activities.

During the 1960s group workers were among those who were active in the use of group experiences, such as sensitivity training, encounter groups, empowerment groups, social action groups, and expressive arts therapies. During this period activity groups were also used for individual change and rehabilitation. A framework for conducting an activity analysis was developed to use programs prescriptively for cognitive and behavioral change (Vintner, 1985; Whittaker, 1985).

However, from the 1960s on the Council on Social Work Education stressed the development of a generic curriculum. Activity and program began to disappear from the curriculum and group work content, increasingly, was neglected or diminished in the social work curriculum.

Middleman (1968/1982), wrote a classic book, *The Non Verbal Method of Working with Groups*. It provided a conceptual foundation for action-oriented group work practice, as well as activities and examples. Her contributions included those focusing on skills needed in doing activities, the importance of purpose, and the group as a change agent.

In the 1970s the journal of *Social Work with Groups* started publishing and the Association for the Advancement of Social Work with Groups began. The value and use of program activity was highlighted through these venues with numerous presentations and articles.

Henry (1981/1992) placed activities in the context of the stages of group development. During this period many articles were written in which writers discussed and proposed the uses of purposeful activity to help the group go through the stages of development and accomplish its goals. Middleman (1980) noted that group workers were using program activity more than ever. However, the language used to explain this included terms and phrasing taken from experiential learning and the non-verbal method.

The pressures of the 1980s and 1990s regarding time and money added to the decline in the use of program activity. The economics of third-party payment and managed care pushed group workers into the therapeutic models of group treatment. Settlements and local "Y"camps struggled to stay open and could not compete with the decline of group membership and funding. Under these conditions group work courses and content suffered a further decline in social work schools (Birnbaum & Auerbach, 1994).

Today, there are major technology advances, mass violence and fears of terrorism. Many individuals are isolated and vulnerable. Activities are being used to learn social skills, experience play, deal with trauma, build community, and find connection with others (Gitterman & Shulman, 2005).

Program activity groups fulfill needs and, as noted in the history, are utilized by different fields in the helping profession. However, as in the past, current workers continue to experience feelings of loneliness, isolation, and of being unprepared (Cusicanqui & Salmon, 2004). Currently, there is a resurgence of interest in the use of program activity as seen in numerous articles being published and the presentations in the yearly symposiums of AASWG.

One could view program and activities as a jewel in the crown of group work. Jewels can be hidden, even lost, but in the end they last forever.

References

Birnbaum, M., & Auerbach, C. (1994). Group work in graduate social work education: The price of neglect. *Journal of Social Work Education, 30*(3), 325–335.

Boyd, N. (1938). Play as a means of social adjustment. In J. Lieberman (Ed.), *New trends in group work* (pp. 210–220). New York: Association Press.

Coyle, G. (1947). *Group experience and democratic values*. New York: The Women's Press.

Cusicanqui, M., & Salmon R. (2004). Seniors, small fry, and song: A group work libretto of an intergenerational singing group. In R. Salmon, & R. Graziano (Eds.), *Group work and aging: Issues in practice, research and education, 44*(1/20), 189–210.

Gitterman, A., & Shulman, L. (Eds.) (2005). *Mutual aid groups, vulnerable and resilient populations, and the life cycle* (3rd ed.). New York: Columbia Press.

Henry, S. (1992). *Group skills in social work: A four-dimensional approach* (2nd ed.). Pacific Grove, CA: Brooks/Cole. Originally published in 1981.

Kurland, R., & Salmon, R. (1998). *Teaching a methods course in social work with groups*. Alexandria, VA: Council on Social Work Education.

Middleman, R. (1980). The use of program: Review and update. *Social Work with Groups, 3*(3), 5–21.

Middleman, R. (1982). *The non-verbal method in working with groups*. Hebron, CT: Practitioners Press. New York: Association Press. Originally published in 1968.

Murphy, M. (1959). *The social group work method in social work education* (A Project Report of the Curriculum Study, vol. XI). New York: Council on Social Work Education.

Schwartz, W. (1985). The group work tradition and social work practice. *Social Work with Groups, 8*(4), 7–27.

Toseland, R., & Rivas, R. (2005). *An introduction to group work practice* (5th ed.). Boston: Allyn & Bacon, Pearson Education Inc.

Vintner, R. D. (1985). Program activities: An analysis of their effects on participant behavior. In Sundel, M., Glasser, P., Sarri, R., & Vinter, R. (Eds.), *Individual change through small groups* (2nd ed., pp. 266–236). New York: Free Press.

Whittaker, J. (1985). Program activities: Their selection and use in a therapeutic milieu. In M. Sundel, P. Glasser, R. Sarri, & R. Vinter (Eds.), *Individual change through small Groups* (2nd ed., pp. 237–250). New York: Free Press.

Wilson, G., & Ryland, G. (1949). *Social group work practice*. Cambridge, MA: Riverside Press.

Activity: Use and Selection

Edna Comer and Kasumi Hirayama

Activities have been used in social work groups since the beginning of the settlement house movement in the late 19th century. Activities, such as games, arts and crafts, dance, singing, story telling, sports, and role plays establish the atmosphere of fun and are used to build group bonds, and influence processes that help members to communicate feelings and manage relationships (Middleman, 1968/1980; Phillips, 1957). Activities are designed to be interesting and enjoyable experiences for members while working toward achieving a particular goal (Toseland & Rivas, 2005). Social group workers have maintained and advanced the notion of "inseparability of content and process" in social work groups (Middleman, 1982). Evidence of the value of the use of activity is noted in the literature (Middleman, 1982; Wilson & Ryland, 1981; Wright, 1999). Conviction regarding the benefits of the use of activities remains "alive and well" in contemporary social group work (Brandler & Roman, 1999; Northen & Kurland, 2001; Toseland & Rivas, 2005).

A social work group is composed of a number of individuals with common concerns or interests who interact with each other toward the achievement of mutual goals. Groups are influential on individuals in shaping their actions, thoughts and feelings (Forsyth, 2005). The social worker must select appropriate activities that promote member interaction, influence group process, and help individual members with their life tasks. The selected activities should be rooted in an ecological conception of the group as the primary means through which members will attain their goals (Henry, 1982; Middleman, 1982; Vinter, 1985). An ecological perspective emphasizes understanding the nature of human beings in continuous exchanges with all elements within a particular physical and cultural context and continuous reciprocal relationship with their environment (Germain & Gitterman, 1995). Proponents of this perspective emphasize the possibilities for growth and change and members' adaptive capacities through mutual aid efforts (Gitterman & Shulman, 2005). Particular activities should promote each member as being important to the group, strengthen the group as a unit, and determine ways of making the group responsive to the individual and environmental needs. Activities differ depending on group purpose, individual interests and skill level, and available resources.

Collective support in working on a common issue among group members is a basic notion in social group work. Activities are used to help foster mutual aid—defined as the efforts of people who face similar problems to provide assistance for one another (Barker, 2003; Schwartz, 1976) so that they will develop a sense of common purpose and dependence on each other and share in common experiences and concerns (Gitterman, 2004). Mutual aid is advanced through the use of activities that help group members to establish trust and feel safe and positive about their environment, and facilitate chances to build on each other's contribution (e.g., ideas, achievements, positive behavior patterns, etc.) and develop ways of working together.

Groups move through various phases over time (Henry, 1992; Northen & Kurland, 2001; Toseland & Rivas, 2005). "Each stage is a differentiable period or a discernible degree in the process of growth and development" (Northen, 1969). Though it is believed that most groups move through phases, they vary across groups. Factors thought to attribute to these differences include group type and purpose, needs of members, and leader orientation.

A selection factor is the inclusion of activities that can be applied at different times and can be responsive to members needs during that period. Some examples of the group's development and corresponding activities are: (1) beginning phase exercises that provide opportunities for members to build relationships and to establish group norms; (2) middle phase activities that are geared toward sustaining the group (e.g., positive communication patterns, problems resolution, conflict management, and decision making); and (3) ending phase activities that focus on clarity and celebration of individual and group achievement, on how experiences gained in the group can be applied in "real life situations," and on evaluation of the group's process and outcomes.

Activities will most benefit the group when they are appropriate and relevant to the members. Their selection must account for the diversities among members, including such elements as gender, religious, ethnic, and racial differences, and variation in social class identification, educational status, and their stage of life, emotional and chronological developmental needs (Northen & Kurland, 2001). For example, with children, drawings are utilized for assessment, simple arts and crafts for improvement of self-esteem, and games for learning rules. Concurrently, activities should demonstrate respect for, and understanding of, the member's culture and, at the same time, provide a structure to reconcile differences and seek common grounds and encourage growth and change. (Delgado, 1982; DeLucia-Waack, 2004; Northen & Kurland, 2001).

Activities also must be compatible with the mission and purpose of the sponsoring organization. For example, community mental health centers provide psychiatric and social services and employ activities for remediation, rehabilitation, and socialization purposes. Particular activities such as role plays are used for social skills training to address deficits of these elements in persons who have interpersonal difficulties (Hepler, 1995). In selecting an activity, the worker must consider the potential for implementation within the agency's practice ideology and intervention techniques (e.g., cognitive-behavioral, short-term or task, open or closed membership groups). Choice of activities should include those that can be carried out within the available facilities (e.g., school, outpatient clinic, community center, etc.), resources (e.g., space, materials, technology etc.), time allotment (e.g., 45- vs. 90-minute group, etc.), and proposed group membership size.

Activities remain a vital intervention technique in social group work. They can be used to influence the group's processes and outcomes, members' interactions and group outcomes. Selecting the appropriate group activity must take into account the person–environment perspective, the group's mutual aid system and phases of group development, and members' individual needs.

References

Barker, R. I. (2003). *The social work dictionary* (5th ed.). Washington, DC: NASW Press.

Brandler, S., & Roman, C. (1999). *Group work: Skills and strategies for effective Interventions*. Binghamton, NY: Haworth Press.

Delgado, M. (1983). Activities and Hispanic groups: Issues and suggestions. In R. R. Middleman (Ed.), *Activities and action in group work* (pp. 85–96). New York: Haworth Press.

DeLucia-Waack, J. L. (2004). *The practice of multicultural group work*. Belmont, CA: Thomson Brooks/Cole.

Forsyth, D. R. (2005). *Group dynamics* (4th ed.). Belmont, CA: Brooks/Cole.

Germain, C. B., & Gitterman, A. (1995). Ecological perspective. In R. Edwards, & J. Hopps (Eds.), *Encyclopedia of social work* (19th ed., pp. 816–824). Washington, DC: NASW Press.

Gitterman, A. (2004). The Mutual Aid Model. In C. Garvin, L. Gutiérrez, & M. Galinsky (Eds.), *Handbook of social work with groups* (pp. 93–110). New York: Guilford Press.

Gitterman, A., & Shulman, L. (Eds.). (2005). *Mutual aid groups, vulnerable populations and the life cycle* (3rd ed.). New York: Columbia University Press.

Henry, S. (1992). *Group skills in social work: A four dimensional approach* (2nd ed.). Itasca, IL: F. E. Peacock.

Hepler, J. B. (1995). Social skills in training. In R. L. Edwards, & J. Hopps (Eds.), *Encyclopedia of social work* (19th ed., pp. 1129–1143). Washington, DC: NASW Press.

Middleman, R. R. (1980). *The non-verbal method in working with groups*. New York: Association Press. Hebron, CT: Practitioners Press. Originally published in 1968.

Middleman, R. R. (1982). *Activities and actions in group work*. Binghamton, NY: Haworth Press.

Nothern, H. (1969). *Social work with groups*. New York: Columbia University Press.

Northen, H., & Kurland, R. (2001). *Social work with groups* (3rd ed.). New York: Columbia University Press.

Phillips, H. (1957). *Essentials of social group work skill*. New York: Association Press.

Schwartz, W. (1976). Between client and system: The mediating function. In R. Roberts, & H. Northen (Eds.), *Theories of social work with groups* (pp. 171–197). New York: Columbia University Press.

Toseland, R. R. W., & Rivas, R. F. (2005). *An introduction to group work practice* (5th ed.). Needham Heights, MA: Allyn & Bacon.

Vinter, R. (1985). Program activities: An analysis of their effects on participant behavior. In M. Sunder, P. Glasser, R. Sarri, & R. Vinter (Eds.), *Individual change through small groups* (2nd ed., pp. 226–236). New York: The Free Press.

Wilson G., & Ryland, G. (1981). *Social group work practice*. Hebron, CT: Practitioners Press.

Wright, W. (1999). The use of purpose in on-going activity groups: A framework for maximizing the therapeutic impact. *Social Work with Groups, 22*(2/3), 31–54.

Activity Therapy for Children

Lorraine R. Tempel

Activity psychotherapy groups for children date back to the pioneering work of S. R. Slavson (1943) who developed them to address the emotional needs of children presenting with a range of symptoms at child guidance clinics in New York City. Heavily influenced by the non-medical psychoanalytic community who had arrived from Europe in the 1920s and 1930s, these settings were a seminal breeding ground for the shift from a child welfare court-dominated view of social work with children to one that integrated developmental theories about childhood and the environment into their approach (Aiello, 1998). This period also followed the heyday of the settlement house movement when the importance of social, educational and recreational groups for children was recognized and included in the proliferation of programs for immigrant families that eventually formed the basis for such organizations as summer camps, neighborhood youth centers and YMCAs (Axinn & Stern, 2008). Social group workers who were involved in these organizations emphasized the use of activities and were instrumental in integrating them into programming from the earliest days of the method (Kurland & Salmon, 1998; Wilson & Ryland, 1949). Thus, it was in an atmosphere characterized by a burgeoning of social group work, a melding of social casework and psychoanalytic theory, and an emphasis on understanding children's developmental needs and difficulties that activity group psychotherapy was first recognized as a viable modality for working with children.

Activity group psychotherapy is particularly well-suited to children in the 6–12-year age range. Although involvement in family relationships is still primary during these years, socialization with peers, cooperative play and gradual distancing from parental figures significantly characterize this period as well (Schiffer, 1984). By providing a vehicle for children to test out new roles, work out conflict, and develop social skills, groups allow children a normative vehicle for supporting identity formation. For children who come to the attention of such settings as outpatient mental health clinics, preventive counseling programs, foster care agencies, school-based programs and residential treatment facilities, there are likely to be varying degrees of ego impairment associated with family conflict and/or trauma such as abandonment, abuse, or neglect. The group framework may be a choice modality for children of this age, often in combination with, or subsequent to, family and individual therapy.

Structurally, children are provided with the freedom to interact with play materials, each other, and the leader. Clear guidelines for screening and "balancing" the group membership, coupled with the special talents and qualities of the group leader, provide the children with a multitude of opportunities to correctively experience new object relationships for potential internalization (Soo, 1992). Through these experiences, internal conflict may be dealt with and/or ego structures may be built to support children in their developmental progress. It is desirable to place children together whose characterological issues may emerge as complementary in the group setting, with special care given to avoid placement of any one child who may be more vulnerable to severe scapegoating by other members. It is also advisable that children be grouped together who roughly fall within a 2-year age span of one another (e.g. 9- and 10-year-olds) although there may be exceptions when clinically indicated.

Although Slavson (1943) advocated for group composition as the primary safeguard against destructive acting out, he and others recognized the need for an expansion of technique to meet the needs of more severely disturbed children whose assessment picture included major compromises with the ability to sublimate destructive impulses into play activity (Lomoanaco, Scheidlinger, & Aronson, 2000). The result—activity–interview group therapy (and other outgrowths)—included a greater degree of leader intervention, group discussion, and scrutiny of the relationship between children's behavioral group interactions and the presenting problems outside of their sessions. Schamess (1986) noted the importance of structuring interventions based upon the specific developmental needs of the individual children, using group observations as well as discussion with other professionals who interface with the family and individual child as informants for deciding how to best do this. Schamess also emphasized how the group's collective potential to replicate and correctively alter elements of a dysfunctional family system may help the children to play new roles and then serve as change agents in those chaotic external systems.

The groups generally meet for an hour, although this may be scaled down for groups of children on the younger end of the age spectrum. Most of the cited authors recommend that the size, location, and furnishings of the group room be appropriate for the children's generally high level of activity and proclivity toward action. Thus, the environment should be simple, durable, safe, fairly well sound-proofed, and spacious enough for the number of participants (approximately 5–6 children). Materials such as arts and crafts, games, and other age-appropriate manipulatives should be available. Additionally, the therapist should be prepared to cultivate and manage naturally emerging peer culture-based activities (e.g., video games) that the children themselves may introduce into the group. This may be particularly useful in involving children who are reluctant to engage. In addition to play materials that encourage fantasy and verbal inquiry, activity–interview therapy groups generally include a snack time. The symbolism of this scenario as a simulation of family mealtime frequently triggers the conflicts with which the children are struggling and provides the leader with powerful opportunities for intervention.

Many of the activity-based structures utilized in this model were also highlighted in a therapeutic context by the prominent social group work literature. For example, Middleman (1968/1982) discussed the centrality of play activities in examining the non-verbal content and meaning behind children's behaviors in groups, and, in a much more formal presentation of the activity setting and its structure, Vinter (1974) described the use of activities for the achievement of specific therapeutic purposes. Although the writings of these and other significant social group workers were not explicitly discussed by the psychodynamically oriented group therapists who developed the model described in this piece (nor did the mainstream of the social group work literature discuss group therapy technique per se), there are clearly strong linkages between the two—certainly in the use of activities and play as a powerful vehicle for psychological growth. As described by Wright (2002), the social group worker interested in psychotherapeutic work may not immediately grasp the crucial importance of play and activity in facilitating change in groups but, through experience and supervision, can learn to appreciate their value. It is quite apparent that the writings from both social work "worlds" form a continuum of complementary viewpoints that certainly coalesce around the placement of children's developmental needs and emotional growth in the forefront of their goals.

References

Aiello, T. (1998). The influence of the psychoanalytic community of émigrés (1930–1950) on clinical social work with children. *Child and Adolescent Social Work Journal, 15*(2), 151–166.

Axinn, J. & Stern, M. J. (2008). *Social welfare: A history of the American response to need* (7th ed). Boston: Allyn & Bacon.

Kurland, R., & Salmon, R. (1998). *Teaching a methods course in social work with groups* (Unit 2, pp.13–22). Alexandria, VA: Council on Social Work Education.

Lomonaco, S., Scheidlinger, S., & Aronson, S. (2000). Five decades of children's group treatment: An overview. *Journal of Child and Adolescent Group Therapy, 10*(2), 77–96.

Middleman, R. (1982). *The non-verbal method in working with groups: The use of activity in teaching, counseling and therapy.* Hebron, CT: Practitioners Press. Originally published in 1968. New York: Association Press.

Schamess, G. (1986). Differential diagnosis and group structure in the outpatient treatment of latency-age children. In A. E. Reister, & I. A. Kraft (Eds.), *Child group psychotherapy: Future tense* (pp. 29–70). Madison, CT: International Universities Press.

Schiffer, M. (1984). *Children's group therapy.* New York: Free Press.

Slavson, S. R. (1943). *An introduction to group therapy.* New York: International Universities Press.

Soo, E. (1992). The management of resistance in the application of object relations concepts in children's and adolescents' group psychotherapy. *Journal of Child and Adolescent Group Therapy, 2*(2), 77–92.

Vinter, R. (1974). Program activities: An analysis of their effects on participant behavior. In P. Glasser, R. Sarri, & R. Vinter (Eds.), *Individual change through small groups* (pp. 233–243). New York: Free Press.

Wilson, G., & Ryland, G. (1949). *Social group work practice: The creative use of the social process.* Boston: Houghton Mifflin.

Wright, W. (2002). But I want to do a real group: A personal journey from snubbing to loving to theorizing to demanding activity-based group work. *Social Work with Groups, 25*(1/2), 105–110.

Anti-Oppressive Practice

Izumi Sakamoto

In recent years, anti-oppressive practice (AOP) has been recognized as a significant approach in social work theory, practice and education in the United Kingdom, as well as in Canada, Australia, New Zealand, and parts of Europe (e.g., Dominelli, 2002; Mullaly, 2002). AOP in general is less recognized in the United States. Despite a limited amount of literature devoted specifically to group work from anti-oppressive perspectives, the framework has much potential in enriching social justice-oriented social work practice with groups.

AOP in social work has a decided focus on analyzing the structural oppressions affecting the lives of individuals, groups, and communities, and on working toward the ultimate eradication of all levels of oppressions. While there is no consensus among scholars and practitioners on a definitive AOP approach, some common features of AOP approaches include the influences of Marxist, socialist and radical ideologies, structural, and critical understandings of intersecting oppressions, and emancipatory and feminist perspectives (e.g., Dominelli, 2002; Mullaly, 2002). AOP has been criticized for its near-exclusive focus on macro contexts and overall lack of practical tools needed to apply its great structural analysis at the micro level (Sakamoto & Pitner, 2005). Subsequently, a more explicit focus on fostering and examining critical consciousness within AOP has been proposed, in which the social worker strives to simultaneously addresses the needs of the service user while critically challenging both the social system's and their own assumptions about the professional role of social work (Sakamoto & Pitner, 2005).

Although scholarly writings explicitly examining AOP in social work with groups (AOP group work for short) are sparse, much of the broader scholarly work on AOP encompasses group-based interventions or actions as a modality of social work practice. Key components of AOP may include critical analysis, consciousness-raising, empowerment, partnership, minimal intervention, advocacy, organizational change, collective action, development of resistance strategies, use of human rights and legal frameworks, and incorporation of indigenous knowledge frameworks (Dalrymple & Burke, 1995; Dominelli, 2002; Mullaly, 2002; Sakamoto & Pitner, 2005).

Additionally, to better reflect the multicultural and transnational realities of both service users and social workers, and to ensure social work is truly anti-oppressive, proposals are made to confront "whiteness" (hegemony based on white privilege) and other hegemonic forces through critical self-reflection (critical consciousness; much of which has been written in the US context, e.g., Gutiérrez & Lewis, 1999) and interrogation of our knowledge base from different ways of knowing (Dylan, 2003, Sakamoto, 2007).

Group work from anti-oppressive perspectives is often linked to collective action, similar to group work within community-organizing and social-action traditions, via such methods as cultural activism, consciousness-raising (Thiara, 2003), and strengthening of communities (Dominelli, 2002). In a more direct-practice-oriented group work, Brown and Mistry (2005) in the United Kingdom examine "mixed membership" groups (wherein men and women, or "black" and "white" members constitute a group), positing that theories such as systems theory do not include an analysis or understanding of the unequal power relations that mixed-group members experience structurally and interpersonally. In addition to commonly understood notions of "good practice" in group work, the authors (Brown & Mistry, 2005) propose an anti-oppressive approach that requires critical analysis and action in the following areas: (1) agency context; (2) group composition and structure; (3) preparation (including worker preparation and preparing responses to oppressive/discriminatory behaviors); (4) workers' non-verbal behaviors ("walking the walk" of anti-oppressive behaviors); and (5) linking group work to the external social environment.

Mullaly (2002) suggests different ways of addressing oppression on the individual, cultural, and structural levels. On the personal level, AOP tasks may include efforts to counteract "the intrapsychic damages associated with oppression" and to foster individual empowerment and possible collective action through critical analysis and consciousnesses-raising (Mullaly, 2002, p. 192). On the cultural level, dominant discourses can be challenged by creating alternative discourses. Mullaly (2002) cites an example of a group of poor people in Vancouver ("End Legislated

Poverty") who successfully applied the negative stereotypes commonly assigned to poor people to their wealthy counterparts (e.g., "are wealthy people too dependent on wealth?"; "would counseling help break the culture or cycle of wealth?", p. 192). Taking actions to challenge oppressive culture/structure as in this example can be an effective tool for re-writing discourses, group/community empowerment, and constructive use of anger toward social action. All of the described tasks are suited for group settings where members share similar kinds of oppressions (and sometimes with their allies).

AOP overlaps with the literature on group work within multicultural social work and empowerment models (Alvarez & Cabbil, 2001; Gutiérrez & Lewis,1999) often written in the United States. However, AOP remains unique in its historical development and unyielding focus on all forms of intersecting oppressions. When "culture" (as in cultural diversity or multiculturalism) is the focus of social work, as opposed to anti-homophobia, anti-ageism or anti-oppression, the commitment to address oppression could be consciously or inadvertently masked or co-opted under a neo-liberal agenda, which funds and legitimizes social services. Instead, AOP group work aims to ensure the eradication of oppression is at the core of the group work rationale, objectives, content (e.g., topics, activities), process (e.g., recruitment, selection), and outcomes (e.g., evaluation of the group and member experiences).

As with every approach, the promise and potential of AOP group work is not without limitations. For example, how can a group worker help prioritize individual issues when all oppressions should be regarded as important? In considering the agency context, how can group work be truly anti-oppressive while operating within oppressive agencies or social policies?

As AOP group work evolves, more empirical and conceptual work is needed both in direct and indirect settings. Such work should include articulation of all aspects of group work, including discussion of when this model should be applied and how. Additionally, there is a need to expand upon the roles of allies in anti-oppressive group work, drawing on existing AOP literature (Mullaly, 2002) and on alternative approaches to addressing differences such as intergroup dialogues (Nagda & Zuniga, 2003; Sakamoto & Pitner, 2005).

References

Alvarez, A. R., & Cabbil, L. M. (2001). The MELD program: Promoting personal change and social justice through a year-long multicultural group experience. *Social Work with Groups, 24*(1), 3–20.

Brown, A., & Mistry, T. (2005). Group work with "mixed membership" groups: Issues of race and gender. *Social work with Groups, 28*(3/4), 133–148.

Dalrymple, J., & Burke, B. (1995). *Anti-oppressive practice: Social care and the law.* Buckingham, UK: Open University Press.

Dominelli, L. (2002). *Anti-oppressive social work theory and practice.* London: Palgrave Macmillan.

Dylan, A. (2003). Talking Circles: A traditional form of group work. In N. E. Sullivan Sullivan, E. S. Mesbur, N. C. Lang, D. Goodman, & L. Mitchell (Eds.), *Social work with groups: Social justice through personal, community and societal change* (pp. 119–133). Binghamton, NY: Haworth Press.

Gutiérrez, L., & Lewis, E. A. (1999). *Empowering women of color.* New York: Columbia University Press.

Mullaly, B. (2002), *Challenging oppression: A critical social work approach.* New York: Oxford University Press.

Nagda, B. A., & Zuniga, X. (2003). Fostering meaningful racial engagement through intergroup dialogues. *Group Processes and Intergroup Relations, 6,* 111–128.

Sakamoto, I. (2007). A critical examination of immigrant acculturation: Toward an anti-oppressive social work model with immigrant adults in a pluralistic society. *British Journal of Social Work, 37,* 515–535.

Sakamoto, I., & Pitner, R. (2005). Use of critical consciousness in anti-oppressive social work practice: Disentangling power dynamics at personal and structural levels. *British Journal of Social Work, 35,* 435–452.

Thiara, R. K. (2003). Difference, collective action and women's groups: South Asian women in Britain. In M. B. Cohen, & A. Mullender (Eds.), *Gender and group work* (pp. 41–52). London: Routledge.

Curricular-Based Approach

Joan Letendre

Curricular-based groups have increased in use in the last decade as the mental health profession has emphasized the use of therapeutic methods that are influenced by evidence-based practice and can be easily evaluated (Galinsky, Terzian, & Fraser, 2006). Groups that use a standardized curriculum are based on the premise that learning specific skill sets can either prevent or alleviate problems that interfere with daily living (LeCroy & Wooten, 2006). The worker in such groups is also a teacher who facilitates the acquisition of specific information and the practice of targeted skills related to the identified problem (Sands & Solomon, 2003; Wayne & Cohen, 2001). Curricular-based groups are used in correctional centers, schools, hospitals, and mental health clinics. The groups focus on specific populations of children, adolescents, and adults, who are experiencing problems that impact daily living (mental illness, substance abuse problems, HIV/AIDS). Violent behaviors, social skill deficits, emotional regulation, and lack of empowerment have all been addressed with curricular models. This entry will discuss the benefits of the use of curriculum in group work; the challenges to implementing this type of group; and the guidelines to help practitioners with the integration of the curriculum with group work knowledge and skills.

The use of curricular group models that have proven effective insures that practitioners are using methods of helping that promote "best practice" for intervening with specific populations and problems. The evidence base for the curriculum influences the development of the activities and exercises that provide the opportunity to practice skills, and often increases the attractiveness of the groups. When members know that they are in a group where other members share the same life experiences, engagement in the group can be facilitated, thus promoting the practice and acquisition of the skills (Rose & Edelson, 1987). Adherence to a format that specifies the content to be delivered over a set number of sessions insures that the designated skills are being delivered across settings and practitioners (Galinsky et al., 2006). The educational structure within the groups provides a pre-determined plan for delivering the curriculum, which emphasizes didactic instruction, modeling, role playing, and reinforcement, elements found to be effective in learning of new ways of thinking and behaving (LeCroy & Wooten, 2006). Modification of the generic curricula to fit with the developmental and cultural uniqueness of group members insures that the curricular lessons are relevant to the lives of the group members and can be generalized to situations outside of the group sessions (Kulis et al., 2005; Letendre, 2007).

The pressures that many agency settings experience as they attempt to serve increased numbers of clients with decreasing resources is often a motivating factor in the use of curriculum-based models of intervention that have proven effective, can be easily evaluated and serve multiple clients at one time. The pressure for fidelity to the models often drives the group sessions, as practitioners focus on covering the material with little attention to the rich opportunities within the group to bring the curricular lessons to life by including group members input and experiences in the sessions (Letendre & Wayne, in press). Pressured by the need for fidelity to a specific model, workers unskilled in the principles of group work enthusiastically embrace curricular models that "teach" skills to client groups (i.e., anger management), and yet fail to understand that the encouragement of group interaction that integrates the designated skills will better promote the acquisition of the very skills that the group seeks to teach. In contrast, experienced group workers, accustomed to facilitating groups with open agendas, may have difficulty integrating the specific skill sets targeted by the program into a time-limited group session. In addition, the generic curriculum models may not always be relevant to the needs of specific age groups, resulting in additional barriers to engagement of members. The prevalence of short-term treatment programs that are most often facilitated in group settings (i.e., substance abuse programs) present further challenges to the group worker, as frequent member turnover can interfere with the normal progression through stages of the group where members experience increased trust and sharing.

As Galinsky et al. (2006) suggest, group work practice with manualized curricula is an "art" but one that can be learned by both the experienced and inexperienced group worker. Training in implementation of curriculum-based group models involves understanding the curriculum, as well as integration of group work skills within the sessions. Such integration results in delivery of the rich material as part of a group work method and less as a dry, classroom lesson. The importance of thoroughly understanding the curriculum and the rationale for the progression of sessions is key to the successful delivery of a group model that has proven effective for specific populations and problems. Thorough understanding of the complete model and each individual component then allows the worker to have ease in its delivery. Rather than reading from a manual, the worker uses the skill-building to engage group members in its relevance to their lives. Understanding the uniqueness of the members and group (age, culture, problem area, setting, etc.) can facilitate modification of the generic lessons to respond to the needs of the group members. For example, teaching children skills for managing conflict or refusing drugs may differ depending on the culture and social contexts of the group members (Kulis et al., 2005; Letendre, 2007). Training in the principles of group work and the related skill sets can prepare inexperienced workers to facilitate a group where members not only learn the specified skills but where they can also develop a sense of camaraderie, have multiple opportunities to practice newly learned skills, hear other ways of coping, and offer positive and negative feedback in non-oppressive ways. Understanding the worker skills that are used to facilitate trust and positive interactions through the stages of the group's development can greatly enhance the group experience for its members and ensure that the learning of skills becomes a dynamic rather than just a didactic experience.

With the emphasis on evidence-based practice and accountability in social service delivery, curricular-based groups are one method that has shown promise in helping persons with problems function more effectively in their daily lives. Facilitating such groups with skill can be an effective way of helping members—many isolated from positive interpersonal relationships—learn how to relate to others in ways that encourage enjoyment, caring, and growth. Workers, both experienced and inexperienced, must be trained to understand how to present the evidence-based skills in ways that engage the members, while integrating the very group processes that promote caring and mutual aid amongst members. Agency commitment to thorough training of facilitation of such groups can provide support for this learning.

References

Galinsky, M., Terzian, M., & Fraser, M. (2006). The art of group work practice with manualized curricula. *Social Work with Groups, 29*(1), 11–26.

Kulis, S., Marsiglia, F., Elek, E., Dustman, P., Wagstaff, D. A., & Hechts, M. L. (2005). Mexican/Mexican American adolescents and keeping it REAL: An evidence-based substance use prevention program. *Children and Schools, 27*(3), 133–145.

LeCroy, C. W., & Wooton, L. (2006). Social skills training in school settings: Some practical considerations. In R. Constable, C. R. Massat, S. McDonald, & J. P. Flynn (Eds.), *School social work: Practice, policy and research* (pp. 598–617). Chicago: Lyceum Press.

Letendre, J. (2007). Take your time and give it more: Supports and constraints to success in curricular school-based groups. *Social Work with Groups, 30*(3), 65–84.

Letendre, J., & Wayne, J. (in press). Integrating process interventions into a school-based curriculum group. *Social Work with Groups.*

Rose, S. D., & Edleson, J. L. (1987). *Working with children and adolescents in groups.* San Francisco: Jossey-Bass.

Sands, R. C., & Solomon, P. (2003). Developing educational groups in social work practice. *Social Work with Groups, 26*(2), 5–21.

Wayne, J., & Cohen, C. (2001). *Group work education in the field.* Alexandria, VA: Council on Social Work Education.

Emergency Crisis Interventions

Ogden W. Rogers

Disaster and mass emergencies are disruptive life events that are of such magnitude that their experience is felt at both the individual and collective level. While the overwhelming nature of traumatic experience can be helped via individual techniques, the opportunity for "normalizing of experience" and "filling in the details" of what is a complex experience, make group-oriented interventions seem a logical approach to helping support persons who have experienced catastrophe.

Grounded in efforts after World War II (S. Bernstein, personal communication, March 1985; Schwartz & Zalba, 1971) emergency group crisis interventions have expanded and developed since. Using group work methods within crisis intervention frameworks augments helping efforts to restore individuals and communities to adaptive function. The types and extent of emergency group crisis interventions have been shaped from the intellectual and practice environments that nurtured them. Steeped in educational, mutual aid, natural groups activity-oriented, and even community organization models, group approaches in the aftermath of disaster cross a spectrum of process from the brief and educative, to efforts with more intensive therapeutic focus (Dunning, 1988). Group crisis interventions tend to be used in two basic ways: groups for people who experience thematically similar, but individual crisis experiences, and group crisis interventions for groups of persons who have experienced a shared crisis event. The former tend to be ongoing in nature, with individuals coming and going from the group, such as self-help support groups. Emergency group crisis interventions tend to be very short-term group experiences for teams, indigenous working groups, or neighborhoods that have shared in a disaster experience.

Most group approaches share features basic to crisis intervention principles (Parad, Selby, & Quinlan, 1971). There is an assumption that persons who survive mass emergency situations are normal people who have had their personal and social frameworks acutely disrupted. They may have experienced loss of property, of significant others, or of a sense of personal control, or experienced a threat to themselves or others. There is also the assumption that the cognitive and emotional response to significant disruption is based in normality, and serves adaptive purposes. The various group perspectives share a notion that the imbalance that persons experience in the wake of disaster is shaped by a temporal sense–that at individual and group levels, the phenomenon of crisis and response has "phases" of experience and is time limited. Building upon this, the various models hold an assumption that the provision of intervention is most helpful when shaped by the needs of persons who have experienced the disaster, and provided at the closest and most appropriate point in time after the mass emergency situation.

Critical incident stress debriefing (CISD) is a short-term group psychoeducative crisis intervention method initially discussed by Mitchell (1983). Designed to use interpersonal strengths of individuals who, as part of an emergency services team, had experienced symptoms of stress response following a difficult event, the technique tended to be a single group intervention that followed seven "phases" of process. It was designed to ameliorate acute stress effects by creating an environment where the relationship between the critical incident (an event stressor) and the psychosocial effects (personal responses) would be identified and discussed within the supportive context of the working team of first responders, such as a fire company, emergency medical services (EMS) team, or a group of policemen that had entered into the event. The technique built upon a natural part of emergency service organizational life, the "operational critique" or "incident debriefing," which tended to be a meeting to discuss the performance of the team. The difference is that CISD was designed to allow for members to discuss their own personal thoughts, feelings, and behaviors during and after a stressful emergency event, rather than just operational performance.

The typical CISD group is a 1- to 3-hour single session experience facilitated with the natural working team requesting debriefing. Group leaders are a "mental health professional" (MSP) and one or more "peer support persons" (PSPs). PSPs were ideally members of the same type of emergency service (fire, police, EMS) who had been cross-trained in the CISD process with the MSP.

The CISD process proceeds in the following format: an *Introductory Phase* for introducing the facilitators and participants, outlining confidentiality and time boundary, and explaining the purpose of the session; a *Fact Phase* for eliciting from members of the group what activities they performed at the incident, and their perceptions at the scene; a *Thought Phase* encouraging a discussion of the initial thoughts that rescue workers had at the scene; a *Reaction Phase* where the facilitator encourages members to share with others the emotional feelings they had at the scene and feelings they had afterward; a *Symptom Phase* where the facilitator explores the psychological and physical after effects that the workers have experienced following the incident; a *Teaching Phase* where the group leaders could discuss normalization and stress management hygiene; and a *Re-entry Phase* to conclude the group's activities, answer questions, and allow the group to plan some future action if it wished.

The intervention model promotes an experience of competence in group sharing and emotional safety among working team members. It builds upon the basic skills of emergency service personnel as observers and reporters of fact, and then moves them into being sharers of emotion, and providers of support to other team members.

CISD gained wide popularity in the 1980s and the technique was being utilized with audiences that were never the method's intended "rescuer" target population. Despite this popularity, there had been little controlled research on the technique (Rogers, 1993). Concern for the method's lack of empirical demonstration of efficacy (Gist & Woodall, 1999) became an academic controversy in the late 1990s and continues.

A modification of the CISD process includes the multiple stressor debriefing (MSD) model discussed by Armstrong, Lund, McWright, and Tichenor (1995). This model was designed for Red Cross disaster workers involved with longer, multi-event disaster situations, who had formed a temporary working team for the disaster. An emphasis on this model was distancing content from "therapeutic" culture.

The National Organization for Victim Assistance (NOVA) uses a debriefing model called "group crisis intervention"(1998). Similar to CISD, the content and the process is oriented to primary survivors of a community disaster, and emphasizes the support and validation that can arise out of existing community membership, and may include organizing opportunities.

Emergency group crisis interventions are likely to continue to be used in the aftermath of mass emergency. Survivors of terrorist events, natural, and human-promulgated disaster will need to be afforded psychosocial supports. Continued research into effectiveness and evidence-based best-practice needs further development and offer broad opportunities for group work practitioners amenable to quick, flexible, and creative response in complex environments.

References

Armstrong, K. R., Lund, P. E., McWright, L. T., & Tichenor, V. (1995). Multiple stressor debriefing and the American Red Cross: The East Bay Hills fire experience. *Social Work*, 40(1), 83–90.

Dunning, C. (1988). Intervention strategies for emergency workers. In M. Lystad (Ed.), *Mental health response to mass emergencies: Theory and practice* (pp. 284–307). New York: Brunner/Mazel.

Gist, R., & Woodall, S. (1999) There are no simple solutions to complex problems: The rise and fall of Critical Incident Stress Debriefing as a response to occupational stress in the Fire Service. In R. Gist, & B. Lubin (Eds.), *Response to disaster* (pp. 211–235). Ann Arbor, MI: Taylor & Francis.

Mitchell, J. (1983) When disaster strikes: the critical incident stress debriefing process. *Journal of Emergency and Medical Services, 8*, 36–39.

National Organization for Victim Assistance. (1998). *Community crisis response team training manual* (2nd ed.). Washington, DC: Author.

Parad, H., Selby, L., & Quinlan, J. (1976). Crisis intervention with families and groups. In R. W. Roberts, & H. Northen (Eds.), *Theories of social work with groups* (pp. 304–330). New York: Columbia University Press.

Rogers, O. W. (1993) *An examination of Critical Incident Stress Debriefing for emergency services providers: A quasi experimental field study.* (Doctoral Dissertation, University of Maryland Baltimore,1993). Ann Arbor, MI.

Schwartz, W., & Zalba, S. (Eds.). (1971). *The practice of group work.* New York: Columbia University Press.

Family Involvement Approach

David S. Crampton

Since the 1980s, an assortment of group approaches have emerged that are designed to engage family and community members in developing plans for the care and protection of children who are at risk of child abuse and neglect. These family involvement groups have become a widely used practice throughout the world. They include family group conferencing (FGC) from New Zealand, family unity meetings (FUM) from Oregon, team decision making (TDM) from Ohio, family team conferences (FTC) from Alabama, and many other variations. The FGC approach is used in Australia, Canada, Finland, New Zealand, Norway, Sweden, the United Kingdom, and many other countries, while there are a variety of different approaches used in the United States (FGC, FUM, and TDM). Within the group work literature, there is acknowledgement of the need for group workers to be familiar with these practices and for family involvement practitioners to be trained in essential group work skills and knowledge (Crampton & Natarajan, 2005; Macgowan & Pennell, 2001).

Family involvement groups are also used in other fields of social work practice, particularly in juvenile justice and school settings. Following principles of restorative justice, a family group conference could be convened to allow a young offender who vandalized a home an opportunity to meet the victim's family. Several other support people, including the youth's family, would be invited to the meeting as well. Together, they talk about the impact of the crime on their lives and the community, and develop a plan to repair the harm. Participants in this type of family group conference frequently say they feel good about the process, believing it to be a very practical way of holding young people accountable (Umbreit, Vos, Coates, & Lightfoot, 2005). Family group conferences are also used in schools to address behavioral and/or attendance concerns. Young people who attend them generally say they appreciate the opportunity to be heard and they often benefit from the plans developed by the group to improve their school experience (Crow Marsh, & Holton, 2004). While this entry focused on the use of family involvement groups in child welfare, many of the points made below are applicable to juvenile justice and education practice.

The growth in the use of family involvement groups in child welfare decision making is due to dissatisfaction with conventional child welfare approaches and positive results from these family involvement groups for including children, youth, and families in service planning. Practitioners have discovered that family meetings improved the child welfare agency's decision making by giving caseworkers access to more information and giving families the opportunity to "buy into" the process by involving them in developing a plan for the child. Practitioners also see the benefits of family members gaining an opportunity to add their own cultural identity and strengths to plans for children (Pennell & Anderson, 2005).

The focus of family involvement groups is a plan for the care and protection of children developed through a meeting of the children's extended family members, community supporters and service providers. Macgowan and Pennell (2001) suggest that these meetings most closely fit the social goals model of group work, with an emphasis on following a group development perspective towards a self-directed objective. In this case, the meeting is used by the participants to develop plans for protecting children who are at risk of maltreatment. A group worker sometimes called a coordinator or facilitator guides the meeting. Macgowan and Pennell (2001) describe the developmental schema of the meeting in three main stages: planning/preparation, convening, and implementation/follow-up. In the planning preparation stage, the purpose of the meeting is determined as well as who should attend. Arrangements are made for a time and place to meet. The convening stage includes the sharing of information about the purpose of the meeting, and the strengths and concerns that must be discussed as part of the meeting. After this information is shared, the group develops their plan. In some models, the family members are left alone to develop their plan, with service providers remaining nearby if any questions come up during their deliberations. In the implementation/follow-up stage the group reviews the proposed plan and determines who will take responsibility for implementing the various parts of the plan.

Although family involvement groups generally follow these stages, there are some differences in the approaches in terms of the purpose, timing, composition, and role of the group worker (Crampton & Pennell, in press). While there are many differences in these family involvement groups, they all include: an emphasis on the need for child welfare agencies to interact with children, families, and communities with mutual respect; an expectation that power will shift from being exclusively held by the child welfare system and the courts to being shared with families and communities; a broad and inclusive definition of who is included in the "family team" that is making these decisions; a meeting place that provides an environment that is supportive of families in the decision-making process; and a commitment to providing sufficient preparation, coordination and facilitation of the family meetings in order to balance the needs of all parties, while remaining focused on the child's safety and well-being (Center for the Study of Social Policy, 2002).

There are several common aspects of family involvement practice and traditional group work concepts, such as mutual aid and social responsibility. Steinberg (2004) describes mutual aid as "people helping one another as they think things through" (p. 3); she further notes that it is both a process and an outcome. In family involvement groups, the members comfort one another and share information throughout the meeting and eventually develop a plan that supports each other and the child or children who are the focus of the meeting. In this way, family involvement groups include mutual aid in both the process and outcome. Macgowan and Pennell (2001) describe how family involvement groups promote social responsibility by developing groups that can promote social goals, such as the care and protection of children or the restoration of justice following a crime. They point out that the use of groups to promote democracy and social goals can be traced back to Grace Longwell Coyle and many other group work theorists.

Given the growing use of these family involvement groups, it would be helpful for group workers to be familiar with these practices so that they can contribute to making them most effective. For example, group work has much to teach about the role of facilitation and group decision making in these sorts of meetings (Crampton and Natarajan, 2005). At the same time, group workers may learn some things about improving their own work by observing the work of family involvement practitioners.

References

Center for the Study of Social Policy (2002). *Bringing families to the table: A comparative guide to family meetings in Child Welfare*. Retrieved December 1, 2007 from http://www.cssp.org/uploadFiles/Bringing_Families.PDF

Crampton, D., & Natarajan, A. (2005). Connections between group work and family meetings in Child Welfare Practice: What can we learn from each other? *Social Work with Groups, 28*(1), 65–79.

Crampton, D., & Pennell, J. (in press). Family involvement meetings with older children in foster care: promising practices and the challenge of child welfare reform. In B. Kerman, A. N. Maluccio, & M. Freundlich (Eds.), *Seeking permanence for children and youths in the Child Welfare System*. New York: Columbia University Press.

Crow, G., Marsh, P., & Holton, E. (2004). *Supporting pupils, schools and families: An evaluation of the Hampshire Family Group Conferences in Education Project.* Retrieved December 1, 2007 from http://www.petermarsh.staff.shef.ac.uk/documents/FGCEducFindings.doc

Macgowan, M. J., & Pennell, J. (2001). Building social responsibility through family group conferencing. *Social Work with Groups, 24(3/4)*, 67–87.

Pennell, J., & Anderson, G. (2005). *Widening the circle: The practice and evaluation of family group conferencing with children, youths and their families.* Washington, DC: NASW Press.

Steinberg, D. M. (2004). *The mutual-aid approach to working with groups.* Binghamton, NY: Haworth Press.

Umbreit, M. S., Vos, B., Coates, R. B., & Lightfoot, E. (2005). Restorative justice in the 21st century: A social movement full of opportunities and pitfalls. *Marquette University Law Review, 89(2)*, 251–304.

Intergroup Dialogue: Introduction

Nancy Rodenborg and Lois A. Bosch

In congruence with social work's core mission, culturally competent social workers must be able to work with diverse groups in varied contexts. Sometimes group work involves conflict (Corey & Corey, 2006) that is based on stereotyping and prejudice. Bargal (2004) advises group workers to develop a "repertoire of interventions" (p. 293) to work directly with intergroup conflict. Instead, however, he notes that group work is largely focused on "intragroup structures and processes (and) . . . interpersonal and intrapsychic problems" (p. 304). Intergroup dialogue is a non-therapeutic group work method designed specifically to address intergroup conflict. It is useful in education, community, advocacy, and other social work contexts involving diverse groups.

Intergroup dialogue consists of "face-to-face, focused, facilitated, and confidential discussions occurring over time between two or more groups of people defined by their different social identities" (Schoem, Hurtado, Sevig, Chesler, & Sumida, 2001, p. 6). Dialogue focuses directly on race, ethnicity, culture, religion, disability or other social identities (Schoem et al., 2001) associated with historical or current intergroup conflict. Dialogue versus discussion or debate is emphasized. Participants are urged to listen deeply to others' experiences to try and understand their meaning rather than to judge, challenge, or debate. Participants are "more likely to think together" if they listen carefully and "create shared meaning" (Dessel, Rogge, & Garlington, 2006, p. 304). This shared meaning contributes to reduced prejudice and conflict. To be successful, intergroup dialogue facilitators must be familiar with long-standing group work concepts, such as the stages of group development and participant contracting, as well as having basic generalist social group work skills.

Intergroup dialogue developed from a large body of theory and research known as contact theory (Allport, 1954/1979; Pettigrew, 1998). Contact theory postulates that if diverse people meet under specific conditions their prejudice is more likely to be reduced than if contact occurs outside of these conditions. Military and athletic contexts provide two good examples of intergroup situations that adhere to the central "contact conditions" and tend to reduce prejudice (Pettigrew, 1998). In both cases, contact occurs under the following five contact conditions in which participants: (a) are of equal status (belong to the same military branch or athletic team); (b) pursue common goals (to succeed in battle or win a game); (c) meet under the auspices of a respected institution, law, or custom (national military, athletic team sponsor); (d) share "common interests and common humanity" (all are soldiers together or athletic team members) (Allport, 1954/1979, p. 281); and (e) are likely to see each other as potential friends (Pettigrew, 1998). Intergroup dialogue is structured to create these five central conditions.

Intergroup dialogue usually involves people from groups that have historical or current conflict or tension. Reduced prejudice is its main goal but its rationale is social justice. The method provides a forum to examine issues associated with inequality, privilege, discrimination, and oppression (Zuniga, Nagda, & Sevig, 2002). It increases the intergroup communication skills required for collaborative social justice work and is well suited to social work's social justice mission.

Within social work, intergroup dialogue has been utilized in educational, community, non-profit, and advocacy settings (Alvarez & Cabbil, 2001; Dessel et al., 2006; Nagda, Kim, & Truelove, 2004; Nagda et al., 1999; Rodenborg & Huynh, 2006). It has been used in a variety of other settings including education, community groups, non-profits, leadership training, public policy, and conflict resolution, and has focused on topics such as abortion, environment, or race (Dessel et al., 2006; Pettigrew, 1998). A large body of international research has documented its effectiveness at reducing prejudice among diverse people (Pettigrew, 1998).

Intergroup dialogue facilitation follows a stage model through which participants learn to see each other as unique individuals as well as representatives of their social group. Similar to many group work methods, facilitation begins by reviewing ground rules and establishing norms of trust, confidentiality, and listening. In the first step, participants learn the difference between dialogue and discussion or debate. Facilitators help participants recognize each other as human beings with unique personal, cultural, and social identities. Participants may begin to see each other as potential, while not actual, friends. A second stage moves to direct sharing of experiences rooted in social identity. Facilitators may ask about experiences of discrimination or privilege and invite participants to share experiences as a child, during pivotal times in their lives, or from their current life. Sometimes a third stage is added that focuses on specific difficult topics, such as affirmative action or abortion. Some groups may address an issue pertinent to their unique context (e.g., discrimination in local government or neighborhood safety). The final stage includes action planning and next steps. Participants may choose to remain together as a continuing advocacy or identity group (Rodenborg & Huynh, 2006) or the group may disband. Either way participants leave the group with personal plans and a greater skill for ongoing social justice work. The overall facilitation goal is to increase understanding and reduce prejudice among diverse people.

Intergroup dialogue is not without its challenges. A critical ethical consideration is the impact of intergroup dialogue on oppressed populations. Some research suggests that dominant groups benefit more than non-dominant groups (Dessel et al., 2006). Especially in non-voluntary settings, practitioners must be careful not to victimize members of oppressed groups by encouraging the sharing of difficult personal experience, which can educate dominant culture listeners but exploit the speakers. Social workers must insure that intergroup dialogue adheres to the two core values outlined in the *Standards for Social Work Practice with Groups*: rigorously respect the autonomy, worth, and dignity of each group participant and remember that the goal of the group is to create a socially just society (Association for the Advancement of Social Work with Groups, 2006).

Documenting the effectiveness of intergroup dialogue through rigorous research is a second challenge. Initial effectiveness data have been anecdotal or case examination. Research rigor should be improved and should examine intergroup dialogue's effectiveness for dominant and non-dominant participants, its flexibility across multiple settings, and its limitations (Dessel et al., 2006).

References

Allport, G. W. (1979). *The nature of prejudice* (25th Anniversary ed.). Reading, MA: Addison-Wesley. Originally published in 1954.

Alvarez, A. R., & Cabbil, L. (2001). The MELD program: Promoting personal change and social justice through a year-long multicultural group experience. *Social Work with Groups, 24*(1), 3–20.

Association for the Advancement of Social work with Groups. (2006). *Standards for Social Work Practice with Groups*. Retrieved August 14, 2007 from http://www.aaswg.org/Standards/standards

Bargal, D. (2004). Groups for reducing intergroup conflict. In C. D. Garvin, L. M. Gutiérrez, & M. J. Galinsky (Eds.), *Handbook of social work with groups* (pp. 292–306). New York: Guilford Press.

Corey, M. S., & Corey, G. (2006). *Process and practice with groups* (7th ed.). Belmont, CA: Thomson Brooks/Cole.

Dessel, A., Rogge, M. E., & Garlington, S. B. (2006). Using group dialogue to promote social justice and change. *Social Work, 51*(4), 303–315.

Nagda, B. A, Kim, C., & Truelove, Y. (2004). Learning about difference, learning with others, learning to transgress. *Journal of Social Issues, 60*, 195–214.

Nagda, B. A., Spearmon, M. L., Holley, L. C., Harding, S., Balossone, M. L., Moise-Swanson, D., & De Mello, S. (1999). Intergroup dialogues: An innovative approach to teaching about diversity and justice in social work programs. *Journal for Higher Education, 35*(3), 433–449.

Pettigrew, T. F. (1998). Intergroup contact theory. *Annual Review of Psychology, 49*, 65–86.

Rodenborg, N. A., & Huynh, N. (2006). On overcoming segregation: Social work and intergroup dialogue. *Social Work with Groups, 29*(1), 27–44.

Schoem, D., Hurtado. S., Sevig, T., Chesler, M., & Sumida, S. H. (2001). Intergroup dialogue: Democracy at work in theory and practice. In D. Schoem, & S. Hurtado (Eds.), *Intergroup dialogue: Deliberative democracy in school, college, community, and workplace*. Ann Arbor, MI: University of Michigan Press.

Zuniga, X., Nagda, B. A., & Sevig, T. D. (2002). Intergroup dialogues: An educational model for cultivating engagement across differences. *Equity and Excellence in Education, 35*(1), 7–17.

Intergroup Dialogue: Overview

Adrienne Dessel

Intergroup dialogue is an innovative and versatile non-therapeutic group work approach that social workers can use to reduce prejudice and conflict, improve communication and relationships, and promote social change (Alvarez & Cabbil, 2001; Miller & Donner, 2000; Rodenborg & Huynh, 2006). Dialogue is a process of exploring one's own perceptions, values, and experiences, and communicating them without either forcing them on others or conforming, as a way to create meaning between people (Bohm, 1992). Intergroup dialogue is a facilitated group experience that is designed to provide a safe space for participants to address divisive social issues (Dessel, Rogge, & Garlington, 2006). Intergroup dialogue may incorporate learning or experiential material, and engages participants in listening, speaking, reflecting on one's own views, and learning about the perspectives of others (Herzig & Chasin, 2006). Such dialogue involves processes of appreciation of difference, engaging self, critical self-reflection, and alliance building (Nagda, 2006). It may also address cultural differences and power imbalances.

Group work pays close attention to participants' personal, cultural, and social identities and dialogues are often co-facilitated by trained facilitators who may represent the social or cultural identities of the groups involved (Brown & Mistry, 2005; Nagda, 2006). The development of group norms is also addressed through the use of established dialogue agreements (Alvarez & Cabbil, 2001; Herzig & Chasin, 2006). Convening and facilitating intergroup dialogues combines the social work micro skills of critical self-analysis and relational engagement with macro skills of systemic and structural change (Dessel et al., 2006). The practice of intergroup dialogue builds upon both the interactional group work model that seeks common ground between individual and group needs (Gitterman & Shulman, 2005) and social action group work that promotes empowerment and social change (Breton, 1995).

Social work with groups has a historical yet under recognized purpose of linking group work with social change (Alvarez & Cabbil, 2001). Intergroup dialogue is employed in academic, community, and international settings to address issues such as racism, interethnic conflict, and civic participation (Dessel et al., 2006). The National Coalition for Dialogue and Deliberation identified four primary intentions of dialogue: exploration, conflict transformation, decision making, and collaborative action. The Public Conversations Project has identified goals of intergroup dialogue that include thoughtful speaking and listening before responding, mutual recognition of the authenticity of others, an inquiring stance, and a sense of safety, security and trust (Herzig & Chasin, 2006). The United Nations Development Programme's (UNDP) Democratic Dialogue Project described the goals of their international dialogues as dealing with critical sociopolitical events, addressing challenges of the times, and promoting long-term change.

Groups are a social microcosm of the larger society and successful intergroup contact has been shown to improve intergroup relationships (Brown & Mistry, 2005). Stages of group process inform how a group functions and illuminate the powerful effects of addressing private issues in a public setting (Drumm, 2006). Allport's (1954/1979) contact hypothesis stated that intergroup contact results in positive effects when four conditions are present: (1) equal group status within the group encounter, (2) common goals (3) cooperative interactions; and (4) support of those with social influence and power. Pettigrew and Tropp (2006) found that change occurs through learning about outgroups, the opportunity for reappraisal and re-categorization of outgroups, the generation of empathy and positive emotion, and the potential for friendships.

Intergroup contact that provides opportunities for "self-revealing interactions" has been shown to facilitate superordinate identity formation and reduce bias (Gaertner, Dovidio, & Bachman, 1996, p. 271). Dasgupta and Rivera (2006) found that the activation of conscious egalitarian beliefs and intention to control prejudicial behaviors can mediate the relationship between automatic prejudice and biased behavior. Furthermore, the provision of a safe and positive opportunity for interactions between different groups may reduce the anxiety and negative attitudes dominant groups have about marginalized groups. Members of non-dominant groups have also reported positive experiences from participating in intergroup education and dialogue.

Interventions that seek to educate and promote self-reflection and empathy, manipulate ingroup and outgroup perceptions, and facilitate intergroup contact and its impact on social identity roles and potential for cross-group friendships have been shown to achieve prejudice reduction through attitude change. Studies in academic settings have shown that dialogue participation has increased white students' perspective taking and sense of commonality with students of color, political involvement, and views of differences as compatible with democracy. For students of color, dialogue participation has been related to perceiving less intergroup divisiveness and holding more positive views of conflict, as well as increased positive relationships with white students (Nagda & Zuniga, 2003). Effects for all students have included learning about the perspectives of people from other social groups, valuing new viewpoints, understanding the impact of social group membership on identity, gaining increased awareness of social inequalities, and developing analytical problem-solving skills, leadership, and cultural awareness (Hurtado, 2005). Results of dialogues in community and international settings have included breakdown of stereotypes, facilitation of personal relationships, the establishment of trust and consensus building leading to critical social policy development, and commitment to social change (Alvarez & Cabbil, 2001; Diez-Pinto, 2004).

The first challenge is to contend with power differentials between majority and marginalized groups. Group work practitioners must take into account inherent privilege and systemic imbalances of power, and their implications for intergroup relationships, when designing and facilitating intergroup dialogues (Brown & Mistry, 2005). The second task is to improve research on intergroup dialogue outcomes. This requires collaboration between dialogue practitioners and researchers, and support for such work from funding sources. Improved research might include studies that use representative samples and random assignment and discuss response rates, attrition and social desirability bias, the use of well-established dialogue intervention protocols and measurement instruments, and employment of rigorous qualitative analysis methods. The final challenge for intergroup dialogue is to expand its potential in both research and practice in order to foster non-traditional means of resolving societal oppression, conflict and violence.

References

Allport, G. (1979). *The nature of prejudice* (25th Anniversary ed.). Reading, MA: Addison-Wesley. Originally published in 1954.

Alvarez, A., & Cabbil, L. (2001). The MELD program: Promoting personal change and social justice through a year-long multicultural group experience. *Social Work with Groups, 24*(1), 3–20.

Bohm, D. (1992). *Changing consciousness: Exploring the hidden source of the social, political, and environmental crises facing our world.* San Francisco: Harper.

Breton, M. (1995). The potential for social action in groups. *Social Work with Groups, 18*(2/3), 5–13.

Brown, A., & Mistry, T. (2005). Group work with "mixed membership" groups: Issues of race and gender. *Social Work with Groups, 28*(3/4), 133–148.

Dasgupta, N., & Rivera, L. (2006). From automatic antigay prejudice to behavior: The moderating role of conscious beliefs about gender and behavioral control. *Journal of Personality and Social Psychology, 91*(2), 268–280.

Dessel, A., Rogge, M., & Garlington, S. (2006). Using intergroup dialogue to promote social justice and change. *Social Work, 51*(4), 303–315.

Diez-Pinto, E. (2004). *Vision Guatemala 1998–2000: Building bridges of trust.* New York: United Nations Development Programme. Retrieved July 31, 2006 from http://democraticdialoguenetwork.org/documents/view.pl?s=13;ss=;t=;f_id=263

Drumm, K. (2006). The essential power of group work. *Social Work with Groups, 29*(2/3), 17–31.

Gaertner, S., Dovidio, J., & Bachman, B. (1996). Revisiting the contact hypothesis: The induction of a common ingroup identity. *International Journal of Intercultural Relations, 20*(3/4), 271–290.

Gitterman, A., & Shulman, L. (2005). *Mutual aid groups, vulnerable and resilient populations, and the life cycle* (3rd ed.). New York: Columbia University Press.

Herzig, M., & Chasin, L. (2006). *Fostering dialogue across divides: A nuts and bolts guide from the Public Conversations Project.* Retrieved June 10, 2006 from http://www.publicconversations.org/jamsdownload.html

Hurtado, S. (2005). The next generation of diversity and intergroup relations. *Journal of Social Issues, 61*(3), 595–610.

Miller, J., & Donner, S. (2000). More than just talk: The use of racial dialogues to combat racism. *Social Work with Groups, 23*(1), 31–53.

Nagda, B. (2006). Breaking barriers, crossing borders, building bridges: Communication processes in intergroup dialogues. *Journal of Social Issues, 62*(3), 553–576.

Nagda, B. A., & Zuniga, X. (2003). Fostering meaningful racial engagement through intergroup dialogues. *Group Processes & Intergroup Relations, 6*(1), 111–128.

Pettigrew, T., & Tropp, L. (2006). A meta-analytic test of intergroup contact theory. *Journal of Personality and Social Psychology, 90*(5), 751–783.

Rodenborg, N., & Huynh, N. (2006). On overcoming segregation: Social work and intergroup dialogue. *Social Work with Groups, 29*(1), 27–44.

Intergroup Dialogue: Principles

Mona C. S. Schatz

Social group work plays a major role in building deeply meaningful and growth-filled opportunities for group members. Dialogue groups, developed as a group approach to promote meaningful group interaction, starts where the group members are, letting the group develop from its own point of departure (Konokpa,

1983). Dialogue group work is a process that promotes validation and support for group members, offering social work an innovative and effective group work approach for working in multinational, multicultural situations as well as in the local community.

Among the vital roles of group work is the opportunity to promote and foster democratization, social action, and leadership (Konopka, 1983; Kottler, 1994). A dual focus on "democracy in action and mental health is very significant in the development of group work itself" (Konopka, 1994, p. 9). Dialogue as a recent group work approach is equally valuable to serving this dual focus in localized, regional, and global settings.

Dialogue gains its movement for the group through members' openness, authenticity, and the opportunities that promote democratic exchanges. Dialogue is an empowering group process, structured to allow members to seek common ground. This is a new social work group work approach, beneficial to the vast array of social agency settings and professional groups within social work.

Dialogue is a process with ancient Socratic roots; yet, dialogue groups in their present form were initiated by the late physicist David Bohm (Bohm, 1996; Bohm & Edwards, 1992) as an avenue to build honest, deeply meaningful, shared discussions addressing vital social and environmental challenges. As conceived, dialogue is a multi-faceted process looking well beyond conventional ideas of conversational parlance and exchange (Nichol, 1996). Nichol's suggests that Bohm hoped to explore the widest range of humanness in this approach. Dialogue has the capability in its process to explore an unusually wide range of human experiences: from our closely held values to the nature and intensity of emotions; to the patterns of our thought processes and the function of memory in which our neuronphysiology structures momentary experiences. Dialogue may foster a process that asks group members to question deeply held assumptions about culture, meaning, and identity. In its deepest sense, dialogue is an invitation to test the viability of traditional definitions of what it means to be human and collectively to explore the prospect of an enhanced humanity (Nichols, 1996, pp. vii–viii).

Dialogue is a conversation among equals and begins with a suspension of thoughts, impulses, and judgments. Dialogue, in seeking common ground, is very open in design and process, usually without an agenda or any expected outcomes. Five key expectations frame the work of dialogue: (1) *authenticity*, as a person in the process of the dialogue group; (2) *respectfulness*, listening fully and completely as each group member speaks; (3) *thoughtfulness*, being one's self, not the labels, degrees, etc., being "there, in the moment" and genuine; (4) *inclusiveness*, fostering opportunities and invitations for everyone to voice their thoughts, ideas, and insights, and 5) *suspending judgment* of ideas and thoughts presented, being totally open and accepting of the whole experience, being willing to suspend the "reactive and combative" conversational debate model, thus, recognizing that closure is not needed or required in the process of finding common ground. Hsai (2005), in her work with Asian "foreign brides," locates this common ground among women of varied nationalities who all come to the recognition that they share the label and accompanying trials and challenges as "foreign brides" in Taiwan.

Dialogue requires listeners to come out of "auto-drive" mode. This group approach invites an experience that is not the ordinary, humdrum style of talking and listening. Bohm (1996) believes that dialogue explores the manner in which *thought* is sustained at a collective level, thus, opening one's thinking to new ideas about cultural development and how cultures can change when thoughts change. The process of exploration for the group actually takes place during listening (Bohm, 1996). It is vital for the group initiator, who may or may not serve as the group facilitator or leader, to introduce these expectations and group elements and give group participants ideas and suggestions in order to use these elements as their "skill basket" for the impending group experience. Dialogue groups can be developed as leaderless groups, as facilitated groups, co-lead groups, and as leader-directed groups.

Dialogue can be a powerful tool for social group workers, useful at different systemic levels. On the micro practice level, dialogue has been shown to be effective as a theoretical orientation for psychotherapy and personal growth (Sharma, 1996). On the mezzo and macro levels, dialogue groups have been utilized to explore social oppression (Hsai, 2005; Schatz, Tracy, & Tracy, 2006) and to facilitate understanding and discussion between groups that historically have been in conflict, e.g., dialogue groups in the United States to understand and deal with the American legacy of racism (St. Louis Community College, 2001) and dialogue groups among Palestinians and Jews (Jewish–Palestinian Dialogue Group (2001).

The use of groups and group discussion to facilitate personal growth and change is an essential intervention approach for social workers internationally. Yet, in some circumstances, individuals are invited into groups that are not overtly organized as clinical or therapeutic. They may be more community oriented. Yalom (Yalom & Leszcz, 2005, p. 525) has addressed "groups for normals," in his group psychotherapy text. Yalom presents the encounter group, providing some description of this group approach and some evaluative data. Dialogue may actually become the type of group that Yalom would categorize as a group for "normals," a group used in non-clinical circumstances where the group members do achieve personal development among other gains.

Dialogue groups are often composed of social leaders, educators, policy-makers. The value of dialogue groups to foster opportunities for transformative experiences as well as strong networking among participants in different countries has been described when used at multinational, multicultural conferences (Schatz et al., 2006; Schatz, Furman, & Jenkins, 2003). In the international dialogue process, participants learn together, find common ground from which to transform their sorrows into joys, problems into solutions, even, new social inventions that may better meet basic human needs.

The dialogue experience has been assessed as very positive for participants (O'Hara & Varga, 1996). Qualitative evaluation instruments document that the dialogue process (a) promotes feelings of trust among group participants that contributes to the success of the group experience, and (b) fosters greater cultural and personal understanding. In promoting egalitarian relationships, dialogue groups are consistent with the core values of the social work profession internationally.

"Among the most important reasons why dialogue groups work is that people's basic needs for human connection and belonging are provided for in the process, simply by its design" (Schatz et al., 2003, p. 489).

References

Bohm, D. (1996). *On dialogue*. New York. Routledge.

Bohm, D., & Edwards, M. (1992). *Changing consciousness: Exploring the hidden source of social, political and environmental crisis facing our world*. New York: Pegasus.

Hsai, H. (2005). Internationalization of capital and the trade in Asian women: The case of "foreign brides" in Taiwan, women and globalization. *Migrant Monitor, 1*, 34–51.

Institute for International Connections (1998). *The Family and beyond: Building community across systems and cultures*. 17–20 June. (Conference monograph.)

Jewish–Palestinian Dialogue Group (2001). Jews and Palestinians cooperate for peace. Retrieved February 21, 2001 from http://www.igc.org/traubman/dg-tlart.htm

Konopka, G. (1983). *Social group work: A helping process*. Englewood Cliffs, NJ: Prentice-Hall.

Kottler, J. A. (2001). *Learning group leadership*. Boston: Allyn & Bacon.

Nichol, L. (1996). Foreword. In D. Bohm, *On dialogue*. New York: Routledge.

O'Hara, J., & Varga, A. (1996). *The ties that no longer bind: Russians and Americans talk to each other*. Notre Dame, ID: Cross Cultural Publications.

Schatz, M. S., Furman, R., & Jenkins, L. E. (2003). Space to grow: Using dialogue for multicultural, multinational learning. *International Social Work, 46*(4), 481–494.

Schatz, M. S., Tracy, J., & Tracy, S. (2006). Overcoming social oppression: Using dialogue and theatre to reveal oppression and foster healing. *Critical Social Work, 7*(2). Retrieved May 9, 2007 from http://www.criticalsocialwork.com/

Sharma, S. L. (1996). *The therapeutic dialogue: A guide to humane and egalitarian psychotherapy*. New York: Jason Aronson.

St. Louis Community College (2001). *Inter-racial dialogue groups*. Retrieved February 21, 2001 from http://www.stlcc.cc.mo.us/fv/ird/

Yalom, I., & Leszcz, M. (2005). *The theory and practice of group psychotherapy* (5th ed.). New York: Basic Books.

Multiple Family Approach*

Geetha Gopalan and Lydia Maria Franco

Multiple family groups (MFGs) developed as a combination of family and group therapy in order to offer families unique opportunities to develop support networks, reduce social isolation, overcome stigma related to mental health difficulties, share information, develop coping strategies, resolve family problems, and ameliorate dysfunctional family interactions (McKay, Gonzalez, Stone, Ryland, & Kohner, 1995; O'Shea & Phelps, 1985). Pragmatic concerns within overburdened mental health facilities further stimulated the use of MFGs as an efficient service delivery option, such that multiple families could be served simultaneously (O'Shea & Phelps, 1985). Despite large variations in theoretical bases, techniques, and client populations used in actual practice, key defining features of MFGs include: (1) involving six to eight families; (2) being facilitated by trained clinicians;

(3) including at least two generations of a family in each session; (4) being problem-focused; and (5) offering psychoeducational and practice activities that foster both within-family and between-family learning (McKay et al., 1995; O'Shea & Phelps, 1985). Moreover, MFGs reflect key features of social group work practice by validating members' strengths, encouraging mutual aid and social support, addressing stigma, acknowledging stages in group development, allowing for conflict to further work, using active problem-solving skills, and integrating varied learning activities (Drumm, 2006; Gitterman & Shulman, 2005; Steinberg, 2004).

MFGs as a social group work approach is specifically exemplified by the MFG service delivery model to reduce disruptive behaviors (MFG-DB), particularly oppositional defiant disorder (ODD) and conduct disorder (CD). This model was designed to meet the needs of families residing in low-income, urban environments (Franco et al., 2008). Given that family-level processes (e.g., parental child management skills, discipline practices, family communication, and interactional patterns; Keiley, 2002; Tolan & Henry, 1996), are the most powerful predictors of the development and maintenance of ODD and CD, counseling involving all family members is crucial. At the same time, stigma associated with seeking mental health services among minority families, and parents' fears of being blamed for children's difficulties frequently impede retention in treatment (for review, see McKay & Bannon, 2004). Moreover, specific factors tied to urban living (i.e., socioeconomic disadvantage, social isolation, high stress, lack of social support, damaging influences within the community or peer group) also contribute to the development of childhood conduct problems (Kazdin, 1995). Consequently, the MFG-DB approach provides culturally congruent care by fostering mutual aid and social support, and reducing stigma for urban families of color (McKay et al., 1995). The family's concerns are optimally validated and normalized when they are able to see and hear from others "who have been there". In this way, the presence of other families maximizes change, as feedback from peers can be less threatening than suggestions offered by clinical facilitators (McKay et al., 1995). Moreover, MFG-DB facilitators validate group members' strengths by emphasizing the varying expertise of different family members in solving difficulties presented in the group.

The MFG-DB approach involves a series of 16 weekly sessions lasting an hour and a half each. Four core conceptual elements organize sessions: (1) rules, (2) responsibility, (3) relationships; and (4) respectful communication (the 4Rs). In addition, "stress" and "social support" conceptual categories were added, as these factors can also impact child mental health service use and outcomes. The MFG-DB manual, while providing an overall curriculum structure, also allows for facilitators to tailor session content to the individual needs of the child and family. Generally speaking, each session is divided into segments that include a family social time, homework review, group discussion, family practice activities, and homework assignment (Franco et al., 2008). The group structure and content differ during the beginning, middle, and end phases. In the first few sessions, activities and discussions focus on establishing group rules, building connections between members, and acknowledging members' strengths. The beginning phase also involves initial psychoeducation around different topics relevant to the 4Rs. In addition to group discussion, role-play exercises, family board games, and group activities reflect the importance of addressing multiple learning styles. The middle phase is marked by increasing group cohesion and family members seeking support from each other. Family conflicts, which are more likely to emerge during this phase, are utilized as opportunities for all group members to provide feedback and suggestions for problem solving. Pervasive throughout sessions, facilitators encourage the ongoing participation of families. For all families, mid-week calls are placed between sessions to address any obstacles to participation, support parenting skills, encourage homework completion, and remind families to attend the next session. For families with frequent absences, additional phone calls, home visits, and letters are recommended. As the sessions continue, a buddy system may also further engagement, mutual aid, and social support (Franco et al., 2008). Such a system would pair family units together to provide support and updates if sessions are missed. A program of incentives (e.g., dinner, transportation money, childcare, periodic prizes, and homework sticker awards) also help to retain families in the group (Franco et al., 2008). Weekly supervision encourages facilitators to connect families to other needed services (i.e., housing, child welfare, medication treatment). Finally, the ending phase focuses on members' feelings towards termination, obtaining feedback about the group structure and content, addressing additional needs of families through referrals, and encouraging group members to maintain ties with each other.

The MFG-DB approach has the potential to reduce child disruptive behaviors and increase family participation in child mental health services. As the number of children in need of mental health treatment far outstrips the availability of service providers (Wolraich, 1995), the MFG-DB service delivery approach can also expand service capacity by helping multiple families simultaneously.

* The authors gratefully acknowledge support from Mary M. McKay, Kara Dean-Assael, Anil Chacko, and the National Institute of Mental Health.

References

Drumm, K. (2006). The essential power of group work. *Social Work with Groups, 29*(2/3), 17–31.

Franco, L. M., Dean-Assael, K. M., & McKay, M. M. (2008). Multiple family groups to reduce youth behavioral difficulties. In C. W. LeCroy (Ed.), *Handbook of evidence-based treatment manuals for children and adolescents* (pp. 546–590). New York: Oxford University Press.

Gitterman, A., & Shulman, L. (Eds.). (2005). *Mutual aid groups, vulnerable and resilient populations and the life cycle* (3rd ed.). New York: Columbia University Press.

Kazdin, A. E. (1995). *Conduct disorders in childhood and adolescence* (2nd ed.). Thousands Oaks, CA: Sage.

Keiley, M. K. (2002). Attachment and affect regulation: A framework for family treatment of conduct disorder. *Family Process, 41*, 477–493.

McKay, M. M., & Bannon, W. M. Jr. (2004). Engaging families in child mental health services. *Child & Adolescent Psychiatric Clinics of North America, 13*, 905–921.

McKay, M. M., Gonzales, J. J., Stone, S., Ryland, D., & Kohner, K. (1995). Multiple family groups: A responsive intervention model for intercity families. *Social Work with Groups, 18*(4), 41–56.

O'Shea, M., & Phelps, R. (1985). Multiple family therapy: Current status and critical appraisal. *Family Process, 24*, 555–582.

Steinberg, D. M. (2004). *The mutual-aid approach to working with groups: Helping people help one another* (2nd ed.). Binghamton, NY: Haworth Press.

Tolan, P. H., & Henry, D. (1996). Patterns of psychopathology among urban poor children: Co-morbidity and aggression effects. *Journal of Consulting & Clinical Psychology, 64*, 1094–1099.

Wolraich, M. L. (1995). Services in the primary care context. In L. Bickman, & D. J. Rog (Eds.), *Children's mental health services: Research, policy, and evaluation.* Thousand Oaks, CA: Sage.

Needs Acquisition and Behavior Change Approach

Tom Caplan

The needs acquisition and behavior change (Needs ABC) approach, developed for group work at the McGill Domestic Violence Clinic, uses an integrated therapeutic perspective combining observation and elucidation of group and client process (Garvin, 1985; Shulman, 2006). The approach uses concepts from cognitive-behavioral (Ellis, 1997), motivational (Miller & Rollnick, 1991), narrative (Wite & Epston, 1990), and emotion-focused models (Greenberg & Johnson, 1988) , and is inspired by the work of Shulman (2006), Doel and Sawdon (1999), Malekoff (1997), Greenberg and Pavio (1997), and Kurland and Salmon (1992) among others. This group work approach is generally consistent with the broader trend towards the integration of methods. The author's personal experience with groups designed for the treatment of domestic violence, substance abuse and anger management underlies this approach.

The Needs ABC approach emphasizes the relational needs behind maladaptive behaviors, rather than the behaviors themselves (Caplan, 2007). Invariably, problematic behaviors spring from relationship needs that are not currently being met in the individual's personal and social life; the problematic behaviors are dysfunctional or non-functioning attempts to meet these needs. Generally, they have their origin in childhood, stemming from strategies that the child implemented in an attempt to meet his or her needs, with a degree of success. Many members of treatment groups present for therapy because of the "immature" problem-solving behaviors they have used in an attempt to solve their adult problems. In other words, the child who achieved the attention he craved by throwing tantrums is likely to become an adult who will similarly "act out" when significant others do not seem to provide the longed-for attention.

The Needs ABC approach (Caplan, 2007) is flexible in terms of application to group work with clients. Its aims are for the members of the group to collaboratively explore an understanding of their social relationships, first within the safety of the group environment and later in the "real world" (Yalom, 1995), and to formulate more constructive ways to react to stress by testing and practicing alternative responses in the context of the group (Doel & Sawdon, 1999; Gitterman, 2001), and by actively providing each other with insight, advice, and problem-solving techniques. The Needs ABC approach encourages group members to work toward insight into the problematic behaviors troubling other members of the group. Once clients understand what is missing from their various relationships, and why they react in certain ways to obtain these relational needs, they can begin, together, to work positively towards acquiring them. The social format of the group provides a forum in which new skills can be acquired and used in practice for the "real world."

The Needs ABC approach involves helping clients to see their personal needs in a broader context by using a vocabulary that centers on what are referred to as "universal themes," or commonly used words to describe relational needs that are easy to understand and empathize with, such as "abandonment," "competence," and so forth (Caplan, 2007). These themes are "universal" in that everyone can relate to them (group worker and group member alike), whether or not they are descriptive of the presenting issues of all group members. They are emotionally (rather than rationally) based (Greenberg & Johnson, 1988; Greenberg & Pavio, 1997) and often express the unresolved issues "left over" from clients' earlier stages of development. In other words, all members of the group will be able to understand the emotional issues troubling any one member, even if their own problems are not "the same." These themes can be used to help define what is lacking with regard to clients' relational needs (needs deficit) and what they have unsuccessfully been trying to get, and help to vocalize these needs to the group and to the group leader. The use of these "easy-to-identify-with" themes enables multiple clients to understand others' needs and emotions, and to ally with these needs rather than the problematic behaviors that result from them (Malekoff, 1997). Maintaining focus on the needs and emotions behind the behaviors in question also minimizes feelings of guilt and shame, which are counterproductive in the group work milieu, and maintains focus on the underlying problem, not the potentially shameful behavior. The group facilitator also seeks to impart the message that when one uses a dysfunctional behavior in an attempt to meet a need, one invariably obtains precisely what is not wanted or needed. He or she helps group members to understand which emotions are more useful than others in dealing with relational issues.

The Needs ABC approach assumes the need for clients to feel safe, if not always comfortable, in the group work setting (Caplan, 2007). By providing an arena for the safe expression of difficult emotions, and a group work framework that is consistent and predictable, a situation is created in which frank dialogue is welcome (Kurland, 2004). The establishment of a safe emotional environment begins with the first contact between worker and client, often over the telephone or in the screening interview, and continues throughout the lifetime of the group. Work is carried out at the clients' pace, rather than the group worker's (Northen & Kurland, 2001), and therapeutic interventions are done, whenever possible, as observations about client and group process and as invitations for the group to engage in the problem-solving process).

The Needs ABC approach is about learning and relearning how to be oneself in a healthy way in a social context and becoming able to negotiate the various demands of personal, familial, and social communication. The client-centred relational approach of the Needs ABC means that the outcome of this collaborative work releases into society individuals who have become better able to negotiate social relationships, while the integrated approach, combining cognitive-behavioral, motivational, client process, narrative, and emotion-focused concepts, gives facilitator and clients alike a wide focus for the discussion, analysis and solution of problems.

References

Caplan, T. (2007). *Needs-ABC: A needs acquisition and behavior change model for group work and other psychotherapies*. London: Whiting and Birch.

Doel, M. & Sawdon, S. (1999). *The essential groupworker: Teaching and learning creative groupwork*. London: Jessica Kingsley.

Ellis, A. (1997). *The practice of rational emotive behavior therapy*. New York: Springer.

Garvin, C. (1985). Group process: Usage and uses in social work practice. In M. Sundell, P. Glasser, R. Sari, & R. Vinter (Eds.), *Individual change through small groups* (pp. 203–225). New York, NY: The Free Press.

Gitterman, A. (2001). Vulnerability, resilience, and social work with groups. In T. Kelly, T. Berman-Rossi, & S. Palombo (Eds.), *Group work: Strategies for strengthening resiliency* (pp. 19–23). Binghamton, NY: Haworth Press.

Greenberg, L., & Johnson, S. (1988). *Emotionally focused couples therapy*. New York: Guilford Press.

Greenberg, L. S., & Pavio, S. C. (1997). *Working with emotions in psychotherapy*. New York: Guilford Press.

Kurland, R. (2004). *Social group work: Five key components of superb practice*. Invitational Workshop presented at the AASWG International Symposium, Detroit, MI.

Kurland, R., & Salmon, R. (1992). Group work vs. casework in a group: Principles and implications for teaching and practice. *Social Work with Groups, 15*(4), 3–14.

Malekoff, A. (1997). *Group work with adolescents: Principles and practice*. New York: Guilford Press.

Miller, W., & Rollnick, S (1991). *Motivational interviewing: Preparing people to change addictive behavior*. New York: Guilford Press.

Northen, H., & Kurland, R. (2001). *Social work with groups* (3rd ed). New York: Columbia University Press.

Shulman, L. (2006). *The skills of helping: Individuals, families, groups, and communities* (5th ed.). Belmont, CA: Thomson Brooks/Cole.

White, M., & Epston, D. (1990). *Narrative means to therapeutic ends*. New York: Norton.

Yalom, I. D. (1995). *The theory and practice of group psychotherapy* (4th ed.). New York: Basic Books.

Psychoeducational Approach

Lynn Turner

Using an educational approach adds another dimension to the power of group dynamics. Psychoeducation is a theme-focused, time-limited, structured group work approach that provides a supportive, experiential environment with education, empowerment, role modeling and skill building. Psychoeducational groups are routinely used in social work with populations as diverse as the mentally ill, sexually assaulted, distressed couples, new parents, and substance abusers.

Psychoeducational groups empower homogeneous cohorts through education about their condition, and skill-building exercises. These didactic groups relieve client stress with sharing of mutual concerns, as well as role modeling by participants and leaders. Exercises, lectures, and homework assignments are developed to create problem-solving, stress management, assertiveness training, empathy development, and cognitive restructuring skills. Working with sexually assaulted university women, for example, VanDeusen and Carr (2004) taught group members: (1) definitions and common effects of sexual assault; (2) relationship issues such as boundaries, trust, sexuality and intimacy, and (3) to develop coping skills. Turner (Turner, Belsher, & Brintzenhofe-Szoc, 2007) taught maritally distressed couples: (1) communication skills; (2) conflict resolution skills; (3) self-understanding exercises; (4) sensuality and sexuality; and (5) development of a satisfying relationship contract for the future. Lethborg and Kissane (2003), for another example, taught women with early stage breast cancer to: (1) debrief each other about the shock of diagnosis and trauma of treatment; and (2) develop coping skills for reintegration back into authentic living.

Several theoretical frameworks undergird the principles of psychoeducation. VanDeusen and Carr (2004) cite cognitive-behavioral, integrative, relational, and psychodynamic theories. Turner (1998) utilizes symbolic interactionism and cognitive, behavioral, and affective theories. The symbolic interactionist sociological model supports individual change through new construction of meaning within a social context. Cognitive and behavioral theories address the creation of coping skills, and affective theories address the amelioration of dysfunctional emotional reactions within the supportive and expressive group environment. Macgowan (1997) focuses on the mutual aid dimensions of "engagement": (1) contracting; (2) attendance; (3) contributing; (4) relating to the group leader; (5) relating to the group members; (6) working on one's own problems; and (7) working on the problems of others.

Tolman and Molidor (1994), reviewing 54 social work studies of group work over 10 years, found that psychoeducational treatments were primarily used with premarital couples and parenting issues, substance abuse, child abuse, and divorce. A recent review of international literature found psychoeducation used in the fields of: (1) mental health (schizophrenic/bi-polar patients, dementia, and Alzheimer patient caregivers); (2) health (cancer and AIDS/HIV); (3) family and children (sexual abuse victims, offenders, parenting, marital distress, divorce, and stepfamilies, psychological and physical abuse); and (4) substance abuse (treatment and continuing recovery).

Psychoeducational groups embody the classic list of group work benefits: instillation of hope, universality, altruism, corrective recapitulation of the primary family, development of socialization techniques, imitative behavior, corrective emotional experience, and dynamic interaction between the person and the group, with transference and insight. The homogeneity of psychoeducational groups reduce isolation and give members a sense of universality and hope (Gitterman, 2005). Through structured exercises, members support each other, develop interpersonal skills, create imitative behavior and rehearse behaviors in the safety of the group. The supportive environment of mutual sharing about past and present difficulties can result in catharsis and emotional healing, as well as a sense of empowerment rather than victimization (Steinberg, 2004).

Research reveals that psychoeducational groups are beneficial for both their group dynamic aspect as well as for their education. Mason and Vasquez (2007) studying psychoeducation for parents with HIV/AIDS suggest that psychoeducational groups are: (1) less stigmatizing than traditional mental health; (2) reduce stress; (3) increase knowledge and techniques; (4) create support; and (5) increase self-esteem. Subramanian, Hernandez, and Martinez (1995) suggest that psychoeducational groups are the most useful method to reach the largest numbers of lower Socioeconomic status (SES) Latina women with HIV infection and are perhaps ideally suited to reach marginalized populations. Turner (1998), studying psychoeducational groups for marital distress using multiple regression analysis of post-test scores, found statistically significant correlations between improvement in marital discord and the participants,' but not the controls abilities to create social support outside the group at the end of treatment. Edelman, Craig and Kidman (2000) using 15 studies of acceptable design comparing the efficacy of psychoeducation versus support groups for cancer patients, found that the majority of the evidence suggested that those attending psychoeducational groups experienced greater benefits than those who attended purely supportive groups. Turner et al. (2007) in a qualitative evaluation of 12 years of psychoeducation for marital distress found that 765 participants recording hand-written answers at the end of treatment revealed 88% positive responses to the program, 97% positive responses to the leaders, more voluntary naming of emotional rather than either behavioral or cognitive components, and a 90% desire for a monthly ongoing group.

Psychoeducational groups appear to be a well-established, beneficial social group work approach. The didactic aspect joined with group dynamics appears to make psychoeducation the treatment of choice for homogeneous populations lacking life skills and support to resolve psychologically and physically threatening issues.

References

Edelman, S., Craig, A., & Kidman, A. D. (2000). Group interventions with cancer patients: Efficacy of psychoeducational versus supportive groups. *Journal of Psychosocial Oncology, 18*(3), 67–85.

Gitterman, A. (2005). Group formation: Tasks, methods and skills. In A. Gitterman, & L. Shulman (Eds.), *Mutual aid groups, vulnerable and resilient populations, and the life cycle* (3rd ed., pp. 73–110). New York: Columbia University Press.

Lethborg, C. A., Kissane, D. W. (2003). It doesn't end on the last day of treatment: A psychoeducational intervention for women after adjuvant treatment for early stage breast cancer. *Journal of Psychosocial Oncology, 21*(3), 25–41.

Macgowan, M. J. (1997). A measure of engagement for social group work: The groupwork engagement measure. *Journal of Social Service Research, 23*, 17–37.

Mason, S., & Vazquez, D. (2007). Making positive changes: A psychoeducation group for parents with HIV/AIDS. *Social Work with Groups, 30*(2), 27–40.

Steinberg, D. M. (2004). *The mutual-aid approach to working with groups: Helping people help one another* (2nd ed.). Binghamton, NY: Haworth Press.

Subramanian, K. Hernandez, S., & Martinez, A. (1995). Psychoeducational group work for low-income Latina mothers with HIV infection. *Social Work with Groups, 18*(2/3), 53–64.

Tolman, R. M., & Molidor, C. E. (1994). A decade of social group work research: Trends in methodology, theory and program development. *Research on Social Work Practice, 4*, 142–159.

Turner, L. (1998). *The impact of a psychoeducational group intervention on marital discord, adult interaction style, projective identification, and perceptive identification.* Unpublished dissertation submitted to the faculty of the National Catholic School of Social Services, The Catholic University of America, Washington, DC.

Turner, L., Belsher, B., & Brintzenhofe-Szoc, K. (2007). A qualitative review of client responses to treatment in PAIRS, a 120-hour psychoeducational group intervention for relationships. Submitted for publication.

VanDeusen, K. M., & Carr, J. L. (2004). Group work at the university: A psychological sexual assault group for women. *Social Work with Groups, 27*(4), 51–63.

Self-Directed Approach

Audrey Mullender and David Ward

As highlighted by Cohen and Mullender (1999), the British model of self-directed groupwork is one of the most fully developed of the empowerment-orientated social action approaches to groupwork. Originally formulated by Mullender and Ward (1985, 1991), it is described by Payne (1997, p. 280) as offering "a clear view of empowerment theory focused on group setting and processes." The approach has continued to evolve through practice and through inductive and grounded research on self-directed groups in action in a wide range of social work, community development, education, and health services settings (Berdan et al., 2006; Cohen & Mullender, 1999, 2003; Fleming & Ward, 1999, 2004; Mullender, 1996; Ward 2000).

A notable feature of the model is a clear value-base, which is outlined in the form of six practice principles (Mullender & Ward, 1991, pp. 30–31). The principles emphasize:

- avoidance of negative labels;
- rights of group members;
- interventions based on a power analysis;
- attainment of collective power through coming together in groups;
- opposition of oppression though practice;
- group workers facilitating rather than leading.

The struggles of the black, feminist, and disability movements afford a sense of direction. They have shown the complex way in which the various dimensions of disadvantage and exclusion are distinctive but still interlink. Each overarches the others at different times and in particular conditions, requiring independent action but within a coherent worldview. The approach recognizes the interwoven nature of personal and structural power relations (Lorde, 1984, p. 183) to mobilize the capacity of a groupwork process to achieve change and transformation at both levels.

Self-directed groupwork conceptualizes the approach as user-centred and the worker's role as a facilitator (Beresford, 2000; Ward and Mullender, 1991). In this way, the approach contrasts with other approaches which stress user-control. Self-directed groupwork does not abrogate practitioner knowledge, responsibility, or skill but is grounded in partnership rather than control. The expertise of the worker lies in the skilled and sensitive implementation of the self-directed groupwork process, whilst group members define the content and outcomes.

Self-directed group workers target external goals identified by group members through a process which involves them focusing, in turn, on *what* are the major problems in their lives, *why* these exist, and *how* to tackle them. This process closely parallels the group-centred approach to social change developed by Paulo Freire (1972). "Why?" is the watchword of self-directed groupwork, setting it apart from other practices, which claim to be participatory and empowering but which too often jump from the question "what?" to the question "how?" without considering the question "why?" in between. By ignoring the "why" question, explanations, responsibilities, and the scope of solutions are unwittingly steered to the private world around people and within their existing knowledge and experience. These have been fashioned by their position in society and the processes that keep them there.

In asking "why?" people are encouraged to pursue an issue until the root causes have been identified and exposed. Asking "why?" gives people the opportunity to "examine the internal bridles and perceived powerlessness which underpin their sense of self and guide their actions in the world" (Young, 1999, p. 88). The focus on "why" enables people to break out of the demoralizing and self-perpetuating narrowness of vision introspection and self-blame created by poverty, lack of opportunity, and exclusion, as well as the post-modern emphasis on the self. With expanded horizons of what is possible, people conceive of new explanations in the wider social, political and economic context and consider how they can identify and engage with these. Asking "why?" directs the spotlight away from people as problems, to the problems they encounter, and enables them to see opportunities to develop a much wider range of options for action and change. Asking the question "why?" is the key that unlocks the process.

The self-directed model of groupwork has five stages:

1. Taking stock: Pre-planning to find a compatible worker team, engage consultancy support, and agree on empowering principles for the work.
2. Taking off: Engaging with users as partners to plan the group jointly through what is referred to as "open planning".
3. Preparing to take action: Helping the group explore *what* issues are to be tackled, *why* these issues exist and *how* to produce change.
4. Taking action: Group members carry out agreed actions.
5. Taking over: Workers move increasingly into the background and may withdraw altogether. The group reviews what it has achieved, exploring the connections between what, why and how. It then identifies new issues, explores these issues and again decides what action to take. This process continues throughout the group's life.

Self-directed groups seek to challenge the fact that group members may have become, or could potentially become, negatively labeled as a result of interventions that inappropriately seek control or change at the individual or family level, rather than empowering the group to tackle wider injustices. However, through its recognition of the interweaving of the personal and structural, intrapersonal and interpersonal change may come about as a result of participation in self-directed groups (Butler, 1994; Cohen & Mullender, 1999; Mistry, 1989).

Self-directed groupwork has achieved wide international currency through adoption, and citation, of Mullender and Ward's original model as a guide for practice in many places in both the developed and developing worlds. Self-directed groupwork has underpinned the development of the *Social Action* approach (separate entry) in which the application of the model has evolved to encompass training, evaluation, and research, in addition to practice, in a wide range of national and cultural settings.

References

Berdan, K., Boulton, I., Eidman-Aadahl, E., Fleming, J., Gardner, L., Rogers, I., & Soloman, A. (Eds.). (2006). *Writing for a change: Boosting literacy and learning through social action.* San Francisco: Jossey-Bass.

Beresford, P. (2000). Service users' knowledge and social work theory: Conflict or collaboration. *British Journal of Social Work, 30,* 489–503.

Butler, S. (1994). "All I've got in my purse is mothballs": The social action women's group. *Groupwork, 7*(2), 163–179.

Cohen, M. B., & Mullender, A. (1999). The personal in the political: Exploring the group work continuum from individual to social change goals. *Social Work with Groups, 22*(1), 13–31. Reprinted in A. Malekoff, & R. Kurland (Eds.). (2005). *A quarter century of classics (1978–2004): Capturing the theory, practice and spirit of social work with groups.* Binghamton, NY: Haworth Press.

Cohen, M. B., & Mullender, A. (Eds.). (2003). *Gender and groupwork.* London: Routledge.

Fleming, J., & Ward, D. (1999). Research as empowerment: The social action approach. In W. Shera, & L. Wells (Eds.), *Empowerment practice in social work: Developing richer conceptual foundations* (pp. 370–389). Toronto: Canadian Scholars. Press.

Fleming, J., & Ward, D. (2004). Methodology and practical application of the social action research model. In F. Rapport (Ed.), *New qualitative methodologies in health and social care research* (pp. 162–178). London: Routledge.

Freire, P. (1972). *Pedagogy of the oppressed,* Harmondsworth, UK: Penguin.

Lorde, A. (1984). *Sister outsider.* Freedom, CA: Crossing Press.

Mistry, T. (1989). Establishing a feminist model of groupwork in the probation service. *Groupwork, 2*(2), 145–158.

Mullender, A. (1996) Groupwork with male "domestic" abusers: Models and dilemmas. *Groupwork, 9*(1), 27–47.

Mullender, A., & Ward, D. (1985). Towards an alternative model of social group-work. *British Journal of Social Work, 15,* 155–172.

Mullender, A., & Ward, D. (1991). *Self-directed groupwork: Users take action for empowerment.* London: Whiting & Birch.

Payne, M. (1997). *Modern social work theory* (2nd ed.). Basingstoke., UK: Macmillan.

Ward, D. (2000). Totem not token: Groupwork as a vehicle for user participation. In H. Kemshall, & R. Littlechild (Eds.), *User involvement and participation in social care: Research informing practice* (pp. 45–64). London: Jessica Kingsley.

Ward, D., & Mullender, A. (1991). Facilitation in self-directed groupwork. *Groupwork, 4*(2), 141–151.

Young, K. (1999) The youth worker as guide, philosopher and friend. In S. Banks (Ed.), *Ethical issues in youth work* (pp. 77–92). London: Routledge.

Spirituality

Carlean Gilbert

The number of articles on religious and spiritual issues in social work has risen significantly since the 1990s, and in 2001 the Council on Social Work Education affirmed the inclusion of religion and spirituality as diversity issues in its *Educational Policy and Accreditation Standards* (Council on Social Work Education, 2001). Despite the increased inclusion of spiritual content in social work literature and curricula, few articles in the group work literature have addressed this topic (Gilbert, 2000). A 2007 literature review of spirituality in groups found that most authors describe pre-planned use of spiritual interventions with specific populations. Conducting spiritually focused groups for persons with severe and persistent mental illness for 25 years, Kehoe (1999, 2007) reported that group members were able to develop trust, to respect differences, to cope, to gain hope, and to find meaning in their suffering. Wong-McDonald (2007) found that persons with severe psychiatric disabilities who participated in a spirituality group were significantly more successful in reaching their treatment goals than the control group. When Revheim and Greenberg (2007) utilized spiritually oriented "emotion-focused coping," such as cognitive reframing, minimizing, and using social comparison, they found that group members with schizophrenia experienced decreased emotions of anger, fear, and despair and increased emotions of hope. Miller (1999) presented evidence of the effectiveness of 12-step programs for substance-related disorders that incorporate the importance of God or a Higher Power. While this literature describes spiritual interventions and supports the efficacy of spiritually focused groups, it does not address issues that arise when clients spontaneously introduce spiritual content in traditional educational, support, and treatment groups.

Processing spiritual content in groups can be discomforting to group workers and members alike. Social workers in the United States tend to be more secular in their spiritual orientations (Sheridan, Bullis, Adcock, Berlin, & Miller, 1992) than the general population. Among the many explanations for this client–clinician disconnect and practitioners' reluctance to address spiritual issues are: (a) the Constitution of the United States legally separates activities of church and state; (b) some social workers insist that a detached, scientific approach is necessary to attain "professional" status; (c) some clinicians have been influenced by Sigmund Freud's teachings on the negative impact of religion on personality development; (d) the misuse of spiritual beliefs has caused harm, such as rare cult tragedies like the mass murder/suicide in Jonestown; and (f) practitioners have feared imposing their own spiritual beliefs onto their clients. In order to get in touch with client systems holistically, however, group workers must develop spiritually competent practice.

Practitioners tend to encounter unique challenges related to countertransference and differential diagnosis when spiritual issues arise. Spiritually oriented group workers may fail to recognize the psychopathology in some spiritual beliefs or activities, such as excessive ritualistic behaviors that fulfill diagnostic criteria for obsessive–compulsive disorder (American Psychiatric Association, 2000). They also may overlook the misuse of spiritual beliefs that support dysfunctional behaviors, such as rationalizing domestic violence, "splitting" persons into good or bad categories, or "being special" in examples of narcissistic personality disorder (American Psychiatric Association, 2000). These practitioners may erroneously assume shared understandings of group members' spiritual references and metaphors and fail to examine their meanings. In contrast, non-spiritually oriented group workers may tend to view culturally accepted spiritual beliefs and practices as pathological or extraneous. Group workers may be unfamiliar with mystical experiences or uncommon behaviors such as glossolalia, "speaking in tongues," which some Christians believe is a gift of the Holy Spirit. They may not recognize or discuss spiritual themes and metaphors and, therefore, convey messages that spirituality is an unacceptable topic and contribute to disengagement of group members. Importantly, workers may miss opportunities to harness beneficial internal and external spiritual resources. Lastly, some group workers who frequently encounter clients with spiritually referenced delusions, hallucinations, language disturbances, and disorganized behaviors may inadvertently pathologize expressions of spirituality. They must maintain skills in differentiating between manifestations of spirituality that enhance coping with mental disorders and those that fulfill clinically significant *DSM-IV-TR* criteria.

While reminding practitioners to eschew the roles of spiritual leaders, Schermer (2006) proposes that group leaders create a "sacred space" in which growth and healing can occur. To create a group culture that is characterized by necessary and mutual trust, respect, and connectedness, practitioners are urged:

1.　to be self-aware of their spiritual orientations in order to guard against harmful countertransferences;
2.　to develop group norms, such as respect for spiritual diversity, avoidance of proselytizing, and, depending on the type and purpose of the group, inclusion or exclusion of prayer, scripture, and spiritual practices;
3.　to value spiritual beliefs as sources of client strengths;
4.　to collaborate with spiritual leaders in order to enhance practitioners' understanding of spiritual issues, to identify resources in the spiritual community, and to ensure practicing within their areas of expertise;
5.　to seek spiritually competent group work supervisors and opportunities for professional development.

Using these guidelines, group workers in various settings can incorporate spiritual matters into group content and create optimal environments in which members can maximize their potentials for growth and healing.

References

American Psychiatric Association. (2000). *Diagnostic and statistical manual of mental disorders* (4th ed.) text revision. Washington, DC: Author.
Council on Social Work Education. (2001). *Educational policy and accreditation standards*. Alexandria, VA: Author.

Gilbert, M. C. (2000). Spirituality in social work groups: Practitioners speak out. *Social Work with Groups, 22*(4), 67–84.

Kehoe, N. C. (1999). A therapy group on spiritual issues for patients with chronic mental illness. *Psychiatric Services, 50*(8), 1081–1083.

Kehoe, N. C. (2007). Spirituality groups in serious mental illness. *Southern Medical Journal, 100*(6), 647–648.

Miller, W. R. (1999). *Integrating spirituality into treatment: Resources for practitioners.* Washington, DC: American Psychological Association.

Revheim, N., & Greenberg, W. M. (2007). Spirituality matters: Creating a time and place for hope. *Psychiatric Rehabilitation Journal, 30*(4), 307–310.

Schermer, V. L. (2006). Spirituality and group analysis. *Group Analysis, 39*(4), 445–466.

Sheridan, M. J., Bulls, R. K., Adcock, C. R., Berlin, S. D., & Miller, P. C. (1992). Practitioners' personal and professional attitudes and behaviors toward religion and spirituality: Issues for education and practice. *Journal of Social Work Education, 28*(2), 190–203.

Wong-McDonald, A. (2007). Spirituality and psychosocial rehabilitation: Empowering persons with serious psychiatric disabilities at an inner-city community program. *Psychiatric Rehabilitation Journal, 30*(4), 295–300.

Systemic Approach

Oded Manor

Systemic group work is a form of working with groups as systems. A system exists when at least two elements are connected within a unifying whole. The whole is expected to be different from the simple sum of the elements comprising it—it has qualities that cannot be identified from simply adding up those elements (Simon, Stierlin, & Lyman, 1985, p. 353).

Systemic group work deals with each group as a system. A boundary is usually drawn between those who are inside that system and those who are outside. Inside are the elements of that system: the members of that group and the group worker. Outside are friendship networks, families, and other groups and organizations. Such detailed partitions enable systemic group workers to methodically pursue changes inside as well as outside each group.

The boundary of each system is upheld by resorting to certain norms. The way in which these norms are structured around certain moral principles is the "paradigm" of that system. The structuring of norms differs from one system to another. Therefore, systemic practice always includes the handling of moral diversity. In addition, each system influences all the others and is influenced by them. Interest in the complexity of such mutual influences has led to detailed analysis. Some of the major features that have evolved are the capacity to open and close boundaries, which Durkin (1981, p. 340) called '*boundarying*', and the consequent *permeability* of boundaries. Interest has focused also on *interface*:—the overlap of boundaries—and, particularly, on *feedback*—relaying at least part of group members' messages back to them. Within the inclusive stance (Manor, 2000a, pp. 47–48) different group work skills are identified with which different types of feedback may be offered. Thus, feedback is clearly differentiated from unilateral interventions, such as a short talk, which is called *"input"*, and certainly from an environmental shock, for example, losing a job, called *"perturbation"*. These ideas have expanded the range of intervention methods so that many types of change may be pursued within and between numerous systems.

The systems approach has long been part of social work (Chetkow-Yanoov, 1992, pp. 133–134). In social group work, various authors, such as Brandler and Roman (1991), as well as Butler and Wintram (1991), have dealt with the relationships between parts and whole, without explicitly identifying their frameworks as systemic. An early reference to systems theory can be clearly seen in the mediating model developed by Schwartz and his followers (Schwartz & Zalba, 1971), where the legacy of Homans (1950) is evident. Shulman (2006), as well as Gitterman and Shulman (2005), greatly expanded the meaning of that model.

Later developments, inspired by cybernetics, and the work of people like Ashby, (1956), and constructivism (Berger & Luckmann, 1967; Simon et al., 1985) can be seen in the work of leading thinkers like Bateson (1979). Those influences have diversified knowledge further. Some, for example Donigian and Malnati (1997), still emphasize the *structural aspects*: the repeated patterns of behaviours that consolidate positions of power in the group (Manor, 2000a, pp. 48–56). Others, such as Sharry (2001), pay far more attention to *processes*: the ever changing moment to moment variations of verbal and bodily influences during each group session (Manor, 2000a, pp. 46–48). A third strand, notably Doel and Sawdon (1999), focuses far more on the *contents*: the verbally symbolized messages exchanged among group members (Manor, 2000a: 57–60).

The inclusive stance (Manor, 2000a) refers to all the above *three perspectives*: structure, process, and contents. All three are seen as manifestations, that is, as parts of the whole group's *dynamics*. In turn, group dynamics is underpinned by a value judgement made about the importance of *human communication*, including its *paradoxical features* (Manor, 2000a, pp. 41–46, 203–212). A central issue is the ways workers choose what to do.

Usually, each group worker is expected to choose to communicate mainly with regard to issues related to the group's agreed goals. Indeed, each group may have its own goals. For example, a group set up to help members with loss and bereavement is likely to have different goals from one that is created to enable members to budget their expenses. It stands to reason that each worker's involvement should serve these different goals, and that work is focused on outcomes that are concrete expressions of these goals (Manor, 2003).

Yet, even the needs of very disparate groups may well have some features in common. Many people seem to experience the wish for a sense of purpose. They also want to know the means of achieving it. Trust, respect, and the handling of power are often major concerns too. These considerations have led to stressing the importance of building a *working alliance* while working with all groups (Manor, 2000b). Coping with this alliance, all time-limited groups are likely to involve pretty similar ways of beginning and ending their lives. It is the middle period of each group that can be expected to vary according to the agreed goals of that group.

However, within the inclusive stance, the middle period is not left to chance. That part of the group experience is logically articulated in relation to the ways the group's goals influence changes of its dynamics over time. These changes are articulated through the concept of *stages of group development*. Each stage itself is conceptualized as a period when group dynamics—the process, the structure and the contents—coalesce into a meaningful whole. A complete range of eight possible stages is conceived in advance, and from that "generic blueprint" practitioners are invited to choose the middle stages that may best serve each group's goals in practice.

Such an "evolving" view of group development means that no existing form of group work is excluded. Any model may be applied within this framework. The only restriction is that each is modified to incorporate the values and concepts that underpin an inclusive systems approach (Manor, 2003), which is itself continuously evaluated and revised.

References

Ashby, W. R. (1956) *An introduction to cybernetics.* London: Methuen.

Bateson, G. (1979). *Mind and nature: A necessary unity.* Glasgow: Wildwood House.

Berger, P., & Luckmann, T. (1967) *The social construction of reality.* London: Allen Lane/Penguin.

Brandler, S., & Roman, C. P. (1991). *Group work: Skills and strategies for effective interventions.* Binghamton, NY: Howarth Press

Butler, S., & Wintram, C. (1991). *Feminist groupwork.* London: Sage.

Chetkow-Yanoov, B. (1992). *Social work practice: A systems approach.* Binghamton, NY: Howarth Press.

Doel, M., & Sawdon, C. (1999) *The essential groupworker.* London: Jessica Kingsley.

Donigian, J., & Malnati, R. (1997). *Systemic group therapy: A triadic model.* Pacific Grove, CA: Brooks/Cole.

Durkin, J. E. (Ed.). (1981). *Living groups: Group psychotherapy and general systems theory.* New York: Brunner/Mazel.

Gitterman, A., & Shulman, L. (Eds.). (2005). *Mutual aid groups, vulnerable and resilient populations, and the life cycle* (3rd ed.). New York: Columbia University Press.

Homans, G. C. (1950). *The human group.* New York: Harcourt Brace.

Manor, O. (2000a) *Choosing a groupwork approach: An inclusive stance.* London: Jessica Kingsley.

Manor, O. (2000b) The working alliance. In M. Davis (Ed.), *The Blackwell encyclopaedia of social work* (pp. 375–376). Oxford: Blackwell.

Manor, O. (2003) Groupwork fit for purpose? An inclusive framework for mental health. *Groupwork, 13*(3), 101–128.

Schwartz, W., & Zalba, S. R. (Eds.). (1971). *The practice of group work.* New York: Columbia University Press.

Sharry, J. (2001). *Solution-focused groupwork.* London: Sage.

Shulman, L. (2006). *The skills of helping: Individuals, families, groups, and communities* (5th ed.). Belmont, CA: Thomson Brooks/Cole.

Simon, F. B., Stierlin, H., & Lyman, C. W. (1985). *The language of family therapy: A systemic vocabulary and sourcebook.* New York: Family Process Press.

Group Stages of Development

Boston Model

Francis Bartolomeo

Garland, Jones, and Kolodny made a major contribution to the theory and practice of social work with groups with their publication, *A Model for Stages of Development in Social Work Groups* (1965). Garland et al.'s model, also known as the "Boston Model" emerged from the authors' direct observations and analyses of process recordings of numerous children's groups conducted in a traditional social service agency. Garland et al. proposed a five-stage model: pre-affiliation, power and control, intimacy, differentiation, and termination.

Their research helped practitioners recognize that a group is a social system that changes over time, and that growth can be facilitated through interventions attuned to the group's stage of development. Group development is conceived as an underlying dynamic process that is manifested in changes in such areas as task performance, group cohesion, role behavior, and capacity for mutual aid (Berman-Rossi, 1993; Garland et al., 1965; Lacoursiere, 1980; Papell & Rothman, 1980). The Boston Model reflects social work's tradition of emphasizing human relationships and connection; its essential theme is that of interpersonal proximity or closeness and its permutations over the course of a group's life.

At the outset of the first stage, pre-affiliation, a collection of individuals with a shared task or identity does not yet exist (Berman-Rossi, 1993; Lacoursiere, 1980). Because trust in others or the situation has not yet developed, anxiety is present and new group members engage in superficial, stereotyped interactions. Group members are, to varying degrees, ambivalent about committing to, and making an emotional investment in, the group. Even when there are positive expectations for the group experience, new members normally need to be self-protective, as manifested in cautious, approach–avoidance behavior and attitudes toward the group and its activities (Garland et al., 1965). In this stage, the social worker attempts to help an aggregate of individuals to become a functioning group. The social worker facilitates this effort by attending to the task needs of the group, especially the group's purpose, and by providing sufficient structure and direction, thereby reducing the level of interpersonal anxiety.

Once members have adequately resolved to be in the group and have established basic trust in the group situation and the other members, the group-as-a-whole theme shifts to concerns about dominance, authority relations, rebellion, and autonomy (Bennis & Shepard, 1956; Garland et al., 1965; Yalom, 1995). If the primary relational dynamic in the first stage of group development was ambivalence, the preoccupation of the second stage is "power and control" (Garland et al., 1965, p. 272). In stage two problems of influence and status also appear. In the attempt to establish a social hierarchy, scapegoating of more vulnerable members may occur, and internal cliques or dyadic alliances form (Garland et al., 1965).

The relationship between the worker (and the authority he or she represents) and the group is central to the power and control stage. Garland et al. (1965) regard the second stage as crucial because it is through the group's grappling with the authority of the worker that power is redistributed to the group itself. The group as a whole may struggle with the group leader through testing limits, nonparticipation, and rebelliousness. The group reacts to the structure or format they previously found necessary to feel safe, but which now feels oppressive, or as an arbitrary expression of the leader's power. It is imperative that the group worker not respond punitively to the group's challenge to his or her authority, which is "a necessary prerequisite to helping members feel more secure in expressing themselves freely and in permitting autonomy in their relations with one another" (Garland et al., 1965, p. 273). The power and control stage, therefore, is profoundly relevant to the value of empowerment in social work practice. A social work group cannot become a system of mutual aid (Shulman, 2006) unless the power and expertise of the group leader, which was vital in the pre-affiliation stage, is dispersed and embraced by the group members.

Following the tumult and high emotionality of the power and control stage, and presuming that redistribution of power was sufficiently successful, the group as a whole enters a harmonious stage, characterized by cohesion, esprit de corps, and camaraderie, i.e., the intimacy stage. With a more realistic perspective of the social worker, the group understands and assumes more responsibility for their work together. No longer preoccupied with the power struggle with the leader, the group can focus on developing more satisfying relationships and accomplishing its goals (Bennis & Shepard, 1956; Garland et al., 1965). Members become more self-revealing and the group climate subsequently grows more intimate. During this third stage, affective bonds are deepened, and the group's capacity for mutual aid is dramatically enhanced.

As individual group members achieve equilibrium between belonging to the group and asserting their individuality, the group has progressed to the stage of differentiation (Garland et al., 1965). Highly functional group norms and member roles allow the group to locate a balance between its task and social–emotional needs. As a mature, interdependent group, members perceive each other as unique individuals who can tolerate and accept differences. The group has also become differentiated in that it has become its own frame of reference. The group is largely self-operational, as the group has flexibly assumed leadership functions; the social worker has fulfilled a practice ideal of making him or herself obsolete.

Having accomplished their agreed-upon goals and with the impending completion of the group experience, the group members must now confront separation from each other as well as the loss of the group. The worker supports the group members in expressing the range of emotions associated with the loss of the group experience and the affective ties between members. The task needs of the group at this stage involve reminiscing, reviewing, and evaluating the collective and individual accomplishments over the course of the group. Areas of further growth and/or need for continued supports are identified.

There is certainly debate as to the applicability of the Boston Model, which was based on long-term, closed-membership groups, for contemporary social work practice in which short-term groups have become the norm (Berman-Rossi, 1993; Dies, 1996; Schaefer, 1999; Steinberg, 1999). The brevity of present-day groups raises questions as to whether these groups progress through the discreet stages of development as described by Garland et al. (1965) and others (Lacoursiere, 1980; Tuckman, 1965; Yalom, 1995).

Although the effect of time on group development in short-term groups is unclear (Dies, 1996), *A Model for Stages of Group Development for Social Work Groups* by Garland, Jones, and Kolodny remains a seminal, pioneering contribution to the theory and practice of social group work. As one of the earliest models grounded in research and practice, it supplied social workers with a structure in which to understand complex group processes, and a framework for interventions consistent with a group's developmental stage (Berman-Rossi, 1993). Garland et al. (1965) established an agenda for future research on group development that led to an examination of variables that impact group evolution, such as group member age, presenting problems, gender, and changes in group composition. The Boston Model's significance went further than the discipline of social work, as it contributed to the fields of social psychology, sociology, and group psychotherapy in the United States and beyond; it has been published in several countries including Brazil and Germany.

References

Bennis, W. G., & Shepard, H. A. (1956). A theory of group dynamics. *Human Relations, 9*(4), 415–457.

Berman-Rossi, T. (1993). The tasks and skills of the social worker across stages of group development. *Social Work with Groups, 16*(1/2), 69–81.

Dies, K. R. (1996). The unfolding of adolescent groups: A five-phase model of development. In P. Kymissis, & D. A. Haperin (Eds.), *Group therapy with children and adolescents* (pp. 35–53). Washington, DC: American Psychiatric Press.

Garland, J. A., Jones, H. E., & Kolodny, R. L. (1965). A model for stages of development in social work groups. In S. Bernstein (Ed.), *Explorations in group work: Essays in theory and practice* (pp. 251–294). Boston University School of Social Work.

Lacoursiere, R. (1980). *The life cycle of groups: Group developmental stage theory.* New York: Human Sciences Press.

Papell, C., & Rothman, B. (1980). Relating the mainstream model of social work with groups to group psychotherapy and the structured group approach. *Social Work with Groups, 3*(2), 5–23.

Schaefer, C. E. (Ed.). (1999). *Short-term psychotherapy groups for children: Adapting group processes for specific problems.* Northvale, NJ: Jason Aronson.

Shulman, L. (2006). *The skills of helping individuals, families, groups, and communities* (5th ed.). Belmont, CA: Thomson Brooks/Cole.

Steinberg, D. M. (1999). The impact of time and place on mutual-aid practice with short-term groups. *Social Work with Groups, 22*(2/3), 101–117.

Tuckman, B. W. (1965). Developmental sequence in small groups. *Psychological Bulletin, 63*, 384–399.

Yalom, I. D. (1995). *The theory and practice of group psychotherapy* (4th ed.). New York: Basic Books.

Relational Model

Linda Yael Schiller

Observing that women's groups developed differently than the majority of traditional models of group development formulated, a new framework for group development emerged. Arising from clinical experiences and qualitative analysis in the field, the relational framework was originally formulated to address the differential yet normative pathway in which women's groups evolved (Schiller, 1995), then expanded to address implications for practice and how facilitation of a group developing along these lines may differ from facilitation of other groups (Schiller, 1997). This framework reflects the growing body of feminist scholarship on women's growth and development (Gilligan, 1982; Miller, Stiver, Jordan, Kaplan, & Surrey 1991; Miller, 1976)

Most recently, the applicability of the relational framework has been expanded to include use with groups composed of vulnerable populations; including loss, trauma, and oppression, regardless of gender (Schiller, 2007). Finally, the concept of "applying" a framework of group stages has been suggested, in contrast to observing them, based on the facilitator's clinical judgment and professional knowledge base.

The relational framework uses as its template the Garland, Jones, and Kolodny (1965) five-stages framework of group development. The first and last stages in both models of pre-affiliation and separation/termination are held to be pretty much constant, while the differences in group development appear in the middle three stages. The relational model suggests that the five stages of group development are: (1) pre-affiliation; (2) establishing a relational base; (3) mutuality and interpersonal empathy; (4) challenge and change; and (5) separation and termination. The pre-affiliation stage in the relational model will also have elements of approach–avoidance, "trying on for size," and testing out the group to see if it is a good enough fit, with an emphasis on the availability of relational connections. The final stage of separation/termination will also occur in each group, either during the final weeks of a time-limited group, or in a revolving and cyclical fashion in open-ended groups, with the work of reviewing, evaluating, saying goodbye consolidating learning, and transitioning occurring as they reflect the specific style of learning and development of each group.

The differences immediately apparent in the two models are the differential placement of the dynamics of connection and of conflict in groups. There is both a qualitative difference in how they emerge and are best dealt with by the worker, as well as a difference in when these dynamics emerge in the life of the group. *Affiliative* connections with both members and workers emerge much sooner, and these connections, including the "felt sense" of safety (Gendlin, 1970) in earlier stages, are necessary prerequisites for the later emergence of challenge or conflict in a productive and growth-enhancing manner. It would seem that the ability to comfortably hold power and engage in conflict is the cutting edge of growth for many women and people experiencing oppression and disempowerment, while the ability to comfortably engage in deep empathic connection and share vulnerabilities is the cutting edge of growth for many men and people used to holding positions of power.

Stage two, *establishing a relational base*, follows pre-affiliation and is a time when members come together to form connections, find similarities between themselves and others, and connect with the facilitators. This is in contrast to the oft-seen power and control dynamics with their conflicts and testing behaviors, jockeying for control and status, and challenges to authority seen when a group is following other developmental models (Garland et. al., 1965, Tuckman, 1965; Tuckman & Jensen, 1977). This mode of development is a normative one for some groups. Conflict is usually part of the life of any group, but when it emerges, and how it is then managed, is salient. The establishment of a felt sense of safety is a pre-requisite for members to sufficiently complete the work of this stage and move on to the next one. This felt sense is simultaneously a visceral as well as cognitive understanding that incorporates a body/mind awareness of the present moment.

Stage three, *mutuality and interpersonal empathy*, incorporates elements of both intimacy and recognition of difference. Here, trust and its accompanying willingness to take risks and expose one's vulnerabilities are paired with the recognition of, and respect for, differences. While not yet engaged in overt conflict or challenges at this stage, members are able to allow and appreciate each other's differences within the framework of their affiliation and connection. A holding environment has developed that has room for both the "oh, me too," and the "I see it differently, but can understand your point of view as well." Important in this phase, as all through the life of a group facilitated through a relational lens, is that the facilitators participate in empathic sharing of responses to the here and now life of the group. The ability for a worker to be moved by the group, and to let the members know when this has occurred, is a central tenet of the healing process that can occur when a group is facilitated in this style. Thus, the mutuality and interpersonal empathy of this stage includes the facilitators empathic presence coupled with appropriate professional boundaries.

The fourth stage is *challenge and change*. This stage of development is often the heart of the work for women and others who have been silenced, oppressed, and disempowered. The ability to hold connection through conflict is at the core of this stage. In fact, for this model, it is the ability to hold connection through similarity (establishing a relational base), through difference (mutuality and interpersonal empathy), and then through conflict (in the challenge and change stage) that is the core principle of a relationally based mode of work. In this stage, conflicts may emerge without sacrificing the bonds of connection and empathy, if the work in the prior stages has been sufficiently managed. While conflict may emerge in an earlier stage, the group is usually not yet ready to handle it without the risk of losing these bonds until this fourth stage. Members now may challenge each other, the facilitators, and themselves, secure in the knowledge that the container of the group will hold. This is not simply a given for members who have a history of trauma, loss, abuse, oppression, and silencing of their authentic voice. Rather, this knowledge must be carefully built within the dynamics of the group, so that members may arrive at this stage with sufficient trust and sense of safety to withstand conflict without it destroying the group or a member's connection to it.

Although the relational framework was originally formulated for work with women's groups, it seems to be particularly applicable to vulnerable populations who have suffered trauma, loss, and oppression prior to their group membership. Members of these groups often share symptomatology of disconnection and alienation, of shame, hopelessness, and a number of classic post-traumatic stress disorder (PTSD) symptoms. This framework, with its emphasis on safety before allowing conflict to emerge fully, and its heightened attention to connection and empathic attunement, seems ideally suited to repair the relational ruptures and counteract these sequelae of loss, trauma and oppression.

References

Garland, J., Jones, H., & Kolodny, R. (1965). A model of development in social work groups. In S. Bernstein (Ed.), *Exploration in group work: Essays in theory and practice* (pp. 17–27). Boston: Milford House.

Gendlin, E. (1970). *Focusing.* New York: Bantam Books.

Gilligan, C. (1982). *In a different voice.* Cambridge, MA: Harvard University Press.

Jordan, J., Kaplan, A., Miller, J. B., Stiver, I., & Surrey, J. (Eds.). (1991). *Women's growth in connection.* New York: Guilford Press.

Miller, J. B. (1976). *Toward a new psychology of women.* Boston: Beacon Press.

Schiller, L. (1995). Stages of development in women's groups: A relational model. In R. Kurland, & R. Salmon (Eds.), *Group work practice in a troubled society* (pp. 117–138). Binghamton, NY: Haworth Press.

Schiller, L. (1997). Rethinking stages of development in women's groups: Implications for practice. *Journal of Social Work with Groups, 20*(3), 3–19.

Schiller, L. (2007). Not for women only: Applying the relational model of group development with vulnerable populations. *Social Work with Groups, 30*(1), 11–26.

Schiller, L., & Zimmer, B. (2005). Sharing the secrets: The power of women's groups for sexual abuse survivors. In A. Gitterman, & L. Shulman (Eds.), *Mutual aid groups, vulnerable populations and the life cycle* (3rd ed., pp. 290–319). New York: Columbia University Press.

Tuckman, B. (1965). Developmental sequence in small groups. *Psychological Bulletin, 63*(3), 384–399.

Tuckman, B., & Jensen, M. A. (1997). Stages of small group development revisited. *Group and Organizational Studies,* 2(1), 419–437.

Group Work Phases of Helping

Preliminary Phase

Lawrence Shulman

Because the helping process in group practice is so complex, it is useful to analyze it against the backdrop of time. The four phases of work are: the Preliminary (or Preparatory) Phase; the Beginning (or Contracting) Phase; the Middle (or Work) Phase; and the Ending and Transition Phases.

Each phase of work—preliminary, beginning, middle, and ending and transition—has unique dynamics and requires specific skills. Jessie Taft (1949), referring to the beginning, middle, and ending phases, was one of the first to draw attention to the impact of time on social work practice. Schwartz (1961), who developed the Mutual Aid Model now commonly in use, incorporated this dimension into his work, adding the preliminary phase and modifying the ending phase to the "ending and transition" phase.

The preliminary (or preparatory) phase is the period prior to the first encounter with the client group. The beginning (or contracting) phase refers to the first sessions in which the worker develops a working contract with the group members, begins developing his or her working relationship with the group, and starts to encourage mutual aid. The middle (or work) phase is the period in which the work is done. Finally, in the ending and transition phase, the worker prepares the client to bring the relationship to an end and to make transitions to new experiences.

The preliminary phase in group work can be divided into two, interrelated sets of tasks. The first, *group formation*, refers to those efforts by the social worker to conceive of a group service and to make decisions about group purpose, size, meeting frequency and duration, membership criteria, meeting place, and other structural, issues such as whether the group should be open-ended (accepting new members while other may be leaving) or closed to new members, or whether the group will incorporate activities—such as in many children's groups, will there be co-leaders and how shall they work together, what will the rules of the group be—for example in relation to attendance and confidentiality. An important part of this work requires meeting with other agency staff to encourage referrals and meeting with prospective members as part of a recruitment and intake process.

The second set of tasks involves a skill called *"tuning in"* and the development of the ability to "respond directly to indirect communications" (Shulman, 2009). The tuning in process involves the worker putting him or herself in the shoes of the prospective group members and attempting to develop some preliminary empathy on a number of levels. These include: the "authority theme" (how members will initially react to the group leader); the "agency theme" (how members feel about the group being offered and the conditions of their involvement such as mandated versus voluntary attendance); "work themes" (the issues the group needs to address, based upon its purpose); and finally the "intimacy theme" (thoughts and feelings about the other members).

The *idea* for a group may emerge in an agency in many ways: from client feedback, a worker who discovers a common concern among individual clients, or a staff team that discovers an important gap in the service. Wherever the idea starts, all involved staff members must have the opportunity to comment honestly on the potential service. A common mistake is for workers to decide on the need for a group and then to set about "selling" colleagues on the idea. Rather than presenting their own views on the need and inviting feedback and discussion, workers may try to influence their colleagues, thereby creating the illusion that they have involved others in the process (Gitterman & Shulman, 2005; Shulman, 2009). Tuning in to staff concerns and issues may be just as important as tuning in to potential group members. In particular, attention to possible hidden sources of resistance and using the skill of reaching for staff ambivalence can lead to a more honest discussion.

Group composition requires close attention in the formation stage (Gitterman, 2005). Group leaders might prefer clear and specific rules to inform the decisions as to who to accept to the group, and who should be excluded. However, the reality is that at times the group leaders must take "who we can get." The worker's experience is of crucial importance in responding to questions that arise about group composition, and the decisions that have to be made.

For example, we know that extremes often lead to problems. Groups can clearly be too large to provide an opportunity for everyone to participate or too small to provide a consistent core of members. Although groups can tolerate some degree of age range, for some populations, such as teenagers, this can create problems. For example, a 12-year-old foster child faces life tasks that differ significantly from the concerns of a 17-year-old who is preparing to leave the care of the agency at age 18. Issues of diversity are also important to address. For example, one person of color in an all-White group—what I call the "only one" problem—may experience a sense of isolation that the addition of another might well alleviate. In another structural example, a group of survivors of sexual abuse may have significant difficulty achieving intimacy if the group is open-ended, with new members constantly joining the group and other members leaving it.

Tuning in is defined as developing preliminary empathy as to what the potential group member (or staff member) may be thinking and feeling about the many issues described earlier. For example, it is not uncommon to have a group leader who has not had the experiences of the group member: leading a parent group when one does not have children; leading a recovery group when one has not "walked the walk" (been an alcoholic) or "talked the talk" (been active in Alcoholics Anonymous); leading a group dealing with serious illness or one for persons grieving the loss of a loved one when the leader has not had experience with the illness or that kind of grief. The group leader would have to tune in to what is often the first question on the minds of new group members: "Who is this group leader and what kind of person will he or she be?" (Shulman, 2009). Genuine tuning in requires that the group leader attempt to get in touch with these feelings by remembering similar experiences in his or her life. This is only possible when the group leader has also tuned into his or her anxieties and feelings about leading the group. With this kind of preparation, when one of the mothers in the group asks the usual question: "And how many children do you have?," instead of responding defensively the group leader can address the underlying questions directly. These are often: "Can you understand my life?" "Can you help me?" "Will you judge me?" An empathic and non-defensive response that recognizes that the group leader lacks that specific knowledge, understands and validates the group members' concern, and invites the members to help the leader to better understand can lead to the development of a positive working relationship that is the medium through which we help (Germain and Gitterman, 1996; Shulman, 1978; Truax, 1966).

In a similar manner, the group leader needs to tune in to the potential "themes of concern" that may be brought into the group related to its purpose. When group members raise issues indirectly, during perhaps a period of "problem swapping" in the first session, the group leader will be better able to reach for the underlying issues and feelings by responding directly. For example, when a husband in a group dealing with grief around the loss of a child indicates "It's been hard on my wife," the tuned-in group leader can respond directly and say: "And it hasn't been easy for you as well."

References

Germain, C. B., & Gitterman, A. (1996). *The Life Model of social work practice: Advances in theory and practice* (2nd ed.). New York: Columbia University Press.

Gitterman, A. (2005). Group formation: Tasks, methods, and skills. In A. Gitterman, & L. Shulman (Eds.), *Mutual aid groups, vulnerable and resilient populations and the life cycle* (3rd ed., pp. 73–112). New York: Columbia University Press.

Gitterman, A., & Shulman, L. (2005). *Mutual aid groups, vulnerable and resilient populations and the life cycle* (3rd ed.). New York: Columbia University Press.

Schwartz, W. (1961). The social worker in the group. In *New perspectives on services to groups: Theory, organization, and practice* (pp. 7–34). New York: National Association of Social Workers.

Shulman, L. (1978). A study of practice skills. *Social Work, 23*(4), 274–281.

Shulman, L. (2009). *The skills of helping individuals, families, groups and communities* (6th ed.). Belmont, CA: Thomson/Wadsworth.

Taft, J. (1949). Time as the medium of the helping process. *Jewish Social Service Quarterly, 26*, 230–243.

Truax, C. B. (1966). Therapist empathy, warmth, genuineness, and patient personality change in group psychotherapy: A comparison between interaction unit measures, time sample measures, and patient perception measures. *Journal of Clinical Psychology, 71*, 1–9.

Beginning Phase

Lawrence Shulman

Many of the uncertainties and fears associated with new beginnings will be increased by the public nature of a first group session. For example, the client's fear of being manipulated by someone in authority may increase at the thought that peers will witness any display of inadequacy, along with the resultant humiliation. For this reason and others, workers must pay special attention to first sessions to set a proper stage for the work that will follow. The first session or sessions can be considered a form of "contracting" between the group members and the agency or setting offering the service. Contracting includes attention to the "authority theme," the relation between the group leader and the members, and the "intimacy theme," the relationship between the members (Schwartz, 1961).

In the beginning phase group members must make a first decision about whether or not to engage with the worker. Even mandatory clients (e.g., child welfare, court ordered, or probation) must make that decision for the work to be effective. There are four basic questions on the group members' minds that need to be answered as part of this "contracting process" in the first session or sessions. First, "Who is this group leader and what kind of person will he or she be?" Second, "What is the purpose of this group?" Third, "Do I see a connection between what I feel I need and the stated group purpose?" And finally, who are these other group members and what kind of people will they be?" (Gitterman & Shulman, 2005; Shulman, 2009).

As the group starts, the members will watch the worker with keen interest. Having experienced the impact of powerful people in authority, they know it is important to "size up" this new authority figure as soon as possible. This leads to the clients' first central question: "What kind of person will the worker be?" Until the group members can understand clearly how this worker operates and will affect them, they will need to test the worker directly or indirectly. Defenses will remain in position until members are certain of their individual safety. The also need to understand the group leader's role which requires that it be clarified as part of the contracting process.

As in individual work, early clarification of purpose is central in the group context. The clients' second question will be: "What are we here for?" Once the boundary of the group experience has been clearly described, members will find the process of selecting appropriate responses easier. When the expectations of the group worker and the setting or agency within which the group takes place are clear, the group members feel much safer than when the purpose remains ambiguous. With clarity about group purpose they can better answer the third question, "Do I see a connection between what I feel I need and the stated group purpose?" It is this overlap between services and needs that defines the common ground and the initial contract (Germain and Gitterman, 1996; Schwartz, 1961; Shulman, 2009).

Even in those situations where attendance is mandated it is important to search out the connection between what the group members perceive they need and the service offered. For example, members ordered by the court to attend a group for driving while intoxicated (DWI), at the start, may only be interested in finding out what they need to do to get the court and the judge off their backs, and to get the driving license returned. That is the place the group leader will begin.

All these dynamics are similar to the ones that emerge in first sessions in individual counseling. The main difference in the group setting involves the presence of other clients. As the group session proceeds, each group member will also be appraising the others. Many questions will arise: "Who are these other people? Do they have the same problems that I do? Will I be embarrassed by finding myself less competent than they are? Do they seem sympathetic and supportive, or are there people in this group who may attack and confront me?" Although the client's primary concern in the first session is the group leader, questions about the other members follow close behind. Not only do members wonder what they can get out of the experience to meet their own needs, they wonder why it is necessary to get help in a group: "How can other people help me if they have the same problems I have?"

With some of these issues in mind, the worker should design the structure of first meetings to meet the following objectives:

- To introduce group members to one another.
- To make a brief, simple opening statement that clarifies the agency's or institution's stake in providing the group service, as well as the potential issues and concerns that group members feel strongly about.
- To obtain feedback from the group members on their sense of the fit (the contract) between their ideas of their needs and the agency's view of the service it provides.
- To clarify the group worker's task and method of attempting to help the group do its work.
- To deal directly with any specific obstacles that may obstruct this particular group's efforts to function effectively, stereotypes that group members may hold concerning group work or people in authority, or group members' anger if attendance is involuntary.
- To begin to encourage intermember interaction rather than discussion only between the group leader and the group members.
- To begin to develop a supportive group culture in which members can feel safe.
- To help group members develop a tentative agenda for future work.
- To clarify the mutual expectations of the agency and the group members. For example, what can group members expect from the worker? In addition, what expectations does the worker have for the members (regarding regular attendance, meetings starting on time, and so forth)? Such rules and regulations concerning structure are part of the working contract.
- To gain some consensus on the part of group members as to the specific next steps. For example, are there central themes or issues with which they wish to begin the following week's discussion?
- To encourage honest feedback and evaluation of the effectiveness of the group.

At first glance, this list of objectives for a first meeting may appear overwhelming. Actually, many of them can be dealt with quickly, and most are interdependent—that is, work on one objective simultaneously affects the others.

Obviously, however, these objectives cannot be achieved in the first session unless a clear structure for work is provided. The approach to creating such a structure is offered as a general statement recognizing that the order of elements and the emphasis may vary depending on the leader, the group members, and the setting.

References

Germain, C. B., & Gitterman, A. (1996). *The Life Model of social work practice: Advances in theory and practice* (2nd ed.). New York: Columbia University Press.

Gitterman, A., & Shulman, L. (2005). *Mutual aid groups, vulnerable and resilient populations and the life cycle* (3rd ed.). New York: Columbia University Press.

Schwartz, W. (1961). The social worker in the group. In *New perspectives on services to groups: Theory, organization, and practice* (pp. 7–34). New York: National Association of Social Workers.

Shulman, L. (2009). *The skills of helping individuals, families, groups and communities* (6th ed.). Belmont, CA: Thomson/Wadsworth.

Middle Phase

Hal Lipton

> In this group I feel I belong ... I need this group because I found out that I am not alone in having problems ... I feel a sense of relief in being with others in the same boat as me ... I can speak out what I feel here—I cannot tell my family or friends what I really feel ... in this group we help each other—it is not just the worker that helps ... there is a sense of caring here that I never got before in my life ....

Powerful, evocative comments, such as those above, are most likely to be expressed during a period of time, in the group's life, that was named by William Schwartz (1971) as the Work Phase. Schwartz, an innovative thinker and theoretician, was an early proponent of mutual aid as an integral component of a framework for helping group members in the small group.

Today, mutual aid is recognized as the hallmark of social work with groups, and many authors have described the process (Gitterman & Shulman, 2005; Shulman, 2006). In the pre-group and beginning phases of group life, group formation is achieved, and the purpose of the group has been discussed and established (Kurland & Salmon, 2005). When the group has moved past the beginning phase of group development, members engage each other more freely, deeply, and openly in the group's task of helping each other. This is the time period when mutal aid can best do its work—in the Middle or Work Phase.

Gitterman (2006) emphasized the importance of developing a "culture of caring" in the early days of the work phase:

Early in a group's life, members usually speak to and through the worker. To facilitate mutual aid processes, the worker directs members' transactions to each other. Initially, members may talk at each other rather than to each other. The worker helps members to build on each other's contributions by linking their comments to each other. The worker identifies and focuses on salient group themes. Common salient group themes are the "glue" that binds members together as they help each other with mutual concerns and issues.

(p. 100)

During this phase, the worker's active role is crucial. The worker's professional tasks are specifically directed toward the successful alleviation of the group's mutual issues or problems. Schwartz (1971) describes five essential tasks:

> Finding through negotiation, the common group between the requirements of the group members and those of the systems they need to negotiate; detecting and challenging the obstacles to work as those obstacles arise; contributing ideas, facts, and values from his own perspective when he or she thinks that such data may be useful to the members in dealing with the problems under consideration; lending his own vision and projecting his own feelings about the struggles in which they are engaged; and, defining the requirements and limits of the situation in which the client–worker system is set.

(p. 17)

While collective themes are emphasized, at the same time, the worker does not neglect the needs of the individual in the group. The group worker needs to be careful not to stifle divergent perceptions and opinions, which, in fact, often enrich the group's life, and strengthen a group norm of accepting individual difference (Gitterman, 2006).

Group members have a great sense of one another as different characteristics emerge. Members take on, and assign to each other, specific roles. Sub-groups form. Differences among members assume increased importance as members speak freely and share opinions and points of view. Conflict can become more frequent and should be expected. Workers have to help group members to constructively address conflict (Kurland & Salmon, 1998). The worker needs a repertoire of professional abilities for the more complex demands. They include (Schwartz, 1971):

> The ability to perceive when work is going on and when it is being avoided; reinforcing the different ways in which people help each other; the ability to reach for opposites, for ambiguities, for what is happening under the good feelings or the bad; partializing large problems into smaller, more manageable pieces; generalizing and finding connections between small segments of experience. Calling not only for talk but talk that is purposeful and invested with feeling; being able to handle not only the first offering, but also the second and third stages of elaboration; and, throughout, being able constantly to make the demand of work inherent in the worker's helping function.

(p. 17)

Middleman and Wood (1990) identify core practice skills that group workers are most likely to use in the middle phase:

Reaching for consensus: to check to see if most members agree on how things are going.

Reaching for difference: to help group members see things from various angles so that a range of viewpoints and possibilities are entertained.

Confronting situations: to involve relevant members in open exchanges of information and affect about a problem or issue as each person perceives it.

Reaching for feeling: to invite members to describe the emotions they are experiencing.

Amplifying subtle messages: to call attention to unnoticed communicative behavior (e.g., words, tone of voice, facial expressions) by commenting on it to others in the group rather than to the particular person.

Reporting own feelings: to describe one's in the moment emotional experience which self-disclosure is likely to be useful in shedding light on others feelings or the situation.

Giving feedback: to repeat the essence of what members have said and to ask if the meaning was in fact, the intended meaning.

Check out inferences: to ask if a certain thought, hunch, or interpretation is valid for members in a particular situation.

Giving information: to offer the group facts, opinions, or ideas that may increase their knowledge of a situation or event.

(p. 67)

Established group workers are likely to be familiar with most of the above skills and strategies; newer group workers may not yet be experienced in applying them. When one is experienced in group work the skills are applied almost without thinking—the worker often uses them spontaneously—when he or she senses the benefit to individual members or to the group as a whole.

References

Gitterman, A. (2006). The Mutual Aid Model. In C. Garvin, L. Gutiérrez, & M. Galinsky (Eds.), *Handbook of social work with groups* (pp. 93–110). New York: Guilford Press.

Gitterman, A., & Shulman, L. (Eds.). (2005). *Mutual aid groups, vulnerable and resilient populations and the life cycle* (3rd ed.). New York: Columbia University Press.

Kurland R., & Salmon, R. (1998). *Teaching a methods course in social work with groups*. Alexandria, VA: Council on Social Work Education.

Kurland, R., & Salmon, R. (2005). Education for the group worker's reality: The special qualities and world view of those drawn to work with group. In R. Kurland, & R. Salmon (Eds.), *Making joyful noise: The art, science and soul of group work* (pp. 73–89). Bringhamton, NY: Haworth Press.

Middleman, R., Wood, R., & Goldberg, G. (1990). *Skills for direct practice in social work* (pp. 91–154). New York: Columbia University Press.

Schwartz, W. (1971). On the use of groups in social work practice. In W. Schwartz, & S. Zalba (Eds.), *The practice of group work* (pp. 3–24). New York: Columbia University Press

Shulman, L. (2006). *The skills of helping individuals, families, groups and communities* (5th ed., pp. 344–353). Belmont, CA: Thomson Brooks/Cole.

Sessional Endings

Martin L. Birnbaum and Andrew Cicchetti

Single sessions have beginning, middle and ending phases. Purposeful sessional endings require evaluation of members goals, group content and process, and the role of the worker. They also serve to establish closure and transition between sessions. The use of the purposeful ending provides a holistic framework for each session, as the group is able to see the interrelationship of beginning, middle, and ending phases. It leads to member reflection, transition between sessions, closure, empowerment, and a sense of satisfaction and accomplishment.

Reflection occurs as members discuss what meaning the group encounter had for them individually and as a group. They reflect on what they can take away and use in their lives outside of the group. The work of the group is enhanced when connections are made between single sessions. Each session should provide direction for the next group encounter. When the session is over, members have a sense of closure and completion of the group experience. Unfinished work is identified for consideration during the next session. When the ending is unproductive and spillover occurs, the worker can use the ending experience as content for the next meeting. The sessional ending provides a context to enhance the development of individual and group empowerment. This occurs as members have a say about group content, how the group functions, and the role of the worker.

Purposeful sessional endings require distinctive group practice skills. They include allocating time, developing norms, soliciting feedback, reaching for discrepant points of view, and attention to both content and process. Practitioners must save sufficient time for sessional endings (Shoemaker, 1960); at times, accelerating group process. The allocation of time allows for a smooth transition between the middle and ending phase.

In establishing norms for sessional endings, initially, members may express surprise, and view it as taking time away from the work of the group. When the sessional ending is a part of the initial group contract, members are usually more accepting than when it is introduced at a later time. As members experience the benefits of sessional endings, they are likely to embrace it.

Workers may fear reaching for feedback about group progress or lack of it. The fear diminishes as workers experience that the members are likely to use the opportunity to provide constructive ideas. In reaching for discrepant points of view, the worker should encourage the expression of different ideas and perspectives. The following type of questions help to elicit differences: "Are there other thoughts, feelings, or opinions about the session?" or "While many of you have pointed out what you liked about group, I am wondering if there are any disappointments or dissatisfactions?" This skill is particularly useful in the beginning stage of group development, as it prepares the group for the expression and resolution of differences and conflict.

In the ending phase, practitioners are likely to focus on the covered group content and avoid dealing with group process. Content refers to the topics or issues covered and the expression of ideas. Process refers to the group as a whole and its interrelated parts, such as social interaction, purpose, relationships, roles, norms, conflict, and group cohesion, that influence group functioning and development (Northen, 1998). Attention to both content and process is necessary if members are to experience the benefits of sessional endings.

The social worker also benefits from reflecting on the content and process of sessional endings, examining his or her role from session to session as well as at the end of the entire group experience. Additionally, the worker is able to more effectively assess the group, as sessional evaluation provides ongoing data about individual and group functioning. Group feedback to the worker in individual sessions enables the worker to correct mistakes and make changes in his or her role and interventions.

The sessional ending phase has special application for short-term and open-ended groups. The short duration of the total group experience underscores the importance of the ending phase for evaluation of individual and group progress, and planning for the next session.

The sessional ending is viewed as a natural part of the group life cycle in each group encounter. Our experience and that of students and practitioners who have made purposeful use of sessional endings is that they contribute significantly to the efficacy of group work practice.

References

Northen, H. (1988). *Social work with groups*. New York: Columbia University Press.
Shoemaker, L. (1960). Use of group work skills with short-term groups. In *Social work with groups* (pp. 74–85). New York: National Association of Social Workers.

Termination Phase

Steven Rose

All groups come to an end. Termination takes place. It is the ending and transition phase of the group's work, "in which the worker prepares to end the relationships and to help the client (group) review their work together as well as to prepare for transitions to new experiences" (Shulman, 2006, p. 609). As there are many different types of groups—treatment, self-help, psychotherapeutic, recreational, educational, and task groups—to name but a few, it is expectable that different types of groups will end in different ways.

However, what is consistent among all types of groups is that endings are particularly complicated because they occur on three levels: "the relationship between group members and the worker is coming to an end; and the group as an entity is concluding and will cease to exist. The worker needs to be cognizant simultaneously of the multiple meanings of endings on all three levels" (Kurland & Salmon, 1998, p. 132).

Also, it should be noted that the group's ending also means that the worker is ending a specific relationship, as leader to the group that has developed over time. Workers, as well as clients, also may find this stage of the group's development particularly difficult, depending on their own personal histories of attachment, separation, loss, and relationships (Roman, 2006, pp. 235–242). The termination process is focused on the ending of the entire group, or on one specific member's departure from the group, while others continue. However, at times, it is the group leader that leaves the group and this has its own powerful impact on the remaining client group. For example, group work students leave their field work placement after an academic year of social work education. Leaving, ending, is as natural and as expectable a part of group life as beginning.

Whenever possible, the group worker needs to call early attention to the imminence of endings as an important and intrinsic part of group life. This helps the process unfold in an unforced, natural manner. Group members' positive and negative feelings about ending are best expressed spontaneously, and over time, thus providing the worker and the group opportunities to explore and consider them. The members' articulation of feelings about endings is important. Encouraging the group to reminisce helps the group relive the group experience. Genuine feelings become expressed during such discussions, and reminiscence helps the group members bring closure to the experience:

- Evaluation of the group experience is an important corollary to reminiscence. This evaluative process provides a frame of reference that group members can use as they move on to new situations.
- It is hard to say goodbye, and particularly so when the group experience has been important to the members, and/or the worker. As a result there often is a tendency to try to cram new material in at the last moment. However, it is best to use the last meeting of the group to talk about the accomplishments of the group, and to consolidate the learning that has taken place, rather than introducing new material.

(Kurland & Salmon, 1998, p. 133)

As the group moves into the ending phase, three kinds of problematic behavior might be seen:

- *Denial*—The worker informs the group of the duration of the group, and periodically reminds the members of the closing date for termination. However, when the ending is imminent, the group members may deny that the worker ever informed them of this.
- *Regression*—Problematic behavior patterns that were apparent in the beginning stage of group development, and seemingly resolved, may return. This can, be understood as one way to deliver a message that the group and/or worker continues to be needed.
- *Flight*—As the group nears its end, some members may start to attend sporadically, or not at all. They may be experiencing a sense of loss, and they choose to leave the group and worker before the group ends, and/or the worker leaves them.

(Kurland & Salmon, 1998, pp. 131–146)

Margaret Hartford (1971, pp. 67–93) used social work practice groups and social science research as the foundation for the development of a five-phase scheme of group development. She began with what she named the *Pre-Group Phases*, which included the period of time, in the beginning, when the idea of forming a new group existed primarily in the mind of the organizer. It proceeded, in steps, to a *Group Formation Phase*, and finally to the *Termination Phase*, which consisted of three parts.

The first part is *Pre-Termination*, which includes acknowledgement that the group really is about to end, and helping members come to term with this reality. *Termination* is the actual ending of the group, and it takes place on the final group meeting. *The Post-Termination Phase* refers to subsequent thoughts, plans, emotions and activities following the actual ending of the group.

There is variety in the way termination takes place. It may be planned or unplanned, expected or unexpected, successful or unsuccessful, abrupt or tapering, individual or group, member or leader, and external or internal. The start of a group may affect the way it ends. Preparatory interviews often do not include a discussion of termination (Hannah, 2000). Kurland (2005) noted that premature termination often is the price of inadequate planning and preparation.

A successful termination is not an emotionally traumatic event for the members. If group members expect termination, they are more likely to have sufficient time to adjust to its ending. Some members arrange to participate in another group or otherwise receive assistance to meet their own needs.

In short-term, time-limited, cognitive groups, educationally oriented thematic type groups, and task groups, such as committees, scant opportunity exists to form a significant social–emotional attachment to the group or the leader. The number of sessions is specified before the group actually begins, and termination is understood and accepted at the onset.

Although termination usually is about the entire group, individuals also may end their relationship with the group. This can be initiated either by the member or by the leader. In some groups, as members achieve their goals, they leave the group. In some circumstances it is not expected that the group member will be replaced. If a member harms himself or others, and the leader is unable to bring about change in the member's behavior, that member is likely to be asked by the leader to leave the group. Under some circumstances, a member may be treated individually by the group leader, after the group ends. Furthermore, while termination is usually thought of in terms of the member, occasionally it is the group worker who leaves the group (Pudil, 2006).

External and internal termination refers to the locus of change, or the impetus for termination. In the former case, the group ends as a result of factors outside of the group; termination is compelled. This includes situations where organizational or fiscal support become unavailable for the continuance of the group. In contrast, internal termination refers to the ending of the group when the impetus for termination stems from the group itself, or from the leader.

References

Hannah, P. J. (2000). Preparing members for the expectations of social work with groups: An approach to the preparatory interview. *Social Work with Groups, 22*(1), 51–66.

Hartford, M. E. (1971). *Groups in social work.* New York: Columbia University Press,

Kurland, R. (2005). Planning: The neglected component of group development. *Social Work with Groups, 28*(1), 9–16.

Kurland, R., & Salmon, R. (1998). *Teaching a methods course in social work with groups.* Alexandria, VA: Council on Social Work Education.

Pudil, J. (2006). I'm gone when you're gone: How a group can survive when its leader takes a leave of absence. *Social Work with Groups, 29*(2/3), 217–233.

Roman, C. P. (2006). A worker's personal grief and its impact on processing a group's termination. *Social Work with Groups, 29*(2/3), 235–242.

Shulman, L. (2006). *The skills of helping individuals, families, groups and communities* (5th ed, pp. 344–353). Belmont, CA: Thomson Brooks/Cole.

Group Work Education

Field Instruction

Carol S. Cohen and Julianne Wayne

Though practicum experiences remain a central component of social work education, special concerns have been identified about the planning and supervision of group work assignments (Cohen, 1998; Knight, 1997; Wayne & Cohen, 2001). Three contemporary trends contribute to this situation. First, is the movement of social work curricula towards generalist rather than method specific practice as the professional foundation (Commission on Accreditation, 2001). Many foundation practice course instructors report providing less knowledge about, and application of, generalist principles to work with groups than to work with individuals (Birnbaum & Wayne, 2000), and not all programs require specialized group work courses. This has resulted in many students entering the field with relatively little academic support for group work practice. Therefore, it falls primarily on field instructors to help students learn and link generalist and specific knowledge and theory to their work with groups.

Yet many field instructors themselves have limited experience and education of group work, and describe using a more apprenticeship rather than conceptual approach to the supervision of their students' group work practice. Many spend little or no time in formal discussion of group assignments and, unlike their supervision of work with individuals, do not require process recordings or other written materials as teaching tools to support students' ability to engage in practice informed by theory (Wayne & Garland, 1990). Social agencies and organizations increasingly look to groups to serve a wide range of client and organizational needs, but often rely on expertise of other professionals and non-professionals. While the widespread use of groups is a positive movement, students must be helped to distinguish between social work with groups and other group practices.

Together, these trends suggest the need for aggressive action from the academic and practice arenas to support field educators as the front line of learning group work practice. Although practical factors such as the availability of groups often influence how assignments are made, each student should either understand or have the opportunity to carry out the group planning processes. Kurland's (1978) widely acknowledged formulation includes the following areas: understanding agency and social context; needs of the target population; specific purpose of the group; group composition; structure; content; formation strategy; and, additionally, evaluation (Wayne & Cohen, 2001). Each of these areas requires serious consideration and is informed by its own body of knowledge.

Direct participation in the planning process lends professional rigor to the process of assessing organizational environments for a group service and identifies elements that will become areas of future inquiry. In modeling the collaborative learning approach, instructors partner with students in planning and gathering resources for the best possible group analysis and generate understanding of an agency's opportunities for, and barriers to, effective group work practice.

Students and field instructors must engage in a thoughtful analysis of "why" a group intervention would be effective, its potential benefits to members and environment, group types that could serve to accomplish its purpose, at which stage the group is functioning, and how they will track process and outcomes. Types and purposes include education, support, socialization, therapy, and task orientation (Wayne & Cohen, 2001). These groups vary in many dimensions, including degree of structure and balance of cognitive and affective material. All group work types, however, rely on mutual aid as a group dynamic (Gitterman & Shulman, 2005).

Groups provide unique benefits (Yalom & Leszcz, 2005) that are not offered in work with individuals. These vary in nature and intensity with group purpose, and need to be considered within the framework of each particular group (Wayne & Cohen, 2001). They include: helping members feel normal (it is the norm in this group to have my problem); providing opportunities to hide (remain silent) until they feel safe; opportunities to see many aspects of each member's personality as they evoke different types of responses from each other; creating new behavioral norms; growth through giving; effective problem solving; reliving and correcting early family experiences; development of social skills; appreciation of diversity; successful task completion; and empowerment. All skilled interventions must take into account the group's stage of developmental tasks and achievements.

Too frequently, students and agencies become locked into automatic thinking, including: fixed ideas that students must observe before facilitating groups (although individual work is assigned immediately); co-leadership as the best choice (overlooking its many complexities); and perennial designation of "student groups" (instead of looking broadly for productive assignments).

The need for solo practice experience, accompanied by regular, intensive supervision is essential for group work, as for other types of assignments in the field (Wayne & Cohen, 2001). Drawing from generalist practice models, individual supervisory conferences and process and other recordings (full verbatim or narrative/verbatim combinations) also serve as the foundations of group work supervision. Field instructors must assess where the student is in relation to their group and practicum, and select educational interventions informed by the knowledge of stages of student learning (Reynolds, 1942; Wayne & Cohen, 2001).

Field instructors need to use and/or adapt a range of reporting and discussion formats in order to highlight and study the generalist principles and specialized dynamics and skills of group work practice (Cohen & Garrett, 1995; Glassman & Kates, 1998). Group supervision can be used as a means of modeling the method and pointing to the parallel processes of members engaging in a mutually supportive learning environment (Cohen, 2004). Students can be helped to compare and contrast elements of their supervisory and practice experiences.

As the "playing field where the knowledge, skills, and values of a profession are transmitted" (Hendricks, Finch, & Franks, 2005, p. xiv), field is the essential arena to integrate classroom learning, build skills, experience agency practice, and form professional values and identity. With immediate investments in students, field instructors, faculty and organization collaborators, we will be able to meet the demand to increase and institutionalize field education with groups, and thus expand the use of, and expertise of, social workers' group work practice in this and future generations.

References

Birnbaum, M., & Wayne, J. (2000). Group work content in foundation generalist education: The necessity for change. *Journal of Social Work Education, 36*, 347–356.

Cohen, C. S. (1998). Building field instructor's skills in planning and supervising group assignments. *Journal of Teaching in Social Work, 16*(2), 99–114.

Cohen, C. S. (2004). Clinical supervision in a learning organization. In M. Austin, & K. Hopkins (Eds.), *Supervision as collaboration in the human services: Building a learning culture*. Thousand Oaks, CA: Sage.

Cohen, M. B., & Garrett, K. J. (1995). Helping field instructors become more effective group work educators. *Social Work with Groups, 18*(2/3), 135–148.

Commission on Accreditation. (2001). *Educational policy and accreditation standards*. Alexandria, VA: Council on Social Work Education.

Gitterman, A., & Shulman, L. (Eds.). (2005). *Mutual aid groups: Vulnerable and resilient populations and the life cycle* (3rd ed.). New York: Columbia University Press.

Glassman, U., & Kates, L. (1988). Strategies for group work field instruction. *Social Work with Groups, 11*(1/2), 111–124.

Hendricks, C. O., Finch, J. B., & Franks, C. L. (2005). *Learning to teach, teaching to learn: A guide for social work field education*. Alexandria, VA: Council on Social Work Education.

Knight, C. (1997). A study of MSW and BSW students' involvement with group work in the field practicum. *Social Work with Groups, 20*(2), 31–49.

Kurland, R. (1978). Planning: The neglected component of group development. *Social Work with Groups, 1*(2), 173–178.

Reynolds, B. C. (1942). *Learning and teaching in the practice of social work*. New York: Farrar & Rinehart.

Wayne, J., & Cohen, C. S. (2001). *Group work education in the field*. Alexandria, VA: Council on Social Work Education.

Wayne, J., & Garland, J. (1990). Group work education in the field: The state of the art. *Social Work with Groups, 13*(2), 95–109.

Yalom, I. D., & Leszcz, M. (2005). *The theory and practice of group psychotherapy* (5th ed.). New York: Basic Books.

Use of Literature in Teaching

Dana Grossman Leeman

Every semester it happens. It is the first day of class and my new students arrive. We introduce ourselves, I facilitate a group-building activity, and then we review the syllabus. I then present a brief history of social work with groups, beginning with the settlement houses and charity organization societies of the progressive era (Axinn & Stern, 2005) culminating with William Schwartz, and the Mutual Aid Model (Schwartz, 1961, 1962, 1971). In this first lecture, it is my mission to establish group work as not only the historical antecedent of social work practice, but to counter the long-standing image of group work as the forgotten and neglected child of social work practice.

And then it happens. A hand is raised: "Excuse me and maybe I missed this, but, what about Yalom? We're doing Yalom, right?" "*Do* Yalom?" I ask. My student continues insistently, "we can't learn group work without Yalom, right?" "We will review Yalom's therapeutic factors (Yalom, 1995) today, but that is it. I respect and admire his work, but Yalom is not a social group worker. He doesn't think like one and he doesn't approach the worker–client relationship in the way that we do. Therefore, I don't teach him." I scan the class, which has descended into an addled silence. I sit comfortably in it for a moment, and then proceed. This is my worldview, and for the ensuing 13 weeks of the semester, I unapologetically impose it upon them.

For the record: I like Yalom (1995). Over the years, I have read much of his published work and have watched his training videos, awed by his artistry. My pedagogical choices, however, have everything to do with the promulgation and survival of social group work, and not anti-Yalom sentiment.

One might call me a militant group worker—perhaps a byproduct of having graduated from Boston University School of Social Work (BUSSW) in 1989, and having been trained by James Garland and Lawrence Shulman, and greatly influenced by the work of Trudy Duffy, Alex Gitterman, Roselle Kurland, Robert Salmon, Linda Schiller, Andrew Malekoff, and Mary Bitel. Their collective works, both in class and in text, taught me that as the worker I could strive to think broadly and progressively about group process, infuse it with poetry, humor, and metaphor without sacrificing the social and political conscience, which guide group work method. My training consolidated my belief that group work was an important and legitimate practice methodology. I discovered my passion and love of group work, which has endured, and which I try to gift to my students.

Lamentably, group work is disappearing from graduate level curricula, and the language of mutual aid is seldom spoken by social workers in the field. After many years of providing consultation to experienced social workers, the paucity of those who are conversant in group work is no longer surprising to me, nor is their inability to articulate what distinguishes group work from group psychotherapy. Specifically: the worker as a mediator and collaborator; the facilitation of mutual aid; an interest in exploring members' differences as well as similarities; maximization of the collective's strengths and innate skills which challenges social and cultural norms of individualism (Drumm, 2006; Gitterman & Shulman, 2005; Kurland & Salmon, 1996); and the group as the potential birthplace of social action. Conversely, Yalom's conceptualization of group psychotherapy is fundamentally pathocentric. It also emphasizes the primacy of the therapist as expert and architect of the group experience, and focal point of each individual's transference. Yalom's work, furthermore, is devoid of the consideration that a client's distress may be the effects of interactions with oft oppressive or marginalizing systems.

In 1996 I created and taught my first group work class. I confess that only half of the assigned readings were from group work, but in class I taught what I practiced—mutual aid. Five years into teaching, the field education department enjoined me to supervise a group of second-year students who were experiencing problems with their groups. I recall one particularly discomfiting conversation with one of my student's supervisors, who criticized my consultation. My method, she complained, was useful for classroom discussion, but had no place in the "real world." She opined that the group was a place for individuals to practice social skills and explore affect, it was not the time or place to discuss social change. She encouraged her student to practice individual casework within the group, and asked that I support this (Kurland & Salmon, 1993). I was stunned. At what point had group work and "the real world" diverged? What could I do to build a bridge between theory and practice, and between the classroom and agency life? This revelation led me to refashion my syllabus, omit non-social work literature, and fervently politicize group work practice in classroom lectures and discussion. And thus it has remained.

In a recent discussion with some senior colleagues, I was asked what I thought would happen if I re-introduced Yalom into my course, in response to student demand. It is my sincere belief that social work students need to learn group work. This does not mean that they should not be introduced to other methods of group facilitation. Yet, we must instill in them the unique philosophy and method upon which our profession was founded. If social work educators do not teach them, who will? As my mentor and esteemed colleague, Dr. Carol Swenson recently said, "each generation who doesn't learn social group work is another generation who can't teach it" (C. Swenson, personal communication, July 2007). This is indeed a disheartening prospect. If we abandon group work as a profession, we divest ourselves of what we historically cared about and endeavored to change since those first socialization groups at Hull House. As an instructor and group worker, this does not seem to be a viable option. And for this reason, I do not "do" Yalom.

References

Axinn, J., & Stern, M. J. (2005). *Social welfare: A history of the American response to Need* (6th ed.). Boston: Allyn & Bacon.

Drumm, K. (2006). The essential power of group work. *Social Work with Groups, 29*(2/3), 17–31.

Gitterman, A., & Shulman, L. (2005). *Mutual aid groups, vulnerable and resilient populations, and the life cycle* (3rd ed.). New York: Columbia University Press.

Kurland, R., & Salmon, R. (1992). Group work versus casework in a group: Principles and implications for teaching and practice. *Social Work with Groups, 15*(4), 3–14.

Kurland, R., & Salmon, R. (2006). Making joyful noise: presenting, promoting, and portraying group work to and for the profession. *Social Work with Groups, 29*(2/3), 1–15.

Schwartz, W. (1961). The social worker in the group. *The social welfare forum* (pp. 146–177). New York: Columbia University Press.

Schwartz, W. (1962). Toward a strategy of group work practice. *Social Service Review, 36*(3), 268–279.

Schwartz, W. (1971). On the uses of groups in social work practice. In W. Schwartz, & S. Zalba (Eds.), *The pactice of group work* (pp. 3–24). New York: Columbia University Press.

Yalom, I. D. (1995). *The theory and practice of group psychotherapy* (4th ed.). New York: Basic Books.

Use of Technology in Teaching

Shirley R. Simon and Kathleen W. Stauber

In the last 20 years, the personal computer and the Internet have drastically changed our methods of seeking information and communicating with one another, as instantaneous communication around the globe has become a reality. Email, online research, and "wired classrooms," have become mainstays of the current educational structure. Distance education has emerged as a burgeoning new offering in higher education, leading to the proliferation of online courses and degree programs. Given the potential economic benefits, the ability to reach new and underserved student markets, and the need to compete with other "wired" universities, it is not surprising that deans and faculties are increasingly called upon to offer individual courses and even entire curricula in an online format. Administrators cite the speed and efficiency of communication between students and faculty, the flexibility in time and format of educational delivery, and the increased organization and accountability in instruction as reasons for promoting distance learning options. This entry (1) summarizes the current use of technology and distance learning in social work education; (2) delineates the challenges, benefits, and significance of incorporating technology into group work education; (3) identifies recent online and hybrid (combination of online and face-to-face) group work offerings; and (4) suggests opportunities for social group work leadership in the development of online communities.

Within social work, distance education options are becoming increasingly widespread. The Council on Social Work Education (CSWE) accepts distance education methodologies for all courses, except field practice and field supervision (*Educational Policy and Accreditation Standards*, CSWE, 2004, www.cswe.org). CSWE has accredited a number of social work programs that use distance education technology to complete a large portion of their master's and baccalaureate degree requirements (CSWE, Office of Social Work Education and Research, 2007, www.cswe.org). Online programs provide access to graduate social work education in underserved areas. Recognizing a significant trend in online education, CSWE organized a full-day Summit on Distance Education as part of its 2007 Annual Program Meeting.

For group work, distance education presents a significant conceptual shift. Not so long ago, the very definition of a small group included a requirement for face-to-face interaction (Schwartz, 1971). With the advent of newer means of group communication, including telephone groups, Internet chat groups, and online support groups, the requirement for direct, face-to-face connections no longer applies. Yet many group work educators have demonstrated considerable reluctance to depart from the traditional standard and embrace the new technology. Such resistance is understandable given group workers' long-term comfort and skill in the face-to-face arena. Moreover, most of the contemporary leaders in group work received their education in the decades before computer literacy.

These leaders, like so many other educators who learned to work with computers later in their careers, have had to expend considerable energy just to keep up with the day-to-day technological demands. Intimidation, lack of time and interest, and the difficulty of keeping abreast of continuously changing software and operating formats, serve as additional deterrents to the ready incorporation of technology in contemporary group work education. Nevertheless, group work educators, of necessity, must confront these changing educational expectations.

Although there is a plethora of literature on the strengths and weaknesses of distance education modalities for the delivery of effective social work education (Coe & Elliot, 1999; Frey, Faul, & Yankelov, 2003; Macy, Rooney, Hollister, & Freddolino, 2001; Siebert, Siebert, & Spaulding-Givens, 2006; Siegel, Jennings, Conklin, Napoletano Flynn, 1998; Thyer, Artelt, Markward, & Dozier, 1998; Wilke, & Vinton, 2006), little has been written about the existence and effectiveness of distance education specifically for social group work. Anecdotal information indicates that group work is being offered in online or hybrid formats at Renison College–University of Waterloo, University of Denver, University of Hawai'i, and Loyola University Chicago. At Renison (Muskat & Mesbur, 2007), and at Loyola, social group work courses are offered in hybrid format, as well as in the traditional face-to-face format. Both Renison and Loyola are engaged in comparison assessments of the effectiveness of these offerings.

The perception that group work can only be taught effectively in a face-to-face environment may be a significant factor in the resistance to offering group work online or in hybrid format. Even institutions that offer online programs cite this concern as a deterrent to offering group courses via distance education. Further research and assessment are needed to determine whether this perception is accurate, and whether there are indeed effective strategies and opportunities for the provision of group work education in online formats.

Social group work educators are in an ideal position to assume a leadership role in facilitating the development of online communities. A significant amount of research is being conducted on how to foster commitment and create online communities with limited or no face-to-face contacts. (Marathe, 2002; Palloff & Pratt, 2007; Parr & Ward, 2006). Group work educators, with their understanding of group process and their historic expertise in developing experiential learning communities, are ideally suited to contribute to the burgeoning body of knowledge regarding best practices in this arena.

The integration of technology and group work education is inevitable (Galinsky, Schopler, & Abell, 1997; Rounds & Galinsky, 1991; Schopler, Abell, & Galinsky 1998; Smith, Toseland, Rizzo, & Zinoman, 2004). The timely and effective inclusion of this modality as a means of delivering quality group work education is a necessity if group work education is to remain viable in today's educational climate. Group work education is already struggling for its rightful place at the educational table. If group work educators do not respond to these changing demands, social group work is even more likely to be marginalized. It is incumbent upon group work educators, despite the inherent challenges, to actively explore opportunities for delivering group work education in online/distance education formats, and to assume a leadership role in determining best practices for the development of online communities.

References

Coe, J. R., & Elliot, D. (1999). An evaluation of teaching direct practice courses in a distance education program for rural settings. *Journal of Social Work Education, 35*(3), 353–365.

Council on Social Work Education. (2004). *Educational policy and accreditation standards.* Alexandria, VA: Author.

Frey, A., Faul, A., & Yankelov, P. (2003). Student perceptions of web-assisted teaching strategies. *Journal of Social Work Education, 39*(3), 443–457.

Galinsky, M. J., Schopler, J. H., & Abell, M. D. (1997). Connecting group members through telephone and computer groups. *Health and Social Work, 22*(2), 181–188.

Macy, J. A., Rooney, R. H., Hollister, C. D., & Freddolino, P. P. (2001). Evaluation of distance education programs in social work. *Journal of Technology in Human Services, 18*, 63–84.

Marathe, J. (2002). Creating online communities. Durlacher Research, Inc. Retrieved February 23, 2005, from http://www.durlacher.com

Muskat, B., & Mesbur, E. S. (2007, October). *Technologically enhanced innovative approaches to group work education.* Paper presented at the Annual Program Meeting of the Council on Social Work Education, San Francisco.

Palloff, R. M., & Pratt, K. (2007) *Building online learning communities: Effective strategies for the virtual classroom.* San Francisco: Jossey-Bass.

Parr, J., & Ward, L. (2006). Building on foundations: creating an online community. *Journal of Technology and Teacher Education, 14*(4), 775–794.

Rounds, K. A., & Galinsky, M. J. (1991). Linking people with AIDS in rural communities: The telephone group. *Social Work, 36*(1), 13–18.

Schopler, J. H., Abell, M. D., & Galinsky, M. J. (1998). Technology-based groups: A review and conceptual framework for practice. *Social Work, 43*(3), 254–266.

Schwartz, W. (1971). On the uses of groups in social work practice. In W. Schwartz, & S. Zalba (Eds.), *The practice of group work* (pp. 3–24). New York: Columbia University Press.

Siebert, D. C., Siebert, C. F., & Spaulding-Givens, J. (2006). Teaching clinical social work skills primarily online: An evaluation. *Journal of Social Work Education, 42*(2), 325–336.

Siegel, E., Jennings, J. G., Conklin, J., & Napoletano Flynn, S. A. (1998) Distance learning in social work education: Results and implications of a national survey. *Journal of Social Work Education, 34*(1), 71–80.

Smith, T. L., Toseland, R. W., Rizzo, V. M., & Zinoman, M. A. (2004). Telephone caregivers support groups. In R. Salmon, & R. Graziano (Eds.), *Group work and aging: Issues in practice, research and education* (pp. 151–172). Binghamton, NY: Haworth Press.

Thyer, B. A., Artelt, T., Markward, M. K., & Dozier, C. (1998). Evaluating learning in social work education: A replication study. *Journal of Social Work Education, 34*, 291–295.

Wilke, D., & Vinton, L. (2006). Evaluation of the first web-based advanced standing MSW program. *Journal of Social Work Education, 42*(3), 607–619.

Group Work Research

Evidence-Based Group Work

Mark J. Macgowan

Evidence-based practice (EBP) has made substantial inroads in social work. There is an expanding literature on EBP in general (Briggs & Rzepnicki, 2004; Cournoyer, 2004; Gibbs, 2003; Roberts & Yeager, 2004) and in special areas such as family work (Corcoran, 2000) and field work (Thomlison & Corcoran, 2007). Yet, until recently, there has been little written about EBP for group work, despite a rich history of research in groups, and strong evidence supporting the efficacy of group work.

Evidence-based group work (EBGW) may be defined as a process of the judicious and skillful application in group work of the best evidence, based on research merit, impact, and applicability, using evaluation to ensure desired results are achieved (Macgowan, 2008). As a critical process, EBGW involves clinical expertise, which consists of weighing the practice context and circumstances (e.g., group situation and context), client preferences and actions, and research evidence (Haynes, Sackett, Gray, Cook, & Guyatt, 1996). EBGW is not a separate approach to group work, but rather builds on a foundation of group work theory and practice by including a structured process to incorporate the best available evidence to improve practice. It evolved out of developments in evidence-based medicine and evidence-based practice and systematically integrates into practice the best available research evidence while at the same time integrating the needs and desires of group members. This entry defines evidence, discusses the rationale for EBGW and how it fits into the history of social group work, outlines the four stages of EBGW, and describes a plan for advancing EBGW in research, practice, and education.

The term "evidence" generally refers to "unobserved as well as observed phenomena if the former reflects signs or indications that support, substantiate, or prove their existence, accuracy, or truth" (Cournoyer, 2004, p. 3). However, phenomena that are unexamined or unobserved are considered less credible than evidence derived from observation, experience, or experimentation (Cournoyer, 2004). Those phenomena subject to observation include clinical experience, results from own practice evaluation, expert opinion, case studies, randomized clinical trials, and meta-analyses (Cournoyer, 2004; Pollio, 2002).

There are differences in the literature as to what is considered the "best" evidence. Some consider the best evidence as strictly research-based. Others suggest a broader conceptualization including all knowledge, such as that acquired from both quantitative and qualitative research studies, expert opinion, and the results of personal practice evaluations, as long as the evidence "yields documentary support for the conclusion that a practice or service has a reasonable probability of effectiveness" (Cournoyer, 2004, p. 14). Many of the definitions agree that evidence must be the most rigorous available and appropriate for the client's situation, preferences, values, and needs. These two areas become part of the essential ingredients in determining the *best available* evidence.

EBGW is important for the advancement of group work for several reasons. First, group workers are increasingly held accountable for what they do in practice. EBGW provides tools to assess, evaluate, monitor, and improve practice. Second, increasing knowledge and skills by using the best evidence available is part of social work's values and Code of Ethics (National Association of Social Workers, 1999, Standard 4.01). The *Standards for the Practice of Social Work with Groups* states that group workers should include in their practice "monitoring and evaluation of success of group in accomplishing its objectives through personal observation, as well as collecting information in order to assess outcomes and processes" (Association for the Advancement of Social Work with Groups, 2006, Section 1F). Third, although most research supports the helpfulness of group work (Burlingame, Fuhriman, & Mosier, 2003), group work can be harmful in certain circumstances (Coyne, 1999; Galinsky & Schopler, 1994; Smokowski, Rose, & Bacallao, 2001). An EBGW perspective requires group workers to be aware of these findings in order to incorporate practices that are beneficial and avoid practices that might cause harm.

Although the term EBGW is new, some of its elements can be seen in the history of social group work and in the empirical practice movement of the last 40 years. For example, the development of schools of social welfare (such as Case Western Reserve University) stimulated the growth of science-based practice (Wilson, 1976). Early research studies involving social group workers identified not only the benefits but also the possible pitfalls of group work (e.g., Lewin, Lippitt, & White, 1939; Newstetter & Feldstein, 1930). Grace Coyle's address to the American Association of Group Workers (Coyle, 1948, pp. 81–97) highlighted the need for social group workers to develop and use a body of knowledge, or evidence, in practice. Other social group work theorists over the decades, such as Margaret Hartford, Helen Northen, and Robert Vinter, advanced an understanding of how groups can be demonstrably helpful to clients (Hartford, 1976). In addition, developments in the empirical practice movement helped to specify how research could be used in practice (Blythe & Briar, 1985; Goldstein, 1962; Jayaratne & Levy, 1979; Reid, 1994).

However, only recently have publications described the process and content of evidence-based practice for group work. In the first publication about EBGW, Pollio defined it as "the conscientious and judicious use of evidence in current best practice" (Pollio, 2002, p. 57). Macgowan (2006, 2008) built on this foundation, and provided a systematic process that included resources for undertaking EBGW.

EBP is a process in which practitioners: (a) use findings based on best available evidence that demonstrates predictable and effective results; (b) use clinical expertise and professional ethics; (c) collaborate with clients with their best interests in mind, considering the values and judgments of clients; and (d) evaluate outcomes to see whether predicted results for clients are achieved (Gibbs, 2003; Haynes et al., 1996; Rosenthal, 2004). EBGW incorporates these themes, which are operationalized through a series of four stages in which group workers: 1) formulate an answerable practice question; 2) search for evidence; 3) undertake a critical review of the evidence (with respect to research merit, impact, and applicability), which yields the best available evidence; and 4) apply the evidence with judgment, skill, and concern for relevance and appropriateness for the group, utilizing evaluation to determine if desired outcomes are achieved (adapted from: Berg, 2000; Rosenthal, 2004; Straus, Richardson, Glasziou, & Haynes, 2005). These four stages may be briefly summarized.

The first stage begins with posing a question of concern or challenge that serves the needs of the group members. Questions must be member-relevant, answerable, and practical (MAP). To be member-relevant, questions must either help group members or be from group members. To be answerable, questions must be answered effectively and efficiently, as quickly as possible. Practical questions are concerned with practice rather than theory and are questions of real concern to the group worker or group members. MAP questions may come from the group worker or group members. Examples of questions from a worker include, "How do I increase verbal participation among group members?" and "What is the most effective group intervention for reducing depression among teens?" An example of a group member question may be, "Will this group really help me?" If the question meets the MAP criteria, then it is further refined to be suitable for a search.

The second stage is to undertake a search for evidence. An important part of EBGW is that it requires one to expand beyond convenient evidence (e.g., one's own experience or one's own possibly antiquated library) and to engage in a systematic collection and appraisal of best available new evidence. Relying only on what one knows and has experienced limits the potential sources of new evidence that may help improve practice. Given that there are millions of articles published annually, searches must be effective in finding the right evidence and efficient in finding the right evidence as quickly as possible. Knowing how and where to look helps speed the process (Macgowan, 2008).

The third stage involves completing a critical review of the evidence, yielding the *best available evidence*. The evidence (e.g., article, book, material) is evaluated in the following three areas: rigor, impact, and applicability. First, workers evaluate the research merit of the evidence, or its trustworthiness or validity (rigor). Group workers also evaluate the impact of the evidence; that is, how powerful and in what direction are the findings. Third, they evaluate the practice relevance and appropriateness (applicability) of the avidence for their own groups. All three elements are essential for determining whether evidence is appropriate for a clinical circumstance. There are many cases in which the quality within the three areas will vary, and group workers must use clinical expertise to determine whether and how they should use the evidence. Conceivably, the best available evidence may not be the most rigorous or impactful research study, but one with stronger applicability (see Macgowan, 2008, for examples).

The fourth stage involves applying the evidence and utilizing evaluation to determine if desired outcomes are achieved. Clinical expertise is again used in weighing the group situation and context, group member preferences and actions, and research evidence. The worker must balance the *research* concern of maintaining fidelity to the essential ingredients of the original evidence (to ensure the delivery of the intervention or technique to achieve success) and the *clinical* concern of ensuring that the evidence is relevant to the group situation. This balancing act has been described as the "art" of evidence-based practice (Pollio, 2006). Once the strategy is applied, the group worker evaluates the effects of the action to determine whether the desired results are achieved, using conventional methods for the evaluation of practice. Application and evaluation are not separate endeavors but are intertwined in a circular and iterative process. Thus, the process does not end with knowing whether the strategy "worked," but continues with a systematic, critical process of improving practice, based on the ongoing results of the application in practice and evaluation.

These stages are described in their ideal form, which is not often achieved in practice due to limitations of the existing research base, barriers in practice, and educational models that are non-facilitative. For EBGW to be considered a regular part of group work there needs to be enhancements and adaptations in these areas.

For EBGW to thrive, developments are needed in research, practice settings, and education. Good research evidence is a foundation of EBGW. More studies are needed to guide practice, especially about unstructured open-ended groups and about questions that group workers regularly face in their practice (e.g., how to increase cohesion). To advance EBGW in clinical settings several recommendations may be made. Time-burdened group workers would benefit from pre-appraised research that is readily available. An example is the synoptic journal, such as the *ACP Journal Club* (www.acpjc.org) and its companion Web site, which summarizes the best evidence from traditional journals. Similar journals and Web sites for group work are needed. The Association for the Advancement of Social Work with Groups at the national or Chapter level could form collaborative practice–research networks that include group work practitioners and faculty. Members of these EBGW journal clubs and networks could find and evaluate evidence related to common group work concerns or issues and post their reviews on a Web site.

There are a couple of avenues for the adoption and development of EBGW in practice settings. Group workers, or the organizations in which they work, may have access to a consultant or research specialist with allotted time to complete a review of rigor and impact. In organizations without any such support, there are ways that group workers could foster at least initial organizational support for EBGW or for implementing particular evidence-based interventions (for strategies, see Macgowan, 2008).

EBGW must also be supported and sustained by education, which may occur in two contexts: as part of degree-granting programs in higher education or as part of continuing education. In either of these contexts, traditional teaching methods are not suitable. The optimal andragogical model combines didactic and problem-based learning/practice-based learning (PBL) approaches. PBL "is an instructional method that encourages learners to apply critical thinking, problem-solving skills, and content knowledge to real-world problems and issues" (Levin, 2001, p. 1). This model is ideally suited for teaching EBGW, as it instructs in the process of critical thinking as students develop evidence-based solutions to real group work problems. EBGW is best taught in a curriculum-wide approach that teaches the principles of EBP across courses and includes internship supervisors who have been trained in EBP (Rubin et al., 2007; Thomlison & Corcoran, 2007).

References

Association for the Advancement of Social Work with Groups. (2006). *Standards for social work practice with groups* (2nd ed.). Retrieved May 2, 2007 from http://www.aaswg.org/

Berg, A. O. (2000). Dimensions of evidence. In J. P. Geyman, R. A. Deyo, & S. D. Ramsey (Eds.), *Evidence-based clinical practice* (pp. 21–27). Woburn, MA: Butterworth-Heinemann.

Blythe, B. J., & Briar, S. (1985). Developing empirically-based models of practice. *Social Work, 30*(6), 483–488.

Briggs, H. E., & Rzepnicki, T. L. (2004). *Using evidence in social work practice: Behavioral perspectives.* Chicago: Lyceum Books.

Burlingame, G. M., Fuhriman, A., & Mosier, J. (2003). The differential effectiveness of group psychotherapy: A meta-analytic perspective. *Group Dynamics: Theory, Research, and Practice, 7*(1), 3–12.

Corcoran, J. (2000). *Evidence-based social work practice with families: A lifespan approach.* New York: Springer.

Cournoyer, B. R. (2004). *The evidence-based social work (EBSW) skills book.* Boston: Allyn & Bacon.

Coyle, G. L. (1948). *Group experience and democratic values.* New York: The Woman's Press.

Coyne, R. K. (1999). *Failures in group work.* Thousand Oaks, CA: Sage.

Galinsky, M. J., & Schopler, J. H. (1994). Negative experiences in support groups. *Social Work in Health Care, 20*(1), 77–95.

Gibbs, L. (2003). *Evidence-based practice for the helping professions.* Pacific Grove, CA: Thomson Brooks/Cole.

Goldstein, H. K. (1962). Making practice more scientific through knowledge of research. *Social Work, 7*(1), 108–112.

Hartford, M. E. (1976). Group methods and generic practice. In R. W. Roberts, & H. Northen (Eds.), *Theories of social work with groups* (pp. 45–74). New York: Columbia University Press.

Haynes, R. B., Sackett, D. L., Gray, J. M., Cook, D. J., & Guyatt, G. H. (1996). Transferring evidence from research into practice: 1. The role of clinical care research evidence in clinical decisions. *ACP Journal Club, 125*(3), A14–A16.

Jayaratne, S., & Levy, R. L. (1979). *Empirical clinical practice.* New York: Columbia University Press.

Levin, B. B. (2001). *Energizing teacher education and professional development with problem-based learning.* Alexandria, VA: Association for Supervision and Curriculum Development.

Lewin, K., Lippitt, R., & White, R. K. (1939). Patterns of aggressive behavior in experimentally created "social climates." *Journal of Social Psychology, 10*, 271–299.

Macgowan, M. J. (2006). Evidence-based group work: A framework for advancing best practice. *Journal of Evidence-based Social Work, 3*(1), 1–21.

Macgowan, M. J. (2008). *A guide to evidence-based group work.* New York: Oxford University Press.

National Association of Social Workers. (1999). *Code of Ethics of the National Association of Social Workers.* Retrieved June 20, 2004 from http://naswdc.org/pubs/code/code.asp

Newstetter, W. I., & Feldstein, M. J. (1930). *Wawokiye camp: A research project in group work.* Cleveland, OH: School of Applied Social Sciences, Western Reserve University.

Pollio, D. E. (2002). The evidence-based group worker. *Social Work with Groups, 25*(4), 57–70.

Pollio, D. E. (2006). The art of evidence-based practice. *Research on Social Work Practice, 16*(2), 224–232.

Reid, W. J. (1994). The empirical practice movement. *Social Service Review, 68*(2), 165–184.

Roberts, A. R., & Yeager, K. (Eds.). (2004). *Evidence-based practice manual: Research and outcome measures in health and human services.* New York: Oxford University Press.

Rosenthal, R. N. (2004). Overview of evidence-based practice. In A. R. Roberts, & K. Yeager (Eds.), *Evidence-based practice manual: Research and outcome measures in health and human services* (pp. 20–29). New York: Oxford University Press.

Rubin, A., Corcoran, K., Gambril, E., Howard, M. O., Allen-Meares, P., Ruffolo, M. C., et al. (2007). Special issue: Conference on improving the teaching of evidence-based practice in social work (Austin, Texas, October 16–18, 2006). *Research on Social Work Practice, 17*(5).

Smokowski, P. R., Rose, S. D., & Bacallao, M. (2001). Damaging experiences in therapeutic groups: How vulnerable consumers become group casualties. *Small Group Research, 28*(1), 9–22.

Straus, S. E., Richardson, W. S., Glasziou, P., & Haynes, R. B. (2005). *Evidence-based medicine: How to practice and teach EBM* (3rd ed.). Edinburgh: Churchill Livingstone.

Thomlison, B., & Corcoran, K. (2007). *The evidence-based internship: A field manual for social work and criminal justice.* New York: Oxford University Press.

Wilson, G. (1976). From practice to theory: A personalized history. In R. W. Roberts, & H. Northen (Eds.), *Theories of social work with groups* (pp. 1–44). New York: Columbia University Press.

Focus Group

Lawrence C. Shulman and Michele G. Shedlin

The focus group session/interview is a *qualitative research method* appropriate to all social and behavioral sciences. There are significant differences between the objectives and methodologies of social work groups and these facilitated interviews designed for the collection of group data.

Social work groups are essentially gateways to helping people who are experiencing stressful life circumstances, events or conditions to move toward health and well-being. They are used for personal, family or community problem solving, social inclusion and empowerment. Social work groups facilitate growth for vulnerable and troubled people, networks and communities by utilizing mutual aid for reducing barriers and improving access, providing resources, and providing safe spaces for experiencing therapeutic resolutions or developing improved coping abilities of major life issues (Gitterman & Shulman, 2005). These groups may be talk-focused or utilize activities as the vehicle for growth; the client system and its needs are central to its purpose.

The "focus group" as a research technique, the term thought to have been coined by Robert Merton in 1956 (Denzin & Lincoln, 1994), was initially developed as an investigative technique, became primary in private sector marketing research, and is now increasingly used by academe and public and non-profit agencies as a qualitative research tool. Prior to the mid-1980s, there was little available literature on the use of focus groups as a social science research method (Stewart, Shamdasani, & Rook, 2007). Since the early 1990s numerous publications have expanded the theory and practice of focus groups for use in social, health, and policy research (Krueger & Casey, 2000; Morgan, 1998; Stewart et al., 2007).

Research focus groups are informal, structured, time-limited discussions, involving a small number of respondents ($n = 6$–12) in homogeneous groups of individuals with similar characteristics and/or experiences (Morgan, 1993; Patton, 1990; Stewart et al., 2007). A single group interview, or a series of groups each with different participants, are carried out in a nurturing and encouraging environment to explore topics central to the research question(s) (Krueger & Casey, 2000; Patton, 1990). Focus groups seek to obtain group rather than individual data. As such, they elicit social norms rather than personal histories. The group data obtained from these exploratory sessions provide insights into the *meanings* of behaviors and events within the research domains as seen by specific groups or communities. The group dynamic and sharing of personal experiences and concerns also provide an understanding of the range of attitudes and perceptions in the larger group they represent. Focus groups utilize group processes to elicit data that would be less accessible through other qualitative research methods, such as individual interviews and participant observation (Linhorst, 2002). According to Kitzinger (1995, p. 299), "The method is particularly useful for exploring people's knowledge and experiences and can be used to examine not only what people think but how they think and why they think that way." Focus groups can be employed in a broad number of contexts and can obtain data that can inform social agency needs assessments, program design, and evaluation. The sessions are used to explore complex issues, to describe the context of other research or program findings, and to discover new ideas, issues, concerns, and connections within research domains (Morgan, 1993). Transcriptions provide descriptive detail and actual quotes from participants, instrumental in illustrating the experiences, concerns, beliefs, and language preferences. Focus group interviews are a cost-effective approach and provide quick access to information from new or understudied areas, topics, or groups. Frequently, such data are used to complement, test, and add rigor to other research techniques ("triangulation") (Morgan, 1993). Focus groups pose certain challenges, disadvantages, and ethical complexities. Group data collection is not anonymous and confidentiality cannot be assured. Moreover, the small number of participants and selection criteria bias create difficulties in generalizing or estimating the prevalence of ideas or behaviors reported in the focus groups. Similarly, misusing the group process to force consensus, resolve differences, or conflicts can also generate invalid conclusions. Generally, quantitative conclusions from focus group data should be drawn most cautiosuly. Essentially, focus groups should be used primarily for exploration and learning rather than for generalizing.

A key to the success of any group process is the skill and flexibility of the facilitator. Social group workers represent an effective cohort from which to recruit focus group research facilitators. They are taught to deal with a range of group dynamics, as well as individual differences among participants. They are also educated to be attentive to verbal or non-verbal cues that indicate that disclosure of information. Social group workers can also provide a unique viewpoint and understanding of ethical issues in research, and the subtleties of discrimination and social/economic justice in our society. Patience, a sense of humor, ability to be non-judgmental, and an understanding of the target population and its environment and risk behaviors are crucial, advanced skills, usually honed in social work education.

Focus group moderators generally follow an interview guide that includes questions, prompts, tasks, and exercises (Krueger & Casey, 2000; Stewart et al., 2007). The moderator must generate interest in the topic, involve all the participants, keep the discussion on track (but also allow for unexpected diversions or new areas into which the discussion may lead), keep dominant personalities from overwhelming other participants, deal with unresolved personal or session issues, and guide participants to appropriate resources if required, all valued social group work skills. Skills, practice, and experience are the critical factors in becoming an effective facilitator/moderator.

Focus group moderators must always remember the purpose of these groups. If the moderator does not maintain a clear research purpose, a focus group session could spontaneously convert to a therapeutic or advocacy session (Shedlin, 2004). Kitzinger and Barbour (1999) caution: "Like any research method ... they are open to careless or inappropriate use, the results may be manipulated and 'subjects' of the research can be exploited" (pp. 1–2).

A considerable literature is presently available to the social work field for building skills and guiding focus group research, including: planning, development of guides, structuring and moderating the sessions, and analyzing and utilizing the data (Linhorst, 2002; Morgan, 1993, 1998; Patton, 1990; Stewart et al., 2007)

An increasing body of social work-generated, methodologically rigorous focus group research will expand the use of this method as it continues to inform both research and practice in the social group work research field (Cohen & Garrett, 1999; Linhorst, 2002). Increasing attention is being given to the complex theoretical, pragmatic and ethical issues of the uses of focus group research. Applying social group work's knowledge of, and sensitivity to, group development, structure and process can inform and modify focus group techniques and add to this qualitative method's rich potential (Cohen & Garrett, 1999).

References

Cohen, M. B., & Garrett, K. J. (1999) Breaking the rules: A group work perspective on focus group research. *British Journal of Social Work, 29*, 359–372.

Denzin, N. K., & Lincoln, Y. S. (1994). *Handbook of qualitative research*. London: Sage.

Gitterman, A., & Shulman, L. (2005). *Mutual aid groups, vulnerable and resilient populations and the life cycle* (3rd ed.). New York: Columbia University Press.

Kitzinger, J. (1995). Qualitative research: Introducing focus groups. *British Medical Journal, 29*(July), 299–302. Retrieved August 10, 2007, from http://www.bmj.com/cgi/content/full/311/7000/299

Kitzinger, J., & Barbour, R. S. (1999) Introduction: The challenge and promise of focus groups. In R. S. Barbour, & J. Kitzinger (Eds.), *Developing focus group research: Politics, theory, and practice* (pp. 1–20). Thousand Oaks, CA: Sage.

Krueger, R. A., & Casey, M. A. (2000). *Focus groups: A practical guide for applied research* (3rd ed.). Thousand Oaks, CA: Sage.

Linhorst, D. M. (2002) A review of the use and potential of focus groups in social work research. *Qualitative Social Work, 1*(2), 208–228.

Morgan, D. L. (Ed.). (1993). *Successful focus groups: Advancing the state of the art*. Thousands Oaks, CA: Sage.

Morgan, D. L. (1998). *Planning focus groups*. Thousands Oaks, CA: Sage.

Patton, M. Q. (1990). *Qualitative evaluation and research methods* (2nd ed.). Thousand Oaks, CA: Sage.

Shedlin, M. G. (2004). Research vs. support: Focus group participants living with HIV/AIDS. In P. R. Ullin, E. T. Robinson, & E. E. Tolley (Eds.), *Qualitative methods: A field guide for applied research in sexual and reproductive health* (2nd ed., pp. 110–111). San Francisco: Jossey-Bass.

Stewart, D. W., Shamdasani, P. N., & Rook, D. W. (2007). *Focus groups: Theory and practice* (2nd ed.). Thousands Oaks, CA: Sage.

Intervention Research

Maeda J. Galinsky and Mark W. Fraser

Intervention research (IR) is a fundamental ingredient in developing evidence-based group work practice. IR involves the design and development of new interventions or fine-tuning existing interventions (Fraser, 2003). Using the methods of IR, new modes of group work practice are formulated, based on experience, theory, and research. These innovations are then tested in the laboratory, clinic, or the field and systematically refined. This process provides the foundation for evidence-based practice (EBP).

EBP uses knowledge as a base from which to derive practice principles and content for individual, family, group, community, or organizational interventions. This knowledge has many sources, and may stem from study findings, from theory, or from practice experience. However, the core idea of EBP is to select and use interventions derived from the results of empirical studies. Practitioners apply evidence-based intervention informed by their own or others' experience with the particular population or the practice setting in which the intervention was tested. If EBP is to penetrate practice widely, conducting an increasing number of studies is imperative to provide a rich data foundation for practice.

IR is foundational for EBP because it not only prescribes a process for developing knowledge about the effectiveness of interventions but also places a premium on creation of practice-related resources. Our concept of IR derives from the work of Rothman and Thomas (1994) that specified a six-stage framework for IR: (a) problem analysis and project planning; (b) information gathering and synthesis; (c) intervention design; (d) early development and pilot testing; (e) evaluation and advanced development; and (f) dissemination. Drawing on their pioneering work, we have further synthesized IR (Fraser, Richman, Galinsky, & Day, in press) and further articulated the development of both the program materials and the research processes, and created a model of IR that includes five steps: (a) specify problem and program theory; (b) create and revise program materials; (c) refine and confirm program components; (d) assess effectiveness in a variety of settings and circumstances; and (e) disseminate findings and program materials. At each step, the intervention is refined and adapted for different populations and settings.

An important aspect of IR is the development of program materials, especially treatment manuals. Treatment manuals serve as guides to practice, and their careful development ensures interventions are sufficiently articulated to produce a testable program that, if found effective, can be replicated (Carroll & Nuro, 2002). Manuals vary in the extent of flexibility practitioners are given to develop content, such as role-plays or discussion. Some manuals require that content be presented in a particular sequence, whereas others permit variation depending on group composition and members' needs. Furthermore, practice manuals often contain tips for implementation, such as suggestions to promote engagement, attendance, or compliance (Fraser et al., in press).

IR is rooted in practice. It is imperative that those designing or testing interventions are actively involved with practitioners at each step in the IR process. Research questions, the design of interventions, and the application of the intervention benefit from practitioner ideas and experience. To this aim, feedback is sought from group workers throughout IR.

Many group work practitioners and researchers are involved in IR (e.g., Fraser et al., 2005; Heimberg & Becker, 2002; Roffman et al., 1997; Rounds, Galinsky, & Despard, 1995; Smith & Toseland, 2006), and many have interventions at various stages of development. We illustrate the five steps of IR with the *Making Choices* intervention, a group-oriented program with which we have been engaged for more than 10 years.

Making Choices began when Mark Fraser recognized a need for programs to help prevent and deal with aggression in children, especially peer rejection. His talks with group workers and a thorough review of the research indicated that using social information processing in designing an intervention might provide a means to reach these goals. A manual for use with children was developed (Fraser, Nash, Galinsky, & Darwin, 2000). Pilot tests of the intervention in small groups and in classrooms showed that the program was feasible, that it produced positive results, and that it could be implemented in the field (Nash, Fraser, Galinsky, & Kupper, 2003). In addition, earlier tests indicated that a separate section on emotions and emotional regulation (i.e., controlling arousal and anger) would be helpful. The intervention manual has seven units, including one on emotional regulation and six units reflecting the six steps of social information processing. Goals, content, and activities are specified for the three to five sessions that make up each of the seven units. Since its initial formulation, design, and pilot testing, the manual has been further revised and retested in public school settings (Fraser et al., 2005). During the revision process, the researchers have paid particular attention to population variations and organizational settings. For example, the manual is being translated into Chinese, with consideration given to ensuring that both content and activities are culturally congruent.

As seen in the creation of *Making Choices*, innovation and creative development are core features of IR. For example, a positive experience with group work in an agency may give practitioners an idea for a new intervention. To test that hunch, the practitioners might begin the IR process by turning to the literature to shore up their ideas, creating a program manual, and fielding it in a pilot test. This kind of innovation is common in practice, and helps to refine practice principles, even if these innovations are not tested further in rigorous research.

Although it is important to have a written manual in IR, practice skill is an important aspect of any intervention (Galinsky, Terzian, & Fraser, 2006). Practitioner experience is one of the three defined parts of EBP, along with research findings and client preferences (Sackett, Rosenberg, Gray, Haynes, & Richardson, 1996). Practitioners must rely on their practice skill to make decisions about how to apply the intervention, based on their assessments of the needs of the group, culture, and organizational characteristics, as well as other factors, such as practice standards and codes of ethics. For example, practitioner experiences and intuitive processes may suggest a different sequence of activities, a less-structured session, or a focus on members' immediate issues. Although group workers need to implement required interventions, they have some flexibility; in fact, some manuals call for flexibility in application. As information is gathered from research, the practice principles may be altered. IR does not require a rigid by-the-numbers approach to practice.

Evidence-based group work practice is not possible without studies that provide information about successful group interventions (Macgowan, 2008). In providing a means to design, develop, and refine interventions, IR uses and, ultimately, strengthens reports of successful practice. Increased examination of interventions using IR will lead to creative new practice principles and promising new programs. Collectively, the results of IR should help to formulate new foundations for best practices in group work.

References

Carroll, K. M., & Nuro, N. F. (2002). One size cannot fit all: A stage model for psychotherapy manual development. *Clinical Psychology: Science and Practice, 9*, 396–406.

Fraser, M. W. (2003). Intervention research in social work: A basis for evidence-based practice and practice guidelines. In A. Rosen, & E. K. Proctor (Eds.), *Developing practice for social work interventions: Issues, methods, and research agenda* (pp. 17–36). New York: Columbia University Press.

Fraser, M. W., Galinsky, M. J., Smokowski, P. R., Day, S. H., Terzian, M. A., Rose, R. A., et al. (2005). Social information-processing skills training to promote social competence and prevent aggressive behavior in third grade. *Journal of Consulting and Clinical Psychology, 73*, 1045–1055.

Fraser, M. W., Nash, J. K., Galinsky, M. J., & Darwin, K. E. (2000). *Making Choices: Social problem-solving skills for children*. Washington, DC: NASW Press.

Fraser, M.W., Richman, J. M., Galinsky, M. J., & Day, S. H. (in press). *Intervention research: Designing and developing social interventions*. New York: Oxford University Press.

Galinsky, M. J., Terzian, M. A., & Fraser, M. W. (2006). The art of group work practice using manualized curricula. *Social Work Practice with Groups, 29*, 11–26.

Heimberg, R. G., & Becker, R. E. (2002). *Cognitive-behavioral group therapy for social phobia*. New York: Guilford Press.

Macgowan, M. J. (2008). *A guide to evidence-based group work*. New York: Oxford University Press.

Nash, J. K., Fraser, M. W., Galinsky, M. J., & Kupper, L. L. (2003). Early development and pilot testing of a problem-solving skills-training program for children. *Research on Social Work Practice, 13*, 432–450.

Roffman, R. A., Picciano, J. F., Ryan, R., Beadnell, B., Fisher, D., Lowney, L., et al. (1997). HIV-prevention group counseling delivered by telephone: An efficacy trial with gay and bisexual men. *AIDS and Behavior, 1*, 137–154.

Rothman, J., & Thomas, E. J. (1994). *IR: Design and development for the human services.* New York: Haworth Press.

Rounds, K. A., Galinsky, M. J., & Despard, M. R. (1995). Intervention design and development: The results of a field test of telephone support groups for persons with HIV disease. *Research on Social Work Practice, 5,* 442–459.

Sackett, D. L., Rosenberg, W. M., Gray, J. A., Haynes, R. B., & Richardson, W. S. (1996). Evidence-based medicine: What it is and what it isn't. *British Medical Journal, 312,* 71–72.

Smith, T., & Toseland, R. (2006). The evaluation of a telephone caregiver support group intervention. *The Gerontologist, 46,* 620–630.

Measurement

Mark J. Macgowan

Measures in group work assess the presence and degree of a wide range of phenomena related to group processes, structures, and outcomes. Although measures have been developed primarily for research purposes, many are suitable for group work practice. This entry describes: a) the function of measurement in social group work; (b) how to select measures for practice; and c) a number of psychometrically sound (i.e., reliable and valid) and practice-suitable (i.e., relatively short and easy to administer and score) measures that can be used by social group workers.

Measurement means "assigning numbers or symbols to things" (Vogt, 1999, p. 173). In group work it involves the use of an instrument that measures a concept related either to group member concerns (typically called "group outcomes") or to group conditions (often called "group processes"). Examples of concepts related to member concerns include depression, anxiety, self-esteem, and social skills. Examples of concepts related to group conditions include cohesion, leadership, and group development.

Measures may serve many functions in group work. One function is assessment and diagnosis. A measure or instrument (the terms are used interchangeably) may be used to record the presence or level of a concept at one point of time. Examples include diagnosing depression among group members, assessing the level of cohesion within the group, and assessing group leader behavior and skills.

A second function is determining effectiveness. When coupled with an appropriate evaluation design, a measure is essential for determining the effectiveness of a particular intervention in reducing member concerns or in improving group conditions over time. For example, the effectiveness of a group intervention in reducing alcohol and other drug use (AOD) may be demonstrated by comparing pre- and post-intervention AOD levels (Battjes et al., 2004). In another example, a worker may evaluate a group member's level of engagement at one point of time, utilize strategies to increase engagement, and re-evaluate engagement at a later time to evaluate the effectiveness of the worker's strategies (Macgowan, 2003).

Related to the function of effectiveness is accountability. Measures may be used to hold group workers accountable to themselves ("how am I doing?"), to group

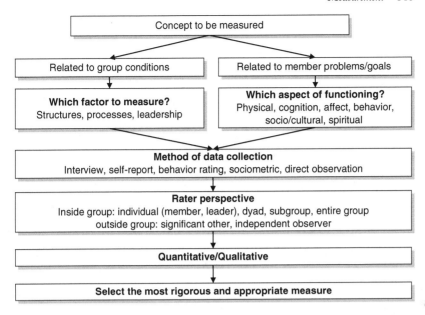

Figure 1 Stages and dimensions of measurement in group work.

members ("this is how our group is doing"), and to administrators ("this is how our service is doing").

In deciding which measure to use and when, how, and with whom it should be used, clinical expertise is needed, which involves weighing the practice context and circumstances (e.g., group situation and context), group member preferences and actions, and research evidence (Haynes, Sackett, Gray, Cook, & Guyatt, 1996). In the hands of a skilled group worker, measures are powerful tools for evaluating the helpfulness of group work (see entry on Evidence-Based Group Work in this encyclopedia).

Figure 1 depicts some of the dimensions of measurement in group work. It also depicts a process in selecting a suitable measure, a process in which group workers might have choices if there are multiple measures of a concept. For example, there are many conceptualizations—and corresponding measures—of group cohesion. Each conceptualization brings a particular bias or view of the concept, and the group worker may need to judge which measure is most fitting with his or her values, knowledge, and skills. The following discussion briefly describes the stages and dimensions noted in Figure 1.

The first step is to identify the concept to be measured. Concepts in group work tend to be related either to member problems/goals or to group conditions (distinguished above). Member problems or goals relate to functioning in the different areas depicted in the figure, and may include reducing problems related to psychosocial diagnostic categories (e.g., depression, anxiety), or achieving a positive goal such as effective coping skills, better knowledge, or stronger spirituality.

Another dimension of measurement is the method of data collection, which will also often dictate from whose perspective the data are to be collected. Group workers may sometimes use a face-to-face interview. An example is the Group Assessment Form (Lynn, 1994) used to screen prospective adolescents for group work. A self-report is useful for assessing personal concerns that group members may not readily disclose face-to-face. An example is the Group Leader Self-Efficacy Instrument (Page, Pietrzak, & Lewis, 2001). Behavior rating scales are a standardized format for making summative judgments about behavior characteristics, completed by another person, such as a group leader. An example is the Group Counselor Behavior Rating Form (Corey & Corey, 1987, pp. 36–38; DeLucia & Bowman, 1991). Sociograms have been used in group work for decades as a method for mapping relations among group members. An example is the Group Therapy Interaction Chronogram (Cox, 1973; Reder, 1978). Direct observation involves raters who collect data by watching others. Examples include the Systematic Multiple Level Observation of Groups (SYM-LOG, Bales, Cohen, & Williamson, 1979; Kutner & Kirsch, 1985; Polley, Hare, & Stone, 1988) and the comparatively simple charts for recording the frequency of group interaction described by Toseland and Rivas (2005, p. 240).

Measures may also be quantitative or qualitative. Quantitative measures require that responses be recorded numerically (e.g., 1 = very untrue, 2 = untrue, etc.) using closed-ended questions. The advantage of these measures is that answers can be ranked or summed and an overall score obtained. Quantitative measures are often constructed out of well-defined theory and empirical research and thus responses fit into pre-defined categories. Most of the examples of measures cited in this entry are quantitative.

Qualitative measures include open-ended questions inviting responses that are in narrative form. These responses can eventually be coded into numbers, but only after careful examination. There are many such qualitative measures in group work. To record what occurs within groups, there is the classic process recording (Wilson & Ryland, 1949, pp. 76–80) and a narrative verbatim record of the session including worker reactions and supervisor analysis (Wilson, 1980, pp. 18–26, 89–98). A structured format that is more selective in what it records is the critical incident record, such as William Schwartz's matrix that analyzes worker responses in group situations (Berman-Rossi, 1994, pp. 764–767). There are also process–outcome instruments such as the Group Work Recording Form (Garvin, 1997, pp. 199–200) and Record of Service (Berman-Rossi, 1994, pp. 768–769; Shulman, 2006, pp. 226, 387–393, 597–599). These methods are helpful for gathering in-depth information about group work, which can be used to supplement information provided by quantitative measures.

The last element in the process is selecting the most rigorous and applicable measure. Measures should have strong rigor; that is, good reliability and validity. Reliability has to do with consistency; reliable measures collect the same information each time in repeated observations of the same phenomenon (Rubin & Babbie, 2008). Types of reliability include internal consistency, interrater reliability, and test–retest. Validity has to do with accuracy; that is, valid measures accurately reflect the concepts they are intended to measure (Rubin & Babbie, 2008). There are many forms of validity, such as face validity, criterion validity (e.g., concurrent and predictive validity), and construct validity (e.g., convergent or divergent validity, factor analysis).

In addition to rigor, a measure should be applicable for the persons or group with which it will be used. Applicability is determined by evaluating variables related to the group work setting (e.g., time to administer and score the measure), group worker (e.g., worker competence, compatibility with professional values and ethics), and group members (e.g., values and socio-demographics). Macgowan (2008) has provided a guide for evaluating the rigor and applicability of group-based measures, which readers may consult for more details.

Although many measures have been developed for groups, few are suitable for practice, which would require them to relatively brief and easy to administer and score. This section describes some measures suitable for practice. Measures related to member problems/goals are first described, followed by a presentation of measures related to group conditions.

A general source for a range of problem-related measures is the comprehensive *Measures for Clinical Practice* (Fischer & Corcoran, 2007). A source of outcome measures specifically for group work is the revised CORE Battery (Burlingame et al., 2006), which also includes measures of group process and tools for pre-group preparation. All the measures included in the CORE Battery have good empirical rigor. Although group workers could gather the instruments themselves, the CORE Battery is a convenient single source for a selection of process and outcome measures for group work. One of the recommended outcome measures is the 45-item Outcome Questionnaire. Both of these excellent sources include reviews and copies of the actual measures.

For measures related to group conditions, there are a number of choices. The revised CORE Battery includes eight instruments that measure the working alliance, worker empathy, group climate, group cohesion (two measures), a critical incidents questionnaire of therapeutic factors, and two group selection/screening instruments. As a selective compendium of measures, however, the CORE does not include measures related to other group factors. A few additional measures may be cited that are suitable for practice, empirically tested, and are available for preview either in the article itself or by contacting the author of the publication. Several useful measures of group leadership include the 36-item Group Leader Self-Efficacy Instrument (Page et al., 2001), the 30-item Group Counselor Behavior Rating Form (Corey & Corey, 1987, pp. 36–38; DeLucia & Bowman, 1991), and the 18-item Skilled Group Counseling Scale (Smaby, Maddux, Torres-Rivera, & Zimmick, 1999). One of the few measures developed by a social worker and which draws from social group work literature is the Group Engagement Measure, available in 37- and 27-item versions (Macgowan, 1997, 2000; Macgowan & Levenson, 2003; Macgowan & Newman, 2005). If social group work is to advance as a special form of group work, there is a critical need for more measures to be developed by social workers, based on the tradition of social group work.

References

Bales, R. F., Cohen, S. P., & Williamson, S. A. (1979). *SYMLOG: A system for the multiple level observation of groups*. New York: Free Press.

Battjes, R. J., Gordon, M. S., O'Grady, K. E., Kinlock, T. W., Katz, E. C., & Sears, E. A. (2004). Evaluation of a group-based substance abuse treatment program for adolescents. *Journal of Substance Abuse Treatment, 27*(2), 123–134.

Berman-Rossi, T. (Ed.). (1994). *Social work: The collected writings of William Schwartz*. Itasca, IL: F. E. Peacock.

Burlingame, G. M., Strauss, B., Joyce, A., MacNair-Semands, R., MacKenzie, K., Ogrodniczuk, J., et al. (2006). *CORE Battery—Revised: An assessment toolkit for promoting optimal group selection, process, and outcome*. New York: American Group Psychotherapy Association.

Corey, M. S., & Corey, G. (1987). *Groups: Process and practice* (3rd ed.). Monterey, CA: Brooks/Cole.

Cox, M. (1973). The Group Therapy Interaction Chronogram. *British Journal of Social Work, 3*, 243–256.

DeLucia, J. L., & Bowman, V. E. (1991). Internal consistency and factor structure of the Group Counselor Behavior Rating Form. *Journal for Specialists in Group Work, 16*(2), 109–114.

Fischer, J., & Corcoran, K. (2007). *Measures for clinical practice and research: A sourcebook* (4th ed., Vols. 1 & 2). New York: Oxford University Press.

Garvin, C. D. (1997). *Contemporary group work* (3rd ed.). Boston: Allyn & Bacon.

Haynes, R. B., Sackett, D. L., Gray, J. M., Cook, D. J., & Guyatt, G. H. (1996). Transferring evidence from research into practice: 1. The role of clinical care research evidence in clinical decisions. *ACP Journal Club, 125*(3), A14–A16.

Kutner, S. S., & Kirsch, R. D. (1985). Clinical application of SYMLOG: A graphic system of observing relationships. *Social Work, 30*(6), 497–503.

Lynn, G. L. (1994). The GAF: The Group Assessment Form: A screening instrument for adolescent group therapy. *Journal of Child and Adolescent Group Therapy, 4*(3), 135–146.

Macgowan, M. J. (1997). A measure of engagement for social group work: The Groupwork Engagement Measure (GEM). *Journal of Social Service Research, 23*(2), 17–37.

Macgowan, M. J. (2000). Evaluation of a measure of engagement for group work. *Research on Social Work Practice, 10*(3), 348–361.

Macgowan, M. J. (2003). Increasing engagement in groups: A measurement based approach. *Social Work with Groups, 26*(1), 5–28.

Macgowan, M. J. (2008). *A guide to evidence-based group work*. New York: Oxford University Press.

Macgowan, M. J., & Levenson, J. S. (2003). Psychometrics of the Group Engagement Measure with male sex offenders. *Small Group Research, 34*(2), 155–169.

Macgowan, M. J., & Newman, F. L. (2005). The factor structure of the Group Engagement Measure. *Social Work Research, 29*(2), 107–118.

Page, B. J., Pietrzak, D. R., & Lewis, T. F. (2001). Development of the group leader self-efficacy instrument. *Journal for Specialists in Group Work, 26*(2), 168–184.

Polley, R. B., Hare, A. P., & Stone, P. J. (1988). *The SYMLOG practitioner: Applications of small group research*. New York: Praeger.

Reder, P. (1978). An assessment of the group therapy interaction chronogram. *International Journal of Group Psychotherapy, 28*(2), 185–194.

Rubin, A., & Babbie, E. R. (2008). *Research methods for social work* (6th ed.). Belmont, CA: Thomson Brooks/Cole.

Shulman, L. (2006). *The skills of helping individuals, families, groups and communities* (5th ed.). Belmont, CA: Thomson Brooks/Cole.

Smaby, M. H., Maddux, C. D., Torres-Rivera, E., & Zimmick, R. (1999). A study of the effects of a skills-based versus a conventional group counseling training program. *Journal for Specialists in Group Work, 24*, 152–163.

Toseland, R. W., & Rivas, R. F. (2005). *An introduction to group work practice* (5th ed.). Boston: Pearson/Allyn & Bacon.

Vogt, W. P. (1999). *Dictionary of statistics and methodology: A nontechnical guide for the social sciences* (2nd ed.). Thousand Oaks, CA: Sage.

Wilson, G., & Ryland, G. (1949). *Social group work practice: The creative use of the social process.* Boston: Houghton Mifflin.

Wilson, S. J. (1980). *Recording guidelines for social workers.* New York: Free Press.

Quantitative and Qualitative Methods

Varsha Pandya

Since the recognition of social work as a profession, expectations for accountability and evidence-based practice have grown. Group work as a method of social work practice also became the focus of effectiveness studies. Unlike the proliferation of social work practice, with individuals increasingly using larger sample sizes and multivariate methods of analysis (Reid, 1995), research on group work practice remains limited in volume and the study methods used. Commonly, studies on group work practice have used small sample sizes and both quantitative methods and qualitative methods equitably. A review of main articles published in the *Journal of Social Work with Groups* from 1998 to 2006 revealed that about 16% (25/158) were research reports. Out of 25 research studies reported, 12 (48%) were quantitative, 10 (40%) were qualitative, and 3 (12%) used mixed methods. Multidisciplinary journals of group work were not examined as the focus was on research done on social work with groups.

Tolman and Molidor (1994) searched and reviewed 54 quantitative social group work research articles published in relevant social work journals during the 1980s. The authors found that the majority of these were outcome studies of closed-ended, time-limited, structured groups informed by cognitive-behavioral theory. The major focus in most studies were summative evaluations that specifically examined the extent to which intended outcomes were achieved. The predominant methods used were pre-experimental or quasi-experimental, where multiple measures were used for outcomes. A few studies tried to incorporate standardization of intervention, which has been reframed as treatment fidelity in contemporary intervention research literature. Tolman and Molidor further state that single-system models of evaluation of group work practice are undertaken by group workers but are not well known because these studies do not often get published. Measures have been selected for the intended behavioral or mood-related outcomes expected of individual group members. Sometimes the scores on outcome measures are available as records, in which case secondary analysis is useful (e.g., Miller & Mason, 2001). The group mean of the scores on these measures is used to report effectiveness of a single group or as a comparison of outcomes of two or more groups (Tolman & Molidor, 1994). Surveys are the next most common method used to find out about the experiences, satisfaction levels, and positive as well as negative consequences of group interventions from the group members' perspectives. They are also a convenient way of studying the opinion of the group members and group facilitators on a number of topics, such as leadership and group development (Gilbert, 2000).

The experimental approaches use either individual data as a unit of analysis or an aggregation of individual data to represent the group. These are useful in determining to what extent group intervention has produced pre-specified outcomes. Using individual data as a unit of analysis does not allow the researchers to discern any consequences of group work climate and activities. Aggregation of data to represent a group can produce erroneous results if within-group variation is greater than between-group variation (Glisson, 1987). Intra-class correlation proposed by Kashy and Kenny (2000) is one of the statistical techniques that could be used in future studies to estimate the influence of the group on individual decision making or change.

Glisson has further noted that quantitative approaches to produce evidence for group interventions have been limited by the lack of use of group measures. Several group measures are available to the social group work researchers: the Group Climate Questionnaire that measures stages of group development [Mackenzie, 1983], the Feelings about the Group Scale that measures group cohesion [Lieberman, Yalom, & Miles, 1973], and the Group Norms Checklist [Bond, 1983] (as cited in Anderson, 1987); the Group Leadership Functions Scale, Group Leadership Styles and the Functions Questionnaire [Hurst, Stein, Korchin, & Soskin, 1978], and Group Process Inventory (as reported and cited in Anderson, 1997); and the Group Engagement Scale (Macgowan & Newman, 2005). Besides these, some researchers have devised and used group measures such as: attraction, defined as a desire to identify with and be an accepted member of the Group (Nickerson & Coleman, 2006); group size, attendance, group structure, and the group processes. Researchers need to include relevant group work related measures in future studies.

The social work profession is gradually recognizing *qualitative* approaches for generating evidence for its practice as not only vital in investigating certain types of questions, but also as complementary to quantitative approaches. Often qualitative studies are able to explain the relationships established through quantitative study, whereas relationships proposed through inductive analysis of data can be tested through quantitative methods (Reid, 1995). Several strategies of qualitative research (observation, focus group, in-depth interview, ethnography, phenomenology, grounded theory, empowerment, etc.), as well as several methods of qualitative data analysis (categorical and theme analysis, narrative analysis, case analysis, content analysis, biographical analysis, matrix analysis), are available to social group work researchers (Miles & Huberman, 1994)). Most published literature on qualitative studies of social work with groups uses qualitative in-depth interview, focus groups, and different types of observations, and employs theme analysis as a primary method of data analysis. Garvin (2001) reviewed qualitative studies that verified different theoretical models of group development, as well as influences of gender, diversity, and the phenomenon of group think, and found that these models predominantly used these three strategies. Different qualitative strategies can be used singly or in combination to answer specific types of effectiveness research questions that focus on finding out about group process, difficulties encountered as the group move through different stages, unanticipated important outcomes, etc. Some authors (e.g., Traver, 2004) emphasize using a participatory action component when researching group work within a community where the social worker's main purpose is to build assets through empowerment of its people.

To encourage evidence-based practice of social work with groups, the volume of research on its effectiveness needs to increase; both newer and traditional methodologies for researching group work needs to be employed, and periodical reviews of findings of the studies done in fields of social work need to be published for their easy utilization by practitioners.

References

Anderson, J. D. (1987). Integrating research and practice in social work with groups. In S. D. Rose, & R. A. Feldman (Eds.), *Research in social group work* (pp. 111–124). Binghamton, NY: Haworth Press.

Anderson, J. (1997). *Social work with groups: A process model.* New York: Longman.

Garvin, C. (2001). The potential impact of small group research on social group work practice. In T. B. Kelly, T. Berman-Rossi, & S. Palombo, (Eds.), *Group work: Strategies for strengthening resiliency* (pp. 51–70). Binghamton, NY: Haworth Press.

Gilbert, M. C. (2000). Spirituality in social work with groups: Practitioners speak out. *Social Work with Groups, 22*(4), 76–84.

Glisson, C. (1987). The group versus the individual as the unit of analysis in small group research. In S. D. Rose, & R. A. Feldman (Eds.), *Research in social group work* (pp. 15–30). Binghamton, NY: Haworth Press.

Kashy, D. A., & Kenny, D. A. (2000). The analysis of data from dyads and groups. In H. T. Reis, & C. M. Judd (Eds.), *Handbook of research methods in social and personality psychology.* New York: Cambridge University Press.

Macgowan, M. J., & Newman, F. L. (2005). Factor structure of the group engagement measure. *Social Work Research, 29*(2), 107–118.

Miles, M. B., & Huberman, A. M. (1994). *Qualitative data analysis: An expanded sourcebook* (2nd ed.). Thousand Oaks, CA: Sage.

Miller, R., & Mason, S. (2001). Using group therapy to enhance treatment compliance in first episode schizophrenia. *Social Work with Groups, 24*(1), 37–51.

Nickerson, A. B., & Coleman, N. M. (2006). An exploratory study of member attraction, climate, and behavioral outcomes of anger-coping group therapy for children with emotional disturbance. *Small Groups Research, 37*(2), 115–139.

Reid, W. J. (1995). Research overview. In R. L. Edwards (Ed.-in-chief), *Encyclopedia of social work* (19th vol., 3 ed.). Washington, DC: NASW Press.

Traver, E. K. J. (2004). A chaotic dance of cultural competence: A participatory oral history project with immigrants and refugees. *Social Work with Groups, 27*(2/3), 3–22.

Tolman. R. M., & Molidor, C. E. (1994). A decade of social group work research: Trends in methodology, theory, and program development. *Research on Social Work Practice, 4*(2), 142–159.

SYMLOG

Saul S. Kutner and Ruth D. Kirsch

SYMLOG, an acronym for Systematic Multiple Level Observation of Groups was developed by Bales (1950, 1970, 1979), and culminates almost six decades of research and testing in the laboratory settings. SYMLOG is a graphic system of observing relationships. Through a field diagram, SYMLOG succinctly captures the dynamics of group interaction. Theoretically, human relationships are described and evaluated through three universal dimensions which are expressed as polarities: dominant versus submissive; friendly versus unfriendly; and instrumentally controlled versus emotionally expressive. The field diagram produces quantifiable data, and represents a graphic representation of these polarities as they apply to relationship patterns between group members, as well as the relationship patterns between the worker and group members. Similar to other means of diagrammatic assessment (e.g., genograms, ecomaps, force field analysis), SYMLOG provides a system for gathering relevant data and visually presenting them. From the ensuing field diagram, the social worker is able to identify dysfunctional patterns, including those at the interface between the worker and group members, and to plan responsive interventions.

Kutner and Kirsch (1983, 1985, 1986) promoted the utility of SYMLOG generally for social work and specifically for social work with groups. In groups, members are asked retrospectively to assess and rate their behavior in specific situations. In addition to the retrospective rating method, an act-by-act scoring method deepens the analysis. Both data collection methods obtain raw scores, which are plotted into three-dimensional field diagrams. The dimension on the vertical plane refers to Instrumentally Controlled versus Emotionally Controlled; the horizontal plane refers to Friendly versus Unfriendly; and the third dimension refers to Dominant versus Submissive. Each circle in the diagram represents the image of a person in the group from a member or worker's perspective. The relative size of the circles represents the perceived potency of the dimension. The larger the circle, the greater the potency. For example, large circles for instrumental, friendly and dominant would suggest a member's perception of another member or of one self as being friendly, task-oriented and dominant. Self-scores are additional sources of data. WISH reflects the behaviors a member wishes to express. AVOID is the behavior a members wishes to avoid.

Additional information can be gained from the field diagram by adding three inscriptions: the Dominant Triangle; the Perimeter and the Polarization–Unification Overlay. The Dominant Triangle is displayed by using a solid line to connect the three members with the highest Dominance scores. This visual transactional pattern provides the social worker with information about who dominates, the type of exhibited behavior, how similar or different they are from each other, and how close or distant they are from other group members. For example, a monopolist may exhibit one type of dominant behavior; while a scapegoater may exhibit a different type (Berman-Rossi, 1993; Galinsky & Schopler, 1994; Gitterman & Shulman, 2005; Steinberg, 1996). The Perimeter inscription, represented by a dotted line, identifies the more marginal (outermost) members. The dotted line alerts the social worker about a source of potential tension in the group. The third inscription, Polarization–Unification Overlay, consists of two large circles, which serve to organize the images in space. Group member images in the Reference circle (R circle) are perceived as being similar to each other and polarized from the members in the Opposite circle (O circle). The opposition of circles reflects the members and areas of potential conflict. Dealing with the dysfunctional communication and relationship patterns becomes a major practice task for the group worker (Gitterman & Wayne, 2003).

In between the two circles are three dotted lines. The outermost dotted line indicates the Swing Area. Members in this area indicate some ambivalence. The ambivalence might be a reflection of either the members' feelings about the group or the rater's feelings about the members. These members hold a fluid position in the group. The center dotted line, the Line of Balance, acts as a pivot for polarization. Members located at the Friendly end of the line have greatest potential for serving as group mediators. These members can be particularly helpful in mediating group development tensions related to intimacy and authority (Garland, Jones, & Kolodny, 1965; Schiller 1997, 2007). In contrast, members located at the Unfriendly end of the line are at risk of being scapegoated.

SYMLOG organizes and graphically portrays wide-ranging perceptions of individual and group processes. The diagram quickly transmits a vast amount of information and provides insights into individual and group dynamics. Transactional patterns between group members (roles, sub-grouping, leadership, conflict) become readily apparent. The ability to visualize adaptive as well as maladaptive group patterns provides the group worker with points of entry and intervention in the group system. Moreover, whereas other methods of visual representation focus principally on the client system, SYMLOG compels the social worker to focus on the interface between him or herself and the group. The diagram provides the social worker with feedback on the gestalt of interactions between group members and him or herself.

References

Bales, R. F. (1950). *Interaction process analysis*. Chicago: University of Chicago Press.

Bales, R. F. (1970). *Personality and interpersonal behavior*. New York: Holt, Rinehart, &Winston.

Bales, R. F. (1979). *SYMLOG: A system for the multiple level observation of groups*. New York: Free Press.

Berman-Rossi, T. (1993). The tasks and skills of the social worker across stages of group development. *Social Work with Groups, 16*(1/2), 69–92.

Galinsky, M. J., & Schopler, J. (1994). Negative experiences in support groups. *Social Work in Health Care, 20*(1), 77–95.

Garland, J., Jones, H., & Kolodny, W. (1965). A model of development in social work groups. In S. Bernstein (Ed.), *Exploration in group work: Essays in theory and practice* (pp. 17–71). Boston: Milford House.

Gitterman, A., & Shulman, L. (2005). The Life Model, oppression, vulnerability and resilience, mutual aid, and the mediating function. In A. Gitterman, & L. Shulman (Eds.), *Mutual aid groups, vulnerable and resilient populations, and the life cycle* (3rd ed., pp. 3–37). New York: Columbia University Press.

Gitterman, A., & Wayne, J. (2003). Turning points in group life: Using high tension moments to promote group purpose and mutual aid. *Families in Society, 84*(3), 433–440.

Kutner, S. S., & Kirsch, R. D. (1983). SYMLOG: A new system for the multiple level observation of groups. In N. Goroff (Ed.), *Reaping from the field: From practice to principle* (vol. 1, pp. 261–271). Hebron, CT: Practitioners Press.

Kutner, S. S., & Kirsch, R. D. (1985). Clinical application of SYMLOG: A graphic system of observing relationships. *Social Work, 30*(6), 497–503.

Kutner, S. S., & Kirsch, R. D. (1986). SYMLOG: A new theory and technology for the therapeutic community. *International Journal of Therapeutic Communities, 7*(2), 121–128.

Schiller, L. (1997). Rethinking stages of development in women's groups: Implications for practice. *Social Work with Groups, 20*(3), 3–19.

Schiller, L. (2007). Not for women only: Applying the relational model of group development with vulnerable populations. *Social Work with Groups, 30*(1), 11–26.

Steinberg, D. M. (1996). She's doing all the talking, so what's in it for me? *Social Work with Groups, 19*(2), 5–16.

Group Work Journals

Groupwork: An Interdisciplinary Journal for Working with Groups

Mark Doel

Groupwork is the only journal based in the United Kingdom that focuses specifically on the method and context of professional practice that we know as groupwork. Allan Brown and Andrew Kerslake, its first editors, and David Whiting (Whiting and Birch, London), its publisher, established the journal in 1988. There have been nine editors and co-editors over the 17 volumes to date (2008), and the current editors are Mark Doel and Pamela Trevithick. *Groupwork* publishes three issues a year.

Groupwork's claim to be an international journal is supported by an analysis of the origin of the 71 articles appearing in the volumes from 2000 to 2006 (Doel, 2007), of which slightly more than half originated from outside the United Kingdom. The English-speaking world dominates, though French Canadian authors wrote two of the five Canadian articles in this period. Notably absent are articles from continental Europe (just two in this period), Africa, Asia (except Hong Kong) and South America.

The 71 articles represent 115 different authors (16 appeared more than once), of whom 57% were female. Of these articles 41% were authored by two or more people, including collaborations between academics and practitioners, between different professions and between researchers and students. However, it is perhaps a surprise that there were no examples of authors collaborating across nations.

In addition to its international base, the journal is also keen to make strong links with groupwork practice in other professions and disciplines. Its strapline reads "An Interdisciplinary Journal for Working with Groups." The breakdown of the authors in the period 2000–2006 indicates that, whilst social work is the largest single professional grouping (58% of all authors), this does leave 42% whose background is not social work. The largest number of non-social work contributions come from psychologists (9%), therapists and consultants (8%) and health workers (7%), with representation also from youth, community and probation/correction work (5%) and school teaching and education (4%).

The journal has been relatively successful in encouraging practitioners to publish, with the result that 21% of these 115 authors are practitioners. It would be interesting to compare this with the figures for the volumes up to 2000. Although the views of group members are often present in the text of the article, none of the articles in 2000–2006 included a group member as a co-author. The peer-reviewed nature of the journal means that some leeway might be needed to encourage writing for publication by people who are likely not to be used to this process. Other journals, for example *Social Work Education*, have produced special issues guest-edited by service users.

The quantity and provenance of articles appearing in *Groupwork* are easily counted. What requires more interpretation are the kinds of topic covered. Clearly, they all focus on groupwork; beyond that what are the main topics? Coding the 71 articles using only one, and occasionally two, principal categories produced this distribution:

Group methods and approaches	21
Mental health	10
Children and families	9
Research and evaluation	8
Education and training	7
Adults	5
Groupwork knowledge and theory	4
Youth work/criminal justice	4
Group leadership	3
Health	3
Conference reports	2
Women's groups	2
Community of practice	1
Ethics	1
Group supervision	1
Involuntary group members	1
Men's group	1
Self-help group	1

Since the journal began publication in 1988 there have been twelve themed issues, usually with guest editors:

Vol. 2, No. 3 (1989) Groupwork in Europe (Ken Heap)
Vol. 3, No. 2 (1990) Child Sexual Abuse (Allan Brown and Andrew Kerslake)
Vol. 4, No. 1 (1991) Groupwork with Offenders (Allan Brown and Brian Caddick)
Vol. 5, No. 3 (1992) Groupwork in Ireland (Robbie Gilligan and John Pinkerton)
Vol. 6, No. 2 (1993) Bereavement and Loss (Lynne Muir)
Vol. 7, No. 2 (1994) Groupwork with Women (Claire Wintram)
Vol. 8, No. 2 (1995) Groupwork in Education (Harold Marchant)

Groupwork offers a commonality for people who, in all other respects, are separated by borders of all kinds—national, professional, specialism, setting, etc. Those who have practised groupwork or researched, taught and written about it know that it has a special potential to transform the rhetoric of anti-oppressive practice and empowerment into reality. *Groupwork* is an eternal force, so it is with some interest that when we consider the title of the very first article to appear in *Groupwork*, "Groupwork with hard to reach clients" (Shulman, 1988), the only terminology that would *not* now be contested is "groupwork"! The terms "hard to reach" and "client" are now highly contested—only "groupwork" endures.

The current editors noted that they "start from a position of wanting to publish your article and we give what help we can in respect of those articles which initially fall short of standards for publication" (Doel & Trevithick, 2004, p. 7). Journals often focus on the authors and contributors, yet the whole purpose of a journal is the *reader*. It is difficult to know who reads *Groupwork*—the list of subscriptions shows a mix of institutions and individuals around the world, but tells us nothing of how useful the journal is nor the extent to which it is used. As the Journal goes on line we will get a better idea of its impact, at least through the numbers of citations. However, this tells us only about the academic referencing to the Journal and nothing about how groupworkers make use of what they read.

It is common for the state of groupwork to be discussed rather like a tide that ebbs and flows, with something of a retreat over the last decade or so, and always the hope that the tide is currently turning. There is no doubt that the profile of groupwork does seem to fluctuate, yet groupworkers know that group processes are essential to almost every aspect of human endeavour. Groups are an inescapable part of our lives, personal and professional, and knowledge of group processes a key to harnessing collective energies and creativity. Whether "social groupwork" is in or out of fashion, *Groupwork* will never cease to fascinate and energize, and learning about groups and groupwork in the pages of *Groupwork* journal will continue to contribute to our growing knowledge and enthusiasm. *Groupwork* play an essential part in developing the evidence base for groupwork, for building theory and for disseminating good practice.

References

Doel, M. (2007). Editorial. *Groupwork*, *17*(2), 3–12.

Doel, M., & Trevithick, P. (2004). Editorial. *Groupwork*, *14*(1), 3–8.

Shulman, L. (1988). Groupwork practice with hard to reach clients: A modality of choice. *Groupwork*, *1*(1), 5–16.

Small Group Research: An International Journal of Theory, Investigation, and Application

Aaron M. Brower, Charles D. Garvin, and Richard Kettner-Polley

Small Group Research (*SGR*) was the brainchild of Charles Garvin, a social worker, and Rick Kettner-Polley, a social and organizational psychologist. It puts out six issues each year and is published by Sage Publications. *SGR* was formed in 1990 from the merger between *Small Group Behavior* (*SGB*), which had recently named Garvin as editor, and the *International Journal of Small Group Research* (*IJSGR*), which had been founded 5 years earlier by Kettner-Polley and Johann Schneider (a German psychologist). Garvin and Kettner-Polley became *SGR*'s co-editors; Aaron Brower (a social worker) and Schneider became associate editors. An editorial board was formed that brought together experts on small group research from all parts of the world.

SGB was founded in 1970 by William Fawcett Hill during the heyday of the study of small groups; it was formed as an outlet for practitioner and empirical articles on T-Groups and Encounter Groups. Hill continued to edit *SGB* for 10 years, at which point its second editor, Fred Massarik, came on board. Massarik continued the focus on experiential groups, and during his 10 years as editor, *SGB* became known as the journal to consult for articles that described observational coding schemes and other techniques attempting to capture in vivo group behaviors.

IJSGR was formed to publish academic articles that were intentionally international and interdisciplinary. The merger of *SGB* and *IJSGR* was an opportunity to build on the strengths of both, and to cultivate and apply knowledge on questions that concern us as small group practitioners and researchers. These questions—about cohesion, development, leadership, individual and group change, observational methods, the role of technology—are all stubbornly, maybe necessarily, interdisciplinary. The complexity of small groups almost guarantees that new discoveries are made at the boundaries and intersection of disciplines. Advances in knowledge are made through the application of basic research as often as they are made when the boundaries of basic science are expanded. New research and applications are made all over the world, and from all disciplines that use groups and study groups. Small group workers and researchers are not a large bunch, after all.

SGR remains intentionally interdisciplinary, intentionally international, and intentionally aimed at both group work practitioners and researchers. The backgrounds of the editors and make up of the editorial board avidly reflect these intentions. The editors and associate editors represent a variety of disciplines—in addition to social work and social psychology, the editorial board members come from communications, management, business, engineering, education, sports psychology, and international relations, among other disciplines, as well as several coming from industry rather than academia. The board members live all over the world—currently over 10% do not live in the United States. *SGR* remains an outlet for issues intrinsic to small group research, and for an international audience that sees themselves as *small group* researchers and practitioners, regardless of their disciplinary affiliation and countries.

Small group researchers and practitioners are interested in examining and using group dynamics to their full advantage, and applying the small group "magic" to all settings, whether with committees or teams in the workplace, in medical settings, or with groups of children in school. Collectively, small group researchers and practitioners are concerned about theoretical and conceptual clarity, measurement issues, and statistical methods—and the resulting dilemmas inherent to the study of complex group interactions regardless of the type of groups studied. Groups remain a microcosm of social interaction that falls at the intersection among individuals, organizations, and community.

By looking at the most cited and most read articles from the *SGR* archive, it becomes clear that *SGR*'s mission is being realized: the journal is consulted for enduring and core small group issues. These are the top 10 themes of articles appearing in *SGR* (not in a rank order):

- group size;
- maximizing group and individual performance;
- issues related to group problem solving leader and member behavior;
- cohesion;
- group identity development and personality trait expression in group;
- issues related to group composition (effects of member; homogeneity/heterogeneity among issues);
- communication patterns;
- issues related to face-to-face vs. technology-mediated groups;
- empirical explorations of group development;
- additionally, these most-cited and most-read articles come from an ever-changing array of practice settings that keep small group behaviors current in our world. Applications come from work teams to therapy groups to sports teams, orchestras and string ensembles; from the training of nurses and social workers, to accountants and realtors.

SGR has supported INGroup, the Interdisciplinary Network for Group Research www.msu.edu/~gwittenb/ingroup.html), since its inception in 2006. INGroup was created to bring together those who study groups and teams, recognizing that they are scattered across many social scientific disciplines, and across the world. In their charter, their aim is to: (1) promote communication about group research across fields and nations; (2) advance understanding about group dynamics through research; (3) advance theory and methods for understanding groups; and (4) promote interdisciplinary research. *SGR* and Sage Publications sponsor an award selecting the publication that best exemplifies the ideal of interdisciplinary, international small group research that can have impact on real-world issues. The annual *SGR Outstanding Research Award* is presented at INGroup, and is highlighted in a yearly special issue of *SGR*.

Why should social workers care about *SGR*? The fact is that social work is a profession based on values, and we are proud of that distinction. Throughout our profession, and particularly in the area of group work, our knowledge and practice are drawn from all disciplines—and they should be. We have learned long ago that to survive, and have an impact on the world, we cannot be insular. *SGR* is virtually the only place where social work researchers dealing with groups can inform other group scholars of their work and receive feedback from them. It is important for group work writers to avoid being cut off from the broad field of group scholarship, and instead to see ourselves as part of a broader flow of information to draw from and contribute to. *SGR* is the *only* journal devoted to small groups that is multidisciplinary and international—exactly those features that will continue to keep group work fresh and relevant.

George Homans said over half a century ago that small groups were at the very center of our lives as human beings (Homans, 1950). The study of small groups is at the very center of our understanding of human behavior and interaction. *SGR*'s mission is to continue to be at the heart of these discussions.

Reference

Homans, G. C. (1950). *The human group*. New York: Harcourt, Brace.

Social Work with Groups: A Journal of Community and Clinical Practice

Andrew Malekoff

In 1978 William Cohen, publisher of The Haworth Press, asked Catherine Papell and Beulah Rothman, then professors at the Adelphi University School of Social Work, to edit a journal concerned with the group work method in the profession of social work (Papell, 2002). The journal, which recently celebrated its 30th anniversary, was entitled: *Social Work with Groups: A Journal of Community and Clinical Practice*. Although Papell and Rothman had no experiences editing a journal, they wholeheartedly agreed and then proceeded to craft an editorial policy statement that reads, in part, as follows:

> It is the intent of *Social Work with Groups* to serve as a vehicle of communication for the several sectors of our profession wherein the small group heritage and the building of knowledge and skills of group work practice are embodied. There are those who represent the early group work tradition from the community and neighborhood centers with a focus on socialization in groups and the contribution of the healthy group to social betterment. There are those who represent the clinical tradition with a focus on the therapeutic

value of the small group and on the family as a small group. There are those who represent the community and planning tradition with focus on mobilizing and developing social resources and neighborhoods through the energies of task groups. Finally there are those who represent administration and social policy with a focus on welding together a humanizing service system through the collective efforts of staff and community groups. It is to the enrichment and dissemination of those professional labors that this journal of group work theory and practice is dedicated.

(Papell & Rothman, 1978, p. 4)

An editorial advisory board that reads like a "who's who" of social group work scholars was formed to review manuscripts and provide guidance and support to the fledgling journal. In all, Papell and Rothman edited 14 volumes of the journal that appeared in print from 1978 through 1991. As Papell (2002) recalls:

> Starting with the earliest issues, we had to solicit papers. Group workers were not yet accustomed to writing about their work ... many special issues followed, each prepared by a social group worker who could elicit a substantive array of papers around the area of group work practice that was his/her expertise.
>
> (p. 11)

Referred to as "Monographs from *Social Work with Groups*," 33 special thematic issues of the journal have been published from 1981 through 2006. They include some of the following themes: co-leadership, alcoholism, frail elderly, permanency planning for children, activities and action, gender issues, ethnicity, children and adolescents, research, violence, poor and oppressed, emotionally disabled, and social action.

In 1990, the founding editors decided to pass the baton to a new editorial team that they decided should include an academic and a practitioner. Consequently, they invited Roselle Kurland, a professor at Hunter College School of Social Work, and Andrew Malekoff, a social work practitioner at North Shore Child and Family Guidance Center, on Long Island, New York. Both had written for the journal and neither had met one another before. They met in Papell's office at Adelphi in 1989 and soon agreed to accept the invitation. They continued to work together as co-editors through June of 2005, editing a total of 13 volumes of the journal up to and including Volume 27 (published in 2004). In 2004 they produced a special issue (Volume 28, Issue 3/4) of the journal entitled, *A Quarter Century of Classics (1978–2004): Capturing the Theory, Practice and Spirit of Social Work with Groups*, a compilation of the "best of" articles, from over 100 issues and 600 articles printed in the journal in its first 25 years. This special issue provides readers with a broad overview of *Social Work with Groups* from four decades beginning with the 1970s.

As Kurland and Malekoff (2002) recalled on the 25th anniversary of the journal:

> One of the most frustrating themes we wrote about is how our profession seems to be losing its way [with] the growing emphasis on research and doctoral programs. ... It seems to us that research is becoming an end in

itself. If the primary aim of doctoral programs is to turn out skillful researchers who can compete with other disciplines for status, prove that social work interventions work, and enhance social work's prestige, then it is not surprising that such programs are having difficulty. Those are not the reasons that most social workers would be interested in seeking doctoral education. Current trends seem to be devaluing quality practice. We need to reverse that direction. We are in danger of losing our profession if we do not.

(pp. 4–5)

The special relationship between the journal and the Association for the Advancement of Social Work with Groups (AASWG), an international professional organization founded in 1979, is a key to understanding the counterforce that this partnership represents to the profession "losing its way" (Middleman, 2000). AASWG is a not-for-profit organization of group workers, group work educators, and friends of group work, who support its program of advocacy and action for professional practice, education, research, training and writing about social work with groups. At its annual symposia AASWG members present papers, many of which are published in symposium proceedings (some of which were published as special issues of the journal). The board of directors of AASWG includes one spot for the Editor of *Social Work with Groups*. And, historically, several AASWG board and general members serve on the Editorial Advisory Board of the journal and many more submit articles for publication and review books and videos for the journal. Although all editorial decisions of the journal are made independently, the interdependent relationship between the journal and the association is critical to promoting social work with groups.

In June 2005, Andrew Malekoff assumed the sole editorship (beginning with the development of Volume 28) when his long time co-editor (for 15 years) Roselle Kurland died suddenly and unexpectedly early that month. In its 30-plus years, the journal has been important in the theory and practice of social work with groups. It has provided a vital place where those in the profession who have a particular interest in and commitment to group work practice can feel at home, have a sense of belonging and an outlet to discuss their own interests and read about those of colleagues. The journal has helped to create a sense of community among group workers.

References

Kurland, R., & Malekoff, A. (2002). Introduction. *Stories celebrating group work: It's not always easy to sit on your mouth* (pp. 1–7). Binghamton, NY: Haworth Press.

Malekoff, A., & Kurland, R. (2004). *A quarter century of classics (1978–2004): Capturing the theory, practice and spirit of social work with groups*. Binghamton, NY: Haworth Press.

Middleman, R. (2000, May). A brief history of AASWG (originally written July 20, 1998, for the One Hundredth Anniversary of Social Work). *Social Work with Groups Newsletter, 16*(1), 17–18.

Papell, C. (2002). Memories of *Social Work with Groups*: Volume I (1978) through Volume 14 (1991). *Social Work with Groups, 25*(1/2), 9–13.

Papell, C., & Rothman, B. (1978). From the editors. *Social Work with Groups, 1*(1), 1–3.

Group Work in Fields of Practice

Community Settings for Adolescents

Maryanne Sabatino

There are many problems that plague our inner city youth today. Students in large cities are twice more likely to leave school before graduating than non-urban youth (Schwartz, 1998). Reasons given for dropping out include failing or getting poor grades, not getting along with teachers and other authorities, little or no family support, drug and alcohol problems, and teen pregnancy. The overall national public high school graduation rate for the class of 2003 was 70%. The graduation rate for White students was 78%, compared with 55% for African-American students, and 53% for Hispanic students (Green & Winters, 2006). In 2001, 46% of high school students reported ever having had sexual intercourse. Black high school students were more likely than Hispanic and White students to have ever had sex—61% of Black students, 48% of Hispanics, and 43% of Whites (Motivational Educational Entertainment, 2007).

The United States still has the highest rates of teen pregnancy and births in the industrialized world. Teen pregnancy costs the United States at least $7 billion annually. In the United States there are nearly 900,000 teen pregnancies annually (Motivational Educational Entertainment, 2007). Girls who are poor students with low educational aspirations are more likely to become teenage mothers than their high achieving peers; in fact one-third of teenage mothers drop out of school before becoming pregnant (Maynard, 1995). In addition, like teenage mothers, the boys and men who father their children tend to be poor, are often continuing an intergenerational practice, live in low-income communities, and have low educational achievement (Lerman, 1993).

Recent estimates in the United States place the number of gangs at 30,533 and the number of gang members at 815, 896 (Vigil, 2002). Drug trafficking, abuse, and violence are often associated with gang involvement. Given the data, minority youth are particularly vulnerable to gang activity, teen pregnancy, school truanting and drug use, and desperately require preventive and rehabilitative services. For our youth today, families, communities, and schools have not been able to meet their needs. Two-parent working households and an increasing divorce rate diminish family resources. Many of at-risk youth grow up in families who have difficulty providing the essential nurturance and structure that adolescents require. Consequently, they have too much unsupervised and unstructured after school time on their hands. Left on their own, they gravitate toward others peers on the streets. In the absence of family supervision, and positive alternatives in the community, their needs to belong are fulfilled by gangs.

In developing programs designed to service teens, holistic approaches must be used. Approaches that take into account the cognitive, emotional, physical, and environmental factors, contributing to the lives of adolescents. Too often, block grants, motivated by politics, have led to fragmented services, focusing on particular issues, rather than a more holistic approach. Thought must be paid to the issues that prevent the achievement of success in teens, lack of self-respect, low or no career and educational aspirations, poor communication and social skills, and an inability to handle stress. In addition, there is often a lack of positive outlets for reduction of stress, little or no appropriate athletic activity and focus on their physical bodies, and a lack of education about normative development in adolescence.

Programs that focus teens on education and career-related activities could achieve positive outcomes (Manlove, Franzetta, McKinney, Papillo, & Terry-Humen, 2004). In addition, programs that emphasize what is important to adolescents—body-image, positive outlets for budding sexuality, education on sex and pregnancy prevention, and avenues for expression of their pertinent issues—have produced success in combating the issues described above.

Finally, these programs and activities should be rooted in group settings. The group is a natural setting for adolescents (Malekoff, 2004). They are taught in groups, live in groups, and often play in groups. For adolescents to become productive members of society, they must have a buffer from exposure to risks inherent when their needs are not being met. A mutual aid group can serve as a buffer, providing adolescents with a sense of positive attachment to each other, and to adults within their world. Group work for adolescents is an ideal choice, as social interaction is a key aspect of the developmental process. Adolescence has, as its pivotal core, the need for peers, to help in the individuation process. Often, these groups, threaded together in a highly structured community setting, have been instrumental in providing teens with a sense of family and belonging, particularly in cases where there is dysfunctional family relationships. In addition, any model for a social institution must respond to needs clearly and commonly visible in typical neighborhoods (Kurland & Salmon, 1993). These groups need to take place within the community setting, for adolescents need to be integrated into the larger community. Coherent models for community-based programs that address the developmental needs of adolescence, while also providing buffers against the high risks that face our urban youth, are essential in promoting social functioning.

These programs must integrate parents and guardians into the services. Family support workshops and other means for family involvement are critical for helping to foster success in teens. Addressing youth issues alone, without addressing parents' understanding and ability to support their own children, provides a disservice to the youth whom we serve. Parent/Guardian Workshops should focus on helping adults to understand the stages of adolescence, the physiological changes that contribute to the mood swings and sometimes rebellious behavior of teens, and their need for separation and individuation, coupled with their contrastingly strong desire to hold on to the security of their close connection to their parents.

References

Greene, J. P., & Winters, M. A. (2006). *Leaving boys behind: Public high school graduation rates.* Civic Report, No. 48 (April). New York: The Manhattan Institute.

Kurland, R., & Salmon, R. (1993). *Group work practice in a troubled society.* Binghamton, NY: Haworth Press.

Lerman, R. I. (1993). A national profile of young unwed fathers. In R. I. Lerman, & T. J. Ooms (Eds.), *Young unwed fathers* (p. 37). Philadelphia: Temple University Press.

Malekoff, A. (2004). *Group work with adolescents: Principles and practice* (2nd ed.). New York: Guilford Press.

Manlove, J., Franzetta, K., McKinney, K., Papillo, A. R., & Terry-Humen, E. (2004). *A good time: After-school programs to reduce teen pregnancy.* The National Campaign to Reduce Teen Pregnancy. Washington, DC: National Campaign to Prevent Teen Pregnancy.

Maynard, R. (1995). Teenage childbearing and welfare reform: Lessons from a decade of demonstration and evaluation research. *Children and Youth Services Review, 17,* 309–332.

Motivational Educational Entertainment. (2007). *This is my reality: The price of sex.* Philadelphia: MEE Productions.

Schwartz, W. (1998). *School dropouts: New information about an old problem.* ERIC Clearinghouse on Urban Education. New York: Columbia University Press.

Vigil, J. D. (2002). *A rainbow of gangs, street cultures in the mega-city.* Austin, TX: University of Texas Press.

Corrections

Karen Green and Robert Green

"Corrections" includes criminal justice programs or services, which focus on the incarceration and/or rehabilitation of accused or convicted offenders. Institutional correctional settings include federal and state prisons and local jails. Community corrections include probation, parole, home detention, electronic monitoring, alternative work programs, day and weekend reporting, community service, and pretrial supervision. As the scope of social work within corrections is quite broad, group workers should be sure to familiarize themselves with their particular facility or setting, as the context will greatly impact their work.

Many groups in corrections focus on behaviors or other factors that are believed to contribute to criminality. In institutional settings, the environment itself presents challenges, which may be addressed through group work—the stress of living in confinement with others, the threat of violence, and other day-to-day group and community dynamics. Violence and substance abuse are common precursors to incarceration, and offenders' childhood histories frequently include parental substance abuse and incarceration, as well as foster care involvement. Histories of physical and sexual abuse, as well as mental health issues are also common among inmate populations (U.S. Department of Justice [DOJ], 2003, 2006, 2007).

Psychoeducational and skills-building groups in correctional settings have demonstrated effectiveness in dealing with mental health issues such as depression and anxiety (Pomeroy, Kiam, & Green, 2000).

Beyond the general population, there are a number of other populations-at-risk within corrections. Rates of arrest and incarceration for women are growing faster than those for men, and there is evidence that incarcerated women's needs may differ from men's (Singer, Bussey, Song, & Lunghofer, 1995). In particular, women are more likely than men to need alternative care for their children during incarceration, as well as support to cope with the issues raised for themselves, their children, and caregivers (Young & Smith, 2000). There is also growing awareness of the need for supports for children of incarcerated parents. Mutual aid groups offer these children a place to share fears and concerns with others who understand the many challenges of having a parent in jail or prison (Springer, Lynch, & Rubin, 2000).

Other populations requiring special consideration for group work include offenders with learning disabilities or academic delays, a sizeable group given that roughly half of jail inmates have not completed high school (DOJ, 2003). Although cognitive restructuring groups have become increasingly popular in corrections (Goodman, 1997), some workers have challenged their appropriateness for all offenders and presented alternatives for use with these and other populations (Cameron & Telfer, 2004; Mishna & Muskat, 2001). Among these other approaches is mutual aid, which is also commonly used as a component of addictions treatment in professionally led groups (Albert, 1994) as well as self-help models such as Alcoholics Anonymous.

Beyond general group work principles, practice in corrections is influenced by contextual factors, including operational policies and organizational attitudes about capacity for growth and change. For example, the growing practice of direct supervision, which posts correctional officers inside housing units in continuous direct contact with inmates, is based on the expectation that relationships and communication between staff and inmates, as well as among inmates, are important for maintaining safety and security of the facility. Facilities using this model generally organize housing units around a common area, with some using the therapeutic community concept. This approach supports and reinforces group work, allowing members to support one another beyond the group session and hold community members accountable to one another.

When selecting members, workers must consider that some individuals (such as men and women, gang members, co-defendants/witnesses) may not be able to attend group together, based on facility policy and/or safety concerns. Furthermore, institutional release/discharge is not always predictable, and may complicate closed groups when members terminate membership prematurely.

Increasingly, institutions use objective classification systems (considering offense, previous incarceration, age, etc.) to determine where inmates are housed and in which programs they may participate. Such classification may determine group eligibility. In facilities using a therapeutic community model for treatment of addiction or mental health issues, groups are often held within housing units, which may limit groups to residents. Occasionally, group eligibility changes because of re-classification, such as segregation for misbehavior.

In addition to workers' time constraints, sessions in correctional institutions must be planned around the facility's schedule (mealtimes, visitation, headcounts, etc.) and may be preempted by attorney visits, medical appointments, court appearances, and lockdowns.

While content of groups in correctional settings includes a wide variety of discussion and artistic/expressive activities, workers in institutions should be aware that certain activities and/or materials may be restricted for security reasons, or by inflexible physical space arrangements. Workers should also consider privacy concerns when using journaling or written homework, and may want to limit discussion of criminal charges, especially for non-sentenced inmates

Group work in corrections frequently involves what Garvin (1997) has called "working with groups in social control situations" (p. 250). Members may be involuntarily attending to meet some mandate, secure "good time" towards early release, or impress the court. Other members may exert social control, in that the "inmate code," which requires solidarity among inmates, will likely affect behavior and other dynamics (Garvin, 1997). Groups are also viewed as a way to make offenders comply with institutional or societal rules. Workers must acknowledge these multiple purposes, obtain informed consent from participants about what benefits the group may provide, and be clear that the group cannot "fix" members.

Concerns about confidentiality are amplified in correctional settings, where few things are private. In addition to awareness of the limits of confidentiality (including attendance/progress reports for those attending to satisfy sentence conditions), group members must understand risks of participation, including legal implications if other members break confidentiality. In institutions, members have to live alongside one another after group is over, and as Wright (2005) points out, leaders should caution members about exposing vulnerabilities prematurely.

References

Albert, J. (1994). Talking like "real people": The straight ahead prison group. In A. Gitterman, & L. Shulman (Eds.), *Mutual aid groups, vulnerable populations, and the life cycle* (2nd ed., pp. 199–214). New York: Columbia University Press.

Cameron, H., & Telfer, J. (2004). Cognitive-behavioural group work: Its application to specific offender groups. *Howard Journal of Criminal Justice, 43*(1), 47–64.

Garvin, C. (1997). *Contemporary group work* (3rd ed.). Boston: Allyn & Bacon.

Goodman, H. (1997). Social group work in community corrections. *Social Work with Groups, 20*(1), 51–64.

Mishna, F., & Muskat, B. (2001). Social group work for young offenders with learning disabilities. *Social Work with Groups, 24*(3/4), 11–32.

Pomeroy, E. C., Kiam, R., & Green, D. L. (2000). Reducing depression, anxiety, and trauma of male inmates: An HIV/AIDS psychoeducational group intervention. *Social Work Research, 24*(3), 156–167.

Singer, M. I., Bussey, J., Song, L. Y., & Lunghofer, L. (1995). The psychosocial issues of women serving time in jail. *Social Work, 40*, 103–114.

Springer, D. W., Lynch, C., & Rubin, A. (2000). Effects of a solution-focused mutual aid group for Hispanic children of incarcerated parents. *Child and Adolescent Social Work Journal, 17*(6), 431–442.

U.S. Department of Justice. (2003). *Education and correctional populations.* Retrieved September 16, 2007 from http://www.ojp.usdoj.gov/bjs/pub/pdf/ecp.pdf

U.S. Department of Justice. (2006). *Mental health problems of prison and jail inmates.* Retrieved September 16, 2007 from http://www.ojp.usdoj.gov/bjs/pub/pdf/mhppji.pdf

U.S. Department of Justice. (2007). *Criminal offender statistics.* Retrieved September 16, 2007 from http://www.ojp.usdoj.gov/bjs/crimoff.htm#jail

Wright, M. W. (2005). Group work with offenders. In G. L. Greif, & P. H. Ephross (Eds.), *Group work with populations at risk* (2nd ed., pp. 287–305). New York: Oxford.

Young, D. S., & Smith, C. J. (2000). When moms are incarcerated: The needs of children, mothers, and caregivers. *Families in Society, 81*(2), 130–141.

Family and Children's Services*

Mary Pender Greene

A Family and Children's Services organization offers a vast array of options to the community covering a wide range of issues on the mental health and social service spectrum. On a continuum of care, services include groups for children, adolescents, and parents, family education and collateral support services, psychotherapy, treatment for substance abuse disorders, vocational and rehabilitation counseling, play therapy, cognitive-behavioral therapy, and other modalities to assist children, adolescents and adults to cope with troubling symptoms such as anxiety, depression, and more serious disorders of mood and thinking. Outpatient, residential and day treatment programs are available for adolescents and adults experiencing more serious symptoms, such as chronic mental illness. Groups play a major role and are continually evolving in order to keep pace with the full range of mental health and social service needs of present-day communities.

The full array of early childhood challenges are best addressed in relationship-based groups. Young children often present with issues of anxiety, depression, attachment disorders, attention disorders, trauma, and elective mutism. Seen as well are young children who are fearful, under responsive, overly active, aggressive, or suffering from a variety of other developmental issues. Groups are also valuable with latency-aged children who suffer from conditions such as attention-deficit hyperactivity disorder, conduct disorder, obsessive–compulsive disorder, phobias, etc. (Buchholtz & Mishine, 1981). Groups for these children are most effective when they are designed to address therapeutic goals that are set by a combination of the group members, the therapists, and the caregivers.

Adolescent groups are crucial for general issues such as socialization, intimacy and transference issues, physical and sexual abuse, eating disorders, suicidal ideation, drug use, etc.; all such groups are beneficial in guiding the young person through the complex terrain of adolescence. Group work with adults is appropriate for a wide range of difficulties, from those who would like to enhance their interpersonal skills to those with emotional problems like anxiety and depression. In urban settings, groups have evolved as new ways are sought to tackle old problems (White, 1994, 2000). Hence, there are support groups for people in similar situations; for example, for participants where English is a second language, where there are issues of loss and bereavement, for emotionally, physically, and sexually abused women, and for a wide variety of related issues (MacKenzie, 1990).

Adolescent day treatment is intensive treatment provided within the context of the therapeutic milieu by a multidisciplinary staff utilizing various treatment modalities and techniques. Generally, these techniques are integrated to give the under-structured adolescent the opportunity to work through and master developmental tasks and strengthen ego functioning. For those adolescents who are in the highest category of community-based special education and mental health services, day treatment is usually the first stop for a youth returning from residential treatment or the last stop before residential treatment or state hospitalization. Group work in this setting has proven to be effective in improving the emotionally disturbed adolescent's self-esteem, and ability to regulate affect, utilize coping skills, and develop libidinal object constancy (Kirman, 1983). The milieu is the medium through which this change occurs, a macro group, a forum for mutual aid and the corrective recapitulation of family and community issues, The role of race and culture must be incorporated into both the milieu and the group in order to offer the most effective services to this population (Blitz & Pender Greene, 2006; Chisom, 2005).

Implementing a successful group therapy program in a Residential Treatment Facility can be a challenging task. Chronically traumatized and psychiatrically impaired adolescents are often over-stimulated internally and frequently come from highly chaotic environments. Consequently, one of the most beneficial aspects of treatment is the highly structured group setting itself. Open-ended psychodynamic group therapy is not the most useful modality with this population. A psychoeducational model, providing information and instruction on various topics for the residents (i.e., trauma, loss and bereavement, race and culture, sexual orientation, creative expression, etc.) creates a greater sense of safety for this population and therefore increases clients' ability to express themselves and communicate with one another in the here and now with far fewer incidents of behavioral opposition (Blitz & Pender Greene, 2006; Bloom, 1977; Malekoff, 1997; Yalom, 1985).

Groups for adults with mental illness are frequently conducted in structured community settings, such as Continuing Day Treatment Programs, (CDT), Intensive Psychiatric Rehabilitation Treatment Programs, (IPRT), or Psychosocial Clubs. The primary purpose of group work in these settings is to improve the level of functioning of each individual. The structured settings help clients develop support systems and maintain themselves in the community. Groups can include educational and pre-vocational readiness, housing and independent living, improving relationships, and symptom management. Clients in these groups translate their losses into positive actions and meaningful activities (Garvin, 1996, Keller, 2006; Kibel, 2003).

Among the many services available within a Children's and Family Services setting, there continues to be a major role for groups where families and children are helped to understand and to modify coping and risk behaviors related to their issues and symptoms. The group provides a useful environment wherein clients can safely begin to cultivate resilience and support systems to counteract possible setbacks while they develop new life skills. The group acts as a useful laboratory where newly learned behaviors can be practiced. In addition, the group offers a place where personal issues are worked through in a supportive, confidential, and non-judgmental environment. As a result, it is safe to say, that the value of groups in a Children and Family Services agency is indeed incalculable.

* The author acknowledges the contributions of several colleagues in the preparation of this entry: Ellen Blaufox; April Harvin; and Julie Sullivan-Redmond.

References

Blitz, L. V., & Pender Greene, M. (Eds.). (2006). *Racism and racial identity: Reflections on urban practice in mental health and social services.* Binghamton, NY: Haworth Press.

Bloom, S. (1997). *Creating sanctuary: Toward the evolution of sane societies.* New York: Routledge.

Bucholtz, E., & Mishine, J. (Eds.). (1981). *Group interventions with children, adolescents and parents.* Northvale, NJ: Jackson-Aronson.

Chisom, R. (2005). *Principles of anti-racist organizing.* Paper presented on September, 15, 2005 at the Anti-Racist Alliance Workshop, New York.

Garvin, C. (1996). Group work with seriously mentally ill people. In G. L. Greif, & P. Ephros (Eds.), *Group work with populations at risk* (pp. 28–41). New York: Oxford University Press.

Keller, J. (2006) Helping families to help their loved ones with serious mental illness. *A white paper of the National Alliance on Mental Illness of New York State.* Retrieved on September 30, 2006 from http://www.naminys.org

Kibel, H. (2003). Interpretive work in milieu groups. *International Journal of Group Psychotherapy, 53,* 303–327.

Kirman, J. (1983). Modern psychoanalysis and intimacy: Treatment of the narcissistic personality disorder. *Modern Psychoanalysis, 8,* 17–34.

MacKenzie, K. R. (1990). *Introduction to time-limited psychotherapy.* Washington, DC: American Psychiatric Press.

Malekoff, A. (1997). *Group work with adolescents: Principles and practice.* New York: Guilford Press.

White, J. C. (1994). The impact of race and ethnicity on transference and countertransference in combined individual/group therapy. *Group, 18,* 89–98.

White, J. C. (2000). Psychoanalytic group psychotherapy with African-American women. In L. C. Jackson, & B. Greene (Eds.), *Psychotherapy with African-American women: Innovations in psychodynamic perspectives and practice* (pp. 208–224). New York: Guilford Publications.

Yalom, D. (1985). *The theory and practice of group psychotherapy.* New York: Basic Books.

Foster Care

Michael Wagner

The development of societies for the protection of cruelty to children marked the beginnings of modern child welfare practices in the United States. Historical and traditional stories of children raised by strangers abound; however, the development of orphanages and then subsidized homes to meet the needs of children and the medically, intellectually or morally fragile did not emerge until the mid-1800s. Charles Loring Brace established The Children's Aid Society in New York City in 1853, which led to the eventual placing out of 120,000 New York City children in free homes across the United States as a precursor to modern voluntary foster care. The signing of the Social Security Act in 1935 provided a federal funding stream that allowed for the subsidizing of foster care through its requirement to fund services to children who had suffered abandonment and abuse. Volunteer foster families were thus eligible to receive funds to support the needs of children placed in their home and the current state of foster care was in place. Other countries around the world developed a patronage system for supporting foster "carers" where provider families are supported by agencies in patronage agreements directly funding children's care (Children's Aid Society, 2007; Herman, 2007).

Social work with groups in foster care represents an effort on the part of the system to provide rehabilitative, educational experiences, or psychosocial interventions for a specific form of child abuse/neglect, or to provide supports for the children, youth, birth families, and resource parents involved in child protective cases. Services are typically offered to each member of the foster care "triad" separately: to resource (foster/adoptive) families, birth parents and children/youth.

Many foster care agencies and programs currently use a "group preparation" model for resource parent pre-certification training. Multiple state models such as The Model Approach to Partnerships in Parenting: Group Preparation and Selection (Bayless and Craig-Oldsen, 1990) and PRIDE (Child Welfare League of America, 1997) are common. Virtually all pre-certification training is provided in group settings to balance resources and to assure adequate numbers of volunteers available to place children with various needs for care and permanency. These programs involve group services to allow foster parenting and adoption applicants to explore the emotional and practical impacts that serving as a resource family will have on them and their children. Exploration of the applicant's understanding of children and their development, of the emotional impact of separation and loss attendant to child protective removal, and the challenges of expanding family boundaries to include children and their birth parents in a model for sharing parenting are frequently part of these programs, as these challenges represent the greatest novel demands on foster and adoptive families.

Social work with groups of birth parents represents an area of creative and innovative responses to the challenges represented in foster care. Because programs like these allow parents to normalize their experiences and to explore their experience of the child protective intervention, groups can be very useful in helping parents plan for their children in care. The use of groups for services such as drug and alcohol treatment, domestic violence interventions, and parenting skills are frequently used and well documented. Often these services are provided outside of the foster care agency and in this way can provide a greater level of individual confidentiality for the client due to the clear need for consent to disclose information that occurs between agencies.

Services meant to assist birth parents to correct abusive, neglectful, or maltreating behavior and to establish healthy ways of interacting with their children are commonly recommended by child protective authorities as a requirement for families to reunify after a foster care removal. These services can be provided both individually in case work but are often mandated in groups. Parenting skills groups, as they are commonly referred to, take on a number of forms. Some are based on psychoeducational models. These groups anticipate that if given a rehabilitative opportunity to explore effective parenting and provided with a motivating supportive experience, the parents will chose better and more effective parenting skills and thereby reduce the risk of future abuse or maltreatment of their children. A review of the literature regarding such groups can be found in Plasse (1995) and Levin (1992). Examples of these groups are numerous and curricula can be found for specific parenting needs such as parenting newborns, young children, and teens. Some parenting groups include deeper emotional exploration of parenting such as The Parenting Journey from the Family Center in Somerville, MA, and are used in other settings than foster care.

Cognitive-behavioral groups often form around specific child-related conditions that require more effective parental responses. A review of these services can be found in Magen and Rose (1994). There are also a number of specialty services for children's particular special needs, such as attention deficit hyperactivity disorder and difficulties with conduct and, more recently, autism spectrum disorders.

The specific area where groups are plentiful and ongoing continues to be in interventions for youth and children, specifically around emotional and mental health services. Groups designed to promote teenagers' readiness for adulthood are widespread and recommended as best practice. Children are recommended to groups for trauma alleviation, survivor services for witnesses of domestic violence, and for other specific abuse-related rehabilitation.

One emerging area of extended group competence is the growing use of the family team conference (family team meeting, family to family conference, etc.) as a strategy for increasing stakeholder participation in child protective proceedings and in planning for permanency. They represent a task-oriented group meeting in which participants are striving to achieve a working plan for a family to meet the safety, well-being, and permanency needs of their children and to activate and maintain services from providers in the conference to achieve effective service plans and discharge objectives. Service planning meetings and crisis interventions for children in care also take on this format and are served in similar ways. Literature reviews are available through the National Resource Center for Family-Centered Practice and Permanency Planning at The Hunter College School of Social Work. The Children's Aid Society in New York has developed a parenting skills program that uses a mediating self-assessment model to prepare and support parents engaged in these kinds of planning conferences by focusing on exploring the skills parents need to successfully plan for their children in foster care (Wagner, 2003).

Support groups for all members of the foster care triad are all identified as instrumental for successful outcomes. Protecting attachment for children and promoting lifetime relationships to assure permanency for children are not activities that unrelated families typically undertake but are necessary to alleviate the impact of separation and loss that are the unavoidable injuries associated with child protective placement interventions. Since these conditions are virtually inevitable in foster care the use of support groups to allow for members to validate their experiences, to illuminate successful strategies, and to demystify the developing relationships between two families around one child are very useful in promoting positive outcomes for children.

References

Bayless, L., & Craig-Oldsen, H. L. (1990). Model approach to partnerships in parenting: Group preparation and selection of foster and/or adoptive parents. In *Implementation guidebook* (4th ed.). Atlanta, GA: Child Welfare Institute.

Child Welfare League of America. (1997). *PRIDE: Pre-service: The process to develop and support resource families practice handbook*. Washington, DC: Author.

Children's Aid Society (2007). *Adoption history and accomplishments*. http://www.childrensaidsociety.org/adoption/historyandaccomplishments

Herman, E. (2007). *Adoption history: Fostering and foster care*. http://www.uoregon.edu/~adoption/topics/fostering.htm

Levin, A. E. (1992). Groupwork with parents in the foster care system: A powerful method of engagement. *Child Welfare, 71*(5), 457–473.

Magen, R. H., & Rose, S. R. (1994). Parents in groups: Problem-solving versus behavioral skills training. *Research on Social Work Practice, 4*(2), 171–191.

The National Resource Center for Family-Centered Practice and Permanency Planning (2007). *Family group conferencing: Resources*. http://www.hunter.cuny.edu/socwork/nrcfcpp/info_services/family-group-conferencing.html

Plasse, B. R. (1995). Parenting groups for recovering addicts in a day treatment center. *Social Work, 40*(1), 65–74.

Wagner, M. W. (2003). Families for reunification: A mediating model for birth parent self-assessment. In J. Lindsay, D. Turcotte, & E. Hopmeyer (Eds.), *Crossing boundaries and developing alliances through group work* (pp. 147–166). New York: Haworth Press.

The Homeless

Sarah Stevenson

The homeless are easy to stereotype. Words like "dead-beat," "drunk," "smelly," "dumb", or just plain "crazy" are used too often. Granted, society often extends its condolences and goodwill towards individuals who become homeless due to those circumstances beyond their control, such as natural disasters or sudden, unforeseen evictions. But the chronic, lifelong homeless, battling both mental illness and substance abuse, are rarely viewed with a sympathetic eye (Brown & Ziefert, 1990; Pollio, 1995). This homeless population can be difficult to work with, especially in a group work setting. They live chaotic, unpredictable lifestyles. Inevitably, they have cultivated a fierce independence, stubborn will and deep mistrust of friend and foe alike. How then does one develop and implement an effective and meaningful group work experience with the homeless?

A group cannot be sold to the homeless (Kurland & Salmon, 1992). They will have little incentive to return to or follow up on anything that is pitched to them, no matter how well intentioned. The homeless are often more focused on meeting their basic needs than on participating in a group. Although a sobriety support group or psychoeducation group may look good on paper and appear to be meeting the needs of the homeless, it could be argued that it is in fact meeting the needs of the worker (Kurland & Salmon, 1998; Lee, 1989; Sachs, 1991). The development and ultimate purpose of the group must acknowledge the strengths of the homeless (Racine & Sevigny, 2001). Their resiliency, willpower, and their coping mechanisms must be viewed as a tool in group development rather than a hindrance. In short, a group worker must not underestimate this population.

In the beginning phase of a group, structure and trust represent particular challenges for the homeless (Stevenson, 2004). Their life experiences and daily lives incorporate neither of these concepts. Bouncing from park bench to shelter, hospital to halfway house, their existence is unpredictable (Brown & Ziefert, 1990). A group worker should strive to provide some semblance of structure in the beginning phase of a group (Garland, Jones, & Kolodny, 1973). However, the worker should also be prepared for some ordered chaos. Some members may dislike or ignore a group contract; they may change the purpose of the group midstream; they may show up late or leave early; they may walk in high or drunk; they may come to the first session and not return until the fifth; there may be conflicts among members that occur outside the group that suddenly become a part of the group (Brown & Ziefert, 1990; Northen & Kurland, 2001, Sachs, 1991; Stevenson, 2004). A group worker must be willing to think outside the box and cling loosely to traditional notions of what a group "should" look, sound, and feel like (Cohen & Mullender, 1999).

Coupled with the challenges of structure comes the challenge of trust. The homeless rarely trust others and sometimes do not trust themselves (Brown & Ziefert, 1990). Although they may still be in touch with some family or have a network of friends, they are basically alone. Genuine social supports are illusive (Martin & Neyowith, 1989). Therefore, a homeless group member may enter a group with mobilized defenses. They often will be suspicious of the group worker, the agency she works for and the government that funds that agency. The homeless have been let down by many institutions, programs, and workers in the past and the group worker may be seen as no different (Sachs, 1991). A group worker needs to take in stride the initial suspicion and distrust that could come from a homeless group member. This means feeling comfortable in her role as an authority figure in the group while still respecting the fear that many homeless members enter a group with (Kurland & Salmon, 1993).

In the middle phases of a group, as barriers are broken down and slivers of trust begin to emerge, the group can offer a home of sorts to this challenging population. The analogy of group as a family resonates powerfully with the homeless and they may take on familial roles, as many group members will do in the middle phases (Garland et al., 1973). The group becomes its own microcosm of society and allows the homeless to find and express a voice (Racine & Sevigny, 2001). They become visible in the group, whereas they are often invisible in our society. The worker must continually acknowledge and promote this sense of equal respect and integrity of all members (Brown & Mistry, 1994; Kurland, 2002; Lee, 1989; Pollio, 1995).

With this new-found connection to others and sense of belonging inevitably comes conflict. The homeless have often had to fight for every inch of space to sleep on, every crumb of food to consume, and every ounce of dignity they have left. Naturally, disagreements within groups emerge, none more so than in a group with the homeless. The art of compromise is not essential in the life of a homeless person. Rather, they often must view the world in black and white terms in order to survive (Brown & Ziefert, 1990). A worker must be confident and comfortable in the midst of conflict within the group and know how to navigate its murky terrain (Northen & Kurland, 2001).

Endings are never easy in groups and they become especially difficult with the homeless. These are individuals who have said goodbye far too often and too prematurely to homes, families, and futures. They may revert, as some group members will do, to those initial feelings of distrust and suspicion. (Garland et al., 1973; Northen & Kurland, 2001). The group worker herself may also have mixed feelings about ending a group with the homeless. As Stevenson wrote, "I felt slightly guilty for leaving, thinking that I was becoming like everyone else in their lives that may have abandoned them or forgotten them" (Stevenson, 2004, p. 78). Sensitivity to these feelings and reactions is paramount. Processing endings for members may offer the opportunity to say goodbye safely and predictably. Appropriate group ending can educate homeless members that not all closure need be sudden, violent, or painful.

When developed and implemented appropriately the life of a group can have a profound impact on the life of the homeless group member. When the group worker starts from a place of deep regard and respect for the homeless group member, a lively, engaging, provocative, and moving group work experience is bound to emerge.

References

Brown, A., & Mistry, T. (1994). Group work with "mixed membership" groups: Issues of race and gender. *Social Work with Groups, 17*(3), 5-21.

Brown, K. S., & Ziefert, M. (1990). A feminist approach to working with homeless women. *Journal of Women and Social Work, 5*(1), 6–20.

Cohen, M. B., & Mullender, A. (1999). The personal in the political: Exploring the group work continuum from individual to social change goals. *Social Work with Groups, 22*(1), 13–31.

Garland, J., Jones, H., & Kolodny, R. (1973). A model for stages of development in social work groups. In S. Bernstein (Ed.), *Exploration in group work* (pp. 17–71). Boston: Milford House.

Kurland, R. (2002). Racial difference and human commonality: The worker–client relationship. *Social Work with Groups, 25*(1/2), 113–118.

Kurland, R., & Salmon, R. (1992). Self determination: Its use and misuse in group work practice and graduate education. In D. Fike, & B. Rittner (Eds.), *Working from strengths: The essence of group work* (pp. 105–121). Miami, FL: Center for Group Work Studies.

Kurland, R., & Salmon, R. (1993). Not just one of the gang: Group workers and their role as an authority. In P. Ephross, & T. Vassil (Eds.), *Social work with groups: Expanding horizons* (pp. 153–169). Binghamton, NY: Haworth Press.

Kurland, R., & Salmon, R. (1998). Purpose: A misunderstood and misused keystone of group work practice. *Social Work with Groups, 21*(3), pp. 5–17.

Lee, J. A. B. (1989). Introduction: Return to our roots. *Social Work with Groups, 11*(4), 5–9.

Martin, M. A., & Nayowith, S. A. (1989). Creating community: Groupwork to develop social support networks with homeless mentally ill. *Social Work with Groups, 11*(4), 79–93.

Northen, H., & Kurland, R. (2001). *Social work with groups* (3rd ed.). New York: Columbia University Press.

Pollio, D. E. (1995). Hoops group: Group work with young "street" men. *Social Work with Groups, 18*(2/3), 107–122.

Racine, G., & Sevigny, O. (2001). Changing the rules: A board game lets homeless women tell their stories. *Social Work with Groups, 23*(4), 25–38.

Sachs, J. (1991). Action and reflection in work with a group of homeless people. *Social Work with Groups, 14*(3/4), 187–202.

Stevenson, S. (2004). Sweethearts and sourpusses: My year with the elderly. *Journal of Gerontological Social Work, 44*(1/2), 53–80.

Partial Hospitalization

Gilan Miller-Gertz and Nancy L. Herron

Partial hospitalization (PH) has taken on a greater role in the past 30 years in the treatment of psychiatric patients due to cost and efficiency pressures from managed care. Hospital workers are encouraged to discharge patients as soon as they are medically stable, although patients are often not ready to resume normal functioning. PH is used as a "step down" from inpatient care. Upon referral to PH, a patient is more receptive to education and therapy because the stabilization process has already begun. Alternately, outpatients with exacerbated symptoms "step up" to PH to stabilize their symptoms and prevent inpatient hospitalization (Witt-Browder, 2000).

PH provides the benefit of intensive daily treatment while patients transition to life at home. The typical length of stay in PH is 4–6 weeks. Group work is the primary method of counseling, because PH patients are usually too symptomatic to benefit from insight-building individual psychotherapy, and the milieu is the treatment unit. The structure, routine, and support of group work enable patients to recover gradually.

On admission, social workers propose goals and treatment plans for each patient individually, and begin discharge planning. In groups, social workers discuss other issues, including education about symptoms, coping skills, and relapse prevention. They also discuss managing family response to illness, as well as resuming normal life and work.

There are particular advantages to using groups in this setting. People can learn from each other: patients with more experience managing their bipolar disorder, for example, can speak about the importance of remaining on medication. Additionally, developing group cohesion is a healing factor for many people who feel very alone. A common feeling of patients is that they alone suffer from their crippling symptoms, and the group provides proof that this is not true. Supportive relationships often last far beyond discharge for individuals who feel stigmatized by their illnesses and have difficulty finding peers in the community.

Groups are also effective for organically mentally ill or psychotic patients, because other patients model appropriate behavior (Yalom, 1995). The setting promotes a culture of tolerance and acceptance of disability, with patients helping each other in many ways. Patients have the opportunity to try out new behaviors in a protected setting. Groups also counter the resistance of new patients as others disclose their initial feelings about being in the program, and report how this changed over time.

PH can also be used to help populations with specific needs beyond mental illness. For example, the PH format adapts well to substance abuse treatment (Cisler & Nawrocki, 1998). Practitioners can adjust group topics to address areas of interest, such as women's roles (Adolph, 1983). They can also encourage patients to raise topics that are relevant to their lives, allowing the program to be tailored to their needs.

Group size varies: from traditional size, 10 or fewer people, to large groups of 30 members. Small groups can focus on the individual's recent life events, goals, and concerns. Often, patients prefer this format for disclosing personal information. The larger groups may be psychoeducational and instructive about skills and medication. Because the composition of the group constantly changes with new admissions and discharges, social workers must make each group a stand-alone unit. For this reason, a short-term, solution-oriented focus is required. Education and skill building are more appropriate than traditional psychodynamic techniques. Instead of relationships being symbolic, they are real time, as patients practice skills of assertiveness and empathy.

Types of groups include medication sessions, recreation groups, psychoeducation on varying topics, and problem solving. Art, music, movement, and activity therapy are offered as well. Psychoeducation covers many issues, including orientation to the mental health care system, basics of diagnosis, symptoms and treatment, and patient rights. In these groups, social workers teach life skills such as emotional regulation techniques, anger management, assertiveness, and stress reduction (Bourne, 2000). Other discussions focus on improved relationships with family members and significant others, and overcoming the stigma of mental illness (Garvin, 1997).

Cognitive therapy techniques are especially useful to PH patients (Witt-Browder, 2000). Many patients are flooded with negative thoughts, which are reinforced by their cognitive distortions. Cognitive-behavioral therapy tools such as thought recording can help PH patients examine and counter negative thoughts and improve self-esteem. Core beliefs can also be explored in the group, though to a lesser extent, due to time constraints.

Given the changing composition of PH groups, social workers in the PH setting need to creatively implement various tools and resources. One such tool is respect for each individual, which workers model in several ways: by calling patients by name, by valuing each comment made, and by tolerating sincere but irrelevant or disorganized comments. Group members follow the social worker's example, listening respectfully and treating each other with consideration. Social workers also demonstrate respect by dressing professionally and presenting material in an engaging and interesting manner. Although some patients do not have advanced education, social workers do not speak patronizingly to patients; rather they address the group at a mid-range intellectual level.

Social workers regularly face challenges. Lack of participation is a common problem due to depression, social anxiety, or psychosis. Social workers encourage participation by making expectations clear and describing topics and discussions from previous groups to orient new patients. They also pose open-ended questions such as, "What is it like to tell relatives or friends how you've been feeling?" When patients see there are no wrong answers and each contribution is valued, they are more likely to participate. To be sure, mental illness can cause patients to act in a disruptive manner, or make inappropriate comments. Social workers can make an effort to locate some positive aspect of the comment, to accept and respond to this, and refocus the patient.

Another valuable technique for handling challenges in PH is bridging, which connects patients to one another by pointing out commonalities in their situations. PH programs draw heterogeneous populations: patients differ in age, economic level, level of functioning, diagnosis, and other personal factors. Social workers help overcome these differences by exploring how the common experience of mental illness has disrupted everyone's life, regardless of economic level or severity of diagnosis. Asking questions such as, "Has anybody else ever felt this way, or had this problem?" invites patients to connect to one another. When patients work together to problem-solve for each other, they overcome their differences.

References

Adolph, M. (1983). The all-women's consciousness raising group as a component of treatment for mental illness. *Social Work with Groups, 6*(3/4), 117–131.

Bourne, E. (2000). *The anxiety and phobia workbook*. Oakland, CA: New Harbinger.

Cisler, R., & Nawrocki, J. (1998). Coping and short-term outcomes among dependent drinkers: Preliminary evidence for enhancing traditional treatment with relapse prevention training. *Alcoholism Treatment Quarterly, 16*(4), 5–21.

Garvin, C. (1997). Group work with seriously mentally ill people. In G. Greif, & P. Ephross (Eds.), *Group work with populations at risk* (pp. 28–40). New York: Oxford University Press.

Witt-Browder, A. (2000). Clients in partial hospitalization settings. In J. White, & A. Freeman (Eds.), *Cognitive behavioral group therapy for specific problems and populations* (pp. 361–383). Washington, DC: American Psychological Association.

Yalom, I. D. (1995). *The theory and practice of group psychotherapy* (4th ed.). New York: Basic Books.

Residential Care Settings for Adolescents

Francis Bartolomeo

Residential care facilities for adolescents are to be found in the major systems of care and rehabilitation: health care, education, social welfare, and criminal justice. These settings often employ a group-oriented approach that emphasizes the shared life-space between those who receive care and those who provide it (Fulcher &

Ainsworth, 2006; Redl & Wineman, 1957). Perhaps in no other agency context is the relationship between the setting and the service more evident than in residential care; therefore effective social group work in residential programs necessitates a systemic and organizational approach (Garland, 1992; Garvin, 1997).

On a continuum of care, residential treatment is frequently conceived as being one step below an inpatient medical facility and is usually reserved for adolescents: who present a persistent danger to themselves and/or others; whose functioning is so impaired that they need round the clock care; whose difficulties are too complex and severe (e.g., self-injurious behaviors, substance abuse, runaway behavior, eating disorders) to safely be contained by outpatient services; or for children removed from their families in cases of severe child abuse and neglect. A distinguishing characteristic of many residential treatment programs is the intentional creation of a therapeutic milieu as an essential treatment element (Redl & Wineman, 1957). Thus, residential treatment is more than a venue for the delivery of an array of intensively provided services. Within a therapeutic milieu every client interaction with every worker, from cook to administrator, is a potential moment for learning and growth for both the care receivers and the caregivers.

Creating a therapeutic culture with a shared mission, philosophy, and values with corresponding services provided by multiple staff members and professionals with diverse and sometimes competing perspectives is a significant challenge. The objective, however, to create a cohesive therapeutic environment is complicated by the ongoing dynamic tension between maintaining cultural and programmatic consistency on the one hand and providing individualized care on the other. Group work is a service that is highly valued in residential program for adolescents, because it is the intervention of choice for a spectrum of adolescent emotional and behavioral disorders (Hoag & Burlingame, 1997; Nadelman, 2005). Additionally, group work is crucial in settings like residential programs that aim to create a therapeutic milieu because the quality of the relationships between and among the various sub-systems (i.e., students, academic, counseling, and community life staff) profoundly impact the degree of program consistency and stability of the overall environment.

The agency purposes (i.e., the functions that an organization fulfills for society, or clients, or both) of residential programs are: to treat, to teach, to nurture, and to control (Fulcher & Ainsworth, 2006, p. 5). Residential care programs for adolescents most frequently have several purposes, for example, to provide youth with an education and mental health rehabilitation. Practice and ethical dilemmas emerge for social workers in these settings when: the agency is unclear about its purposes internally and externally (which can result in client–agency mismatch); the agencies purposes conflict or when one purpose dominates to the detriment of others (e.g., a corrections or control approach with youth who have significant mental health needs and vulnerabilities). Common social work practice and ethical tensions in residential care for youth are: client self-determination versus coercion; necessary limits versus excessive control; group or client empowerment versus authoritarianism; and imposed group purposes that may never be accepted by the group members (Garvin, 1997).

In addition to the ethical and practice challenges posed by the agency context is the fact that adolescents in residential programs present with overlapping areas of educational, social, familial, and psychiatric needs. Consequently, creating social work groups to reflect the agency purposes and the needs of the population is a formidable task. Further, since the majority of adolescents in residential treatment programs do not choose, at least initially, to enroll in such programs, they correspond with Rooney's (1992) description of *invisible involuntary or non-voluntary clients* (p. 5). Groups for non-voluntary and involuntary (i.e., legally mandated) clients, Rooney observes, "often start, end, or persist indefinitely in power struggles between leaders and participants" (p. 290). Social work with legally and non-legally coerced clients involves appreciable power disparities that can trigger client reactions to equalize the power imbalance (Rooney, 1992). This dynamic adds technical and ethical complexities to the clinical challenges already posed by the population and the agency context.

An organizational and systemic approach results in a social group work service that is integrated and culturally consistent with the agency context. To establish an integrated group program in residential care social workers need an approach that is both "systemic and systematic—i.e., every element of the agency system must be analyzed and assessment and implementation must be systematically done" (Garland, 1992, p. 89). An integrated group program produces group work services that are more congruent with the agency mission. The purpose of specific groups becomes clearer, and the groups tend to be more efficient and effective than when using adjunctive, idiosyncratic approaches to the delivery of group services. In addition, integrated groups programs have expectations for participation and involvement that are more apparent and consistent, which reduces the degree of power struggles potentially evoked from compulsory services.

Since group purpose emerges from client needs and agency purpose, assessment of group members' needs is a primary planning task included in the systematic analysis of the agency context (Garland, 1992; Garvin, 1997; Kurland & Salmon, 1998). With respect to group purposes for adolescent groups, Malekoff (1997) suggests that social work groups with adolescents be formed following an assessment of three overlapping need domains: *normative needs*, *specific needs*, and *contextual needs* (p. 54). Social workers in residential treatment have very effective ways of assessing need, which are: (a) access to clients; (b) informal time with students; and (c) opportunities to observe student interaction in a variety of situations. Since many adolescents may be unable or unwilling to articulate what they need, social workers in residential programs have the powerful advantage of participating in the life-space of the residents, and thereby, can be more attuned to their needs.

References

Fulcher, L. C., & Ainsworth, F. (Eds.). (2006). *Group care practice with children and young people revisited.* Binghamton, NY: Haworth Press.

Garland, J. A. (1992). Developing and sustaining group work services: A systemic and systematic view. *Social Work with Groups, 15*(4), 89–98.

Garvin, C. D. (1997). *Contemporary group work* (3rd ed.). Boston: Allyn & Bacon.

Hoag, M. J., & Burlingame, G. M. (1997). Evaluating the effectiveness of child and adolescent group treatment: A meta-analysis review. *Journal of Clinical Child Psychology, 26*, 234–246.

Kurland, R., & Salmon, R. (1998). Purpose: A misunderstood and misused keystone of group work practice. *Social Work with Groups, 21*(3), 5–17.

Malekoff, A. (1997). *Group work with adolescents: Principles and practice.* New York: Guilford Press.

Nadelman, S. A. (2005). Sharing the hurt: Adolescents in a residential setting. In A. Gitterman, & L. Shulman (Eds.), *Mutual aid groups, vulnerable and resilient populations, and the life cycle* (3rd ed., pp. 220–245). New York: Columbia University Press.

Redl, F., & Wineman, D. (1957). *The aggressive child.* Glencoe, IL: Free Press.

Rooney, R. H. (1992). *Strategies for work with involuntary clients.* New York: Columbia University Press.

Schools

Steven Rose

The purposes of group work in schools include: to help children acquire and develop essential social and cognitive skills in order to make best use of available school resources; to enhance communication and mediate between students, families, schools, and communities; and to improve school learning/teaching cultures.

Recent legislative developments such as "No Child Left Behind" have increased testing and the accompanying pressure to improve performance. Educational issues, such as optimal class and school size, impact group work in elementary, middle, and senior high schools. Schools vary in regard to: auspices (public-secular, private, and parochial); educational program (regular and special education); grade levels (elementary, middle, and senior); size (large, medium, and small); geographical location (rural, urban, suburban, and exurban); pupil population (heterogeneous and homogeneous), and social class (rich, middle-class, and poor). The outcome of the current debate whether middle schools should become more like elementary schools or senior high schools will also affect group services. The administrative, teaching, and pupil personnel service professions impact inaugurating and maintaining group work services in the schools. This represents a significant challenge when using unconventional, spontaneous group work approaches (Jagendorf & Malekoff, 2005). The degree of diversity present in the school population and the quality of intergroup relations within and between schools contribute to how much need exists for group work to promote harmonious relationships between youth of different ethnic and cultural backgrounds. These and other factors influence the availability, receptiveness, and type of offered group work services.

The culture of schools directly influences how group work is provided, as group work frequently mirrors the values and climate of the setting in which it is practiced (Wayne & Gitterman, 2003). Many schools are highly structured and value organization. The school environment is ruled by time, encompassing the school year, which defines the lifespan of most school groups, school day, and the seasons.

Ongoing prevention, intervention or treatment groups, which are offered on an ongoing basis as part of a special education programs are often scheduled to begin early in the school year.

Social work groups address serious, sensitive, and difficult social, mental health, and substance abuse problems experienced by children and youth. Social work groups differ from counseling groups in the schools in that they consider a wide variety of social factors and conditions, and are more likely to consider serious, sensitive, and difficult social, mental health, and substance abuse problems experienced by children and youth as the focus of the group. Violence, pregnancy, and suicide prevention, as well as issues of sexual orientation, discrimination, prejudice, and racism, are the focus of group work in the schools. Group work is used to promote child and youth development, encourage peaceful conflict resolution, prevent dropping out of school, acquire social and cognitive skills, and cope with family change, especially parental divorce. Evidence exists of effectiveness of group work in schools for various populations, purposes, and types of group work. In particular, evidence exists for social skills training groups and groups for children of divorce (Fraser, Day, Galinsky, Hodges, & Smokowski, 2004).

At times, school social workers co-lead groups with teachers and other pupil personnel professionals. The role of the leader of social work groups with adolescents includes awareness of authority issues and taking extra efforts to understand and communicate with members (Doel, 2005). Three confidentiality issues exist in group work with adolescents in schools, namely: (1) confidentiality is limited and is prescribed by legislation pertaining to educational records; (2) the potential exists for serious threats to health and well-being associated with adolescent behavior; and (3) adolescence is normatively a developmental period of increased independence, and shifts in interdependence.

References

Doel, M. (2005). Difficult behavior in groups. *Social Work with Groups, 28*(1), 3–22.

Fraser, M. F., Day, S. H., Galinsky, M. J., Hodges, V. G., & Smokowski, P. R. (2004). Conduct problems and peer rejection in childhood: A randomized trial of the Making Choices and Strong Families programs. *Research on Social Work Practice, 14*, 313–324.

Jagendorf, J., & Malekoff, A. (2005). Groups-on-the-go: Spontaneously formed mutual aid groups for adolescents in distress. *Social Work with Groups, 28*, 229–246.

Wayne, J., & Gitterman, A. (2003). Offensive behavior in groups: Challenges and opportunities. *Social Work with Groups, 26*(1), 23–34.

Group Work with Specific Populations

Adolescents with Co-Occurring Mental Health and Substance Use Problems
Marvin W. Clifford

Adolescents typically do well in groups in which the members have similar problems and ages (Sugar, 1986). Adolescents with mental health problems and simultaneous drug, alcohol, and excessive behavioral addictions require a comprehensive approach for treatment (Riggs, 2003). The approach should include group work to help the adolescents interact with each other, to offer support, and to meet the developmental needs of adolescents to identify with a peer group. Other services included in a comprehensive approach are individual therapy, family therapy, educational approaches, and medical and psychiatric interventions as are appropriate (Anderson & McNelis, 2006). A team approach is helpful provided services from varied agencies and programs provide a safety net called the wrap-around concept to help the adolescent with complex problems to succeed (Kerbs, Gaylor, Pullman, & Roe, 2004).

Groups designed to help adolescents with combined mental health and addictive disorders present unique issues for the social worker leading these groups. These issues include the skills and knowledge needed by social workers to lead this type of group, team-work skills to collaborate with other agency and community professionals, and knowledge of evidence-based practices that are effective with adolescents having co-occurring disorders (Bryan, 2003).

In addition to group process (Malekoff, 1993), mutual aid (Steinberg, 2004), and peer group identification, the following theories and techniques can also be helpful for working with adolescents in groups: motivational interviewing (Miller & Rollnick, 2002), motivational enhancement therapies (New Orleans Practice Improvement Collaborative, 2004), cognitive-behavioral therapy (Bryan, 2005), harm reduction (Rotgers, Little, & Deanney, 2005), and solution focused therapy (Metcalf, 1998; Tellerman, 2001). Family system approaches are useful for working with the adolescent and his or her family within this context while the adolescent attends group therapy (Walsh, 1997).

A well-designed group for this population is important. Clients need to be carefully selected for appropriate group member composition. An ideal co-occurring disorder adolescent group would include an equal number of boys and girls, be diverse in population, and have group members aged 13 to 17 who have had some type of previous treatment, have strong family or agency support for the need to be in group treatment, and would be willing to make a long-term commitment and to follow the group's guidelines. For those in recovery from addictions, they must agree to remain clean and sober, and for those on medications, they need to continuously follow their doctor's recommendations for prescription medicines and dosage. Group members are expected to interact and contribute to the group process, goals, and purpose. It is expected that group members would also be in other social work services, for example, individual casework, family work, and possibly Alcoholics Anonymous or Narcotics Anonymous meetings for teens, when appropriate.

Adolescents with combined mental health and addictive disorders can be helped, and social groups provide a method when comprehensive services and skills, provided by trained social group workers, can address the group members' complicated problems (Malekoff, 2007). A co-therapy team, composed of two social workers who are trained in co-occurring disorders intervention present an effective professional team to help these adolescents. This also offers the group workers support, influencing group members with their expertise, information, ideas, and interventions (Reid, 1997).

An example of a recent group, where the names have been changed and the scenario does not include the actual clients, is as follows:

Michael (age 14):	I wonder what it is like to use marijuana again?
Cascio (17):	You do not want to know!
Michael:	I want to get high!
Jessica (16):	Why?
Michael:	I just want to get high!
Worker:	Michael, what is going on in your life to make you want to use?
Michael:	I want to feel good! My life is bad.
Cascio:	Don't do what I did. Look at me. Don't be like me.
Worker:	What is bad about your life, Michael?
Michael:	I don't know! Just feel bad all the time. School, people, everybody bugs me. I hate it!
Jessica:	Michael, it scares me when you talk this way like you need to get your feelings out here and not on weed.
Worker:	Michael, what do you hear group members saying to you?
Michael:	That I should not use weed! And maybe talk more in group.
Cascio:	Do not relapse like me. It really set me back – school, family, probation. It was like starting all over.
Franchesca (17):	Michael, tell us you won't get loaded! Take my number. Call me if you feel shaky. I'll talk to you. I need support too, you know.
Jessica:	Michael, we care! Tell us about yourself, man.
Worker:	Michael, everyone wants you to open up and agree not to use again.
Michael:	Well, I'll think about this.
Worker:	What does Michael want for Michael?

Working with adolescents with complex mutual health and addictive disorders can be demanding work. The group worker must demonstrate enthusiasm with this population and in group sessions. Emphasizing members' strengths helps in engaging adolescents and their families (Yip, 2003).

References

Anderson, T. B., & McNelis, D. N. (2006). *Co-occurring substance use and mental health disorders in adolescents: Trainer's manual* (revised. ed.). Pittsburgh, PA: Northeast Addiction Technology Transfer Center.

Bryan, M. A. (Ed.). (2003). Co-occurring disorders: Implementing evidence-based practices. *Addiction Messenger, Fall*, Special Issue.

Bryan, M. A. (June 2005). CBT and adolescent marijuana dependence. *Addiction Messenger, 8*(6), 1–3.

Kerbs, J., Gaylor, R., Pullman, M., & Roe, P. (2004). Wraparound and juvenile justice: Making a connection that works. *Focal Point, Summer*, 19–22.

Malekoff, A. (1993). A guideline for group work with adolescents. *Social Work with Groups, 17*(2), 5–19.

Malekoff, A. (2007) *Group work with adolescents* (2nd. ed.). New York: Guilford Press.

Metcalf, L. (1998). *Solution focused group therapy*. New York: The Free Press.

Miller, W. R., & Rollnick, S. (2002). *Motivational interviewing* (2nd ed.). New York: Guilford Press.

New Orleans Practice Improvement Collaborative. (2004). *Motivational enhancement therapy with substance involved individuals: A clinical research guide*. New Orleans, LA: Author.

Reid, K. E. (1997). *Social work practice with groups: A clinical perspective* (2nd ed., p. 99). Pacific Grove, CA: Brooks/Cole.

Riggs, P. A. (2003). Treating adolescents for substance abuse and comorbid psychiatric disorders. In D. Anderson (Ed.), *Science and practice perspectives* (Vol. 1, No. 2, pp. 18–29). Rockville, MD: National Institutes of Health.

Rotgers, F., Little, J., & Deanney, P. (2005). Harm reduction and traditional treatment: Shared goals and values. *Addiction Professional, 3*(4), 20–26.

Steinberg, D. (2004). *The mutual-aid approach to working with groups* (2nd ed.). Binghamton, NY: Haworth Press.

Sugar, M. (Ed.). (1986). *The adolescent in group and family therapy* (2nd ed.). Northvale, NJ: Jason Aronson.

Tellerman, J. S. (2001). Solution oriented groups for teens, pre-teens, and their families. In: L. Vandercreek (Ed.), *Innovations for clinical practice: A source book* (Vol. 20). Sarasota, FL: Professional Resources Press.

Walsh, F. (1997). Family therapy: Systems approaches to clinical practice. In J. F. Bondell (Ed.), *Theory and practice in clinical social work* (pp. 132–163). New York: The Free Press.

Yip, K.-S. (2003). A strengths perspective in working with adolescents with dual diagnosis. *Clinical Social Work Journal, 31*(2), 187–203.

Adults with Co-Occurring Mental Health and Substance Use Problems

Brian E. Perron and Kimberly Bender

The epidemiological and services research consistently shows that co-occurring psychiatric and substance use disorders (also referred to as "dual diagnosis" and "comorbidities") are the rule rather than the exception. That is, persons with a psychiatric disorder are likely to have a substance use disorder, and vice versa.

Treating co-occurring psychiatric and substance use disorders involves considerable challenges, as they are associated with multiple treatment needs, loss of support systems, increased symptom severity, poor treatment retention, and frequent relapses and hospitalizations.

Historically, treatment for persons with co-occurring disorders has been limited. Mental health programs often do not provide counseling to clients who are active substance abusers, and many addiction treatment programs are not designed to address psychiatric disorders. Thus, persons with co-occurring disorders have often been excluded from one or both systems of care. Recent efforts in the field of social work have been devoted to improving the quality of care for this population. Existing research shows that treatment for co-occurring disorders can be effective through integrated or highly coordinated services. This approach considers both disorders as primary disorders and treats them concurrently. Social work groups are an important part of the overall set of strategies for helping this population (Hendrickson, Schmal, & Ekleberry, 2004). Outlined below are different types of groups that are commonly used.

Persons with co-occurring disorders commonly have functional impairments that present as barriers to independent living, employment, and socialization. A variety of skills groups have been developed to help overcome these impairments (Psychiatric Rehabilitation Consultants, 2000). Skills groups typically involve a structured curriculum that is administered by a professional or paraprofessional service provider. There are both proprietary (i.e., commercial) and non-proprietary curriculum materials. Some materials include specific scripts that can be read by the group leader and/or supplemental videos that provide additional learning context or specific examples of the skills taught. The group leader then uses a series of behavioral principles (e.g., coaching, modeling, role-playing, and feedback) to promote acquisition of the target skills.

The group approach provides a safe environment for practicing specific skills that can be generalized to everyday experiences. These groups are often used to target short-term objectives while working toward long-term outcomes. For example, some clients may need to develop core social skills in order to benefit from other skills-based groups such as vocational groups or peer support groups (described below). Thus, skills groups can easily be arranged sequentially to achieve various outcomes.

Peer support groups, sometimes referred to as "self-help" groups, provide a way for persons with co-occurring disorders to interact with and support other persons with similar disorders and problems (Davidson et al., 2001; Gitterman, 2006). Treatment programs may organize peer support groups, but persons with experience successfully coping with the disorders typically lead these groups. Co-occurring support groups vary slightly from traditional 12-step groups of Alcoholics Anonymous by focusing both on maintaining sobriety and on coping with symptoms of mental illness. Peer support groups are an effective way of normalizing experiences, reducing social isolation, and promoting the development of new and healthy relationships. The group format also provides an opportunity for mutual problem solving. That is, members experienced in their own recovery can offer specific strategies derived from their personal experiences. Thus, participants can provide mutual aid to one another, benefiting from the support of others while offering tools, support, and challenge to fellow group members (Gitterman & Shulman, 2005; Steinberg, 2004).

Groups exist for dealing with both substance use and psychiatric problems. Unlike peer support groups, therapy groups are facilitated by a professional and are goal oriented. They commonly use a cognitive-behavioral and problem-solving orientation for addressing specific symptoms and challenges associated with co-occurring disorders (Kopelowicz, Liberman, & Zarate, 2002). Therapy groups provide a safe setting for patients to explore behaviors, emotions, and thoughts related to reaching individual goals for improved functioning (Hendrickson et al., 2004).

By coordinating services with other providers, leaders of therapy groups can help address specific goals that may be part of the client's overall treatment plan. Therapy groups can be especially important to clients who have been recently hospitalized or are presently unstable in their recovery. Specifically, group leaders can monitor emerging problems and help coordinate a plan to avoid relapse or hospitalization.

Co-occurring disorders can place significant social and economic burdens on families. Families commonly report that they do not understand the complexities of co-occurring disorders, which can lead to significant discord among family members. An effective way of helping families understand the complexities of co-occurring disorders is through family psychoeducation (Dixon et al., 2001). This is the process of working with families to support the recovery of their family member with co-occurring disorders. Family psychoeducation is typically administered in a group format, involving multiple families. Groups may be facilitated by a human service professional or a family member experienced in this area.

Family members are taught about the various illnesses, which helps dispel myths associated with stigma. Family members also learn specific strategies for coping with the various stressors, delivering effective support, and planning ways of dealing with crisis situations (Hendrickson et al., 2004). A notable advantage of the group format is that it helps normalize experiences for families and addresses the stigmas commonly associated with psychiatric and substance use disorders (Kelsey, 2004).

Similar to adult treatment, therapy groups, skills groups, and peer support groups are important for the treatment of adolescents with co-occurring disorders. However, in order for social work groups to be effective, adult-oriented treatment should be tailored to the developmental needs of the adolescents (Lysaught & Wodarski, 1996; Malekoff, 2005). This includes making the treatment environment inviting and comfortable; involving important individuals to the adolescent such as family members, friends, and school personnel; and using language and experiential techniques that are developmentally appropriate.

The group format is particularly advantageous for treating adolescents with co-occurring disorders, as they tend to place a high value on peer interaction. The group format also provides an opportunity to incorporate a wide array of didactic treatments (e.g., decision-making skills, communication skills, impulse control) in the context of social activities. This can help improve treatment engagement and retention, thereby increasing the likelihood of achieving desired outcomes (Crome, 2004; Flanzer, 2005).

References

Crome, I. B. (2004). Comorbidity in youth people: Perspectives and challenges. *Acta Neuropsychiatrica, 16*, 47–53.

Davidson, L., Chinman, M., Kloos, B., Weingarten, R., Stayner, S., & Tebes, J. K. (2001). Peer support among individuals with severe mental illness: A review of the evidence. *Clinical Psychology: Science & Practice, 6*(2), 165–187.

Dixon, L., McFarlane, W. R., Lefley, H., Lucksted, A., Cohen, M., Falloon, I., Mueser, K., Miklowitz, D., Solomon, P., & Sondheimer, D. (2001). Evidence-based practices for services to families of people with psychiatric disabilities. *Psychiatric Services, 52*(7), 903–910.

Flanzer, J. (2005). The status of health services research on adjudicated drug-abusing juveniles: Selected findings and remaining questions. *Substance Use & Misuse, 40*, 887–911.

Gitterman, A. (2006). Building mutual support in groups. *Social Work with Groups, 28*(3/4), 91–106.

Gitterman, A., & Shulman, L. (Eds.). (2005). *Mutual aid groups, vulnerable populations and the life cycle* (3rd ed.). New York: Columbia University Press.

Hendrickson, E. L., Schmal, M. S., & Ekleberry, S. C. (2004). *Treating co-occurring disorders: A handbook for mental health and substance abuse professionals.* Binghamton, NY: Haworth Press.

Kelsey, A. (2004). Healing through companionship. *Social Work with Groups, 27*(2/3), 23–34.

Kopelowicz, A., Liberman, R. P., & Zarate, R. (2002). Psychosocial treatments for Schizophrenia. In P. Nathan, & J. Gorman (Eds.), *Treatments that work: Evidence-based treatments for psychiatric disorders* (2nd ed., pp. 201–228). New York: Oxford University Press.

Lysaught, E., & Wodarski, J. S. (1996). Model: A dual focused intervention for depression and addiction. *Journal of Child and Adolescent Substance Abuse, 5*(1), 55–71.

Malekoff, A. (2005). *Group work with adolescents: Principles and practice* (2nd ed.). New York: Guilford Press.

Psychiatric Rehabititation Consultants (PRC). (2000). Skills training modules of the Psychiatric Rehabititation Consultants. Camarillo, CA: Author.

Steinberg, D. M. (2004). *The mutual-aid approach to working with groups: Helping people help one another* (2nd ed.). Binghamton, NY: Haworth Press.

Adult Survivors of Childhood Sexual Abuse

Carolyn Knight

Sexual abuse is associated with a host of difficulties in adulthood including mental health problems like posttraumatic stress and diagnoses of dissociative identity and borderline personality disorders, behavioral and emotional problems such as depression, eating disorders, suicidal ideation, and substance abuse, and physical problems such as chronic pain. Sexual abuse also leads to distortions in thinking about self and others, resulting in chronic feelings of inadequacy, guilt, powerlessness, mistrust of others, and depersonalization.

Both men and women experience the more common long-term consequences of sexual abuse. There are differences in how men and women respond to and experience sexual victimization. Men are more likely to struggle with sexual identity issues and possess particularly intense feelings of inadequacy. In response to these feelings, male survivors may have greater difficulty managing feelings of anger.

Relative to other types of traumatic exposure that have been studied, sexual victimization in childhood is less likely to lead to any sort of adversarial growth. However, certain factors have been found to contribute to resilience among survivors of sexual abuse. Families in which there is a high level of cohesiveness among members protect members from sexual abuse in the first place, as well as mitigate its effects, should it occur. In contrast, survivors who characterize their family of origin as lacking in cohesiveness and support, controlling of members, and engaging in frequent conflict display more pathology and experience more distress.

When a child discloses the abuse and is believed and supported, and the abuse stops, the long-term impact of the abuse also is mitigated. However, when disclosure results in anger at and/or blame of the child and the abuse continues, this enhances its harmful effects, and may be more damaging than no disclosure at all.

Group participation provides survivors of childhood sexual abuse with several therapeutic advantages. First, the experience of being with others with a similar history serves to normalize survivors' experiences, reactions, and present-day difficulties. Members can learn and grow from one another. Second, group membership lessens survivors' isolation and feelings of being alone and different. Third, as survivors develop a connection to others, their sense of worth and esteem is enhanced and sense of self validated. Fourth, participation in a group can assist survivors in developing a different, more realistic perspective on their victimization, themselves, and others; distortions in thinking become apparent as members interact with one another and can be challenged directly in a group context. It is both the content of group members' discussions as well as the process of their interacting with one another that are beneficial to adult survivors of sexual abuse.

Research supports the efficacy of groups for survivors of childhood sexual abuse (Wright, Woo, Muller, Fernandes, & Kraftcheck, 2003). However, this research is largely focused on groups for women. Further, groups described in the literature also tend to be time-limited, between eight to ten sessions, and structured, with an emphasis on education and support.

Groups for adult survivors of sexual abuse exist on a continuum, from those that are focused on present-day challenges on the one hand to those that are focused on the underlying childhood sexual abuse on the other. Research suggests that for many survivors of sexual abuse, a more structured group that has a psychoeducational component, and focuses on present-day challenges and normalization of feelings and experiences is a necessary starting point for treatment. A group with a more trauma-centered focus, in which members are encouraged to disclose their victimization and confront their feelings, is more appropriate for individuals who are more stable in their functioning and achieved some basic insight into their difficulties (Spiegel, Classen, Thurston, & Butler, 2004).

Regardless of the overall focus, groups for survivors of sexual abuse should be small, generally six to eight members, to encourage intimacy and honest discussion.

Groups in which members start and finish together also are preferable. The group worker also will need to attend to composition issues and adhere to Gitterman's "not the only one" principle (2005) such that no one member should stand out in a way that isolates him or her from others in the group. Further, in any group for survivors of sexual abuse, the group worker must be prepared to help members contain or express feelings and focus on their here-and-now interactions with one another, as is appropriate to the group's overall purpose and members' needs.

Several themes are common in groups for survivors of sexual abuse. Tentative optimism, and a superficial reaching out to others characterize early sessions. It also is likely that members will assume that everyone in the group but them is a victim who did not deserve the abuse and therefore warrants the care and concern of the group. As the group progresses, it becomes harder for members to maintain the view that they were somehow to blame for their victimization. The worker must be prepared to point out the discrepancy between members' views of themselves and others in the group, paving the way for members to assume this responsibility.

As members develop greater comfort with one another, it is likely that they will begin to talk more openly about their abuse and its effects. Therefore, strong emotional reactions are most likely to surface in the group's middle phase. As the work becomes more difficult, two other dynamics are likely to emerge. Optimism about the group often is replaced by disillusionment and may be manifested by members desiring to quit or missing sessions. Dissociation, either by individual members or the group as a whole, also may occur. The group worker should be prepared to directly discuss both of these dynamics with members and, in the case of dissociation, help members understand the protective role that it serves. A fourth theme in the middle phase reflects members' attempts to reconcile behaviors and choices they made as adults. As members talk about taboo subjects and are met with acceptance, their ability to understand how their actions connect to their abuse is enhanced, thus lessening their guilt and shame. Finally, members' increasing comfort with one another will allow them to interact more genuinely with one another. Therefore, transference is likely to abound in this phase and will be apparent in members' relationships with and reactions to one another and the worker.

The ending is likely to be difficult for members. They have developed a level of comfort with one another that is reassuring and affirming. Therefore, denial of the group's ending can be a prominent theme in this last phase. The group worker will need to assist members in talking about their work together, their fears about going on without the support of the group, and identify the gains they have made. In cases where a member leaves an ongoing group, the worker will need to help the member end with the group and the group to end with the member, thus minimizing potential feelings of abandonment, guilt, and anger.

References

Gitterman, A. (2005). Group formation: Tasks, methods, and skills. In A. Gitterman, & L. Shulman (Eds.), *Mutual aid groups, vulnerable and resilient populations, and the life cycle* (3rd ed., pp. 73–110). New York: Columbia University Press.

Spiegel, D., Classen, C., Thurston, E., & Butler, L. (2004). Trauma-focused versus present-focused models for women sexually abused in childhood. In L. Koenig, & L. Doll (Eds.), *From child sexual abuse to adult sexual risk: Trauma, revictimization, and intervention* (pp. 251–268). Washington, DC: American Psychological Association.

Wright, D., Woo., W., Muller, R., Fernandes, C., Kraftcheck, E. (2003). An investigation of trauma-centered inpatient treatment for adult survivors of abuse. *Child Abuse and Neglect, 27*, 393–411.

Blind Adults

Faith Fogelman

Group work with totally blind adults thrusts sighted facilitators into new levels of sensitivity and awareness. Regardless of objectives, undercurrents of visual loss are present. General group work dynamics apply, but there are outstanding variables due to the unique role assigned to blindness, considered the most severe sensory loss.

From the ancients to modern times fascination with blindness has contributed to distorted assumptions. The blind have been portrayed from the pitiful to mystical. Although these depictions have been culturally internalized, industrious blind individuals are eclipsing strongly held negative stereotypes (Kirtley, 1975). Agencies for the blind do not usually attract these individuals, since they have reputations for reinforcing passive and even grateful behavior. Newly blinded adults are more inclined to affiliate for rehabilitation and socialization, among other reasons (Scott, 1969). Therefore, group participants in agencies for the blind do not reflect the wide spread of functioning levels among the blind population. Even so, there is broad enough diversity to contribute to an interesting mix.

One omnipresent common denominator in groups for blind adults is the deprivation of sight and its individualized meaning to each member, whether congenital or adventitiously blind. Sighted workers have a unique physical perspective— they can see. The split is severe, based on permanence and personal beliefs about blindness held by facilitators and members. Visual advantages can create imbalances contributing to covert negative feelings for sighted workers and questions about their ability to empathize, but these feelings may subside if workers use themselves well. Workers with other populations may not necessarily share challenges with participants, but the possibility of situation reversal is realistic. For example, cancer patients may recover. With permanency, like blindness, sighted workers have something that participants do not.

Sensitivity to vision calls upon skill to minimize or maximize the disability, based on the needs of participants or for one participant at poignant times. This challenge begins even prior to group sessions. Facilitators can see physical appearances and can provide feedback, but should they? Does small talk about appearances reinforce the split between what is available to the facilitator and to group participants? Some say it is unnatural to refrain since everyday conversation among the blind and sighted includes visual references. Additionally, language includes literal and figurative visual references (watch TV, see the point). Why be unnatural?

Avoidance of visual subject matters reflects bias and the discomfort of sighted workers who may sway discussions to maintain their own comfort levels. For example, blind adults, congenital or adventitious, are usually interested in appearance. Discussions of appearance reinforce that the subject is not bound by sight. This discussion should not be viewed as anything but for what it is—adults discussing a subject of interest from their own points of view and life experiences (Kaplan-Myrth, 2000).

Working with blind adults translates to relating to individuals and not to the disability. Successful group work leaders respect that blind adults are adults first and blindness may not even be their primary identity, an important point to remember in professional and casual interactions. Ethnicity and sexual orientation also contribute to identity and may be a stronger source of self-identification. Group members also reflect a mix of emotional adjustment levels and life experiences, based on many other variables including congenitally blind status, age of visual loss if adventitiously blind, and pace of loss (Saino, 2003). Blind adults including those serviced by agencies are not monolithic. Personalities vary.

Even still, the issue of blindness is prevalent, although group objectives with blind adults do not always have to center on visual loss. Groups can be current events discussion groups and groups focused on learning or performing task objectives, which have nothing to do with blindness. Blind participants are very capable of moving from self and offering intelligent opinions about world events, even though blindness ultimately informs the frame of reference. Mutual support groups are especially helpful to the newly blinded, who may be struggling with role confusion. Group members who have adjusted, are living full lives, and are confident adults serve as role models. Interacting with those who have moved beyond baseline rehabilitation can be more therapeutic than just working with a sighted caseworker. Support groups can also focus on other commonalities, including age-related issues (Baird, 2005; Orr, 2005).

Agencies servicing the blind are usually inclusive of the legally blind (visual acuity no greater than 20/200 with the better eye and the best correction or a circumference field of no greater than 20 degrees). This range runs from shadow vision to those who navigate life without detection of blindness. Legally blind group members add to diversity and high partials have the challenge of straddling both the blind and sighted worlds. One outstanding concern among the legally blind is the fear of losing all residual vision (which can parallel fears of sighted workers).

This anxiety can play itself out in group dynamics with disguised hostility, scapegoating, and a status claim based on having residual vision. Sighted facilitators should not assume that legally blind participants function on higher levels than totally blind counterparts. Some totally blind participants have a better relationship with themselves than those with partial visual loss. Although those with some vision may not necessarily be more intelligent or better adjusted, workers may gravitate towards them. Legally blind participants can offer what totally blind participants cannot: interactions with eye contact and facial expressions. Workers also must decide whether to employ visible ambiances which can be helpful to those with residual vision but can also reinforce visual divides.

A developed sensitivity to disability nuance suggests that agency groups be initiated only after facilitators have had casework experience. It is important to know general life experience differences between the congenitally and adventitiously blind. This background prepares workers with knowledge of trends in discrete blindness cultures. Agency support is critical for initiating new groups since workers need supervision to ensure a positive group experience for all (Goodman & Munoz, 2004).

Group work with the blind should not be focused on the needs of sighted workers and their possible discomfort or anxiety raised by interactions with this population. Sighted facilitators utilize a highly developed sense of self to do the validating and to facilitate optimal functioning among members. Sighted facilitators foster group dynamics in meaningful ways, which includes minimal use of visual cues and stimuli, but not unnatural dialogue. While hope for seeing or seeing better is not realistic, overt and covert messages about good lives without vision are always part of the agenda.

References

Baird, J. K. (2005). Reflections on the effects of group work with older people with impaired vision. *International Congress Series, 1282*, 360–364.

Goodman, H. & Munoz, M. (2004). Developing social group work skills for contemporary agency practice. *Social Work with Groups, 27*(1), 17–34.

Kaplan-Myrth, N. (2000). Alice without a looking glass: Blind people and body image. *Anthropology and Medicine, 7*(3), 277–299.

Kirtley, D. (1975). *The psychology of blindness*. Chicago: Nelson Hall.

Orr, A. (2005). Dealing with the death of a group member: Visually impaired elderly in the community. In A. Gitterman, & L. Shulman (Eds.), *Mutual aid groups, vulnerable and resilient populations and the life cycle* (3rd ed., pp. 471–492). New York: Columbia University Press.

Saino, M. (2003). A new language for groups: Multilingual and multiethnic group work. *Social Work with Groups, 26*(1), 69–82.

Scott, R. A. (1969). *The making of blind men*. New York: Russell Sage Foundation.

Children with Traumatic Grief

Alison Salloum

Social workers need to be prepared to provide effective services for children who are experiencing traumatic grief, whether due to disasters, terrorist attacks, war, accidents, suicide, homicide, or disease. While many children are resilient after traumatic loss, some children will need professional intervention. In a landmark study of an incident where a sniper killed a child on a school playground, Nader, Pynoos, Fairbanks, and Frederick (1990) found that exposure to the event and closeness of the relationship to the deceased were associated with higher levels of posttraumatic stress, which persisted over time. Since that study, advances in understanding both childhood bereavement and posttraumatic stress after death have occurred. Traditionally, bereavement research with children has explored psychosocial distress such as depression, anxiety, and social adjustment (e.g., Cerel, Fristad, Verducci, Weller, & Weller, 2006; Worden & Silverman, 1996). However, researchers have found that some bereaved children and adolescents are also at risk for experiencing posttraumatic stress (Stoppelbein & Greening, 2000). In fact, scholars are currently studying and defining constructs such as childhood traumatic grief (Cohen, Mannarino, Greenberg, Padlo, & Shipley, 2002) and childhood complicated grief (Melhem, Moritiz, Walker, Shear, & Brent, 2007), which are seen as syndromes distinct from posttraumatic stress disorder and depression. In childhood traumatic grief, whether the death is unnatural or natural, the child perceives the death as traumatic and posttraumatic symptoms interfere with the bereavement process (Cohen et al., 2002). Similarly childhood complicated grief may occur even in the absence of exposure to the dying or a traumatic life-threatening event and the child may experience symptoms such as constant thoughts of the deceased, avoidance of death and loss reminders, loss of security and control, and anger (Melhem et al., 2007). As in the adult bereavement literature, there is controversy about the definitions of clinical bereavement conditions. However, researchers are continuing to examine the characteristics, measurement, and interventions for childhood traumatic grief.

Many group work interventions with children and adolescents experiencing traumatic grief utilize structured, closed, time-limited formats. These short-term group approaches have specific goals of facilitating grief, and more specifically, improving symptoms and functioning that may be complicating the bereavement process. Sessions range from 4 to 18 meetings and some utilize individual and family meetings in conjunction with the child-only group sessions. While there are different types of time-limited group interventions after death, such as crisis interventions, support groups, expressive arts groups, and psychotherapy (Webb, 2003), the research on outcome effectiveness is limited. Nonetheless, with the evolving practice of manualized and evidence-based practices (Galinsky, Terzian, & Fraser, 2006), time-limited group treatment with children and adolescents experiencing traumatic grief post disaster (Goenjian et al., 2005) and violent death (Pfeffer, Jiane, Kakuma, Hwang, & Metsch, 1997; Salloum, Avery, & McClain, 2001; Saltzman, Pynoos, Layne, Steinberg, & Aisenberg, 2001) is promising. These studies have been conducted in schools, detention centers, and community agencies with children and adolescents from low to middle socioeconomic status and from various racial and ethnic backgrounds. However, additional research on group models with specific populations in various contexts is needed.

When incidents occur resulting in death(s) affecting groups of children, crisis intervention groups such as Psychological First Aid or more universal prevention programs that can be delivered to large groups of children may be offered. Screenings may also occur with all children potentially affected to identify children experiencing significant grief and posttraumatic stress. After large group interventions or screenings, children who are experiencing traumatic grief and other psychosocial difficulties need to be referred to small group and/or individual or family interventions that address their specific needs.

Individual premeetings to further assess appropriateness for group participation and to conduct a brief biopsychosocial–spiritual assessment, including death-related factors, are warranted. In fact, it may be that children who are experiencing high distress and psychosocial and behavioral problems will benefit the most. Bereaved children who are not experiencing traumatic stress and who are in groups with other traumatized children may worsen (Jordan & Neimeyer, 2003), although more research in this area is needed.

Group work models for children experiencing traumatic grief need to be grounded in current research and theory on childhood bereavement and trauma. Other theories and approaches used to inform group therapies include risk and resilience literature, cognitive-behavioral therapy, attachment theory, ecological perspective, and group work theory. Group interventions also need to be developmentally specific and be implemented in ways that are culturally congruent with bereavement and trauma responses of specific populations. Perhaps as childhood traumatic grief research advances, additional theories will be used to guide group interventions.

Common components of childhood grief and trauma groups include parental involvement, grief and traumatic stress psychoeducation, death or traumatic event education, coping and promoting resilience, stress management techniques, increasing a sense of safety, constructing a trauma narrative of the dying and traumatic circumstances, correcting cognitive distortions, commemorating the deceased's life and restoring positive memories, reducing traumatic stress, affect expression, addressing changes and adjustments post-loss, connecting or reconnecting with supports and interests, promoting developmental tasks, and evaluating the group. Social workers should consider addressing these components in group work with children who are experiencing traumatic grief.

References

Cerel, J., Fristad, M. A., Verducci, J., Weller, R. A., & Weller, F. B. (2006). Childhood bereavement: Psychopathology in the 2 years postparental death. *Journal of the American Academy of Child and Adolescent Psychiatry, 45*(6), 681–690.

Cohen, J. A., Mannarino, A. P., Greenberg, T., Padlo, S., & Shipley, C. (2002). Childhood traumatic grief: Concepts and controversies. *Trauma, Violence and Abuse, 4*, 307–327.

Galinsky, M. J., Terzian, M. A., & Fraser, M. W. (2006). The art of group work practice with manualized curricula. *Social Work with Groups, 29*(1), 11–26.

Goenjian, A. K., Walling, S., Steinberg, A., Karayan, I., Najarian, L. M., & Pynoos, R. (2005). A prospective study of posttraumatic stress and depression reactions among treated and untreated adolescents five years after a catastrophic disaster. *American Journal of Psychiatry, 162*, 2302–2308.

Jordan, J. R., & Neimeyer, R. A. (2003). Does grief counseling work? *Death Studies, 27*, 765–786.

Melhem, M. N., Moritiz, G., Walker, M., Shear, K. M., & Brent, D. (2007). Phenomenology and correlates of complicated grief in children and adolescents. *Journal of the American Academy of Child and Adolescent Psychiatry, 46*(4), 493–499.

Nader, K., Pynoos, R.S., Fairbanks, L., & Frederick, C. (1990). Children's PTSD reactions one year after a sniper attack at their school. *American Journal of Psychiatry, 147*, 1526–1530.

Pfeffer, C. R., Martins, P., Mann, J., Sunkenberg, M., Ice, A., Damore, J. P., Gallo, C., Karpenos, I., & Jiang, H. (1997). Child survivors of suicide: Psychosocial characteristics. *Journal of the American Academy of Child and Adolescent Psychiatry, 36*(1), 65–74.

Salloum, A., Avery, L., & McClain, M. (2001). Group psychotherapy for adolescent survivors of homicide victims: A pilot study. *Journal of the American Academy of Child and Adolescent Psychiatry, 40,* 1261–1267.

Saltzman, W. R., Pynoos, R. S., Layne, C. M., Steinberg, A. M., & Aisenberg, A. M. (2001). Trauma-and-grief-focused intervention for adolescents exposed to community violence: Results of a school-based screening and group treatment protocol. *Group Dynamics: Theory, Research, and Practice, 5,* 291–303.

Stoppelbein, L. M. A., & Greening, L. (2000). Posttraumatic stress symptoms in parentally bereaved children and adolescents. *Journal of the American Academy of Child and Adolescent Psychiatry, 39,* 1112–1119.

Webb, N. B. (2003). Play and expressive therapies to help bereaved children: Individual, family and group treatment. *Smith College Studies in Social Work, 73*(3), 405–422.

Worden, W. J., & Silverman, P. R. (1996). Parental death and the adjustment of school-age children. *Omega, 33,* 91–102.

Domestic Violence Survivors

Patricia O'Brien

Each year, almost two million women in the United States suffer from domestic violence (Tjaden & Thoennes, 1998). Before shelters, national hotlines, or formalized and funded programs existed, self-help support groups met in church basements, hospital waiting rooms, and late-night eateries. In these settings, women from every type of background came together to validate their reality of being physically battered and emotionally abused. In these support groups, members shared information and learned from each other how to get free of controlling and abusive relationships. Sometimes peer led, sometimes facilitated by altruistic social workers in after-hours work, the group members would first discuss the warning signs of violence, how to create safety plans, and where to go in a crisis. A feminist perspective often informed these support groups (Cohen, 2003).

The support groups also provided a combination of consciousness-raising, education, problem solving, mutual aid, and a social context for deciphering the violence in women's lives. The groups focused on women knowing they were not alone in the experience of being abused—that as they named the violence and abuse they had suffered, they could hear that someone else had experienced the same or worse. The naming of the violence provided an initial point of validation and an opening for how they could regain their capacity for controlling their own lives. They also learned from each other that they were not responsible for their partner's abusing them, and they gained crucial information about how they could begin rebuilding their lives for themselves and their children, sometimes in new cities and states. As they continued in the groups, they learned about how they could heal from the abuse they had experienced. They learned they could tell other people about what they had experienced and, by the telling, reclaim connection to others who would remind them that they deserve better. They learned from each other how to listen and believe in each woman's ability to be healthy and strong and safe. Members were encouraged to look to themselves for an understanding of their problems, as well as working together toward individual and collective solutions. A gendered analysis facilitated the women moving from individualized stories of victimization to processes of empowerment (Cohen, 2003). Consistent with the basic principles of mutual aid, the role of the facilitator/leader in these early groups was to help members help one another.

The Self-Help/Mutual Aid Model (Steinberg, 1997) that informed the early development and implementation of the support groups was not a perfect model. It provided a solid and initial core of empowering support, but women and their families often had many acute problems that transcended the capabilities of other similarly situated members to address within the group context, particularly the need for immediate and safe shelter. Furthermore, due to the group being by its nature, open-ended for women in crisis, women were less likely to develop the level of connection that Schiller (1995) describes as common to women's group development over time.

In addition to a direct line of support, many members moved from the support groups to collective action, by building the base of advocacy that assisted in making the case for protective policies. One of the first times that organizing by battered women and advocates made a major difference in policy formulation was the organized hearings sponsored by the Attorney General's Task Force on Family Violence championed by Assistant Attorney General Lois Haight Herington (Attorney General's Task Force, 1984). These Hearings provided visibility and voice to the plight of battered women, a phenomenon that had been "hidden" behind closed doors and often ignored or minimized by legal and social institutions. The public testimony provided in six cities by nearly 300 witnesses resulted in multiple recommendations for the legal system that became the bedrock for the treatment of battered women today as victims of a crime.

The early analysis of the battering of women was based on a feminist recognition of male dominance that was reinforced through the threat and use of violence. As an antidote to this analysis, early support groups as well as statewide and national advocacy organizations developed an empowerment and anti-oppression philosophy. One of the earliest national coalitions, the National Coalition Against Domestic Violence (NCADV) operated for many years using consensus decision making and held clear policies for inclusionary membership, with a special focus on former victims of abuse, women of color, and lesbians (Schechter, 1982). These early coalitions provided a powerful and cohesive voice for making the hidden issue of wife battering visible, as well as, drawing upon feminist tenets, actualizing the connection between the personal and the political by using group models focused on empowerment (Cohen, 2003).

Battered women's groups are still an important service component of shelters and programs serving battered women. The basic recognition of being "in the same boat" that is basic to mutual aid processes is the starting point for individual and collective transformation (Gitterman, 2004).

References

Attorney General's Task Force on Family Violence. (1984). Washington, DC: Department of Justice.

Cohen, M. B. (2003). Women in groups: The history of feminist empowerment. In M. B. Cohen, & A. Mullender (Eds.), *Gender and groupwork* (pp. 32–40). London: Routledge.

Gittterman, A. (2004). The Mutual Aid Model. In C. Garvin, L. Gutiérrez, & M. Galinsky (Eds.), *Handbook of social work with groups* (pp. 93–110). New York: Guilford Publications.

Schechter, S. (1982). *Women and male violence: The visions and struggles of the battered women's movement.* Boston: South End Press.

Schiller, L. Y. (1995). Stages of development in women's groups: A relational model. In R. Kurland, & R. Salmon (Eds), *Group work practice in a troubled society* (pp. 117–138). Binghamton, NY: Haworth Press.

Steinberg, D. M. (1997). *The mutual-aid approach to working with groups: Helping people to help each other.* Northvale, NJ: Aronson.

Tjaden, P., & Thoennes, N. (1998). *Prevalence, incidence and consequences of violence against women: Findings from the National Violence against Women Survey.* Washington, DC: U.S. Department of Justice.

Family Violence Survivors

Wendy Bunston

Social work's contribution to the development and delivery of group work to address family violence within the Australian context appears to be significant (Bunston & Heynatz, 2006; Gevers & Goddard-Jones, 2003, 2004; Jackson & Dilger, 1995; Laing, 2001; McMaster, 2004). Workers "on the ground," usually in collaboration with other health and welfare professionals, targeted diverse cultural groups within non-indigenous and indigenous Australia, as well as across metropolitan, rural and outback settings. Adult perpetrator and victim groups, parenting groups, young people and/or children's groups are provided in a variety of community settings.

Australian perpetrator programs began to emerge in the late 1980s. An early and significant influence was the Duluth Model, originating out of the Domestic Abuse Intervention Project (DAIP) in Duluth, MN (Pence & Paymar, 1993; Younger, 1995). This model focuses on power and control as instrumental to the exercise of violence by men in intimate relationships. Largely psychoeducational, the model emphasizes accountability not just through court-mandated attendance at programs but also through partner contact. What distinguishes Australian perpetrator programs from other countries, however, is they are largely "stand alone," voluntary and located within community, rather than judiciary systems.

Many community organizations offering men's behavior change programs also offer support groups for their women partners; however, women's groups can often operate in isolation from men's programs. They are generally based on feminist values and educational approaches, which incorporate concepts such as the cycle of violence (Walker, 1979). These organizations offer "mutual aid" and "empowerment" through a supportive group approach (Jackson & Dilger, 1995), as well as "strengths-based" parenting programs (Jewell & Blackmore, 2004). More comprehensive "family approaches" offering treatment groups for men, women and children are often run in partnership with other organizations and some provide social work staff to supervise ongoing, "community-led" support groups.

In the 1990s Australian social worker and family therapist Michael White and New Zealander David Epston developed a very popular, alternative narrative therapy approach. This approach recognized that people were the "experts in their own lives" and aimed to "externalize problems," seeing them as "separate to" rather than "part of" a person (White & Epston, 1990). This view revolutionized the way many Australian, New Zealand and international social workers practice, ushering in group work programs that "invite" men who use violence to take full responsibility for their own behaviors (Jenkins, 1990) and encouraging other "solution focused", "anti-oppressive" and "strengths-based" perspectives (McMaster, 2004), whilst also actively involving women partners, and even "outsider witnesses" in the group process (Wirtz & Schweitzer, 2003).

Narrative practices, as well as more inclusive, capacity-building and holistic approaches, have been embraced as more culturally relevant by indigenous populations, as they endeavour to challenge past oppressive practices that have dispossessed the native inhabitants of this country and to recognize the broader political and racial ramifications that have contributed to the very high rates of violence recorded in Australian indigenous communities (Memmot, Chambers, Go-Sam, & Thomson, 2006; Taylor, Cheers, Weetra, & Gentle, 2004). Similarly, in casting indigenous communities as their own experts, these approaches honour their right and authority in determining their own solutions, and expands their definition of "family" to include "community" (Taylor et al., 2004). The involvement of social workers in past practices of removing aboriginal children from their families during the greater part of the last century has, however, left many indigenous communities ambivalent about the involvement of social workers, other professionals, and their interventions.

Groups for children and young people exposed to family violence have been more creative and diverse in their design. Different mediums used have included art, music, dance, storytelling, puppetry, drama and play with the range of approaches being just as varied, such as cognitive-behavioural, educational, systems, psychotherapy, strengths-based and narrative (Gevers & Goddard-Jones, 2003). These groups primarily focus on middle childhood upward, involve their mother/carer and are often con-joint in their delivery. "School-based" and "peer-educational" or "peer support" programs are more popular for young people. In essence, most interventions aim to give children and young people space to make sense of their familial trauma, enhance their self-esteem, appropriately manage strong emotions, strengthen their relationship with the non-perpetrating family member/s and build their networks of support.

Groups promoting child-sensitive practices and embracing a "child up" approach to family group work have also been developed, undertaking some work with non-perpetrating fathers and fathers who have been through behavior change programs, acknowledging the ongoing attachment children may still have with the perpetrator (Bunston & Heynatz, 2006). Further to this, psychotherapeutic "infant-led" groups for infants and mothers affected by family violence have been developed (Bunston, 2006, Thomson-Salo, & Paul, 2007). This approach recognizes the infant as "subject" in, and of, his or her own right, and mother's are encouraged to observe, reflect upon and be available to allowing their infants to guide their interactions.

References

Bunston, W. (2006). The Peek a Boo Club: Groupwork for infants and mothers affected by family violence. *DVIRC Quarterly, Autumn* (1), 3–8.

Bunston, W., & Heynatz, A. (Eds.). (2006) *Addressing family violence programs: Groupwork interventions for infants, children and their families.* Melbourne, Australia: Royal Children's Hospital Mental Health Service.

Gevers, L., & Goddard-Jones, M. (2003). *Working with children and young people living with domestic violence.* Canberra, Australia: Commonwealth of Australia.

Gevers, L., & Goddard-Jones, M. (2004) *National audit of training in Australia for working with men who use violence.* Canberra, Australia: Commonwealth of Australia.

Jackson, M., & Dilger, R. (1995). An empowering approach to women's domestic violence groups. *Australian Social Work, 48*(1), 51–59.

Jenkins, A. (1990). *Invitations to responsibility: The therapeutic engagement of men who are violent and abusive.* Adelaide, Australia: Dulwich Centre Publications.

Jewell, P., & Blackmore, P. (2004). *From strength to strength: A manual for professionals who facilitate diverse parent groups.* Camberwell, Victoria, Australia: ACER Press.

Laing, L. (2001). Working with woman: Exploring individual and group work approaches. *Australian Domestic & Family Violence Clearinghouse* (Issues Paper 4). Sydney, Australia: The University of New South Wales.

McMaster, K. (2004) Facilitating change through groupwork. In J. Maidment, & R. Egan (Eds.), *Practice skills in social work and welfare* (pp. 207–223). Sydney, Australia: Allen & Unwin.

Memmott, P., Chambers, C., Go-Sam, C., & Thomson, L. (2006). Good practice in indigenous family violence prevention: Designing and evaluating successful programs. *Australian Domestic & Family Violence Clearinghouse* (Issues Paper 11). Sydney, Australia: The University of New South Wales.

Pence, E., & Paymar, M. (1993). *Education groups for men who batter: The Duluth Model.* New York: Springer.

Taylor, J., Cheers, B., Weetra, C., & Gentle, I. (2004). Supporting community solutions to family violence. *Australian Social Work, 57*(1), 71–83.

Thomson-Salo, F., & Paul, C. (Eds.). (2007). *The baby as subject* (2nd ed). Melbourne, Australia: Stonnington Press.

Walker, L. (1979). *The battered woman.* New York: Harper & Row.

White, M., & Epston, D. (1990). *Narrative means to therapeutic ends.* New York: Norton.

Wirtz, H., & Schweitzer, R. (2003). Groupwork with men who engage in violent and abusive actions. In Dulwich Centre (Eds.), *Responding to violence: A collection of papers relating to child sexual abuse and violence* (pp. 187–202). Adelaide, Australia: Dulwich Centre Publications.

Younger, B. (1995). *Stopping men's violence in the family.* Richmond, Victoria, Australia: V-Net Inc.

Lesbian, Gay, Bisexual, and Transgender Individuals

Mitch Rosenwald

Individuals who are lesbian, gay, bisexual, transgender, and queer/questioning (LGBTQ), as well as intersex, share in common a sexual orientation or gender identity that is not congruent with societal norms. Despite some progress in more enlightened social views and increasing equal protection statutes among some states and municipalities, the social and political climate for this population remains far from ideal. Social workers conducting group work with this population should be attentive to this context and anticipate that group members' needs will represent a continuum of responses to living in a society still laden with stigma, prejudice, and discrimination.

Although professional group work conservatively began to convert "homosexuals" to a heterosexual orientation as early as the 1950s, an empowerment perspective dominated group work with lesbian and gay individuals began in the early 1980s (Conlin & Smith, 1982). This perspective continues to this day in group work, with the emphasis on honoring their individual and collective dignity, and helping them meet their needs and achieve their goals. Scholarship includes broad discussion of group work, with this population (Getzel, 1998; Rosenwald, in press) as well as attention to the largest focus—group work addressing individuals and HIV/AIDS (e.g., Getzel, 1991; Martin, Riopelle, Steckart, & Geshke, 2001; Sandstrom, 1996). Additionally, research attends to subpopulations including lesbians, bisexual, and transgender individuals (e.g., Firestein, 1999; Groves & Schondel, 1997/1998; Klein, 1999), racial and ethnic minorities (De Vidas, 1999; Masequesmay, 2003), youth and young adults (DeLois & Cohen, 2000; Peters, 1997), and seniors (Drumm, 2004; Moore, 2002).

A broad array of issues emerges when facilitating group work with this population. These include: identity formation, "coming out" to relatives and peers, reconciling sexual orientation/gender identity with religion, discussing civil rights, promoting safety, managing romantic and platonic relationships, discussing sexual behavior, gaining satisfactory housing and employment, and promoting health and mental health. Members' abilities to resolve their issues depend on their own development, their ability to live in a discriminatory society, and the support they have from others, including the power of the group itself.

Group work with this population is both professionally and lay-facilitated. Opportunities for social workers to facilitate groups are typically found through LGBTQ-friendly non-profit agencies such as AIDS-prevention agencies and outpatient mental health clinics, colleges and universities, community centers, and private practice. Unlike group work with other populations, the social worker interested in work with this population may find that existing groups do not exist because the work is too "controversial." For example, an agency-based worker might know that the agency serves a number of LGBTQ clients but no group exists because no one ever thought to form it. Upon probing, the social worker learns that a latent rationale of prejudice is behind the group's absence. Therefore, social workers should play a strong role in advocating for the creation of such groups. They should be prepared for some organizational resistance to their ideas; therefore, careful planning including conducting a needs assessment and allying with supportive staff in leadership roles is both vital and strategic.

When recruiting members for group, gauging the openness of a community and knowing where to advertise the group are crucial considerations that intertwine. A community with civil rights protection, low incidences of homophobic and transphobic crimes, and a visible LGBTQ community are relatively good indicators that the larger community is somewhat supportive. Therefore, openly advertising the group in general community spaces such as agencies, libraries, cafes, bookstores, and senior centers, in addition to lesbian and gay community centers and bar outreach, is a good strategy. If the community is less supportive, advertising "below the radar" is necessary; here bar outreach coupled with collaborating with supportive staff at agencies might be the strongest method to advertise.

Once the group begins, the theoretical perspective a social worker employs with this population, like with all populations, depends on the purpose of the group. A cognitive-behavioral approach is used when the worker assumes a stronger teaching role, in addition to facilitating; this method is used, for example, in harm reduction groups that teach healthy sexual behavior when working with gay and bisexual men. A narrative approach concentrates on members sharing their "stories" and particularly coincides with the need to empower a population that has frequently faced personal and societal hurdles through stigma. A solution-focused approach can be used when working with youth, for example, who need advice from the group on making decisions about the coming out process. Despite the perspective used, mutual aid (Gitterman & Shulman, 2005) is a hallmark approach to group work in which the worker, and then the group members themselves, nurture a number of dynamics that maximize group cohesion and positive change. Mutual aid dynamics such as mutual support, mutual demand, and strength in numbers help members feel comforted, challenged on their thoughts, feelings and actions, and understand that they have power to effect change in society outside of the group structure.

For many group members, the group is the safest social space in which they have ever resided because they can feel truly comfortable that they will not be judged based on their sexual orientation or gender identity. The social worker needs to realize the power of this dynamic. To ensure that such a feeling of safety continues, the attentive group worker includes in ground rules both an affirmation of diversity and a requirement of mutual respect, particularly because dynamics of racism, sexism, and other prejudices occur in this population. In addition to skillful facilitation of the group following mutual aid principles, workers should be versed in the community resources available that are "gay-friendly" to this population. Many members will rely on the group as their sole or primary method for information and referral, as well as support.

Group work with the LGBTQ population is essential in promoting the needs of a portion of society that has historically been excluded from the rights and dignity that all human beings deserve. Social workers attentive and skilled in conducting group work with this population promote the mental health and social welfare of these individuals.

References

Conlin, D., & Smith, J. (1982). Group psychotherapy for gay men. *Journal of Homosexuality, 7*(2/3), 105–112.

DeLois, K., & Cohen, M. B. (2000). A queer idea: Using group work principles to strengthen learning in a sexual minorities seminar. *Social Work with Groups, 23*(3), 53–67.

De Vidas, M. (1999). Childhood sexual abuse and domestic violence: A support group for Latino gay men and lesbians. *Journal of Gay & Lesbian Social Services, 10*(2), 51–68.

Drumm, K. (2004). An examination of group work with old lesbians with a lack of intimacy by using a record of service. *Journal of Gerontological Social Work, 44*(1/2), 25–52.

Firestein, B. A. (1999). New perspectives on group treatment with women of diverse sexual identities. *Journal for Specialists in Group Work, 24*(3), 306–315.

Getzel, G. (1991). Survival modes for people with AIDS in groups. *Social Work, 36*(1), 7–11.

Getzel, G. (1998). Group work practice with gay men and lesbians. In G. P. Mallon (Ed.), *Foundations of social work practice with lesbian and gay persons* (pp. 131–144). Binghamton, NY: Harrington Park Press.

Gitterman, A., & Shulman, L. (Eds.). (2005). *Mutual aid groups, vulnerable and resilient populations, and the life cycle* (3rd ed.). New York: Columbia University Press.

Groves, P. A., & Scholdel, C. (1997/1998). Feminist groupwork with lesbian survivors of incest. *Groupwork, 10*(3), 215–230.

Klein, R. (1999). Group work with transgendered male to female sex workers. *Journal of Gay & Lesbian Social Services, 10*(3/4), 95–109.

Martin, D. J., Riopelle, D., Steckart, J., & Geshke, N. (2001). Support group participation, HIV viral load and sexual-risk behavior. *American Journal of Health Behavior, 25*(6), 513–527.

Masequesmay, G. (2003). Negotiating multiple identities in a queer Vietnamese support group. *Journal of Homosexuality, 45*(2–4), 193–215.

Moore, W. R. (2002). Lesbian and gay elders: Connecting care providers though a telephone support group. *Journal of Gay & Lesbian Social Services, 14*(3), 23–41.

Peters, A. J. (1997). Themes in group work with lesbian and gay adolescents. *Social Work with Groups, 20*(2), 51–69.

Rosenwald, M. (2008). Group work practice with LGBTQ people. In G. P. Mallon (Ed.), *Social work practice with lesbian, gay, bisexual, and transgender people* (2nd ed., pp. 221–239). Binghamton, NY: Haworth Press.

Sandstrom, K. L. (1996). Searching for information, understanding, and self-value: The utilization of peer support groups by gay men with HIV/AIDS. *Social Work in Health Care, 23*(4), 51–74.

Nonresidential Fathers

Glenn Stone

Many nonresidential fathers experience a great deal of pain and anguish as a result of their separation from their children following divorce and/or separation. An early longitudinal study of the effects of divorce on fathers (Hetherington, Cox, & Cox, 1978) identified three primary adaptation challenges for divorced fathers: (a) practical problems of daily living; (b) interpersonal problems in the areas of social life, intimate relationships, and in relating to the children and former spouse; and (c) problems related to self-concept and identity. As a result of these life stressors, nonresidential fathers are at particular risk for long-term adjustment problems such as suicidal behaviors and substance abuse (Umberson & Williams, 1993). Even never-married fathers seem to be at risk for higher rates of depression and social isolation (Vaz, Smolen, & Miller, 1983).

Adapting to a life transition and traumatic event is often complicated for men due to a socialization process that limits their ability to verbalize their painful emotions and to ask for help (Dudley & Stone, 2001). In seeking help, men/fathers often fear that others may view them as a failure (Jordan, 1992). They believe that it is "unmanly" and unacceptable to seek help and admit to having problems (Heppner & Gonzales, 1987). Men/fathers may not have the words to express loss nor the tools to even process the loss. Levant (1992) refers to this problem as a mild form of "alexithymia," which literally means "without words for emotions."

Group work is an ideal approach for helping nonresidential fathers to help each other deal with stressful life transitions and traumatic events (Germain & Gitterman, 1996; Gitterman, 2005). Interactional groups represent a potential source of support and mutual aid for fathers coping with separation from their children. Nonresidential fathers experience considerable emotional distress from a divorce or uncoupling experience as well as from seeing their children intermittently and according to a prescribed schedule. Interactional groups provide a safe place for fathers to explore these issues with other fathers in a way that provides a sense of community support of men. Mutual aid groups provide an important substitute for lost support, restore a diminished self-image, develop new associations, and maximize strengths.

Mutual aid groups for nonresident fathers also provides them the opportunity to not only "receive" assistance, but also to "provide" help to other members (Gitterman & Shulman, 2005). The help may come in the form of advice, shared experiences, support, guidance, or even mentoring. In a paradoxical way, giving help to others makes it easier for men to use help for themselves. This opportunity to be the "helper" assists men in feeling less intimidated by the helping process. They are equal collaborators in the work of the group, and feel empowered rather than being in a "one-down" position. Through these exchanges, nonresidential fathers develop new interpersonal, communication, and relationship skills.

References

Dudley, J., & Stone, G. (2001) *Fathering at risk: Helping nonresidential fathers*. New York: Springer.

Germian, C. B., & Gitterman, A. (1996). *The Life Model of social work practice: Advances in knowledge and practice* (2nd ed.). New York: Columbia University Press.

Gitterman, A. (2005). Developing a new group service: Strategies and skills. In A. Gitterman, & L. Shulman (Eds.), *Mutual aid groups, vulnerable and resilient populations, and the life cycle* (2nd ed., pp. 73–112). New York: Columbia University Press.

Gitterman, A., & Shulman, L. (2005). The Life Model, mutual aid, oppression, and the mediating function. In A. Gitterman, & L. Shulman (Eds.), *Mutual aid groups, vulnerable and resilient populations, and the life cycle* (3rd ed., pp. 3–37). New York: Columbia University Press.

Heppner, P., & Gonzales, D. (1987). Men counseling men. In M. Scher, M. Stevens, G. Good, & G. Eichenfield (Eds.), *Handbook of counseling and psychotherapy with men* (pp. 30–38). Newbury Park, CA: Sage.

Hetherington, E. M., Cox, M., & Cox, R. (1978). The aftermath of divorce. In J. H. Stevens, Jr., & M. Mathews (Eds.), *Mother–child, father–child relations*. Washington, DC: National Association for the Education of Young Children.

Jordan, P. (1992). Counseling men confronted by marital separation. *Journal of Divorce and Remarriage, 18*, 109–126.

Levant, R. (1992). Toward the reconstruction of masculinity. *Journal of Family Psychology, 5*, 309–315.

Umberson, D., & Williams, C. (1993). Divorced fathers: Parental role strain and psychological distress. *Journal of Family Issues, 14*, 378–400.

Vaz, R., Smolen, P., & Miller, C. (1983). Adolescent pregnancy: Involvement of the male partner. *Journal of Adolescent Health Care, 4*(4), 246–250.

Parents

Janet Seden

Social groupwork is critical in supporting and enhancing parenting capacities (the abilities of parents to meet children's developmental needs). Groupwork with parents (and other carers) has embraced a full range of models of practice (self-help, mutual aid, problem-solving, and task-centred (Brown, 1992). Diverse group-work methods have had positive outcomes (Angelini, 1994; Fernandez, 2004; Harrison, Parker, & Honey, 2005; May, Hamilton, & Elderkin, 1999; Neville, Beak, & King 1996, 1998; Scott & O'Neill, 1996). At the same time, however, debates continue about the extent to which such groupwork is empowering or coercive (Mullender & Ward, 1991; Preston-Shoot, 2007) and whether the direction varies, according to the practitioner's interventions and style (Habermann, 1990).

Groupwork has an important function, working in partnership with parents, by enabling parents/carers to maintain children safely at home with their own families and communities wherever it is possible. While it may remain goal directed and aim to achieve change, such group work can recognize the relevance of personal strengths (Saleebey, 1992) and of social networks (Preston-Shoot, 2007); as such it fits well with ecological and partnership approaches to child welfare. For example, groups for parents whose children have a disability and complex social and emotional needs can strengthen their abilities to support their children and obtain necessary services. The mutual aid achieved can be empowering (Mullender & Ward 1991; Steinberg, 2004). Group workers therefore can aim to build community strengths and resilience in parents, thus empowering them to parent well and reduce stresses (Berry & Letendre, 2004; Pritlove, 1990). Groups can also initiate community action and self-direction (Bretcher, Kurtz, & Lamout, 1999; Payne, 2005). Examples are: play activity groups, parent to parent support groups, groups on health, welfare entitlements, baby massage classes, or other activities which enhance the social capital of a particular community or focus on a troubling aspect of parenting.

Where longstanding and complex problems exist or where parental lack of skill or impaired functioning serves as a detriment to children, groupwork plays a special role. For example, teaching parenting skills to parents who maltreat children has been found to be effective (Gottleib & Hughes, 2004; Lyons, Henly, & Schuerman, 2005). Also, groups can be formed to improve impaired functioning including: alcohol or drug misuse, and anger management. Others groups are formed to develop motivation for improving skills (Day, 2005). Yet other parental groups focus on gaining insights into parental depression, or with the parents' own adverse childhood experiences and traumas which may be affecting their ability to parent. Finally, family groups focus on dealing with dysfunctional interactions and improving the family's ability to problem solve, communicate and relate with each other (e.g., give and take affection, praise or criticism) (Barnes, 2004).

Where poverty and poor community resources are the main barrier to effective parenting, supportive community groups can build capacity. Where parents lack skills but are well motivated, behaviourally based parent training groups can assist parents to manage child behaviours and to provide basic home safety and practical care. Where inner psychological issues are impairing a parent's ability to focus on their child, the enhancement of parenting capacity through groupwork may be more complex, especially where mental ill-health or substance misuse are involved. Groupwork remains a creative tool for non-stigmatizing and empowering intervention in the area of enhancing parenting skills where practitioners have the expertise to work in this way using behavioural, educative, psychotherapeutic or community models depending on what is required.

Governments have taken an interest in parent training groups. While the additional resources can be beneficial, the danger exists that such projects become simply a tool of controlling state intervention. These programs may lose their spontaneity, become oppressive and lose effectiveness with marginalized groups (Mullender & Ward, 1991). Moreover, resources may be diverted from other kinds of parental support (Edwards, 1995), especially from building supportive partnerships with parents. However, so long as groupwork values are retained (Brown, 1996) such work can be beneficial.

References

Angelini, N. (1994). Facilitating parenting skills in vulnerable families. *Health Visitor, 67*(4), 130–132.

Barnes, G. G. (2004). *Family therapy in changing times.* Basingstoke, UK: Palgrave Macmillan.

Berry, M., & Letendre, J. (2004). Lambs and lions: The role of psychoeducational groups in enhancing relationship skills and social networks. *Groupwork, 14*(1), 30–45.

Bertcher, H. J., Kurtz, L. F., & Lamont, A. (Eds.) (1999). *From local to global: Groups at the heart of the community.* Binghamton, NY: Haworth Press.

Brown, A. (1992). *Groupwork.* Aldershot, UK: Ashgate.

Brown, A. (1996). Groupwork into the future: Some personal reflections. *Groupwork, 9*(1), 80–96.

Day, P. (2005). Coping with our kids: A pilot evaluation of a parenting programme delivered by school nurses. *Groupwork, 15*(1), 42–60.

Edwards, J. (1995). Parenting skills: Views of community health and social services providers about the needs of their clients. *The Journal of Social Policy, 24*(2), 237–259.

Fernandez, E. (2004). Effective interventions to promote child and family wellness: A study of outcomes of intervention through children's family centres. *Child & Family Social Work, 9*(1), 91–105.

Gottleib, L. N., & Hughes, J. R. (2004). The effects of the Webster-Stratton parenting program on maltreating families. *Child Abuse and Neglect, 28* (10), 1081–1097.

Habermann, U. (1990). Self help groups: a minefield for professionals. *Groupwork, 3*(3), 221–235.

Harrison, C., Parker, P., & Honey, S. (2005). Stepping stones: Parenting skills in the community. *Community Practitioner, 78*(2), 58–61.

Lyons, S. J., Henly, J. R., & Schuerman, J. R. (2005). Informal support in maltreating families: Its effect on parenting practices. *Children and Youth Services Review, 27* (1), 21–38.

May, H., Hamilton, J., & Elderkin, H. (1999). Group support for parenting skills: Taking first steps. *Community Practitioner, 72*(4), 86–87.

Mullender, A., & Ward, D. (1991). *Self directed groupwork: Users, take action for empowerment.* London: Whiting and Birch.

Neville, D., Beak, D., & King, L. (1996). *Positive parenting.* Aldershot, UK: Ashgate.

Neville, D., Beak, D., & King, L. (1998). *Positive parenting with teenagers.* Aldershot, UK: Ashgate.

Payne, M. (2005). *Modern social work theory.* Basingstoke, UK: Palgrave Macmillan.

Preston-Shoot, M. (2007). *Effective groupwork*. Basingstoke, UK: Palgrave Macmillan.

Pritlove, J. (1990). Evaluating a group for mothers under stress. *Practice*, 4(2), 96–109.

Saleebey, D. (1997). *The strengths perspective in social work practice*. New York: Longman.

Scott, D., & O'Neill, D. (1996). *Beyond child rescue, developing family centred practice at St Luke's*. Sydney, Australia: Allen & Unwin.

Steinberg, D. M. (2004). *The mutual-aid approach to working with groups: Helping people help one another*. Binghamton, NY: Haworth Press.

People with AIDS

George S. Getzel

Group work practice has been an integral aspect of service delivery to people living with AIDS, beginning with the earliest recognition of the pandemic in 1981. The founders of the first voluntary service organization, the Gay Men Health Crisis in New York City developed a support group for themselves because they were overwhelmed when life partners and friends came down with a then mysterious, fatal illness, unknown to the medical experts The need for social support for themselves was coupled with the necessity for social action to raise money for research and to challenge the callous, if not hostile, response of the health care system to the mounting numbers of gay men and others falling ill. Similar newly developed service organizations throughout North America began reaching-out to emerging populations, including persons with histories of intravenous drug use and their partners, women, and persons of color in large urban epicenters of the disease (Getzel & Willroth, 2000). By 2005 in the United States, there was more than a million cumulative AIDS cases of which more than half have died (Centres for Disease Control, 2007).

Group work practice models during the AIDS pandemic reflect distinct continuities over the last 25 years. The first major continuity is the group functions of providing ongoing social support to people infected with HIV and affected by AIDS psychosocial consequences, including to kin, friends, and informal and formal service providers. A second functional continuity of group work services is education about the disease and treatment options, through cognitive-behavioral approaches, to prevent the transmission of HIV (Getzel, 2005; Getzel & Willroth, 2000).

A major source of change and innovation in the design and content of group work services is due to shifts in the epidemiology of AIDS cases and HIV infection, from primarily white gay men to persons of color, including men who have sex with men and do not identify as gay, growing numbers of women infected by heterosexual contact, and a smaller number of women with histories of intravenous drug use. A larger numbers of adolescents and young adults have been diagnosed with HIV and AIDS. Pediatric HIV infections, as well as cases from unmonitored, tainted blood products, have dropped dramatically in North America. A second major area of change influencing the structure of group services is related to medical breakthroughs in treatment that have slowed viral replication and the appearance of deadly opportunistic infections. Treatment of opportunistic infections and cancers also has become more effective. AIDS has moved from an incurable syndrome with acute, fatal disease events to a more chronic condition, no less serious but more manageable. Generally, people are living significantly longer after an AIDS diagnoses than ever before (CDC, 2007).

The early period of the pandemic beginning in the 1980s through the middle 1990s is associated with the formulation of the Classical Model of Group Work with People Living with AIDS (PLWAs). The model evolved when an AIDS/HIV diagnosis was tantamount to a life expectancy of weeks, months, or at best a year or two. The disease trajectory featured exacerbating biopsychosocial symptoms resulting in physical incapacitation, bodily disfigurement, psychological distress, mental disorientation, and eventual death. In this early period, the stigma attached to an diagnosis resulted in harsh treatment by providers and by communities fearful of contagion and judgmental of homosexuality and substance use (Getzel, 1991; Getzel & Mahony, 1991). There were frantic efforts to find cures and to provide palliation of associated illnesses. Researchers were perplexed about AIDS multifarious symptom presentations and rapid disease trajectory. Support groups of gay men and their caregivers offered the only venue where the disease could be discussed in relative safety and with the assurance others would understand and be sympathetic (Grossman & Silverman, 1993; Meier, Galinsky, & Rounds, 1995). During this period, large groups were used to provide forums for affected populations to learn what was known about AIDS and transmission. Groups that were cognitive-behavioral emphasized sex-positive approaches to the use of condoms and other safer sex strategies, including negotiating safer sex, meaning the non-exchange of body fluids (Kelly & St. Lawrence, 1990).

In the middle 1990s, PLWAs who thought they were going to die shortly discovered that was not the case and they had to contend with prospect of getting on with their lives—the so-called "Lazarus Effect." Consequently, group services tended to be more short-term, not to "death do we part." Short term groups were started for person with recent HIV diagnoses or later with their first serious opportunistic infections. Help was offered to AIDS survivors who now could contemplate going to work and generally getting on with life, less punctuated by AIDS-related preoccupations. Specialized support and HIV prevention groups offered by community-based organizations began to proliferate and focus more intensively on women including lesbians, persons of color, subsets of persons with addictions, transgendered men and women, youth, immigrants and others all of whom were seen to have particular needs and risks of infection (Richey, Gillmore, Balassone, Gutiérrez, & Hartway, 1997). Culturally sensitive practice, more innovative outreach efforts that emphasized strengths, and the autonomy of consumers became increasingly important in group design and content (Shulman, 2005).

The group work model of the beginning of the 21st century, and nearly 30 years after recognition of the pandemic, consists of groups that deal thoughtfully and empathetically with populations of the poorest and most oppressed living with HIV/AIDS; person who have histories with substance abuse, mental illness, domestic violence, homelessness, incarceration, illiteracy, societal prejudices, and multiple current life stressors. The Survive Model must simultaneously seeks to understand and to assist group members prioritize issues arising from aforementioned psychosocial problems in supportive groups located within their living space, be it their housing setting, neighborhood, or community-based service center. The Survival Model simultaneously provides nutrition, on-site support and advocacy, and crisis management in a warm caring environment with staff that reflects gender, ethnic, and life style characteristics of members. HIV prevention education is integrated into all the support functions. The model harkens to the safe harbor that settlement houses provided immigrants in their neighborhoods 150 years ago. Survival groups can only exist if there is a strong advocacy and member engagement.

References

Centers for Disease Control. (2007). *A glance at the HIV/AIDS epidemic*. Retrieved July 15, 2007 from the Department of Health and Human Resources, Centers of Disease Control and Prevention web site: http://www.cdc.gov/hiv/resources/factsheets/At-A-Glance.htm

Getzel, G. S. (1991). Survival modes of people with AIDS in groups. *Social Work, 36*, 7–11.

Getzel, G. S. (2005). No one is alone: Group work during the AIDS pandemic. In A. Gitterman, & L. Shulman (Eds.), *Mutual aid groups, vulnerable and resilient populations and the life cycle* (3rd ed., pp. 249–265). New York: Columbia University Press.

Getzel, G. S., & Mahony, K. F. (1991). Confronting human finitude: Group work with people with AIDS. *Journal of Gay and Lesbian Psychotherapy, 1*, 105–120.

Getzel, G. S., & Willroth, S. (2000). Acquired immunodeficiency syndrome (AIDS). In A. Gitterman (Ed.), *Handbook of social work with vulnerable and resilient populations* (2nd ed., pp. 39–63). New York: Columbia University Press.

Grossman, A. H., & Silverman, C. (1993). Facilitating support groups for professionals working with people with AIDS. *Social Work, 38*, 144–151.

Kelly, J. A., & St. Lawrence, J. S. (1990). The impact of community-based groups to help persons reduce HIV infection risk behaviors. *AIDS Care, 2*, 25–35.

Meier, A., Galinsky, M. J., & Rounds, K. A. (1995). Telephone support group for caregivers of persons with AIDS. *Social Work with Groups, 18*, 99–108.

Richey, C. A., Gillmore, M. R., Ballassone, M. L., Gutiérrez, L., & Hartway, J. (1997). "Straight Talk": Developing and implementing a group skill training intervention to reduce HIV/AIDS risk among sexually active adolescents in detention. *Journal of HIV/AIDS Prevention and Education for Adolescents & Children, 1*, 71–101.

Shulman, L. (2005). Persons with AIDS in substance abusing recovery: Managing the interaction between the two. In A. Gitterman, & L. Shulman (Eds.), *Mutual aid groups, vulnerable and resilient populations and the life cycle* (3rd ed., 266–289). New York: Columbia University Press.

People with Cancer

Rachel M. Schneider

Patients with acute and chronic illnesses have for many years attended support groups to reduce social isolation, decrease stigmatization (Lieberman & Yalom, 1992), and provide an outlet for the complex feelings and functional changes following a diagnosis. In the oncology setting, groups are often the best vehicle in the provision of support and education for patients. Although support groups are not appropriate for all patients, they are a resource worth considering when working with patients whose lives are affected by cancer.

Oncology groups, most often facilitated by social workers, create opportunities for exploring issues that arise with diagnosis, treatment, and the aftermath of the cancer experience. For many, such groups represent the first opportunity to have personal interactions with other cancer patients. This, in itself, can significantly decrease a sense of loneliness. Within a group context, members can explore changes in their physical function, while also identifying newly developed points of emotional strength. Patients can model for one another the methods by which they cope with the uncertainties of disease and its treatment.

Since there are many, and sometimes divergent needs, served in such groups, workers should pay attention to group purpose so that members have a clear understanding of what might be gained from participation (Kurland & Northen, 2001). As Spiegal and Classen (2000) note, it is critical to establish "cancer" as the central focus of such groups, while remaining cognizant that cancer can affect all aspects of life. Therefore, when a group begins to process other areas of interest it is useful for facilitators to remain attuned to the ways in which those aspects are directly affected by the illness as well as the ways in which the group may need to be redirected.

There is no one-size-fits-all oncology support group. The types of groups available represent a wide range, varying in size, duration, and focus. Generally, groups are offered based on specific diagnosis or stage of disease and/or by gender or age. However, consideration should be the given to the structure and duration of group sessions. In referring to support groups, one must balance a patient's needs with his or her ability to tolerate exposure to other people's medical experiences.

Diagnosis-specific groups can foster a strong sense of connection, since the particulars of the illness are largely known and understood by all members. Adjusting to physical changes and the emotional impact of the disease, as well as understanding how to identify clinical trials and resources, are often key areas of discussion. Diagnosis-specific groups are often co-facilitated by a medical professional in order to provide patients with information and education on self-care during and after treatment. Such groups are often topic-specific. For example, a neuro-oncologist may address concerns regarding the ongoing use of steroids after treatment to a group for primary brain tumor patients. A bone-marrow-transplant survivors' group can benefit from the presence of a nurse who can instruct members on methods of protecting an impaired immune system.

Alternatively, patients can participate in a support group focused on *stage* of disease, rather than on *type* of cancer. People diagnosed with an "early stage" cancer may struggle with different issues from patients with Stage IV illness. It can be frightening to patients with more treatable cancers to be faced with the reality of others' metastases and, conversely, patients with later-stage illness may find it irrelevant and/or unbearable to stay in a group with people diagnosed with lower-grade or earlier-stage disease.

Oncology support groups can also be divided by gender or age. A young adult group may face concerns related to, for example, infertility, dating after diagnosis, or navigating the world of work while undergoing cancer treatment. Their discussions, unique to their stage of life, are typically not appropriate for those approaching retirement, for example, or who have grown children. Similarly, a gathering of senior citizens will be likely to focus on the emotional and physical affects of cancer diagnosis and treatment specific to *their* stage of life. Group cohesion and intimacy tends to increase in direct proportion to the degree of commonality in life experience.

Along these lines, patients may choose a *gender-specific* support groups. Some people are more able to speak openly in a same-sex group. For example, men who experience erectile disfunction after prostatectomy may not feel comfortable sharing the nuances of their difficulties with women present. Moreover, they may gain comfort from a room full of men who understand the complex feelings associated with the effects of prostate surgery.

Length and frequency of group meetings are important considerations. Some oncology groups are *"drop-in"*; open to new members at each meeting. A drop-in group typically meets monthly and accepts any patient who fits the advertised description (e.g., "breast cancer survivors" or "men being treated for prostate cancer"). Open groups tend to alter their texture based on attendance at a given session. Intimacy is usually limited in this context; however, other benefits can be more apparent. In a monthly lung cancer support group, for example, patients may quickly exchange practical methods of coping with the anxiety-induced shortness of breath.

In *time-limited* groups, members are typically asked to commit to attend for the duration. They tend to be *closed*; not accepting new membership during the course of the group's lifespan, to prevent disruption to group process. Many organizations require an intake interview prior to participation. The duration of such groups can vary depending on clinical setting. These groups can promote intimacy, mutual aid and personal attachment; something harder to achieve in an open group.

Physical and/or geographic limitations may make it impossible for some patients to attend an in-person support group. Whereas in the past, these patients would remain without access to counseling services, "virtual" groups are making marked changes in the provision of psychosocial care to this population. Technological advances make *telephone and online* support groups invaluable resources. Patients can become part of a community and receive much needed support and education without leaving home or an inpatient setting.

References

Kurland, R., & Northen, H. (2001). *Social work with groups* (3rd ed.). New York: Columbia University Press.

Lieberman, M., & Yalom, I. (1992). Brief group psychotherapy for the spousally bereaved: A controlled study. *International Journal of Group Psychotherapy, 42*(1), 117–132.

Spiegel, D., & Classen, C. (2000). *Group therapy for cancer patients: A research-based handbook of psychosocial care.* New York: Basic Books.

People with Mental Health Problems

Kathi R. Trawver

An estimated 1 in 17 Americans experience a serious mental health disorder, such as major depression, bipolar disorder, or schizophrenia spectrum disorder (Kessler, Chiu, Demler, & Walters, 2005). The consequences of mental illness can be substantial without appropriate interventions. Serious mental health disorders are associated with higher rates of unemployment, poverty, homelessness, substance abuse, involvement with the criminal justice system, and inadequate health care. Individuals can become isolated, develop impaired social skills, and experience problems in social relationships. They are subjected to stigma, prejudice, and discrimination.

As the largest provider of mental health services in the United States, social workers (National Association of Social Worker, 2007) face unique challenges in providing services to individuals with serious mental health disorders. Group services allow mental health consumers to share experiences and discover that others feel the same way, and have had many of the same experiences, and to learn how others in similar circumstances cope with their disorders. Furthermore, groups can be used to simulate employment, family and other life situations, or learn to relate and practice social interactions with others, while allowing consumers to participate at their own level of readiness (Garvin, 1997).

A variety of group approaches are effective in providing education, skill building, support, and treatment to consumers of behavioral health services with serious mental health disorders. Groups are frequently used in an integrated approach for treating co-occurring mental health and substance use disorders. Additionally, group services also provide support and education to family members.

Psychoeducation groups focus on building participants' knowledge and skills in the effective management of their disorder, accompanying symptoms, medications, and learning about treatment options (Burlingame et al., 2007). Groups are offered to educate and provide information to consumers about their specific disorder. By understanding their disorder, they are able to explore a variety of coping skills and illness management techniques. For example, the Life Goals Program offers group education for bipolar disorder, teaching management skills and addressing the ways bipolar disorder affects psychosocial and occupational aspects of participants' lives (Bauer & McBride, 2003).

Individuals with serious mental disorders may experience a variety of troubling psychiatric symptoms that interfere and impair their everyday functioning, such as significant anxiety, unstable moods, and a decrease in normal cognitive functioning. They may also experience abnormal thoughts, delusions, and hallucinations. *Symptom education and management groups* seek to improve participants' overall functioning by providing education and support, enabling participants to better identify symptom triggers, and offering opportunities to learn and practice skills for managing problematic symptoms.

Medication education and management groups inform group members about how medications work and common side effects. Non-adherence to prescription medication is thought to be one of the leading causes of relapse of psychotic illness and a barrier to effective treatment. Researchers estimate medication non-compliance in up to 50% of outpatient consumers (Fernandez, Evans, Griffiths, & Mostacchi, 2006). Psychotropic, anti-depressant, and anti-manic medications can produce negative side effects including drowsiness, dizziness, skin rashes, rapid heart beat, weakness, nausea, diminished sexual desire, anxiety, confusion, and weight gain (National Institute of Mental Health, 2007). These groups also help members develop strategies in managing the problematic side effects of medications.

Support and self-help groups allow members to share common experiences that are associated with serious mental health disorders. Many behavioral health programs and consumer advocacy organizations sponsor groups that can be flexible in purpose and responsive to the unique needs of group members. Support groups focus on providing support, socialization, and problem solving for group members with serious mental disorders in a supportive milieu. Support groups provide mutual acceptance and understanding. These groups may be structured and topic specific or flexible. For example, the National Alliance for Mental Illness (NAMI) Connection provides support groups across the United States. This weekly recovery support group allows members to learn from each other's experiences, share coping strategies, and offers encouragement and understanding (National Alliance for Mental Illness, 2007).

Several types of 12-step self-help groups with a philosophy of recovery provide mutual support to individuals with serious mental health disorders. Examples include Mental Illness Anonymous, Schizophrenics Anonymous, and Depressed Anonymous. More recently, on-line self-help support groups are becoming popular and provide support, practical information, education, and advocacy to users.

Social workers may use a group as a therapeutic intervention for *treating* individuals with serious mental health disorders. A cognitive-behavioral group approach can be used where social workers target participants' negative thoughts or experiences about any number of barriers, such as negative self-image, problematic relationships, or other self-limiting thoughts, and help group members learn different ways of controlling identified problems.

Epidemiological studies estimate that at least one-half of individuals with serious mental health disorders have a *co-occurring substance use disorder* (Mueser, Noordsy, Drake, & Fox, 2003). The combination of the two disorders exacerbates accompanying problems of each individual disorder, creating a more serious impact on individuals than would either disorder alone (Evans & Sullivan, 2001). Integrated treatment in which both problems are treated simultaneously by one entity is considered best practice. An integrated group treatment format provides participants needed support, allows for shared experiences, identifies coping strategies, and provides education surrounding the unique treatment needs of individuals with co-occurring disorders (Mueser et al., 2003). Double Trouble in Recovery and Dual Recovery Anonymous ™ are examples of 12-step self-help fellowship groups that focus on relapse prevention and recovery, developing peer support, and education for individuals who have both a mental illness and substance dependence.

Family members frequently need to learn how to best support their loved one as well as needing support for themselves. Across the United States treatment providers and consumer groups, as well as state Chapters of the National Alliance for Mental Illness (NAMI), provide *education and support for family members* of people with serious mental health disorders.

References

Bauer, M. S., & McBride, L. (2003). *The life goals program* (2nd ed.). New York: Springer.

Burlingame, G. M., Earnshaw, D., Ridge, N. W., Matsumo, J., Bulkley, C., Lee, J., & Hwang, A. D. (2007). Psycho-educational group treatment of the severely and persistently mentally ill: How much leadership training is necessary? *Journal of Group Psychotherapy, 57*(2), 187–218.

Evans, K., & Sullivan, J. M. (2001). *Oral Diagnosis Counseling the mentally ill substance abuser* (2nd ed.). New York: Guilford Press.

Fernandez, R. S., Evans, V., Griffiths, R. D., & Mostacchi, M. S. (2006). Educational interventions for mental health consumers receiving psychotropic medication: A review of the evidence. *International Journal of Mental Health Nursing, 15*(1), 70–80.

Garvin, C. (1997). Group work with seriously mentally ill people. In G. L. Greif, & P. H. Ephross (Eds.), *Group work with populations at risk* (pp. 28–41). New York: Oxford University Press.

Kessler, R. C., Chiu, W. T., Demler, O., & Walters, E. E. (2005). Prevalence, severity, and comorbidity of 12-month DSM-IV disorders in the National Comorbidity Survey Replication. *Archives of General Psychiatry, 62*(6), 617–627.

Mueser, K. T., Noordsy, D. L., Drake, R. E., & Fox, L. B. (2003). *Integrated treatment for dual disorders: A guide to effective practice.* New York: Guilford Press.

National Alliance for Mental Illness. (2007). NAMI Connection: *Recovery Support Group.* Retrieved August 9, 2007 from http://www.nami.org/Content/NavigationMenu/Find_Support/Education_and_Training/Education_Training_and_Peer_Support_Center/NAMI_Connectio/About_NAMI_Connection.htm

National Association of Social Workers. (2007). *Social workers: Strong role in children's mental health.* Retrieved August 9, 2007 from http://www.socialworkers.org/pressroom/2007/050207.asp

National Institute of Mental Health (2007). *Medications.* Retrieved August 9, 2007 from http://www.nimh.nih.gov/publicat/medicate.cfm

People with Problematic Alcohol Use

Meredith Hanson

Epidemiologic findings from a nationally representative sample in the United States reveal that nearly one-third of all Americans have had an alcohol use disorder at some time during their lives (Hasin, Stinson, Ogburn, & Grant, 2007). Less than one-fourth of those suffering from alcohol dependence ever receive professional treatment (Hasin et al., 2007). If they seek assistance it is likely to be from non-specialized treatment facilities and for conditions like symptoms of mental and physical disorders, interpersonal conflicts, and economic problems associated with alcohol use disorders (Hanson, 2001).   A robust body of research suggests that alcohol abuse and dependence are manifestations of problems in living for most individuals. Life stressors (Brown, Vik, Patterson, Grant, & Schuckit, 1996) and poor coping skills (Marlatt & Donovan, 2005) are major factors in the emergence and maintenance of drinking problems. Given the quality of this evidence, problem drinking may be conceptualized as a socially learned and acquired maladaptive coping mechanism, one that should lend itself readily to group work interventions.

Currently, group-based interventions are among the primary modalities of treatment in both inpatient and outpatient alcoholism treatment facilities, and many professionals believe that group services are the "treatments of choice" for problem drinkers (Anderson, 1983; Fisher, 2004). Historically, however, most "recovery" efforts occurred in self-help groups like Alcoholics Anonymous (AA). Professional health care providers and social workers were involved minimally in the treatment of problem drinking. In fact, when Bill Wilson, one of the co-founders of AA, sought advice about his and others' alcoholism from Carl Jung, Jung indicated that medical and other professional treatments were of little value. Instead, he suggested that a "genuine conversion" or spiritual transformation was required (Alive and Free, 2000). For Wilson and countless other problem drinkers this transformation occurred through the group processes and mutual aid they encountered in AA.

Over the years professionals "discovered" problem drinking and its associated problems in living. Drawing on the perceived success of AA and other self-help approaches, many professionally led groups were "disease" or "recovery" oriented. They incorporated the traditions and steps of AA to promote the spiritual, emotional, and interpersonal transformation that many believed was necessary to lead an alcohol-free life (Cook, 1988). Recovery-focused groups help participants "accept" that they have a disease over which they are powerless, take "responsibility" for their actions, and develop a greater "understanding" of themselves as persons who can live lives as recovering alcoholics. Educational materials, homework assignments, AA attendance, and group discussions are used to achieve the group's purposes.

Group approaches, most notably Twelve-Step Facilitation (TSF; Nowinski, 2003), are effective in preparing and encouraging participants to take part in AA and other self-help groups. Although TSF was originally developed as an individually oriented approach to treatment, it has been adapted successfully to a group format. TSF is a highly structured, time-limited (12–15 sessions) approach to group work in which participants review their "recovery weeks," including attendance at AA, learn about the principles and traditions underlying 12-step fellowships, discuss "triggers" that place them at risk for relapse, practice strategies for coping with pressures to drink, and consider ways to make the most effective use of AA. Each session concludes with a "wrap-up" that includes assigned readings and other tasks, like AA attendance, that the participants are expected to complete before the next group meeting.

In addition to "disease/recovery" models, other models of group work are used in the treatment of drinking problems, for example, alcohol and drug education groups, interactional group therapy, and cognitive-behavioral/learning theory approaches to group work. Didactic alcohol education groups that present general information about alcohol and its adverse consequences are common in alcoholism treatment settings. Yet, they have limited evidence of effectiveness (Miller, Wilbourne, & Hettema, 2003). Their effectiveness can be improved, however, if informational feedback is personalized so that participants can see more clearly how the information relates to their own experiences, and if the information is combined with other treatment tactics like skill development (Bien, Miller, & Tonigan, 1993; Hanson, 1997).

Interactional group therapy draws on the ideas of Irwin Yalom and is framed by the notion that dysfunctional interpersonal processes contribute to problem drinking. The focus is here-and-now, with the members using the group as a mini-laboratory in which they can identify and correct maladaptive communication patterns. It is assumed that patterns, which emerge in the group, are representative of those that occur outside the group and that clients will be able to transfer their group experiences to their lives outside the group. Interactional approaches to group therapy tend to be open-ended. Interventions are process-oriented and provide constructive feedback (confrontation) designed to address both group and individual obstacles to recovery (Brown & Yalom, 1977; Fisher, 2004).

Cognitive-behavioral and other learning theory approaches to group work with problem drinkers are among the most widely studied, with a robust body of effectiveness evidence (e.g., Litt, Kadden, Cooney, & Kabela, 2003). They draw on empirical research, which demonstrates that problem drinking represents a learning process in which individuals develop maladaptive behaviors to cope with pressures to drink. Thus, to establish and maintain sobriety individuals must not only become more aware of situations in which they are likely to drink (i.e., develop cognitive vigilance), they must also learn more adaptive cognitive and behavioral skills to avoid relapse and to maintain sobriety. Cognitive-behavioral and learning theory approaches tend to be time-limited and highly structured with both in-group and homework assignments. Among the strategies used are assessment of high-risk drinking situations and their consequences, coping skills training (e.g., anger management, drink-refusal behaviors, communication training), and behavioral rehearsal. Because problem drinking is primarily an interpersonal process characterized by cognitive, social, and behavioral coping deficits, its treatment should lend itself to group-based interventions. Mutual aid provides a major rationale for the use of group interventions with problem drinkers (Gitterman & Germain, 2008). Groups generate therapeutic forces, like affiliation and peer support, that encourage clients to "bond with a culture of recovery" (Center for Substance Abuse Treatment, 2005). Participation in group services gives group members opportunities to develop new interpersonal skills, receive social support, and be exposed to vicarious learning that help them adopt non-drinking lifestyles. As in self-help groups, individuals who take part in professionally facilitated groups help themselves and strengthen their own recovery by helping and learning from others. Thus, group intervention provides a "natural" platform for attaining alcohol-free lifestyles.

References

Alive and Free (2000, August 28). *Jung, Oxford Group helped influence spiritual roots of AA*. Retrieved August 23, 2007 from http://hazelden.org/Web/public/ade00828.page

Anderson, S. C. (1983). Group therapy with alcoholic clients: A review. *Advances in Alcoholism and Substance Abuse, 2*(2), 23–40.

Bien, T. H., Miller, W. R., & Tonigan, J. S. (1993). Brief interventions for alcohol problems: A review. *Addiction, 88*, 315–336.

Brown, S. A., Vik, P. W., Patterson, T. L., Grant, I., & Schuckit, M. A. (1996). Stress, vulnerability and adult alcohol relapse. *Journal of Studies on Alcohol, 56*, 538–545.

Brown, S. A., & Yalom, I. D. (1977). Interactional group therapy with alcoholics. *Journal of Studies on Alcohol, 38*, 426–456.

Center for Substance Abuse Treatment. (2005). *Substance abuse treatment: Group therapy.* (Treatment Improvement Protocol (TIP) Series 41). Department of Health and Human Services Publication No. (SMA) 05-3991. Rockville, MD: Substance Abuse and Mental Health Services Administration.

Cook, C. C. H. (1988). The Minnesota Model in the management of drug and alcohol dependency: Miracle, method or myth? Part I. The philosophy and the programme. *British Journal of Addiction, 83*, 625–634.

Fisher, M. S. (2004). Groups for substance abuse treatment. In C. D. Garvin, L. M. Gutiérrez, & M. J. Galinsky (Eds.), *Handbook of social work with groups* (pp. 259–274). New York: Guilford Press.

Gitterman, A., & Germain, C. B. (2008). *The Life Model of social work practice* (3rd ed.). New York: Columbia University Press.

Hanson, M. (1997). The transition group: Linking clients with alcohol problems to outpatient care. *Journal of Chemical Dependence Treatment, 7*(1/2), 21–35.

Hanson, M. (2001). Alcoholism and other drug addictions. In A. Gitterman (Ed.), *Handbook of social work practice with vulnerable and resilient populations* (2nd ed., pp. 64–96). New York: Columbia University Press.

Hasin, D., Stinson, F. S., Ogburn, E., & Grant, B. F. (2007). Prevalence, correlates, disability, and comorbidity of DSM-IV alcohol abuse and dependence in the United States: Results from the National Epidemiologic Survey on Alcohol and Related Conditions. *Archives of General Psychiatry, 64*, 830–842.

Litt, M. D., Kadden, R. M., Cooney, N. L., & Kabela, E. (2003). Coping skills and treatment outcomes in cognitive-behavioral and interactional group therapy for alcoholism. *Journal of Consulting and Clinical Psychology, 71*, 118–128.

Marlatt, G. A., & Donovan, D. M. (Eds.). (2005). *Relapse prevention: Maintenance strategies in the treatment of addictive behaviors* (2nd ed.). New York: Guilford Press.

Miller, W. R., Wilbourne, P. L., & Hettema, J. E. (2003). What works? A summary of alcohol treatment outcome research. In R. K. Hester, & W. R. Miller (Eds.), *Handbook of alcoholism treatment approaches: Effective alternatives* (3rd ed., pp. 13–63). Boston: Allyn & Bacon.

Nowinski, J. (2003). Facilitating 12-step recovery from substance abuse and addiction. In F. Rotgers, J. Morgenstern, & S. T. Walters (Eds.), *Treating substance abuse: Theory and technique* (2nd ed., pp. 31–66). New York: Guilford Press.

People with Problematic Alcohol Use and Their Children

Neta Peleg-Oren

Parental alcohol abuse affects the life of the whole family. Having a parent with a history of alcohol problems has been associated with increased risk for negative emotional, cognitive, social, and behavioral outcomes, including substance abuse problems of the children. Epidemiological data (Ramisetty-Mikler & Caetano,

2004) indicate that the number of children in the United States under the age of 18 exposed to their parents' alcohol problems is 11.6 million, and an additional 2 million children are exposed to an alcohol-dependent parent. This means that 19% of children in the United States may be identified as children of alcoholics.

Parental alcoholism has been recognized as an emotional, cognitive, behavioral and social risk in child adjustment and development (Andreas & O'Farrell, 2007; Kuperman, Schlosser, Lidral, & Reich, 1999; Peleg-Oren & Teichman, 2006; Sher, Walitzer, Wood, & Brent, 1991). According to the *DSM-IV-TR* American Psychiatric Association, (2000), children of alcoholics are up to four times more likely to develop alcohol-related problems than children in the general population.

In view of the problems these children face, they are a high-risk population in need of special attention and therapeutic intervention. Group work is one such therapeutic intervention. Group work for elementary- and high-school-aged children of alcoholics is developmentally appropriate because of the significance of the peer group. The group offers the children the possibility of reducing social isolation, because they can meet with other children suffering from the same dysfunctional family situations, in a "holding environment" (Winnicott, 1971) provided by the group workers. Furthermore, sharing experiences with other children who are "in the same boat" can be helpful to increase peer relations (Shulman, 2006). Hearing other group members may help to reduce the feelings of guilt and shame that these children often have for their parent's alcoholism. The group provides an opportunity for the children to react to others in a supportive environment and to learn new coping skills from children who face the same situation (Gitterman & Shulman, 2005). The group worker can educate the children about the concept of alcohol as a disease.

The importance of group work for children of parents with a history of alcoholism is well described in the literature (Deckman & Downs, 1982; Emshoff, 1989; Hawley & Brown, 1981; LePantois, 1986; Mahon & Flores, 1992; Rhodes, 1995) and the group work services for children are mostly delivered through schools or community centers. A range of models are also identified and described (Arman, 2000; Cwiakala & Mordock, 1996; Goldman & Rossland, 1992; Roosa, Gensheimer, Short, Ayers, & Shell, 1989). Generally, two group workers for a group of six to eight children within a 2-year age range are recommended (Arman, 2000). The younger the children and the more severe the difficulties they face, the smaller the recommended group size. Similarly, since younger children usually have a limited capacity for concentration, the length of each group session should be limited to a half hour. Older children can sustain sessions up to one and a half hours. The developmental stages and the objectives are similar whatever the age of the children, but the focus and the techniques for presenting the objectives need to be age-appropriate. The objectives of the group are achieved through play, hands-on activities, and verbalization. The emphasis is on the development of relationships between the members through gaining corrective experience, and on fostering problem-solving ability in a caring environment (Shulman, 2006).

The preliminary stage of recruiting children to the group is a critical one. The group worker needs to interview the children and their parents and receive informed consent from the parents. This is a great challenge because the parents are usually afraid that talking about alcoholism might "harm the children." At this stage the group workers must consider the motivation of the child to participate, as well as the composition of the group.

In the beginning stage of the group, common objectives are creating group rules, norms, and contracting (Kurland & Salmon, 1998). Children learn to recognize different emotions (such as fear, happiness, anger) and to observe how the emotions affect them, through developing relationships with other members. They also learn the differentiation between secret and confidentiality. As these children have difficulties in developing normal social and coping skills and trusting others, this stage might be longer than in other types of groups.

As the group processes to the formative stage, there is more intimacy and comfort between the members, and the objectives focus on self-identity, the secret of alcoholism, reducing self-blame for the parent's drinking, and developing closer relationships between the group members. The children practice new ways to cope with the parent's alcoholism, and develop positive social skills and adaptive coping skills.

The termination and separation stage should be given adequate time. This is usually the most difficult stage because of the repeated separations from parents that these children experience. Reactions such as anger toward the group workers, regression to an early stage, and denial are very common (Gitterman & Shulman, 2005). The objectives in this stage are showing the strength that the members gain through the group process, what they can control in their lives given their age, expressing emotions such as anger, fear of separation, and rejection, and learning to cope with these emotions. In addition, the members also learn to approach a trusted adult outside of the family, if they need help.

References

American Psychiatric Association. (2000). *Diagnostic and statistical manual of mental disorders* (4th ed.). Washington, DC: Author.

Andreas, J. B., & O'Farrell, T. J. (2007). Longitudinal associations between father's heavy drinking patterns and children's psychosocial adjustment. *Journal of Abnormal Child Psychology, 35*(1), 1–16.

Arman, J. F. (2000). A small group model for working with elementary school children of alcoholics. *Professional School Counseling, 3*(4), 290–294.

Cwiakala, C. E., & Mordock, J. B. (1996). Let's discover health and happiness play groups: A model for psychoeducation of young children with parents in addiction recovery. *Journal of Child and Adolescent Group Therapy, 6*, 147–162.

Deckman, J., & Downs, B. (1982). A group treatment approach for adolescent children of alcoholic parents. *Social Work with Groups, 5*, 73–77.

Emshoff, J. G. (1989). A preventive intervention with children of alcoholics. *Prevention in Human Services, 7*, 225–253.

Gitterman, A., & Shulman, L. (2005). *Mutual aid groups, vulnerable and resilient population, and the life cycle.* (3rd ed.). New York: Columbia University Press.

Goldman, B. M., & Rossland, S. (1992). Young children of alcoholics: A group treatment model. *Social Work in Health Care, 16*, 53–65.

Hawley, N. P., & Brown, E. L. (1981). The use of group treatment with children of alcoholics. *Social Casework, 62*, 40–46.

Kuperman, S., Schlosser, S. S., Lidral, J., & Reich, W. (1999). Relationship of child psychopathology to parental alcoholism and antisocial personality disorder. *Journal of American Academy of Child and Adolescent Psychiatry, 38*, 686–692.

Kurland, R., & Salmon, R. (1998). *Teaching a methods course in social work with groups*. Washington, DC: Council on Social Work Education.

LePantois, J. (1986). Group therapy for children of substance abusers. *Social Work with Groups, 9*, 39–51.

Mahon, L., & Flores, P. (1992). Group psychotherapy as the treatment of choice for individuals who grew up with alcoholic parents: A theoretical review. *Alcoholism Treatment Quarterly, 9*, 113–125.

Peleg-Oren, N., & Teichman, M. (2006). Young children of parents with substance use disorders (SUD): A review of the literature and implication for social work practice. *Journal of Social Work Practice in the Addictions, 6*(1/2), 49–62.

Ramisetty-Mikler, S., & Caetano, R. (2004). Ethnic differences of children exposed to alcohol problems and alcohol dependence in the United States. *Journal of Studies on Alcohol, 65*(5), 593–607.

Rhodes, R. (1995). A group intervention for children in addictive families. *Social Work with Groups, 18*, 123–133.

Roosa, M. W., Gensheimer, L. K., Short, J. L., Ayers, T. S., & Shell, R. (1989). A preventive intervention for children in alcoholic families: Results of a pilot study. *Family Relations, 38*, 295–300.

Sher, K. J., Walitzer, K. S., Wood, P. K., & Brent, E. E. (1991). Characteristics of children of alcoholics: Putative risk factors, substance use and abuse and psychopathology. *Journal of Abnormal Psychology, 100*, 427–448.

Shulman, L. (2006). *The skills of helping: Individuals, families, groups, and communities* (5th ed.). Belmont, CA: Thomson Brooks/Cole.

Winnicott, D. W. (1971). *Playing and reality*. London: Tavistock.

People with Problematic Substance Use—Adults

Andrew Cicchetti

Group services are the cornerstone of most abstinence-based programs in the United States (Stinchfield, Owen, & Winters, 1994). The popularity of group services for people with substance use disorders (SUDs) can be best explained by the resonance of mutual aid with the demands of achieving and maintaining abstinence. The power of mutual aid processes, including the combined effect of mutual support and demand, in helping people get sober was phenomenologically discovered by the originators of Alcoholics Anonymous, whose success is likely to have lent credence to early efforts at providing group services to this population (Blume, 2002; Flores, 1997). Furthermore, collaborative, non-exploitive, mutual aid based relationships assuage the isolation, shame, and stigma experienced by people with SUDs. Quite simply, mutual aid heals! At the same time, people with SUDs are likely to experience difficulty in trusting others and forming healthy attachments, a point which should inform the interventions of the worker. This entry will apply concepts and practice principles drawn from the Mutual Aid Model that can be integrated with a variety of group approaches with this population (Gitterman, 2004; Shulman, 2006).

Substance use disorders are best conceptualized as chronic, relapsing brain diseases with biopsychosocial antecedents and consequences (Leshner, 1999).

Recovery from SUDs is an ongoing, perhaps *life-long process* with discrete developmental tasks and challenges to be found in early, middle, and ongoing stages. Typically, clients in agency-based substance abuse treatment are in the early or middle stage of recovery. The primary goals of the early and middle stages of recovery include achieving and maintaining abstinence. The nature of the work is primarily cognitive and behavioral, as opposed to being insight oriented (Centre for substance Abuse Treatment, 2005).

Common early recovery tasks include enhancing motivation for behavior change; learning about SUDs and recovery; identifying and verbalizing feelings; strengthening coping skills; cultivating self-esteem and self-care; and developing a sober support network (CSAT, 2005). Additional work exists for group members who have been mandated to treatment, which can be characterized as "transforming to clienthood" (Rooney & Chovanec, 2004).

The effectiveness of group work is enhanced when the worker possesses knowledge both about group work as well as substance use disorders. Salient *orienting knowledge* includes an understanding of the biopsychosocial implications of SUDs; the concepts, principles and structure of 12-Step Fellowships; the Transtheoretical Model of the Stages of Change; and the principles and skills of motivational interviewing (Flores, 1997; Miller & Rollnick, 1991; Prochaska, DiClemente, & Norcross, 1992; CSAT, 2005).

Empowerment-oriented practice necessitates that the worker view the group member from a *strengths* perspective. Furthermore, the mutual aid based group provides an opportunity for members to identify and experience their own and each other's strengths. The opportunities that exist in group work to experience mutual aid both strengthen self-esteem and affirm the value of a sober network of peers. Members should be encouraged to view their capacity to share feelings, life experiences and taboo topics as individual and collective strengths. Furthermore, the quality of mutual aid becomes enriched as members move through the recovery process and draw upon their accumulated experience in navigating "life on life's terms" sober.

Preparation is enhanced when the worker tunes in to the members' needs and feelings regarding both their being in treatment and in recovery. The stage of change model provides a useful framework for conceptualizing the needs of members as they engage with the change process. Accurately tuning in to these factors will help the worker identify topics that need to be addressed in early group sessions.

Workers should plan to respond to queries about their own recovery status. However, worker disclosure is secondary to the sub-text of such a query. Often members are really wondering if the worker will be helpful, trustworthy and non-judgmental. Additionally, such a request for self-disclosure provides an opportunity for the worker to clarify worker role and member role. Of note, evidence indicates that worker recovery status has no impact on treatment outcome (Culbreth, 2000).

The worker in the beginning phase should actively attend to enhancing motivation for change and issues related to trust and safety. Members are likely to have ambivalent feelings about getting sober (Milgram & Rubin, 1992). The use of the mutual aid process, the dialectic process, is resonant with principles of motivational interviewing. Members can be encouraged to discuss the pros and cons of being in treatment and of getting sober. As the worker responds empathically and points out member commonalties, organic opportunities arise to foster safety and trust as well as enhance motivation for change.

The work of the group is enhanced when member strengths and contributions are both encouraged and recognized. In an outpatient setting the worker stimulated the strengths in numbers phenomenon when the group agreed to accompany one member to his first Alcoholics Anonymous meeting, as he had been afraid to go on his own. In a residential setting, as members began looking for apartments in the community, they often were shown dilapidated apartments in drug-infested neighborhoods. In one session, Francis shared her despair and stated, "I felt like getting high; I got sober to live in a crack-house! But instead of getting high, I called my sponsor." In the next session another member recounted the same experience but added, "I thought of you Francis. I thought to myself I couldn't let you or the group down. So, I followed your lead and instead of getting high I called my sponsor." The worker asked Francis what she felt in knowing that she had helped someone protect their sobriety. Her eyes welled up with tears as she said, "it feels good to help. All my life I had no help to offer anyone; if anything I was a taker."

As most groups in substance abuse treatment settings are open-ended, typically members leave but the group continues. Variations on endings exist when members relapse and prematurely leave the program against medical advice. Ample time should be allotted for members to express their feelings and for the member who is leaving to consider their ongoing relapse prevention plan.

Finally, sessional work is enhanced when the worker helps the group review the purpose and format of the group in each session, in part because of the short-term memory loss associated with early recovery and to help distinguish the work of one group from that of another. Sessional endings provide an opportunity for members to identify the salience of the group encounter with their own recovery process.

References

Blume, S. (2002). Group psychotherapy in the treatment of addictive disorders: Past, present and future. In D. W. Brook, & H. I. Spitz (Eds.), *The group therapy of substance abuse* (pp. 411–428). Binghamton, NY: Haworth Medical Press.

Centre for Substance Abuse Treatment (CSAT). (2005). *Substance abuse treatment: Group therapy.* (Treatment Improvement Protocol (TIP) Series 41). Department of Health and Human Services Publication No. (SMA) 05-3991. Rockville, MD: Substance Abuse and Mental Helath Services Administration.

Culbreth, J. R., (2000). Substance abuse counselors with and without a personal history of chemical dependency: A review of the literature. *Alcoholism Treatment Quarterly, 18*(2), 67–82.

Flores, P. J. (1997). *Group psychotherapy with addicted populations: An integration of twelve-step and psychodynamic theory* (2nd ed.). Binghamton, NY: Haworth Press.

Gitterman, A. (2004). The Mutual Aid Model. In C. Garvin, L. Gutiérrez, & M. Galinsky (Eds.), *Handbook of social work with groups* (pp. 93–110). New York: Guilford Press.

Leshner, A. I. (1999). Science-based views of drug addiction and its treatment. *Journal of the American Medical Association, 282*(14), 1314–1316.

Milgram, D., & Rubin, J. (1992). Resisting the resistance: Involuntary substance abuse group therapy. *Social Work with Groups, 15*(1), 95–110.

Miller, W. R., & Rollnick, S. (1991). *Motivational interviewing: Preparing people to change addictive behaviors.* New York: Guilford Press.

Prochaska, J. O., DiClemente, C. C., & Norcross, J. (1992). In search of how people change: Applications to addictive behaviors. *American Psychologist, 47*(9), 1102–1114.

Rooney, R., & Chovanec, M. (2004). Involuntary groups. In C. Garvin, L. Gutiérrez, & M. Galinsky (Eds.), *Handbook of social work with groups* (pp. 212–226). New York: Guilford Press.

Shulman, L. (2006). *The skills of helping individuals, families, groups, and communities* (5th ed.). Belmont. CA: Thompson.

Stinchfield, R., Owen, P., & Winters, K. C. (1994). Group therapy for substance abuse: A review of the empirical research. In A. Fuhriman, & G. Burlingame (Eds.), *Handbook of group psychotherapy: An empirical and clinical synthesis* (pp. 458–488). New York: John Wiley.

People with Problematic Substance Use—Older Adults

Loretta Hartley-Bangs

The issue of increased use and abuse of alcohol, prescription medication, and illicit drugs by older individuals is a growing concern for the field of substance abuse treatment. The challenge for clinicians is how to adequately treat addiction in this age group, while being sensitive to the unique developmental needs in the later stages of life.

According to the Substance Abuse and Mental Health Services Administration (SAMHSA), approximately 17% of Americans 55 or older knowingly or unknowingly abuse alcohol and/or prescription drugs. This older population is expected to increase to 20% by the year 2030 (NYS Office for the Aging, 2007). Because baby boomers currently consume more alcohol and drugs, this pattern will likely continue into older age. In addition, this generation used illicit drugs more than their predecessors and will continue to be prescribed medications for all ailments presented to the medical field, resulting in increased abuse and dependence on prescriptions drugs.

Much is known about the benefits of social group work when treating younger substance abusers. All individuals struggling with addiction need to identify with, and gain support from, others who are struggling with similar issues. The individual needs to feel that change can occur and to experience the sense of empowerment that comes from achieving individual goals. Older individuals in our society often feel isolated in a culture focused on youth. This sense of isolation and helplessness is often fueled by a commonly held misconception that people are incapable of change after a certain age. Loss is a major issue for the elderly and is something experienced by many individuals in early recovery as they part with their long-time companion, alcohol and drugs.

When working with the older substance abuser, treatment parts ways with that of the younger client in regard to the length of treatment. The elderly need a sense of accomplishment at this stage in their lives. Therefore, treatment planning needs to take this into consideration. With younger clients the issue of major life losses and transitions is often not addressed until the person has substantial sober time (1–2 years). Due to the reality of ageing these are better addressed sooner than later. The individual is doing developmental work that deals with loss and transition and to delay these issues is to ignore where the client is at.

Mutual aid (Gitterman & Shulman, 2005) is well suited for working with this population. In working with the older addict, we need to recognize the many adjustments the individual is making as they enter or continue through this later stage of development. The older individual is constantly adjusting to change within themselves and their lives, as well as in the world around them. For many older addicts this is the start of their substance use. It is a recently developed maladaptive coping mechanism. For others this coping mechanism has been in place for many years and is now interfering with their later age developmental work.

Like all other age groups, the elderly want to be able to identify with others, but not be totally isolated from society. They need to know that they continue to serve a role and are contributing to the larger society. They are trying to master the challenges presented by aging. The issue of substance abuse, while shameful for all ages, is particularly shameful for older clients who often feel they should be beyond such issues and are already struggling with changing roles such as retirement, role reversal with children, etc. The difference for older addicts is that due to physical changes they metabolize substances differently, resulting in a quicker progression, and thus more damage in less time. Their physical detoxification is more complicated and external pressures are different. What could initially present as cognitive dysfunction needs to be closely assessed as the individual is medically stabilized and begins group treatment. In many cases symptoms that appear to be those of dementia gradually subside as the individual recovers from detoxification. Groups for seniors are usually shorter, 55 minutes compared to 90 minutes for younger clients.

The optimum treatment for the older client consists of psychodynamic and psychoeducation groups. The psychodynamic group is age specific with the goal of providing a forum for members to discuss not only their substance use, but also other life events and adjustments. It is not unusual for this group to focus on loss, family issues, and medical problems, as well as politics. The common thread is how these issues impact the individual and the interplay of their substance use. The goal of the psychoeducation group is to provide information about all aspects of substance abuse and the impact on the individual. These two groups should work in conjunction with each other, allowing individuals to process information from psychoeducation in the psychodynamic group. (Clients can also be encouraged to incorporate community self-help groups such as Alcoholics Anonymous into their recovery plan.)

The clients who attend these groups often cite their appreciation of the information provided in the psychoeducation group, which is often processed in the therapy group. Hearing the information in this format often is received in a less threatening way. They appreciate having information provided in an organized way with the assumption that they are still thinking individuals with the capacity to learn new information.

Older individuals are adjusting to a regular stream of change in their lives. Friends and family members move or pass away. Work and/or children are no longer the focus of their lives. Physical changes require adjustments to be made in the home and their routine. The need to ask for, and accept, help from others, especially from children often becomes a blow to their ego, that sense of independence and pride at having cared for themselves and families for so long. Being a part of a group brings them back into a community of people to whom they can relate. It is the interaction with others that provides a sense of purpose for many and begins to counter the isolation they have been living in.

The experience of the staff of Odyssey House, a long-term residential program with specialized services for seniors, validates this. In their experience, "Close peer relationships allow residents to feel more comfortable in group treatment, to be candid about their problems in individual counseling, and to recover from their addictions" (Guida, Unterbach, Tavolacci, & Provet, 2004).

Whether an individual has been struggling with substances all their lives, or it is a relatively new issue for them, their use is interfering with this stage of their life. Treatment is most effective for this age group when balanced. Information and education needs to be provided and can be done within mixed groups, but they need specific groups to address their age-specific issues and addiction.

References

Gitterman, A., & Shulman, L. (Eds.). (2005) *Mutual aid groups, vulnerable and resilient populations, and the life cycle* (3rd ed.). New York: Columbia University Press.

Guida, F., Unterback, A., Tavolacci, J., & Provet, P. (2004). Residential substance abuse treatment for older adults: An enhanced therapeutic community model. In R. Salmon, & R. Graziano (Eds.), *Group work and aging: Issues in practice, research and education* (pp. 95–105). Binghamton, NY: Haworth Press.

Korper, S. P., & Council, C. L. (Eds.). (2002). *Substance use by older adults: Estimates of future impact on the treatment system* (Series A-21.). Department of Health and Human Service Publication No. (SMA) 03-3763, Analytic Series A-21). Rockville, MD: Substance Abuse and Mental Health Services Administration.

NYS Office for the Aging (NYSOFA). (2007). Federal Funding and Policy Priorities for the First Session of the 110th Congress.

People with Problematic Substance Use–In Crisis

Leslie Temme and Maurice Lacey

Chemical dependency continues to be a major health problem in the United States and elsewhere. Rising health care costs and decreased funding have resulted in the need for more cost effective treatment at all levels of care. Group work has been recognized as cost-effective with favorable outcomes within the chemical dependency treatment arena. Group work approaches are the cornerstone of most outpatient chemical dependency treatment programs (Fisher, 2004). However, while a majority of chemically dependent clients initially present themselves to treatment facilities in crisis there is virtually no literature that examines crisis groups with this population. Chemically dependent clients in crisis present specific needs and the nature of the crisis can impact group process. This entry examines how the crisis group typically functions, and presents methods of group development and facilitation for optimal interaction and intervention for the chemically dependent crisis group.

When a person seeks help for a crisis situation they may be more apt to accept and benefit from counseling as they recognize they are in trouble. Conventional chemical-dependency treatment would focus on where the client is in relation to understanding the impact of their use. This approach requires direct confrontation regarding the consequences of the client's use. However, Morley and Brown (1969) caution against using direct confrontation in a crisis situation, as clients are often fragile and may not be able to absorb this kind of intervention. Instead they suggest that the social worker maximize the leverage provided by the actual crisis situation as a means to motivate the client for change without intensifying the crisis.

A crisis entails the breakdown in predictable patterns of adaptation to the inner and external environment. When resources to cope are no longer available, or nor longer work, people become vulnerable to crisis reactions. Traditionally, the goal of crisis intervention is to stabilize the individual and restore functioning to at least a pre-crisis level. However, for the chemically dependent individual restoration to pre-crisis level is not indicated, as pre-crisis level often includes continued substance use and behaviors that were most likely responsible for the crisis. Therefore, for this population, the breakdown of patterned coping can be an opportunity for growth and transformation. Caplan's crisis model (as cited in Aguilera, 1998) postulates that a crisis will spontaneously resolve itself within 4–6 weeks. Therefore, social workers must focus clients to work within this time frame.

Five group models are responsive to chemically dependent clients in crisis:

- Psychoeducational groups to educate clients about the nature of addiction, with connections to the current and past crisis.
- Problem solving and skills development groups, in order to cultivate the skills needed to deal with the current crisis as well as achieve abstinence.
- Specialty groups (acupuncture, yoga, mediation) and topic groups (mental health and recovery, women issues in addiction, pain medication in recovery, homelessness, and serious medical problems), in order to relieve stress and cravings, and to help client to focus more on "self in process."
- Support/mutual groups lead by clients and recovering persons, which allow clients to share feelings and thoughts about the crisis for the purpose of identification and emotional support. Clients also make connections with supportive individuals that can offer support in the community.
- Caseload groups, with 5–10 clients, to deal more specifically with current identified problems related to the crisis and substance use. The smaller size and generic approach can allow for more in-depth sharing of experiences, thoughts, and feelings.

Strickler and Allgeyer (1966) describe a three-phase process in crisis group work. The first phase includes assessment of the crisis and determination regarding why previous coping has failed. Identification and validation of the crisis situation often results in alleviation of some of the stress. According to Aguilera (1998), traditional crisis intervention treatment employs the philosophy that the client needs to feel relief as soon as possible. While relief from critical aspects of the crisis is necessary, the social worker must be careful to maintain accountability with the chemically dependent client. Chemically dependent clients must not feel released of the responsibility to better manage their lives and address their addiction. In working with this population a balance must be found between alleviating the pain of the crisis while also allowing the discomfort to remain as a primary motivator.

Strickler and Allgeyer's (1966) second and third phases of crisis group work involves the group. A crisis group is often open-ended and ongoing, with clients rotating in and out. Each member's specific crisis may be different and, therefore, there may be a tendency for the focus to shift from one crisis to another. A "going around" procedure helps to identify common issues and engage members with each other. While group members are encouraged to share with each other the nature of their crisis, the group leader must assume a very active role in defining commalities to facilitate group process. Cultivation of group process allows curative factors such as universality and hope to emerge (Gitterman & Shulman, 2005). Universality occurs as members recognize their common areas of need. The pervasive common factor in a crisis is fear of loss. The group worker identifies and illuminates this profound commonality. According to Strickler and Allgeyer (1966), "the universal feeling of crisis quickly welds the group into a working unit. The social worker creates an atmosphere of hope that change can take place" (p. 32).

It is essential that the social worker understand the turmoil, chaos, self-destruction, and suffering of substance abuse clients in crisis. To be an effective group leader with this population one needs to be prepared to deal with behaviors such as manipulation, distorted cognition, and anger, as well as understand the workings of denial, rationalization, and projection, which are the prominent defense mechanisms for individuals who are chemically-dependent. Flores and Georgi (2005) state that group leaders in chemical-dependency treatment should have the following skills:

- be able to cool down runaway affect and/or turn a crisis into an opportunity;
- be able to convert conflict into positive energy that powers the group;
- be able to deal with disruptive group members;
- be confident and have excellent active listening skills;
- be flexible and spontaneous;
- effectively use humor.

A crisis can provide a unique opportunity for an individual to be challenged and motivated to change. The crisis can provide increased leverage for change and the group process can be instrumental in supporting the motivation and support necessary for transformation. Group work with chemically dependent individuals in crisis is a viable and useful treatment modality when understood in the context of crisis group work.

References

Aguilera, D. C. (1998). *Crisis intervention: Theory and methodology.* New York: Mosby.

Fisher, M. S. (2004). Groups for substance abuse treatment. In C. D. Garvin, L. M. Gutiérrez, & M. J. Galinsky (Eds.), *Handbook of social work with groups* (pp. 259–274). New York: Guilford Press.

Flores, P. J., & Georgi, J. M. (2005). *Substance abuse treatment: Group therapy.* (Treatment improvement protocol (TIP) Series 41). Department of Health and Human Service Publication No. (SMA) 05-3991. Rockville, MD: Substance Abuse and Mental Health Services Administration.

Gitterman, A., & Shulman, L. (Eds.). (2005). *Mutual aid groups,vulnerable and resilient populations, and the life cycle* (3rd ed.). New York: Columbia University Press.

Morley, W. E., & Brown, V. B. (1969). The crisis-intervention group: A natural mating or a marriage of convenience? *Psychotherapy: Theory, research and practice, 6,* 30–36.

Strickler, M., & Allgeyer, J. (1966). The crisis group: A new application of crisis theory. *Social Work, July, 12*(3), 28–32.

Police Officers

George T. Patterson and Grace A. Telesco

Social workers attempt to help law enforcement officers better respond to social problems, improve the services they provide within communities, and manage work and life stress that result from police work. Social workers provide information about how human service agencies functions, how to make referrals, and how to intervene when responding to interpersonal problems. All of these interventions are best provided in groups. Sociodramatic, informational, and stress management groups are particularly effective. In these groups, members may all share the same police rank and perform the same duties, or they may hold different ranks and perform different duties, including administrative duties. Many groups are single session. In general, not more than two to three group sessions are provided to the same group of officers. These temporal constraints are related to the difficulties in scheduling officers to be away from their duties, and the costs of paying overtime to officers who may be off-duty when a group is scheduled.

Group workers confront the challenges of capturing and maintaining the attention of group members. Law enforcement officers share a unique occupational culture and it is often a challenge when social workers find themselves facilitating a group of officers. When officers are in a group setting, they may manifest behaviors such as posturing and defensiveness. The group experience can provoke member anxiety. The unique culture of law enforcement has certain expectations of its members. Social workers can be viewed as "soft," and non-important. Engaging police officers is a challenging experience. In their daily work, police officers are active and pragmatic. Therefore, group services have to be active and practical. Sociodramatic techniques engage law enforcement officers. The group worker sets up a scenario, that emulates real life situations—situations that the officers may face. Group members try out various ways to handle and respond to situations

Sociodramatic scenarios can be effectively used to help police officers to explore their biases and prejudices (O'Keefe, 2004; Solomon & Telesco, 2001). "Hot topics" such as racism, brutality, and cultural diversity can be explored in a non-threatening and non-confrontational setting. "Stepping in," a particularly effective technique provides police officers the opportunity to join the simulated situation, enter into a scene that is already in progress, and present alternatives to behaviors or actions being employed by fellow officers. Law enforcement officers report that this type of hands-on, practical approach invites free group discussion (Telesco, 2006).

Another technique, "freezing the scene," also allows the social worker to highlight for the officers the multiple issues and situations that are being portrayed by the scenario. In these groups, police officers have attested to the greater empathy they experienced for the mentally ill and the victims of a rape (Solomon & Telesco, 2001).

Informational presentations can be augmented by sociodramatic techniques. The officers are given the opportunity to bridge the gap between theoretical concepts and practical application. Law enforcement topics relating to procedures, such as the handling of child abuse cases, crisis intervention with sexual assault victims, effective police response to people with mental illness, and proper handling of domestic violence, are better understood when the theories, concepts, and procedures come alive for the officers and can be applied in a simulated real life setting.

Stress management groups have been conceptualized as educational groups (Zastrow, 2001), and educational groups as treatment groups because of the socio-emotional assistance provided in the group (Toseland & Rivas, 2005). The goals of the stress management groups are to provide information to officers about the sources, types, and effects of work and life stress that they are likely to experience and how to cope with them (Patterson, in press). The coping strategies need to be practical for managing their work and life stressors.

References

O'Keefe, J. (2004). *Protecting the republic: The education and training of American police officers.* Saddle River, NJ: Prentice Hall.

Patterson, G. T. (in press). A framework for facilitating stress management educational groups for police officers. *Social Work with Groups.*

Solomon, A., & Telesco, G. (2001). Theater of the recruits. *Theater, 31,* 55–61.

Telesco, G. (2006). Using sociodrama for radical pedagogy: Methodology for education and change. *Radical Pedagogy.* Retrieved July 26, 2007 from http://radicalpedagogy.icaap.org/content/issue8_2/telesco.html

Toseland, R. W., & Rivas, R. F. (2005). *An introduction to group practice* (5th ed.). Boston: Allyn & Bacon.

Zastrow, C. (2001). *Social work with groups: Using the class as a group leadership laboratory.* Pacific Grove, CA: Brooks/Cole.

Police Officers and Their Spouses

Linda Openshaw

Group work with police officers and their spouses is an emerging area of social work practice that helps combat marital discord caused by police work. Law enforcement is one of the most stressful occupations (Ansel, 2000, p. 375). This stress has an adverse impact on family life, particularly the social life of police spouses (Alexander & Walker, 1996). Most programs developed to assist police officers deal with stress and sick leave issues and teach coping strategies. Group work provides an educational and supportive environment where police officers and their spouses can improve their marital relationships.

The stress of police work is caused by "the ambiguous framework in which discretionary decisions are made, the danger of dealing with lawbreakers, public suspicions and disdain, and the lack of community and organizational support" (Woody, 2006, p. 97). When stress causes police officers to become physically and emotionally exhausted, they begin to treat family members the same way they treat suspects at work (He, Zhao, & Archbold, 2002, p. 693). Alexander and Walker (1994) found that 40% of police officers admitted taking stress out on their families.

While the National Center of Health Statistics and the U.S. Census Bureau report that the national divorce rate is somewhere around 50%, divorce rates among police officers are much higher than the rate of the general population (Witkin, 1999, p. 32). Unfortunately, officers resist seeking help because a request for assistance may show up in their personnel files and adversely affect their advancement (NYC Patrolmen's Benevolent Association, 2000, p. 27). Webster and Lyubelsky (2005) report that officers do not want the stigma of a psychological disorder on their employment records, avoid professional services, view individuals outside their culture with suspicion, and are less likely to trust outsiders (p. 51).

Law enforcement officers work within a closed culture that is untrusting of outsiders. Facilitators of officer–spouse groups must possess knowledge about police culture and should have the ability to work effectively with educational, reciprocal, and remedial groups (Toseland & Rivas, 2001). Group facilitators should ride along with an officer during a shift to gain a firsthand understanding of police values and the situations that police officers encounter daily, which also will help the officers trust them.

The following principles help assure successful group interactions with law enforcement officers and their spouses:

1. Tailor the intervention to values and attitudes endorsed by the police culture.
2. Capitalize on the positive aspect of the officers' career choice and competence to promote the officers' personal identity, ego strength, and coping abilities.
3. Help the officers understand intimate relationships and gain skills for meaningful, rewarding relationships outside job interactions (Woody, 2006).

4. Structure the group to embrace a theoretical approach that will allow exploration and intervention with police officers' unique problems associated with authoritarianism, cynicism, and aggression (Craig, 2004).
5. Help family members understand their integral role as an officer's primary support system (Woody, 2006).

A group with law enforcement officers and their spouses is most successful when the police department sponsors it and allows officers to attend voluntarily. When groups are sponsored by the police department, officers and spouses know that the department is investing in helping their marriages by making such programs available (Youngcourt & Huffman, 2005).

Each group takes place in several sessions over one weekend, from Friday evening through Sunday at noon. The group is closed, with the same officers and spouses staying for the entire weekend. The number of participants is limited to 12 officers and their respective spouses. The group begins with a welcome from the chief of police and a group dinner. After dinner, there is an icebreaker to introduce the group members to each other. Each subsequent session begins with an icebreaker. The remainder of the Friday night session is an education group. Topics include the importance of friendship and fun in the marriage relationship, the effects of stress, and stress reduction techniques. Couples stay overnight in the hotel or conference center where the group is being held.

Saturday begins with an education group addressing communication skills and police culture. The group is then divided into two support groups, one for the officers and one for the spouses. Each group identifies how the pervasiveness of law enforcement culture has affected family rules, dress, holidays, roles, beliefs, and values. The two groups reconvene and discuss the differences in the officers' and spouses' perspectives. Lunch is provided, after which another education group addresses stages of relationships, power struggles and control, debriefing, and defusing. In a therapy session, each couple works together on improving their problem-solving skills and specific problems in their relationship.

Officers and their spouses typically have little time alone together. Accordingly, each officer and spouse is sent to dinner as a couple on Saturday night at the expense of the department with instructions to work on goal-setting and to enjoy what is for many a rare time alone together.

On Sunday morning, group leaders answer questions about marriage relationships previously submitted anonymously by group members. The group leaders then talk about forgiveness and renewal. As a closure activity, the group members discuss what they have learned. Finally, the group members take the same test that was administered at the beginning session and complete an evaluation of the group.

The group sessions help the officers understand how their job affects the family and the importance of planning and scheduling family time. Spouses realize the importance of a peaceful and positive home environment where the officer can decompress and enjoy the family. The benefits from these groups are being measured with pre-and post-tests and follow-up studies several months after the weekend group sessions. Responses from those who have attended the groups have been positive.

The group work techniques relevant to this population are mutual support, peer support, and education. The officers and spouses are taught how to build and maintain a successful relationship. Officers receive peer support over their pride in law enforcement and the pressures associated with it, and the spouses find value in the mutual support they receive from each other as they share their experiences with the law enforcement culture.

References

Alexander, D. A., & Walker, L. G. (1994). A study of methods used by Scottish police officers to cope with work-induced stress. *Stress Medicine, 10,* 131–138.

Alexander, D. A., & Walker, L. G. (1996). Perceived impact of police work on police officers' spouses and families. *Stress Medicine, 12,* 239–348.

Ansel, M. H. (2000). A conceptual model and implications for coping with stressful events in police work. *Criminal Justice and Behavior, 27*(3), 375–400.

Craig, R. J. (1996). *Theory and practice of counseling and psychotherapy* (5th ed.). Pacific Grove, CA: Brooks/Cole.

He, N., Zhao, J., & Archbold, C. A. (2002). Gender and police stress: The convergent and divergent impact of work environment, work–family conflict, and stress coping mechanisms of female and male police officers. *Policing, 25*(4), 687–708.

NYC Patrolmen's Benevolent Association. (2000). Program for the reduction of stress for New York City police officers and their families, final report. A Final Report to the Office of Justice Program Grant #96-FS-VX-0007. Retrieved August 2, 2007 from http://www.NEJES.gov/PDFiles1/NIS/GRANTS 1185845.PDF

Toseland, R. W., & Rivas, R. F. (2001). *An Introduction to group work practice* (4th ed.). Boston: Allyn & Bacon.

Webster, S. R., & Lyubelsky, J. (2005). Supporting the thin blue line: Gender-sensitive therapy with male police officers. *Professional Psychology: Research and Practice, 36*(1), 51–58.

Witkin, G. (1999). Cops under fire. *U.S. News and World Report, 109,* 32.

Woody, R. H. (2006). Family interventions with law enforcement officers. *The American Journal of Family Therapy, 36,* 95–103.

Youngcourt, W. W., & Huffman, A. H. (2005). Family-friendly policies in the police: Implications for work–family conflict. *Applied Psychology in Criminal Justice, 2*(2), 138–162.

Rape Survivors

Shantih E. Clemans

Most American women and girls have either first or second hand knowledge of the crime of rape. Somewhere in the United States a sexual assault occurs every two and a half minutes (Rape, Abuse and Incest National Network (RAINN), 2007). The vast majority of these victims are female. Approximately 1 in 6 American women is a victim of a sexual assault in her lifetime compared with 1 in 33 men (Bureau of Justice, 2006). Still, rape is a seriously underreported crime. Although police have been trained to be sensitive to victims, more than half of sexual assaults go unreported. Experts agree that a significant reason for underreporting is the relationship between the victim and the perpetrator. A family member, an intimate, or an acquaintance commits two-thirds of the rapes in the United States (RAINN, 2007). Survivors who are raped by a known assailant face less vigorous criminal justice efforts and less sensitive responses from police and other service providers (Campbell, Wasco, Ahrens, Sefl, & Barnes, 2001). Although no one is immune, rape affects young women in much greater numbers. Of rape survivors 44% are under 18; about 15% are under 12 (RAINN, 2007). White women experience the majority of rapes, but women of color are disproportionately represented among victims and report poorer treatment from the criminal justice system (Campbell et al., 2001). Of all offenders arrested on rape charges 99% are male. The average age of these rapists is 31; however, 16% of those arrested for rape are teenagers (RAINN, 2007).

Since the beginning of the anti-rape and battered women's movements, groups have been used to help survivors (Schechter, 1982). Traumatic events question the safety and reliability of basic human relationships. A woman who has experienced rape may feel that her personal relationships or her judgment can no longer be trusted (Herman, 1997). Groups help survivors heal this broken trust, tell their stories, and connect with others (Clemans, 2005; Knight, 2006). A successful group requires careful attention to purpose, planning, membership, and structure. Purpose refers to the means and objectives the group will collectively pursue (Kurland & Salmon, 1999). The primary purpose of this group model is to educate women on rape dynamics, to reduce isolation, and empower members in a trusting, all-female environment.

Groups for rape survivors have many purposes including as to providing a safe forum in which to discuss taboo subjects and to rehearse new behaviors. A mutual aid group affords rape survivors with important opportunities to meet with other women who have gone through similar experiences. Emotional and psychological growth is fostered through the dynamic process of "give and take," characteristic of mutual aid. Secrecy and shame continue to define the post-rape experience for many women. In a group, however, these same survivors have the rich opportunity of sharing and hearing stories of rape and rape recovery. Under the leadership of a group worker who ensures safety, non-judgmentalism, and honesty, this "truth-telling" process is especially cathartic as a reciprocal group experience.

Groups for women trauma survivors have been in existence since the 1970s (Mason & Clemans, in press; Schechter, 1982). However, even with an all-female membership, these groups are not necessarily feminist. There are several specific components that distinguish feminist group work from general social group work practice. First, there is an explicit emphasis on women's lives and experiences as the focal point. Woven into the group process is an inherent critique of sociocultural forces, such as sexism and racism, on women's lives, combined with a commitment to reduce isolation caused by sexism. Next, there is an emphasis on skill development and empowerment (Gottlieb, Burden, McCormick, & NiCarthy, 1983; Israeli & Santor, 2000; Valentich, 1996). Mutual aid and feminism are complimentary elements in this group model. Mutual aid is enlivened specifically through these dynamics: 1) discussing taboos; 2) the "all in the same boat" phenomenon; 3) developing a universal perspective (Shulman, 2006).

A feminist group has, at its core, opportunities for consciousness-raising, a process that helps women realize that they are not the sole cause of their distress. In the case of rape, there are other forces at work, such as patriarchy and misogyny (Israeli & Santor, 2000). Consciousness-raising emphasizes a heightened awareness, primarily through peer discussion, of the particular pain of sexism and of the desire to improve society based on this changed awareness. Framed by a gender analysis, this process mirrors mutual aid, where peers offer and receive aid in a dynamic exchange.

In addition to consciousness-raising, female empowerment is a core function of this group. The trauma of rape affects survivors in many complex ways. Depression, anxiety, shame, isolation, and fear are a handful of examples (Herman, 1997). Women routinely experience sexism, misogyny, and oppression, and rape survivors in particular are vulnerable and marginalized. A group experience offers members opportunities to talk openly about gender-specific injuries. A group worker is instrumental in guiding this process. The group worker may ask members to reflect on these questions: What causes rape? What do you have in common as women? What are your differences? How have you been harmed as women? Here, women are empowered through talking openly about the rape, in advocating for themselves, and through learning self-care strategies such as starting new friendships (Clemans, 2005).

References

Bureau of Justice. (2006). National crime victimization survey. Retrieved October 26, 2007 from http://www.rainn.org/docs/statistics/ncvs_2005.pdf

Campbell, R., Wasco, S. M., Ahrens, C. E., Sefl, T., & Barnes, H. E. (2001). Preventing the "second rape": Rape survivors' experiences with community service providers. *Journal of Interpersonal Violence, 16*, 1239–1259.

Clemans, S. E. (2005). A feminist group for women rape survivors. *Social Work with Groups, 28*(2), 59–75.

Gottlieb, N., Burden, D., McCormick, R., & NiCarthy, G. (1983). The distinctive attributes of feminist groups. *Social Work with Groups, 6*(3/4), 81–93.

Herman, J. (1997). *Trauma and recovery*. New York: Basic Books.

Israeli, A. L., & Santor, D. A. (2000). Reviewing effective components of feminist therapy. *Counselling Psychology Quarterly, 13*(3), 233–247.

Knight, C. (2006). Groups for individuals with traumatic histories: Practice considerations for social workers. *Social Work, 51*(1), 20–30.

Kurland, R., & Salmon, R. (1999). *Teaching a methods course in social work with groups*. Alexandria, VA: Council on Social Work Education.

Mason, S. E., & Clemans, S. E. (2008). Participatory research for rape survivor groups: A model for practice. *Affilia: Journal of Women and Social Work, 23*(1), 66–76.

Rape, Abuse and Incest National Network (RAINN). (2007). Statistics. Retrieved October 19, 2007 from http://www.rainn.org/docs/statistics/ncvs_2005.pdf

Schechter, S. (1982). *Women and male violence: The visions and struggles of the battered women's movement*. Boston: South End Press.

Shulman, L. (2006). *The skills of helping: Individuals, families, groups, and communities* (5th ed.). Belmont, CA: Thomson Brooks/Cole.

Valentich, M. (1996). Feminist theory and social work practice. In F. Turner (Ed.), *Social work treatment: Interlocking theoretical approaches* (pp. 282–318). New York: The Free Press.

Sexual Offenders

Steven Hartsock and Karen Harper-Dorton

On any given day in the United States as many as 234,000 convicted sexual offenders are incarcerated or in custody of correctional facilities, while many others are returning to community living (Stalans, 2004). In 2007, sexual registries provided public access to approximately 500,000 offenders who are predominantly male and known to their victims in at least 80% of offenses. Sexual offenders are feared, hated, and labeled as the lowest of humankind in communities and in prisons as well. Low self-esteem, denial, a lack of responsibility, and low victim empathy are commonly found in this manipulative and difficult to treat population that is shunned by families and society. Group counseling is the modality of choice for treating, managing, and containing sexual offenders as they leave secure settings and return to community living (Hilarski & Christensen, 2006; Hudson, 2005; Levenson & Macgowan, 2004).

Social group work practices and theory inform processes for participation, feedback, confrontation, and education in groups (Bates, Falshaw, Corbett, Patel, & Friendship, 2004; Ephross & Vassil, 2005; Kimberley & Osmond, 2003). The group provides an avenue for delivering treatment from a cognitive-behavioral therapy (CBT) approach as the method of choice for realizing the goal of preventing sexual reoffending in the future. Integration of group processes and CBT techniques have been demonstrated to be effective in treating numerous behavioral and emotional disorders (Bieling, McCabe, & Antony, 2006). The group setting allows offenders to bring distorted thought processes and fantasies into the controlled structure provided by CBT where they can hopefully be restructured. CBT and group therapy combine to provide structure and process for the development of normative behaviors and thought processes. Mandated to receive community-based treatment as part of parole or probation requirements, sexual offenders often lack interpersonal skills and exhibit manipulative behaviors that are difficult to treat in individual therapy. Offenders frequently uncover painful gaps in empathy, attachment, and self-awareness. Group members have the task of identifying thoughts and events that trigger inappropriate sexual images and behaviors and reporting these to the group where they can be processed. Not defined as a psychiatric or physical disorder, sexual offending is viewed as a behavioral disorder involving behaviors under the conscious control of the offender. CBT facilitates cognitive restructuring so that responsibility for offending behaviors, victim empathy, and ability to identify triggers and development of safety plans to prevent reoffending can occur.

Despite the stigma and stereotyping targeting sexual offenders, social group workers must respect their humanity. In the case of sexual offenders, recognizing that they are not alone, but that there are others like them in treatment for having committed sexual offenses as well is a powerful factor toward recovery. Yalom (1995) identifies 11 primary therapeutic factors central to group therapy: instillation of hope, universality, imparting information, altruism, corrective recapitulation of the primary family group, development of socializing techniques, imitative behavior, interpersonal learning, group cohesiveness, catharsis, and existential factors. While the factor of hope is necessary for growth to occur, according to Yalom, universality or the sense of being with others is the primary factor in group therapy. Group therapy permits universality to occur for whatever population is involved in treatment. Group work literature establishes the nature of group treatment as involving processes that support sharing, feedback, and mutual aid where group members can: (1) name their taboo subject, (2) find they are not alone; (3) broaden understanding of their behaviors and contributing factors; and (4) mutually gain support and reciprocate by acquiring and helping others to build empathy and social skills (Shulman, 2006). Interaction in the group helps members to address their own denial systems as they learn to identify triggers that can escalate into sexual offending and develop safety plans to de-escalate sexual fantasies and imagery. The group can be confronting to members who are moving into negative emotional, behavioral, cognitive, and interpersonal behaviors. Simultaneously, offenders provide support and survival information to one another in the process of treatment to manage their thoughts and behaviors. The group milieu provides the unique opportunity to interrupt denial, minimization, and depersonalization that are common among offenders.

Unique features of group treatment with sexual offenders include open-ended and semi-structured groups with male and female co-leaders. Leaders must establish their leadership and provide structure with this often manipulative population. Open-ended groups have changing membership and must accommodate new members who are joining for the first time as well as provide termination and endings for those who leave (Schopler & Galinsky, 2005). Typically all members are required to report their offenses and punishment, be punctual, and pay for treatment. Male and female co-therapists provide structure and balance for appropriate gender relationships (Nosko, 2002). Co-leadership calls for competence in group therapy, maintenance of co-therapy relationships, understanding of human behavior and psychopathology, and cognitive-behavioral therapy in leading sexual offender treatment groups. Tasks that co-therapists must attend to in sexual offender groups include building social competence, reducing cognitive distortion, providing sex education, teaching anger management, providing support and non-specific counseling, involving family systems, preventing relapse, increasing commitment to accountability and responsibility, and enabling positive community re-entry. Co-therapists must be familiar with various types of sexual crimes, and report absences or suspected episodes of re-offending to probation or parole officers. Providing mandated treatment and partnering with correctional systems where aberrant behaviors must be reported places restrictions on confidentiality, a requirement that needs to be understood by group members (Hartsock & Harper-Dorton, 2007).

Research studies support the value of CBT group therapy in reducing recidivism of sexual offenders who are preparing to return to community living (Abel, 2006; Hanson & Harris, 1998). Nevertheless, there is great variability and lack of consensus about long-term effectiveness of treating sexual offenders. There are numerous issues of public safety, privacy rights of offenders, and rights of victims for protection and privacy. In the absence of a "cure" or assured remediation for sexual offending, group treatment is valued as the most efficient and effective approach to attaining the overall goal of preventing re-offending in the future by this difficult to treat population. More longitudinal studies continue to be needed to determine lasting outcomes from treatment.

References

Abel, G. G. (2006). The Abel Assessment for sexual interest-2 (AASI-2). Retrieved March 15, 2007 from http://www.abelscreen.com/tests/aasi.html

Bates, A., Falshaw, L., Corbett, C., Patel, V., & Friendship, C. (2004). A follow-up study of sex offenders treated by Thames Valley Sex Offender Groupwork Programme, 1995–1999. *Journal of Sexual Aggression, 10*(1), 29–39.

Bieling, P. J., McCabe, R. E., & Antony, M. M. (2006). *Cognitive-behavioral therapy in groups*. New York: Guilford Press.

Ephross, P., & Vassil, T. (2005). *Groups that work* (2nd ed.). New York: Columbia University Press.

Hanson, R. K., & Harris, A. J. R. (1998). Dynamic predictors of sexual recidivism. (User Report 1998-01). Ottawa: Department of the Solicitor General of Canada. Retrieved January 10, 2007 from http://www.sgc.gc.ca

Hartsock, S., & Harper-Dorton, K. (2007, July 26). *Group treatment of sexual offenders living in rural communities*. Presentation at the 32nd National Institute on Social Work and Human Services in Rural Areas, Montgomery, AL.

Hilarski, C., & Christensen, C. W. (2006). Adult male sex offenders. In C. Hilarski, & J. Wodarski (Eds.), *Comprehensive mental health practice with sex offenders and their families* (pp. 47–69). Binghamton, NY: Haworth Press.

Hudson, K. (2005). *Offending identities*. Portland, OR: Willan Publishing Co.

Kimberely, D., & Osmand, L. (2003). Night of the tortured souls: Integration of group therapy and mutual aid for treated male sex offenders. In J. Lindsay, D. Turcotte, & E. Hopmeyer (Eds.). *Crossing boundaries and developing alliances through group work*. Binghamton, NY: Haworth Press.

Levenson, J. S., & Macgowan, M. J. (2004). Engagement, denial, and treatment progress among sex offenders in group therapy. *Sexual Abuse: A Journal of Research and Treatment, 16*(1), 49–63.

Nosko, A. (2002). Adventures in co-leadership in social group work practice. *Social Work with Groups, 25*(1/2), 175–183.

Schopler, J. H., & Galinsky, M. J. (2005). Meeting practice needs: Conceptualizing the open-ended group. *Social Work with Groups, 28*(3/4), 49–68.

Shulman, L. (2006). *The skills of helping: Individuals, families, groups, and communities* (5th ed.). Belmont, CA: Thomson Brooks/Cole.

Stalans, L. J. (2004). Adult sex offenders on community supervision. *Criminal Justice and Behaviour, 31*(5), 564–608.

Yalom, I. D. (1995). *The theory and practice of group psychotherapy* (4th ed.). New York: Basic Books.

Siblings of Children with Autistic Spectrum Problems

David Strauss and Daniel Aaron

Autism can be characterized as being on a continuum. With severe autism, infants may shrink from the touch of their parents, fail to smile or imitate expressions, or mouth the syllables of language. Autistic children show little interest in needs and feelings of others. They have no apparent wish to share or communicate experiences, exhibit almost no spontaneous or imaginative play, and prefer monotonous solitary activities. They fear novelty and try to establish rigid routines, and may panic or explode in rage when faced with slight changes. At the other end of the spectrum is a disorder called Aspbergers. Children with Asbergers often have a pattern of social ineptitude, unusual obsessions, limited imagination, and difficulty in understanding the perspectives and feelings of others (Attwood & Wing, 1997).

Siblings of children with autism must cope with particular demands that impact their growth and development. All aspects of a child's life are affected by exposure to autistic spectrum disorder in the family. The typical children in the family are constantly confronted with painful feelings of isolation, loneliness, disconnection, and lack of empathy. In addition, children experience disturbing emotions resulting from exposure to their sibling's often overwhelming affects and bizarre behaviors. These experiences can overwhelm the coping mechanisms of the sibling, leading to greater anxiety, withdrawal, aggression, and compromised opportunities to deal with competition.

The typical child's social development is often challenged, as the desire to form relationships with the peer group conflicts with feelings of loyalty toward the family. Fearing exclusion and rejection, children struggle to form positive peer relationships while maintaining a healthy connection to family (Seligman & Darling, 1989). This dilemma may lead to a lower level of participation in outside activities and loss of companionship. In addition, typical children assume a caretaking role with their sibling and therefore give up an age-appropriate relationship.

The reality of the stress on a family with an autistic member can decrease the effectiveness of the family system and subsequently intensify the child's anxieties of family disintegration. The natural life cycle of the family may be altered as the expectation for children to grow and leave the family changes, i.e., placement of an autistic child in an institution or continuing stay within the family of origin. The possibility of fragmentation and isolation within the family heightens ambivalence around separation for the typical child (Erickson, 1963).

The growing prevalence and awareness of this diagnosis has revealed a need to provide help for children affected directly by this complex situation. Naylor and Prescott (2004) acknowledge the unique needs of children who have a disabled sibling and identified group as a preferred modality of treatment. These children feel isolated and may be unaware for various reasons of others who share their experience. Group is an effective intervention as it lowers resistance to beginning treatment and provides a unique normalizing experience, given the fact that all members share a common issue. The group experience also mirrors the natural propensity for children and adolescents to join groups and may diminish the stigma associated with individual treatment.

Various group approaches can be used to address the needs of children living with autistic siblings. Braucher (2002) states that social work groups tend to emphasize self-empowerment, peer relations, and self-discovery. Depending on the age and degree of impairment, groups may focus on the experience of self-exploration, with the group process serving as a means of developing a sense of self-worth. The group may also serve as an environment to facilitate adaptive peer relations and help members acknowledge the comfort of support. Group can also provide socialization skills through the use of limit setting and skill building.

Both Sugar (1974) and Soo (1992) discuss intrapsychic group approaches that aim to modify the internal dynamics of the members through understanding collective group defense mechanisms and interpreting unconscious group processes. As members reveal themselves in the group's environment, they internalize greater self-acceptance and experience more adaptive ego integration.

Activity group therapy (AGT) encourages the reliving and resolving of interpersonal patterns in a permissive environment. Slavson (1979) and Slavson and Schiffer (1975) argue that the curative factors of AGT include abreaction, controlled regression, and reintegration, based on new identifications and opportunities to develop new sublimations.

One treatment model for siblings of autistic spectrum disorder that is being practiced incorporates an eclectic approach and consists of an initial time-limited experience that is followed by an open-ended group. The initial time-limited group is comprised of an assessment interview, 12 group sessions, and an exit interview. The assessment interview is conducted in the home of the client so that the group facilitator can gain a unique understanding of the client and the home environment. It also provides the opportunity for the facilitator to meet the child with autism and assess the extent of the disability and the impact this child has on the family's functioning (El-Ghoroury & Romanczyk, 1999).

The purpose of the 12 sessions is to give the group members an opportunity to experiment with revealing personal and family information. By sharing information in a group that resembles the natural peer group, the members have an opportunity to replicate that behavior outside. Also, the group provides help with connecting thoughts, feelings, and behavior. The didactic component of the 12 sessions can be helpful in correcting distortions and misconceptions that members may have about their autistic sibling. Finally, the 12-session group will help members normalize their reaction and validate the experience of growing up with an autistic sibling. The goals of the group will be achieved through the modalities of free play, structured play, didactic activities, and verbal discussions (Winnicott, 1971).

After the initial 12 sessions, each group member will receive an exit interview with the group leader. Naylor and Prescott's (2004) research notes the importance of individual interviews to supplement the group experience. The exit interview will be a collaboration of the group leader, family, and group member. It will consist of a summary of the experience, assessment of the group member's progress, and a discussion of future treatment options.

The purpose of the ongoing group will be to provide a forum in which to work through those issues and themes that emerged in the initial group. As in the initial group, the sessions will be comprised of both play and discussion activities. The emphasis will be more aligned with Slavson's (1979) approach who advocates a permissive environment in order to relive and resolve problematic interpersonal patterns.

References

Attwood, T., & Wing, L. (1997). *Asperger's syndrome: A guide for parents and professionals*. London: Jessica Kingsley.

Braucher, D. (2002). *Clinical social work practice with acting-out pre and early adolescents in groups: Intervening in the collective use of primitive defensive mechanisms*. Dissertation, New York University School of Social Work.

El-Ghoroury, N. H., & Romanczyk, R. G. (1999). Play interactions of family members towards children with autism. *Journal of Autism and Developmental Disorders*, 29, 249–258.

Erickson, E. H. (1963). *Childhood and society*. New York: Norton.

Naylor, A., & Prescott, P. (2004). All about my brother. *Community Care, 1538*, pp. 34–35.

Seligman, M., & Darling, R. B. (1989). *Ordinary families special children*. New York: Guilford Press.

Slavson, S. R. (1979). *Dynamics of group psychotherapy*. New York: Jason Aronson.

Slavson, S. R., & Schiffer, M. (1975). *Group psychotherapies for children*. New York: International Universities Press.

Soo, E. S. (1992). The management of resistance in the application of object relations concepts in children's and adolescents' group psychotherapy. *Journal of Child Adolescence Group Therapy, 2*(2), 77–92.

Sugar, M. (1974). Interpretive group psychotherapy with latency children. *Journal of the American Academy of Child Psychiatry, 13*(4), 648–666.

Winnicott, D. W. (1971). Playing. In *Playing and reality* (pp. 51–71). London: Routledge.

Street Youth

Steven Kraft

Street work is the term used to describe activities, or interventions, group workers use in their efforts to engage, and work effectively with hard to reach youth in their own environment. The client population may consist of gangs, juvenile delinquents, alcohol and substance abusers, street youth, homeless individuals, or the persistently mentally ill. These client groups often are described as hard to reach, and hard to work with once contact is established. They tend to be underserved or not served at all.

Working with groups of this kind is a particularly important part of social work practice. It allows workers to engage group members who have demonstrated some problem-solving potential (Schopler & Galinsky, 1978). The importance of helping people on the "streets" in their own environment is based on the premise that this is an effective way to establish a working relationship with people who create problems for the larger society and who also are at high risk of self-destructive behaviors. Moreover, these populations tend to resist seeking or accepting help and often are hostile towards helping institutions. The dynamics of the group are used to guide the street workers' interventions. If the group dynamics are ignored, the effects often are negative suppression of opinions (Galinsky & Schopler, 1994).

Social work in general, and social group work, in particular, has a long-term commitment to serve the most vulnerable, most needy and most oppressed members of society. "The primary mission of the social work profession is to enhance human well-being and help meet the basic human needs of all people, with particular attention to the needs and empowerment of people who are vulnerable, oppressed, and living in poverty" (National Association of Social Workers, 1999). However, unfortunately, in many ways, social work has abandoned this important mission (Specht & Courtney, 1995). This situation has elevated the importance of street work to work with this difficult population.

The combined effort of a large urban settlement house, and three police precincts, to prevent juvenile delinquency illustrates the power and potential of street work. A coordinator, a social worker, a precinct liaison, and three street workers staffed the program. The street workers involved themselves directly with at-risk youth. They participated with the young people in street activities such as informal athletics, or at times, just engaged in hanging out with them. The street workers used the settlement house and other community resources such as the local schools to provide opportunities for more structured activities. In the course of these contacts, relationships developed that encouraged the young people to communicate more specifically about what they wanted and what they felt they needed. Bonding between street workers and group members took place, and helping relationships were created. The street workers used these relationships to bring about changes in the way the young people related to each other, to the workers, and to the community agencies.

At times, street workers were able to connect the youth to the programs, to other social workers, and, also, to more structured activities offered by the host agency and by other community agencies. Frequently, the street workers became involved with the youths' families and were able to make referrals for needed services. The precinct liaison often introduced arrested youth to the street workers who, in turn, would attempt to involve them in the informal and formal group work that they were practicing.

The program was able to offer services in four ways:

1. Recruitment: Group members were recruited and directed to the relevant agency programs that were offered.
2. Help within informal street structure: The street worker's use of self and relationships formed on the streets was used to help the clients become self-reflective about their behavior and, subsequently, to develop in ways of relating that were better for themselves and others.
3. Development of more formal structured activities: i.e., basketball and other athletic leagues, creative dramatics including playwriting, arts and crafts, fine arts programs, and involvement in community service.
4. Referral of clients and families for specific programs, as well as to therapeutic services.

Street work with youth uses recreational interventions (Goldstein & Huff, 1993). The activities need to be selected for specific purposes, such as strengthening group cohesiveness, or for providing an opportunity for a less-valued group member to excel. Demonstrating interest in, and commitment to, issues of importance to the youth, and the ability to work with people of different lifestyles are essential skills. For example, in working in the street with substance abusers, whose lifestyles often include engaging in illegal activities, the street worker must accept their reality while communicating concern about their high-risk behaviors. Other fundamental group skills that are employed during street work include support, listening, confronting, lending a vision, affirming the affirmable, and engaging the reality of the moment. Oppressed street people can be angry and often are intimidating. The ability to reach for, and deal effectively with their anger, is an important and difficult skill. In the process of building relationships with individuals and with groups, the street worker must demonstrate the capacity to bring feelings out in the open and to respond to them effectively. Productive relationships cannot be established without a consistent, direct, and honest approach.

The street worker must learn to deal effectively with the lack of a supportive structure. In traditional social work settings, the worker has a more clearly defined role, which also provides the foundation for the helping relationship he hopes to develop. In street work, the role is much more fluid and must be created primarily out of the relationships that are established on the street. In traditional counseling, the assumption is that in order to help a person change, the client must want to change. However, in street work, the assumption is that in order to help a person change, the street worker must motivate the person to change.

Street workers must be able to manage conflict and to deal with adversaries. In the course of their work, street workers often experience active resentment and resistance from agency representatives, as well as from group members. A combination of tact, firmness, and persistence are qualities that are essential for successful street work.

References

Galinsky, M. J., & Schopler, J. H. (1994). Negative experiences in support groups. *Social Work in Health Care, 20*(1), 77–95.

Goldstein, A., & Huff, C. (1993). *The gang intervention handbook.* Champaign, IL: Research Press.

National Association of Social Workers. (1999). *Code of Ethics of the National Association of Social Workers.* Retrieved January 20, 2008 from http://www.socialworkers.org/pubs/code/code.asp

Schopler, J. H., & Galinsky, M. J. (1978). Social group work. In A. E. Fink (Ed.), *The field of social work* (pp. 179–201). New York: Holt, Rinehart & Winston.

Specht, H., & Courtney, M. E. (1995). *Unfaithful angels: How social work has abandoned its mission* (pp. 106–129). New York: Free Press.

Trauma Survivors

Carolyn Knight

Exposure to trauma, particularly if it involves interpersonal victimization like childhood sexual or physical abuse, has been linked to numerous challenges in adulthood, including substance abuse, health problems, and eating disorders, and psychiatric problems, such as depression, posttraumatic stress, dissociative identity, and borderline personality disorders (Breslau, 2002). Recent research suggest that one of the most deleterious effects of trauma, particularly when it occurs in childhood, is the distorted views of self and others that often result (Garfield & Leveroni, 2000).

Group work is well suited to meeting the treatment needs of individuals with traumatic histories and has been found to reduce the intrusive symptoms associated with a history of trauma, enhance self-esteem, and reduce depression and isolation (Schnurr et al., 2003). Group membership normalizes and validates survivors' experiences, thus maximizing the mutual aid benefit of being "all in the same boat." When survivors discover they are not alone, their sense of isolation is decreased, which enhances their ability to constructively manage the challenges they face. Groups provide trauma survivors with the opportunity to connect with others, which enhances self-esteem and begins to alter distorted views of social relationships. In addition, as they provide assistance to, and learn from, one another, trauma survivors' sense of mastery and self-efficacy is enhanced.

Groups for survivors of trauma exist on a continuum, and research underscores the importance of distinguishing groups that are primarily focused on members' present-day challenges from those that are more focused on members' underlying traumatic experiences (Bisson, 2003). A related consideration is whether the group's primary emphasis will be on the expression or containment of feelings, since expression of intense affect can be re-traumatizing (Speigel, Classen, Thurston, & Butler, 2004).

Groups that are more structured, time-limited, and have a clear educational component have been found to be most appropriate for more fragile, socially isolated individuals and those new to treatment (Klein & Schermer, 2000). Feelings are acknowledged and validated, but also are contained. Such groups normalize members' experiences and decrease their sense of isolation and "different-ness." Emphasis is placed upon helping members understand the effects of the trauma more so than on helping them confront the experience itself and the feelings associated with it. Members' commonality of experience associated with their victimization, their current difficulties, or both, coupled with similar treatment needs for stabilization and education would guide composition decisions.

Research suggests that participation in such groups is an appropriate starting point for many survivors of trauma, because of the safety provided by their structured format (Foy, Eriksson, & Trice, 2001). Further, the effectiveness of structured psychoeducational groups focused on present-day challenges that are common among survivors of trauma, such as a diagnosis or symptoms of posttraumatic stress or dissociative identity disorders or substance abuse, has been demonstrated (Fournier, 2002). In these groups, emphasis is placed on helping members manage their symptoms and understand the connection to the underlying trauma.

Individuals who have some previous experience in counseling, who have developed a basic understanding of their traumatic reactions and are more stable in their functioning would be appropriate candidates for groups that are less structured and that focus both on the traumatic event itself and the affective reactions that resulted from it (Klein & Schermer, 2000). Disclosure is encouraged and members are assisted in confronting and managing the intense affect that results. Members are helped to learn new, more effective ways of coping both with the past trauma and its present-day effects.

In sructured groups, members will typically share similar traumatic experiences, though wide variation could exist with respect to the circumstances surrounding the event and ways members have coped and adapted. These more psychodynamically oriented groups may be time-limited, though they need to be long enough to allow members to develop the level of intimacy and comfort necessary to engage in intense emotional work. This sort of group could be open-ended, though frequent turnover in membership would be counterproductive and limit its therapeutic potential.

The social worker should be familiar with six challenges that typically accompany group work with adult survivors of trauma. First, trauma survivors tend towards social isolation; therefore, they may be difficult to engage in group work treatment. An essential task of the group worker, particularly in the beginning phase, is to help members connect and feel comfortable with one another and with the worker. Gitterman's "not the only one" principle (2005) should guide the selection process. No one member should stand out in a way that intensifies, rather than diminishes, the members sense of isolation.

Second, trauma survivors' mistrust of self and others is likely to be reflected in groups as intense and ongoing transference reactions. The group worker needs to be prepared to assist members in adopting a here-and-now focus, allowing them to examine their interactions with, and reactions to, one another. Third, even in groups that focus more on containment rather than expression of feelings, the worker should be prepared to identify and respond to manifestations of intense affect and the impact this has on the group as a whole and each individual member. The group worker must balance encouraging explicit disclosures on the one hand and avoiding overwhelming individual members' and the group-as-a-whole's coping capacities on the other. The worker also should anticipate that sharing his or her emotional reactions often will be necessary as a means of validating members' feelings and conveying acceptance and understanding. The worker's actions model a more adaptive way of managing feelings and encourage members to risk doing the same.

Expression of feelings and disclosures about members' past traumas are associated with a fourth challenge, which is the possibility that members may individually and/or collectively dissociate in the group as a way of insulating and protecting themselves from strong feelings. The group worker will need to be alert to this possibility and prepared to normalize and validate the dissociative coping as well as the feelings and experiences that led to it.

Given the demanding nature of group work with trauma survivors, countertransference is yet another challenge associated with this work. The range, intensity, and complexity of transference reactions, the likelihood that group-as-a-whole transference may be directed at the worker, as well as the content of the discussions in these groups, suggest that the worker must constantly attend to and monitor his or her affective reactions.

Finally, the social workers who facilitates groups for survivors must anticipate that they will be indirectly traumatized by the work. The group worker's repeated exposure to trauma through group members' experiences results in challenges that are similar to those of the members themselves, including intrusive thoughts of clients and distortions in thinking about self and others (Knight, 2006). Compassion fatigue is another manifestation of indirect trauma. Minimizing the impact of indirect trauma is a more realistic and appropriate goal than is prevention. Research findings underscore the importance of, and need for, social workers to seek out and use professional support and consultation and to cultivate and protect their personal relationships (Baird & Kracen, 2006).

References

Baird, K., & Kracen, A. (2006). Vicarious traumatization and secondary traumatic stress: A research synthesis. *Counselling Psychology Quarterly, 19*, 181–188.

Bisson, J. (2003). Trauma-focused group psychotherapy is not effective for posttraumatic stress disorder in Vietnam veterans. *Evidence-based Mental Health, 6*, 124–125.

Breslau, N. (2002). Epidemiological studies of trauma, posttraumatic stress disorder, and other psychiatric disorders. *Canadian Journal of Psychiatry, 47*, 923–929.

Fournier, R. (2002). A trauma education workshop on posttraumatic stress. *Health and Social Work, 27*, 113–124.

Foy, D., Eriksson, C., & Trice, C. (2001). Introduction to group interventions for trauma survivors. *Group dynamics: Theory, research, and practice, 5*, 246–251.

Garfield, D., & Leveroni, C. (2000). The use of self-psychological concepts in a Veterans Affairs PTSD clinic. *Bulletin of the Menninger Clinic, 64*, 344–364.

Gitterman, A. (2005). Group formation: Tasks, methods, and skills. In A. Gitterman, & L. Shulman (Eds.), *Mutual aid groups, vulnerable and resilient populations, and the life cycle* (3rd ed., pp. 73–110). New York: Columbia University Press.

Klein, R., & Schermer, V. (2000). Introduction and overview: Creating a healing matrix. In R. Klein, & V. Schermer (Ed.), *Group psychotherapy for psychological trauma* (pp. 3–46). New York: Guilford Press.

Knight, C. (2006). Groups for individuals with traumatic histories: Practice considerations for social workers. *Social Work, 51*, 20–30.

Schnurr, P., Friedman, M., Foy, D., Shea, T., Hseih, F., Lavori, P., Glynn, S., Wattenberg, M., & Bernardy, N. (2003). Randomized trial of trauma-focused group therapy for posttraumatic stress disorder: Results from a Department of Vetrans Affairs cooperative study. *Archives of General Psychiatry, 60*, 481–489.

Spiegel, D., Classen, C., Thurston, E., & Butler, L. (2004). Trauma-focused versus present-focused models for women sexually abused in childhood. In L. Koenig, & L. Doll (Eds.), *From child sexual abuse to adult sexual risk: Trauma, revictimization, and intervention* (pp. 251–268). Washington, DC: American Psychological Association.

Women with Advanced Breast Cancer

Fiona McDermott and Christine Hill

Social workers working in the health field are well placed to offer group work services for patients, families and caregivers. Social work practice with groups draws on a variety of theoretical perspectives, models and approaches, many of which are appropriate in the health field (see Kurland & Salmon, 1999; McDermott, 2002; Shulman, 2006). The foci of the group work services are health issues with the patients' experiences placed within the context of family, community, medical condition, and providers and hospital. Clarity of purpose and focus are essential to these groups (Kurland & Salmon, 1998).

Improving and maintaining the health and emotional well-being of participants facing a chronic and eventually terminal illness represents a significant objective for these groups. Group work interventions attend to issues of great importance to these women—motherhood, femininity, and sexual identity—all challenged by advanced breast cancer and its treatments. Losses associated with bodily changes caused by the disease and its treatments, losses of quality of life, sometimes losses of relationships, and eventually loss of life itself are ever present in these groups. Group participants also deal with, and learn from, the losses of group members who leave the group when they are too sick to participate or when they die.

Supportive-Expressive Group Therapy (SEGT) is a group work intervention particularly designed for this population. SEGT has seven purposes: to build bonds; express emotions; detoxify death and dying; redefine life's priorities; increase support of family and friends; improve doctor–patient relationship; and improve coping skills. Spiegel and others (Spiegel, Bloom, Kramer, & Gottheil, 1989) offered SEGT to an experimental group. Group members reported improvement in quality of life and reduction in pain. Unexpectedly, experimental group members lived at least 1 year longer. Incorporating an existential perspective, group members were invited to talk openly about death and dying, By confronting and "detoxifying" death, their fears were lessened (Spiegel & Spira, 1991). Knowledge enhanced a sense of control; mutual support countered isolation; sharing fears and concerns nurtured courage and confidence in choices made. Relationships improved, families felt supported, and the quality of life was improved (Edmonds, Lockwood, & Cunningham, 1999; Kissane et al., 2007).

Ideally, groups are open-ended (members can join at any point) and consist of 7 to 9 members. Participants are assessed beforehand to ascertain their capacities for group work and pertinent issues in their lives that may affect their attendance. There is no set agenda for the group and each session is open for participants to raise issues of concern to them. The groups have co-leaders, who enable members to explore and understand challenges being faced, and to deal with stressful life transitions (leaving the workforce, preparing for death, death of group members) and particularly difficult emotions (despair and anger) (Germain & Gitterman, 1996). Advanced breast cancer places profound emotional demands on group workers, necessitating co-leadership and the capacity for collaborative and shared leadership roles.

Group members are encouraged to build cohesion both within and outside the group. Groups meet weekly for one and a half hours, after which participants socialize over coffee. Outside of group time, members frequently contact one another for expressive, instrumental and social reasons. Should a member be too ill to attend a meeting, the leaders may organize the group to meet in their home or hospice. Members and leaders attend funerals on the basis that the commitment to one another continues for as long as is required, reassuring members that, just as they offer ongoing support to each other, they can expect the same.

Group work with women with advanced breast cancer has a rich history of research, principally derived from randomized controlled trials, but also includes qualitative studies and narrative accounts from group participants (The Thursday Girls, 2004). In a number of countries, studies of both short-term and long-term group programs have used manualized treatments (Bordeleau et al., 2003; Cunningham et al., 1998; Edmonds et al., 1999; Kissane et al., 2003; Kissane et al., 2007; Llewelyn et al., 1999). These studies coincide with an increasing interest in developing an evidence base for social work with groups (McDermott, 2005; Pollio, 2002). Evidence-based models for working with women with advanced breast cancer offer social workers valuable opportunities for contributing to knowledge development.

References

Bordeleau, L., Szalai, J. P., Ennis, M., Leszcz, M., Speca, M., Sela, R., et al. (2003). Quality of life in a randomized trial of group psychosocial support in metastatic cancer: Overall effects of the intervention and an exploration of missing data. *Journal of Clinical Oncology, 21*(10), 1944–1951.

Cunningham, A. J., Edmonds, C. V. I., Jenkins, G. P., Pollack, H., Lockwood, C. A., & Warr, D. (1998). A randomized controlled trial of the effects of group psychological therapy on survival in women with metastatic breast cancer. *Journal of Psycho-Oncology, 7*(6), 508–517.

Edmonds, C. V. I., Lockwood, G. A., & Cunningham, A. J. (1999). Psychological response to long-term group therapy: A randomized trial with metastatic breast cancer patients. *Journal of Psycho-Oncology, 8*, 74–91.

Germain, C. B., & Gitterman, A. (1996). *The Life Model of social work practice: Advances in knowledge and practice* (2nd ed.). New York: Columbia University Press.

Kissane, D. W., Bloch, S., Smith, G. C., Miach, P., Clarke, D. M., Ikin, J., Love, A., Ranieri, N., & McKenzie, D. (2003). Cognitive-emotional group psychotherapy for women with primary breast cancer: A randomised control trial. *Journal of Psycho-Oncology, 12*, 532–546.

Kissane, D., Grabsch, B., Clarke, D., Smith, G., Love, A., Bloch, et al. (2007). Supportive-expressive group therapy for women with metatastic breast cancer: Survival and psychosocial outcome from a randomized controlled trial. *Journal of Psycho-Oncology, 16*, 277–287.

Kurland, R., & Salmon, R. (1998). Purpose: A misunderstood and misused keystone of group work practice. *Social Work with Groups, 21*(2), 5–17.

Kurland, R., & Salmon, R. (1999). *Teaching a methods course in social work with groups.* Alexandria, VA: Council on Social Work Education.

Llewelyn, P., Murray, K., Johnston, M., Johnston, W., Preece, E., & Dewar, A. (1999). Group therapy for metastatic cancer patients: Report of an intervention. *Psychology, Health & Medicine, 4*(3), 229–231.

McDermott, F. (2002). *Inside group work.* Sydney, Australia: Allen & Unwin.

McDermott, F. (2005). Researching group work: Outsider and insider perspectives. *Groupwork, 15*(1), 91–109.

Pollio, D. E. (2002). The evidence-based group worker. *Social Work with Groups, 25*(4), 57–70.

Shulman, L. (2006). *The skills of helping: Individuals, families, groups, and communities* (5th ed.). Belmont, CA: Thomson Brooks/Cole.

Spiegel, D., Bloom, J. R., Kraemer, H. C., & Gottheil, E. (1989). Effect of psychosocial treatment on survival of patients with metastatic breast cancer. *Lancet, 2*(8668), 888–891.

Spiegel., D., & Spira, J. (1991). *Supportive-expressive group therapy: A treatment manual of psychosocial intervention for women with metastatic breast cancer.* Stanford, CA: School of Medicine, Stanford University.

The Thursday Girls. (2004). *A life to live: A group journey with advanced breast cancer.* Melbourne, Australia: PsychOz.

Youth at Risk

Sam Copeland

The small group is an ideal setting for youth as they grow and develop. They have been socialized, learned to trust, and developed peer relationships in these group settings. The group provides the opportunity for young people to experience the normal progression of familiar interactions that promote positive social learning. Group work is widely accepted as an effective method to bring about positive change. Still, there are precautions to be observed with at-risk youth (Toseland & Rivas, 2005). Group development includes attempting to provide a structure designed to achieve success for the members. This includes identifying strengths that the members bring to the group, which, when combined with the skills of the leader, promote the development of mutual aid and interdependence in a timely manner.

Trust must be addressed in the early stages of group development. In mandated, short-term groups, the challenge is to develop trust in an abbreviated format. Developing trust is a process and can be hindered by the fact that group leaders are perceived as authority figures. Short-term groups have the potential for members to move quickly to identification of goals, universality, and socialization (Dies, 1996). Short-term groups may avoid some of the harmful effects of delayed group cohesion that *can* occur in groups of longer duration.

To prevent and eliminate youth crime in the United States, few programs have focused on short-term group strategies to help at-risk youth. Myers and colleagues (2000) suggested focusing on minimizing recidivism and developing cost-effective measures for new youth offenders. Efforts must be made by social workers to utilize social group work approaches where youth are engaged and empowered to accept the helping role to meet their specific needs (Getzel, Kurland, & Salmon, 1987).

Re-socialization or group counseling for at-risk youth is not a new method for juveniles awaiting probation or detention. Over 40 years ago, Faust (1965) reported that professionally prepared group leaders usually ran most programs or groups, and funding was generally limited by many of the juvenile courts. The juvenile authorities attempted to rehabilitate youth of that day by providing partial counseling programs facilitated by probation officers. However, there are few examples in the literature about the effectiveness of early prevention or group counseling with at-risk youth (Myers et al., 2000). A short-term approach allows for the efficient facilitation of consensus building, which moves quickly to mutual aid. Mutual aid lays the foundation, orients, and prepares group members for success prior to starting re-socialization programs. Short-term groups by definition and duration are cost-effective. This allows for group facilitation within the 10 days to 2 weeks that generally occur while youth offenders await sentencing. Professionally trained group leaders, social workers, psychologists, sociologists, or a combination of leaders from the juvenile justice system personnel are recommended to facilitate short-term groups.

Youth who enter into courts and rehabilitation situations do so filled with anxiety and anticipation. Gitterman and Wayne (2003) suggest that *high-tension* in groups provides opportunities to promote mutual aid and improves the relationship between members and group leaders. The ongoing process of developing a conceptual framework for diverse populations, including learning new group expertise, has been evolving since the 1980s (Toseland & Rivas, 2005). African-American and Hispanic youth at risk for a lifetime of crime represent special groups in need of specific and immediate skills, which can be identified in short-term groups.

Communities, whether they are rural or urban, are concerned about developing effective strategies to reduce and eliminate juvenile crime. Youth are being incarcerated at alarming rates across the United States. Educating juveniles can protect them from engaging in criminal behavior (Office of Juvenile Justice and Delinquency Prevention, 2006). It remains unclear which interventions have worked effectively to bring about enduring change that leads to productive citizenship. Programs designed to improve juvenile anti-social behavior must include coordinated prevention and intervention efforts. Short-term groups can be utilized in combination with court-ordered counseling for first-time and early offenders in rural and urban settings. In an effort to understand which risk and protective factors are involved in providing pro-social family intervention, there must be an effective use of the incarceration experience and the development of community-based resources for these youth. One strategy for eliminating the ongoing influx of juveniles into adult prison is to develop preventive programs for youth as they enter into the juvenile justice system (Patrick, Marsh, Bundy, Mimura, & Perkins, 2004). It stands to reason that the short-term group can help prepare first-time and early offenders to utilize and negotiate the many re-socialization strategies that lead to successful youth outcomes.

The short-term group can help lay the foundation for youth rehabilitation. According to Dies (1996), group process theory combined with a Directive Facilitation Model can help first-time juvenile offenders become oriented and prepared to face the challenges of probation, detention, or incarceration. The group can be developed to help youth manage their behavior, and prepare for specific programs. Short-term group contracting is straightforward and brief, allowing members to *buy in*, utilize the right to self-determination, take responsibility for their own programs, and engage in mutual aid with others. This approach allows group members to give equal attention to such issues as the development of identity, self-concept, the management of peer relations, and authority issues. The short-term group also can facilitate preparation for good decision making and lay the foundation for effective problem solving in preparation for unforeseen events.

The goal of the short-term group is to help young people avoid becoming adult criminals, and to assist them in their efforts to become productive individuals. The re-socialization of youth offenders, historically by the juvenile justice system, has been guided by labeling theory. According to Longres (2000), labeling adolescents as delinquent may plant the seeds that grow into a life of habitual crime. The approach of short-term groups and utilization of new and innovative approaches helps social work group leaders and youth offenders move beyond labeling, to improving decision making, problem solving, and empowering today's youth in their efforts to succeed.

References

Dies, D. R. (1996). The unfolding of adolescent groups. A five-phase model of development. In P. Kymissis, & D. A. Halperin (Eds.), *Group therapy with children and adolescents* (pp. 35–53). Washington, DC: American Psychiatric Press.

Faust, F. L. (1965). Group counseling with juveniles. *Crimes & Delinquency, 11*(4), 349–354.

Getzel, G., Kurland, R., & Salmon, R. (1987). Teaching and learning the practice of social group work: Four curriculum tools. In J. Lassner, K. Powell, & C. Finnigan (Eds.), *Social group work: Competence and values in practice* (pp. 35–38). Binghamton, NY: Haworth Press.

Gitterman, A., & Wayne, J. (2003). Turning points in group life: Using high-tension moments to promote group purpose and mutual aid. *Families in Society, 84*(3), 433–440.

Longres, J. F. (2000). *Human behavior in the social environment* (2nd ed.). Itasca, IL: F. E. Peacock.

Myers, W. C., Burton, P. R., Sanders, P. D., Donat, K. M., Cheney, J., Fitzpatrick, T. M., & Monaco, L. (2000). Project back-on-track at 1 year: A delinquency treatment program for early-career juvenile offenders. *Journal American Academy of Child and Adolescent Psychiatry, 39*(9), 1027–1034.

Office of Juvenile Justice and Delinquency Prevention (2006). Juvenile offenders and victims: *2006 National Report*. Washington, DC: Author. Retrieved August 7, 2007 from http://ojjdp.ncjrs.org/ojstatbb/nr2006

Patrick, S., Marsh, R., Bundy, W., Mimura, S., & Perkins, T. (2004). Control group study of juvenile diversion programs: An experiment in juvenile diversion—the comparison of three methods and a control group. *The Social Science Journal, 41*(1), 129–135.

Toseland, R. W., & Rivas, R. F. (2005). *An introduction to group work practice* (5th ed.). Boston: Allyn & Bacon.

Group Work Over the Life Course

Children

Carolyn Knight

Children of all ages—from pre-kindergarten through latency—can derive unique benefits from participating in a mutual aid group. Whether facing normative tasks such as beginning puberty or accommodating the birth of a new sibling, coping with unforeseen circumstances such as the death of a parent, or dealing with individual challenges like aggressive behavior, group membership provides children with the opportunity to connect with others who are "all in the same boat."

The findings from numerous studies support the mutual aid benefits of groups for children of various ages in a range of practice settings (Hoag & Burlingame, 1998; Lomonaco, Schleidlinger, & Aronson, 2000). Contemporary research and theory suggest that the nature of mutual aid in children's groups is similar to that found in adult groups and revolves around a group's ability to normalize members' feelings and reactions and validate their experiences (Shechtman & Gluk, 2005). Depending upon the particular group's purpose and members' unique needs, additional advantages of group participation include increasing members' problem-solving abilities and feelings of self-esteem and self-efficacy, improving their social skills, promoting greater understanding of themselves and others, and enhancing their ability to empathize with others (Hirayama & Hirayama, 2001).

More so than in groups for adults, decisions about composition in children's groups must take into account members' ages and developmental stages, given the significant differences in cognitive, intellectual, social, and emotional functioning between younger and older children. Children under the age of six are characterized by pre-operational thought. Children at this stage are egocentric in their thinking, assuming that events that occur in their world are due to something they did or did not do. At this stage, a child's ability to think abstractly or to view a situation in more than one way is more or less non-existent, while his or her ability to translate thoughts and feelings into words is just beginning to develop.

Emotions are more likely to be acted out rather than talked about. Finally the pre-operational child has only a limited ability to be self-reflective or take the perspective of another.

Older children, ages 7 to 11, move into the stage of concrete operations. At the beginning of this stage, children's thinking and understanding of their world is bound by their immediate experiences. However, throughout this period, they become increasingly able to anticipate the consequences of their actions and to take the perspective of others. The ability to identify internal processes like thoughts and feelings also begins to develop during this stage, as does the child's ability to evaluate him or herself. Early in this stage, children tend to see things in black and white terms; as they mature, however, they begin to develop the ability to think in more relative terms.

Regardless of age, groups for children are, of necessity, based in activity, since "play is [their] natural expressive language" (Jones, 2002, p. 379). In the early stage of the group, play with toys, art and music activities, games, sports, and the like provide a vehicle for the development of cohesion and a sense of connection among members. In some groups, particularly those that include younger children, activity may remain the vehicle through which mutual aid and the work of the group takes place. Groups for older children, however, may become less reliant on activity; as members develop greater comfort with one another, they may be able— and can be encouraged—to talk about their concerns rather than just acting/playing them out.

Activity can be used in two different ways in children's groups. In the directive approach, the group worker structures the group around different topics and selects activities that relate to these themes. These groups tend to have a psycho-educational focus. A group for latency age children who lost a loved one, in which a different art activity is introduced each week to help members understand their grief reactions, would be of this type (Knight, 2005). In non-directive groups, the group worker refrains from making decisions in advance about what will be the topics for discussion. A selection of toys, activities, and games are available to children, and their play, either alone or cooperatively, is more or less unguided and unstructured. A group for severely traumatized pre-schoolers, in which members engage in make-believe play with a variety of toy props like dolls, telephones, kitchen utensils, and dress-ups, would be characteristic of this type (Jones, 2002).

In fact, many groups for children employ both directive and non-directive approaches. For example, in the early stage of a children's group, a non-directive approach might be appropriate as a non-threatening way of engaging members. As the group progresses, the group worker might introduce different topics and activities as a way of helping the group do its work. The group worker's decisions in this regard should reflect the developmental level of the members, as well as the group's purpose, and stage of development.

Regardless of the approach that is adopted, the group worker must recognize that activity in groups for children is a means to an end, rather than the goal of the group (Malekoff, Salmon, & Steinberg, 2006). Activity should be used purposefully and flexibly. For example, group members may be similar in age, but at different levels of development. Therefore, the group worker should be able to offer members a number of ways to express themselves and work through their difficulties. Similarly, if one set of activities is not accomplishing its desired purpose, the worker should be prepared to introduce another.

In addition to the role that activity plays in children's groups, three other considerations are important. First, the group must be held in a space that is conducive to the ways in which children work, interact with the environment, and express feelings. Second, the group worker must establish and uphold expectations for members' behavior that allow them to express themselves, but also foster mutual aid. The group worker's decisions in this regard should be viewed as setting therapeutic limits for members' behaviors as opposed to simply disciplining them (Landreth, 2002; Malekoff, 2002). Third, the size of the group and number and length of sessions must reflect the developmental needs of group members as well as the group's purpose and the sorts of activities that will be employed. Groups that include younger children need to be small, consisting of three or four members. Groups for older children can be slightly larger, but still should be held to six members.

Depending upon the age of the members, session length can vary from 30 to 40 minutes for younger children to 45 minutes to an hour for older children. Providing a snack time as a part of the session can enhance mutual aid. Groups for children generally will be time-limited, reflecting members' capacities, particularly in the area of motivation and staying on task (Tyndall, 2001). For younger children, groups that last four to six sessions would be advisable, while six to ten sessions would be appropriate for older children.

References

Hirayama, H., & Hirayama, K. (2001). Fostering resiliency in children through group work: Instilling hope, courage, and life skills. In T. Kelly, T. Berman-Rossi, & S. Palombo (Eds.), *Group work: Strategies for strengthening resiliency* (pp. 71–83). Binghamton, NY: Haworth Press.

Hoag, M., & Burlingame, G. (1998). Evaluating group treatment for children. *Harvard Mental Health Letter, 15,* 6–8.

Jones, K. D. (2002). Group play therapy with sexually abused children: Group behaviors and interventions. *Journal of Specialists in Group Work, 27,* 377–389.

Knight, C. (2005). Healing hearts: Bereavement groups for children. In A. Gitterman, & L. Shulman (Eds.), *Mutual aid groups, vulnerable and resilient populations, and the life cycle* (pp. 113–138). New York: Columbia University Press.

Landreth, G. (2002). *Play therapy: The art of the relationship* (2nd ed.). New York: Brunner-Routledge.

Lomonaco, S., Schleidlinger, S., & Aronson, S. (2000). Five decades of children's group treatment. *Journal of Child and Adolescent Group Therapy, 10,* 77–96.

Malekoff, A. (2002). The power of group work with kids: Lessons learned. *Social Work with Groups, 25,* 73–86.

Malekoff, A., Salmon, R., & Steinberg, D. (2006). What could happen and what couldn't happen: A poetry club for kids. *Social Work with Groups, 29,* 121–132.

Shechtman, Z., & Gluk, O. (2005). An investigation of therapeutic factors in children's groups. *Group Dynamics: Theory Research, and Practice, 9,* 127–134.

Tyndall, L., & Landreth, G. (2001). Intensive short-term group play therapy. In G. Landreth (Ed.), *Innovations in play therapy: Issues, processes, and specific populations* (pp. 203–215). New York: Brunner-Routledge.

Adolescents

Andrew Malekoff

Social work with adolescents in groups emerged from needs that were generated in the mid-1880s Industrial Revolution. Dramatic population shifts and an influx of immigrants moving to large cities forged a crucible—a melting pot—of poverty, overcrowding, disease, illiteracy, and unhealthful living and working conditions that plagued many of the people who lived in ever-deteriorating neighborhoods, for the most part located in large urban centers. As a counterforce, organizations including settlements houses (Addams, 1912), the YMCAs and YWCAs, national scouting groups, and boys' clubs emerged to address the spiritual, leisure time, and social needs of young people.

The camping movement, for example, made it possible for youngsters to experience nature and to find ways to relate to the broader environment, as many of them needed respite from the exhausting hours and harsh conditions of factory work. Settlement houses, located centrally in neighborhoods, were a major force in addressing the health and educational needs of children and adolescents. The recreation and progressive education movements, along with the settlement movement, were significant historical developments that helped to carve a path for how social work with adolescents in groups would be practiced for a century-plus to come (Breton, 1990).

The recreation movement celebrated the whole person or what we refer to today as promoting emotional wellness and positive youth development (Benson, 1997). This movement offered important insights about the use of program or activity in groups, such as the core dual concept that activity may emerge (a) spontaneously, sparking the creative potential of individuals and the group and leading to a range of imaginative pursuits, or, (b) activity may be planned, promoting critical thinking, rationality, decision making, and problem solving in the group; or it may comprise some integration of the two (Malekoff, 1997). Neva Boyd (1971), who founded the Recreational Training School at the Hull House in Chicago in the early 1900s, was a major force in encouraging group workers to transcend the singular use of formal verbalized aspects of expression, and to see that uncalculated and spontaneous expression were critical to deepening relationships and enhancing social learning. Grace Coyle, another major figure in the history of group work with youth, captured the essence of recreation as it relates to group work with adolescents in her landmark book *Group Work with American Youth* (1948).

John Dewey, the driving force in the progressive education movement, advocated for children through educational reform (1910, 1916, 1938). As with the settlement and recreation movements, the small group was viewed as the vehicle for growth and change in progressive education. The essence of this movement was to help students to learn skills for living and to prepare them to become active participants in community affairs. The progressive education movement, in its efforts to reform the school system, contributed to group work's theoretical orientation.

Some of the concepts from this movement that influenced the development of group work as a method are: the emphasis on the group rather than the individual child in the classroom; the importance of interaction between children, rather than only with the teacher, as a source of learning; development of mutual aid through peer learning; role of the teacher as facilitator rather than rigid autocrat; and learning by doing through problem solving.

In the late 1930s and early 1940s, Gisela Konopka (1949) in Pittsburgh and Fritz Redl and David Wineman (1951, 1952) in Detroit developed approaches, rooted in settlement house and community center practice with "normal youngsters," for helping emotionally disturbed children and adolescents. Henry Maier carried this tradition forth in his work with child and youth development in the group care context (1987). The core of their orientation was programming for ego support, approaches in which activities normal to childhood (i.e., crafts, games, planned discussion, field trips) were employed to bring each member's difficulties in relationships to the surface so that they might be addressed and modified. This process, referred to as the "clinical exploitation of life events," proved applicable across many settings in addressing the day-to-day concerns of the classroom, residential camp, residential treatment facility, and settlement house.

In 1965, A Model for Stages of Development in Social Work Groups, also known as The Boston Model, was first presented in the first of two landmark books (*Explorations in Group Work* and *Further Explorations in Group Work*) edited by Saul Bernstein (1973a and 1973b) who convened the Group Work Theory Committee at Boston University School of Social Work in 1959. The article was written by three practitioner/scholars: James Garland, Hubert Jones, and Ralph Kolodny (1973), colleagues at Boston University School of Social Work. The model was formulated through observation in clinical practice settings and review of records of young-adolescent groups. It consists of five stages of group development—*preaffiliation, power and control, intimacy, differentiation, and separation.* The authors postulate that *closeness* is the central theme running through all five stages. This seminal model, although derived from observations of adolescents, has informed practice with all age groups (Garland & Kolodny, 1981).

As we approached the end of the 20th century, decreasing dollars for human services, the privatization of mental health, and the advent of managed care contributed to a clamor for short-term "solution-focused" interventions for troubled youth. As a result, the cognitive–behavioral approaches for change moved into the foreground. The central organizing principle of this orientation is that behavior, emotions, and cognitions are learned and therefore can be changed by new learning. The emphasis is on addressing problematic behavior as a target for modification, rather than as a symptom of an underlying condition or situation.

The leading proponent of the socio-behavioral approach in the field of group work is Sheldon Rose (1998), who developed the multi-method approach of behavioral group therapy. In this model, the small group is the context for social reinforcement of pro-social behavior, a concept most germane to working with adolescents. As the child begins to step beyond the family circle in adolescence, there is growing affinity for the peer group. Included among the various behavioral methods of teaching children and adolescents coping skills are problem-solving and socio-recreational methods, both derivatives of the progressive education and recreation movements.

Andrew Malekoff, a social work practitioner and editor of the journal *Social Work with Groups* since 1990, formulated a strengths-based approach for group work with adolescents in 2004 (Malekoff, 2004), an expansion and tightening of the eclectic approach he presented in 1997. There is a rich tradition of group work with adolescents with origins in settlement houses, community centers, neighborhood clubs, and camps. Early group work practice promoted democractic and reciprocal interactions among group members. The use of social–recreational activity, as well as reflection, aimed at preparing young people to become socially responsible young adults and active citizens in community affairs. The approach adheres to seven practice principles that are deeply imbedded in the long history of social work with adolescents in groups. The seven principles are: (1) form groups based on members' felt needs and wants, not diagnoses; (2) structure groups to welcome the whole person, not just the troubled parts; (3) integrate verbal and non-verbal activities; (4) develop alliances with relevant others of group members; (5) decentralize authority and turn control over to group members; (6) maintain a dual focus on individual change and social reform; and (7) understand and respect group development as key to promoting change. This approach emphasizes finding and tapping in to what young people have to offer, rather than a narrow focus on deficits.

There is a rich tradition of group work with adolescents, with origins in settlement houses, community centers, neighborhood clubs, and camps. Early on in their development, group workers working with youth focused on promoting democratic, reciprocal, self-help transactions among group members and with the worker; the use of social–recreational activity as well as reflection; and practice that pays attention to young people as citizens, getting ready to participate as socially responsible young adults. The lessons from these traditions are as vital today as they were when they first emerged and provide today's group workers with a solid foundation for contemporary practice.

References

Addams, J. (1912). *The spirit of youth and the city streets.* New York: Macmillan.

Benson, P. (1997). *All kids are our kids: What communities must do to raise caring and responsible children and adolescents.* San Francisco: Jossey-Bass.

Bernstein, S. (1973a). *Explorations in group work.* Boston: Milford House.

Bernstein, S. (1973b). *Further explorations in group work.* Boston: Milford House.

Boyd, N. (1971). Social group work: A definition with methodological note. In P. Simon (Ed.), *Play and game theory in group work: A collection of papers by Neva Leona Boyd* (p. 149). Chicago: Jane Addams Graduate School of Social Work at the University of Illinois at Chicago Circle.

Breton, M. (1990). Learning from social work traditions. *Social Work with Groups, 13*(3), 21–34.

Coyle, G. (1948). *Group work with American youth: A guide to the practice of leadership.* New York: Harper.

Dewey, J. (1910). *How we think.* Boston: Heath.

Dewey, J. (1916). *Democracy and education.* New York: Macmillan.

Dewey, J. (1938). *Experience and education.* New York: Macmillan.

Garland, J., Jones, H., & Kolodny, R. (1973). A model for stages of development in social work groups. In S. Bernstein (Ed.), *Explorations in group work* (pp. 17–71). Boston: Milford House.

Garland, J., & Kolodny, R. (1981). *The treatment of children through social group work: A developmental approach* [uncorrected advance proof]. Boston: Charles River.

Konopka, G. (1949). *Therapeutic group work with children.* Minneapolis: University of Minnesota Press.

Maier, H. (1987). *Developmental group care of children and youth: Concepts and practice.* Binghamton, NY: Haworth Press.

Malekoff, A. (1997). *Group work with adolescents: Principles and practice.* New York: Guilford Press.

Malekoff, A. (2004). *Group work with adolescents: Principles and practice* (2nd ed.). New York: Guilford Press.

Redl, F., & Wineman, D. (1951). *Children who hate.* New York: Macmillan.

Redl, F., & Wineman, D. (1952). *Controls from within: Techniques for the treatment of the aggressive child.* New York: Macmillan.

Rose, S. R. (1998). *Group work with children and adolescents: Prevention and intervention in school and community systems.* Thousand Oaks, CA: Sage.

Adults

Esta Glazer-Semmel

Group work with adults offers endless possibilities and opportunities for clients as well as social workers. The potential combinations of purpose, setting, duration, membership, leadership, process, and program suggest that goodness of fit may be found within the group work continuum for a wide variety of client needs.

All social work groups, regardless of type, share certain curative factors. When working with adults, perhaps the most important of these are universalization and mutual aid. Many cultures encourage their adults, especially males, to be self-reliant and to identify and manage an array of challenges on their own, without reaching out to, or relying on, others for significant guidance and support. This model of emotional competence may result in an inaccurate sense that most, if not all, problems are uniquely individual; that others neither share nor can be of help in confronting and resolving difficulties. Groups for adults offer their members safe environments in which to be relieved of the burden of "only I have this problem" and "no one else can possibly understand what I am going through." Members are able to identify within others the same or similar feelings and issues, opportunities and challenges that they, themselves, are experiencing. Then, they are encouraged to accept from, and offer to, their peers support, information and resources to help themselves while also helping each other. In adult groups, as appropriate, members may be encouraged to continue these relationships outside of the group meetings and beyond the life of the group (Gitterman & Shulman, 2005; Steinberg, 1977).

The typologies of group work that are appropriate for work with adults are described somewhat differently by various authors, but they usually fall into five general categories. Psychoeduational groups focus on knowledge acquisition; they also acknowledge and begin to address members' emotional responses that may be linked to the new information (Mason & Vazquez, 2007). For example, in a group for adults recently diagnosed with diabetes, members can learn about necessary diet and lifestyle changes, and discuss the feelings that are triggered by their new diagnosis and its requirements. Skill development groups target the expansion of a particular repertoire of members' behaviors, and often include behavior rehearsal and role-plays. A socialization group for schizophrenic young adults is an illustration of this type of group; it can assist its members in learning or relearning a repertoire of accepted, effective social skills. Support groups invite members to seek and provide mutual aid around particular, shared issues (Gitterman & Shulman, 2005). Brain tumor patients and their partners may choose to join a support group because they appreciate the understanding and encouragement that is often difficult to find in others who are not making their same journey. Counseling or psychotherapy groups use the group process as a microcosm of everyday experiences; the here and now in the group assists members to work through more complex issues, and gain insight into their etiology and resolution (Yalom & Leszcz, 2005). A group for incest survivors provides a safe environment in which members may struggle with feelings of betrayal and anger, and re-establish basic trust of themselves and others. Community development and organizational groups bring together members who share neighborhood or agency issues (Abramson & Bronstein, 2004; Ephross & Vassil, 2005). Working caregivers (child or elder) will likely have a greater chance of increasing licensed care resources in their community when they work together toward a common goal.

These group types are neither rigid nor mutually exclusive; a particular group may reflect elements of more than one type, and the prominence of one type over another may change over time. It is a needs assessment that drives the design and implementation of a new group, not a helpful but artificial typology. Answers to questions ranging from who owns the problem and how will they respond to offers of help, what kinds of knowledge and experiences will likely help them to make progress with or resolve their problems, and what kinds of resources (space, time, money, transportation, facilitators, etc.) are available to support the group experience are some of the initial queries that guide the development process. Answers to these questions will, in turn, lead to another set of important considerations: Will an open or a closed membership style be a better fit? What will the eligibility requirements be and how will the group be marketed to potential members? How will member selection be accomplished? Will there be a set fee, sliding fee scale or no fee? Will a time-limited or open-ended group format be more likely to meet the target population (and agency, if appropriate) needs? Will a solo or co-facilitation model better meet the needs of the members and complement the strengths of the facilitator(s)?

In addition to the dilemmas that are regularly faced by responsible social workers in any practice setting, groups for adults present the most challenging milieu for dealing with at least four important issues. First, non-voluntary and legally mandated clients run counter to the social work theme of client self-determination. However, adult groups in particular settings (e.g., inpatient mental health, substance abuse treatment) or with targeted themes (e.g., parenting skills) often include members who are directed to participate and have little choice but to comply. Their anger is predictable and deserved. The group leader must acknowledge the anger, rather than discount or challenge it, and then encourage them to choose to make good use of the opportunities that the group experience offers to them. Second, maintaining appropriate boundaries between the facilitator(s) and members can be very difficult in adult groups. Despite defined differences in leader and member roles, similarities in age, life experience, and issue may be pronounced. This, combined with the central group dynamic of mutual aid, demands that the facilitator be especially vigilant regarding transparency during the group and contact outside of the group. Another challenge that agency-based practitioners, in particular, are likely to experience is the pressure to provide cost-effective intervention. To non-group workers, group work may seem to be the efficient methodology of choice. However, the professional social worker is ethically bound first to consider what is the most appropriate and effective intervention model for a particular client at a specific moment in time, and then try to shape that model to meet the reality constraints of the setting—not vice versa. Finally, the leader must consistently evaluate the appropriateness for particular members and for the group, itself, to continue. In many settings, ongoing adult groups risk becoming institutionalized for other than clinical reasons. They may meet training, research, and budgetary needs. While these are certainly valid considerations, it is the social worker's responsibility to remain attentive and responsive to the core reason(s) for the group's existence.

Group work with adults, when done well, is a challenging, growth inducing and rewarding experience for all the members of the group, regardless of their assigned roles. Although everyone shares responsibility for the success of the group, it is the group leaders who must hold themselves accountable to the highest levels of established practice guidelines.

References

Abramson, J. S., & Bronstein, L. R. (2004). Group process dynamics and skills in interdisciplinary teamwork. In C. Garvin, M. Galinsky, & L. Gutiérrez (Eds.), *Handbook of social work with groups* (pp. 384–399). New York: Guilford Press.

Ephross, P. H., & Vassil, T. V. (2005). *Groups that work: Structure and process* (2nd ed.). New York: Columbia University Press.

Gitterman, A., & Shulman, L. (Eds.). (2005). *Mutual aid groups, vulnerable and resilient populations, and the life cycle* (3rd ed.). New York: Columbia University Press.

Mason, S., & Vazquez, D. (2007). Making positive changes: A psychoeducation group for parents with HIV/AIDS. *Social Work with Groups, 30*(2), 27–40.

Steinberg, D. S. (1997). *The mutual-aid approach to working with groups: Helping people to help each other.* Northvale, NJ: Jason Anderson.

Yalom, I., & Leszcz, M. (2005). *The theory and practice of group psychotherapy* (5th ed.). New York: Perseus Books.

Older Adults

Ronald W. Toseland

Group work for older adults is used very extensively in both community and institutional settings. Group work can be used for support, therapy, socialization, recreation and education, service, and advocacy. It can also be used to support family caregivers, many of whom are elderly spouses caring for their frail partners.

It is unclear when group work with older adults began in the United States. The first published reports of group work appeared around 1950, but some of these reports mention work in the 1930s. Theses reports focused on work in psychiatric hospitals, community centers, and nursing homes. For example, James Woods (1953) described his early work to develop group work programs for the elderly in "golden age centers," supported by the Benjamin Rose Institute and Case Western Reserve University in Cleveland, Ohio, in the 1930s. Similarly, Gertrude Wilson and Gladys Ryland (1949) and Jean Maxwell (1952) described their group work activities in community centers for older people. Maurice Linden (1953) was one of the early pioneers in developing group work for older people with dementia in psychiatric hospitals. Group work was also being conducted in homes for the aged by Herbert Shore (1952), Gisela Konopka (1954), and others.

A review of the literature in 1996 revealed that from 1970 to 1996 there were 451 articles, dissertations, and other publications about group work with older adults, a rate of only about nine per year (Aday & Aday, 1997). However, it is somewhat difficult to conduct a complete search of the literature about group work with older adults, because many support groups, socialization groups and cognitive-behavioral groups focus on the topic of the group rather than the fact that they contain mostly older adults. Still, group work with older adults continues unabated as seen in a recent book on the topic by Salmon and Graziano (2004).

Although there are many aspects about group work that are similar across age groups, work with older adults differs in some important ways from group work with younger adults. Group workers may need a bit more preparation for group work with older adults because, unlike their work with younger people, they have not experienced the developmental tasks faced by older adults. Therefore, group workers must be aware of their own stereotypes about older people that may come from their interaction with grandparents and other elders. Group workers should be especially vigilant to guard against negative stereotypes that may have to do with older people with disabilities, and those with terminal illnesses.

Group workers should familiarize themselves with the developmental tasks faced by older adults. Age-related changes, for example, can be very variable within and among groups of older adults. Although the chronic illnesses and disabilities increase with age, most older people compensate for these loses without appreciable affect on their functioning. Gradually, however, reaction time decreases and the acuity of senses decline. Therefore, group workers have to assess group members carefully, taking into consideration whether they need to slow down the pace of groups, or make physical or other changes to accommodate to disabilities.

Because of variable rates of aging, chronic disabilities vary greatly among older people of the same age. Also, varied life experiences mean that chronological age tends to be less important than with group work with younger adults. Still, chronological age is important because it affects the shared life experiences of older adults. These shared life experiences or cohort effects can be used in activity programming as group workers attempt to make groups meaningful for older adults of different ages.

Although personality traits can change with age, there is a great deal of continuity in the personality traits of most older people as they age (Mroczek, Spiro, & Griffin, 2006). Group workers can use this continuity by building on the positive aspects of older people's personality traits using a strengths-based empowerment approach rather than trying to change traits that have developed over a lifetime (Saleebey, 2006). Despite a great deal of continuity, developmental changes take place as people age. Environmental mastery and autonomy become increasingly important as older people attempt to compensate for physical losses. Group work can help older adults meet the challenges of losses by discussing and sharing ways to maintain mastery and autonomy. This may include the group worker helping older adults to connect to family and community supports to maintain their independence. Older people also tend to use more emotion-focused rather than problem-focused coping styles than younger people. Therefore, they are less likely to be aggressive problem solvers and more likely to seek social support, positive reappraisal of past events, and distancing to help them cope with painful experiences (Toseland & Rizzo, 2004). There is also more interiority, especially among the very old. Thus, there is more concern about physical functions, and more concern about accepting and making sense of life as they have lived it. There also tends to be more blending of the past and the present. Therefore, life review, journaling, and reminiscence can help older people put there lives in perspective. Group discussion and reflection can help older people to place their lives in a positive context and to face aging developmental tasks.

There are also some themes that come up more prominently in groups of older people than in groups of older adults. These themes include: (1) continuity with the past; (2) understanding the modern world; (3) independence; (4) physical and cognitive impairments; (5) loss of family and friends; (6) spouses and other family of origin issues; (7) pride and/or worry about children and grandchildren; (8) resources; (9) environmental vulnerability and adjustment; (10) religious conviction and ethnic pride, and (11) leisure pursuits (Toseland, 1995). Group workers should be aware of these themes because they can affect the content of group meetings and what older people want to get out of participating in groups.

Because there is much variability in the population of older adults, one has to be very cautious when generalizing about differences in leading groups of older adults as compared to younger groups. In fact, until older adults reach advanced old age there may be very few differences in leading groups of older persons than middle-aged persons. As physical and cognitive disabilities increase, group workers may need to slow the pace of meetings. Greater emphasis may be placed on wisdom and experiences accrued over time, rather than learning new information or coping skills. When new information is presented, it may be helpful to slow the pace of presentation, and to use visual, sensory and other cues to stimulate older adults and to help them absorb the material using their preferred sense. It is also important to help older adults to reaffirm and revitalize existing coping skills to address current life situations. Family members can also be an important source of support and encouragement as older adults address current developmental issues and challenges.

Finally, special strategies may be needed to help maintain communication and interaction with cognitively impaired older adults. Group workers should be cautious about mixing older people with cognitive impairments with older people without cognitive impairments, not only because older people with cognitive impairments may have special needs in groups but also because older people without cognitive impairments often find it difficult and even threatening of their own sense of self to be in groups of older people with significant cognitive impairments.

References

Aday, R., & Aday, K. (1997). *Group work with the elderly: An annotated bibliography*. Westport, CT: Greenwood Press.

Konopka, G. (1954). *Group work in the institution*. New York: Association Press.

Linden, M. (1953). Group psychotherapy with institutionalized senile women: Study in gerontologic human relations. *International Journal of Group Psychotherapy, 3*, 150–170.

Maxwell, J. (1952). *Centers for older people: A project report*. New York: National Council on the Aging.

Mroczek, D., Spiro, A., & Griffin, P. (2006). Personality and aging. In J. E. Birren, & K. W. Schaie (Eds.), *Handbook of the psychology of aging* (6th ed., pp. 363–378). Burlington, MA: Elsevier Academic Press.

Saleebey, D. (Ed.). (2006). *The strengths perspective in social work practice* (4th ed.). Boston: Pearson Education.

Salmon, R., & Graziano, R. (Eds.). (2004). *Group work and aging: Issues in practice, research and education*. Binghamton, NY: Haworth Press.

Shore, H. (1952). Group work program development in homes for the aged. *Social Service Review, 26*(2), 181–194.

Toseland, R. (1995). *Group work with the elderly and family caregivers*. New York: Springer.

Toseland, R., & Rizzo, V. (2004). What's different about working with older people in groups? *Journal of Gerontological Social Work, 44*(1/2), 5–23.

Wilson G., & Ryland, G. (1949). The Friendship Club. In G. Wilson, & G. Ryland, *Social group work practice: The creative use of the social process* (pp. 514–529). Boston: Houghton Mifflin.

Woods, J. (1953). *Helping older people enjoy life*. New York: Harper.

Transgenerational Relationships

Scott P. Anstadt

Transgenerational groups connote the process of bridging beyond, and moving across, what is often perceived as barriers in relationships between generations. More specifically, this community-based group concept is designed to engage and mobilize the considerable and often untapped resources of the older adult population in effective and sharing interaction with a targeted younger population. The younger population may consist of cohorts of various age ranges, i.e., toddlers, children, adolescents, or younger adults. The focus of activities and interactions is strength-based leading to both recognition of what each generation can offer to a group activity and what each may learn in the process (Roodin,

2005; Slaght & Stampley, 2006). Transformation away from a negative thought framework is commandeered through the development of mutual appreciation of commonality and generativity at all ages (Hermoso, Rosen, Overly, & Tompkins, 2006). Members become both mentors and learners alike in a holographic context whereby members solidify self-concept through reciprocal positive regard (Wrenn, Merdinger, Parry, & Miller, 1991).

These groups are primarily open-ended and based in a community setting such as daycare settings, schools, senior centers, houses of worship, and recreational centers. The structure and theoretical orientation of the group may vary according to overall purpose and group goals. Most transgenerational groups are task or activity oriented with an atmosphere of synergistic interaction (Cusicanqui & Salmon, 2004). Studies have found the temperament of the members often dictates the formal and informal member roles, which are consciously included in tackling group projects; thus microcosmic development of a sense of community can be generalized to applications in everyday life. The facilitator often encourages the group to divide into subgroups to carry out their portion of the activity and then later come back together as a total group to share progress, personal satisfaction, mutual regard, and to hear positive feedback from the group as a whole.

Built into this multidimensional affirming group process is a procedure of self and group evaluation. Each generation looks at interpersonal strengths and capacities in a contrapuntal and harmonious discovery of ways to relate across a generation gap from which they may have previously felt cast adrift and segregated (Ghose, Williams, & Swindle, 2005). Self-efficacy around having purpose and a place in humanity expands members perceptual, cognitive, spiritual, and social boundaries and offsets perceptions of aloneness, obsolescence, and self-isolation. The stage for this process often includes a short educational component with printed material readily accessible to all the members. Examples of activities include: a wellness education focus, caregiver supports, sharing vocational expertise and skills, life story reminiscence, parenting skill building (such as foster grandparents), tutoring school work, crafts, and volunteerism. Using the medium of narrative self-expression or "storytelling" in its many natural forms, members come to appreciate and understand generational idiosyncrasies of expression around group tasks and reminiscent sharing, thus encouraging members to stretch themselves into a deeper appreciation of generational cultural diversity (Wenzel, Pinquart, & Rensen, 2000). A spiritual appreciation for all persons and accompanying lightness of mood in the group is often the product of this process. All of the above speak to social work values and principles. Therefore these groups serve well in social work field education (Wilson & Simson, 1991).

Facilitators take on an eclectic team-building role, engage all members, assess both group and individual needs, and encourage rapport and social skill building. Staffs are trained to be culturally friendly and non-discriminatory, as well as knowledgeable and competent in understanding the learning and communication styles of the elderly as well as younger generations (Vandsberger & Wakefield, 2005). Transportation and payment for these groups are potential barriers but can be overcome with creative efforts such as pooling resources of those members who can drive, public transportation, and/or outreach workers, and tapping into state and federal money often available in the form of grants or entitlement assistance programs through the Older Americans Act, as well as other sources.

The benefits of this group process are several folds. Mutual assistance in both expressive and task-oriented skill building can kindle faith, appreciation, and conviction in a common foundation for all humanity. Cultural traditions and legacy can be passed on and better incorporated into emerging modern behavioral trends (Hatchett, Holmes, & Ryan, 2002). Practical skills learned through experience can be shared and taught so current challenges may be tempered by wisdom and experience of the elders and by current attunement with advancing technology on the part of the younger generation (Fredriksen-Goldsen, Bonifas, & Hooyman, 2006). The patience and maturity of the elders is suited well for infant and toddler daycare as well as being a good listening ear for older children and adolescents. Younger adults may look to the elder as a mentor role model. The kinship or parent role may help extend the feelings of security, comfort, and accountability that come with being present for others who may use their guidance (Ingersoll-Dayton & Amdt, 1990). Each generation may find emotional and spiritual anchorage through a feeling of extended family (Cooper & Lesser, 2005). Positive interactive and trustworthy companionship reflects back in a cyclical mirror effect, leading to self-evaluative ratings describing increased self-efficacy, sense of well-being, and self-esteem.

On a macro community level, the benefits mentioned above help reduce the national trends of resorting to tertiary care for the elderly and discriminatory ageism with its effects of segregating the elderly and their treasures from other generations and subjecting them to a role of primary disability. A strong and consistent social support system, which comes to the elder consumer, is a protective factor and reduces the risk of inpatient medical and mental health hospital utilizations, chronic physical illnesses such as cardiovascular diseases, and the need for nursing home placements. Increasing an elder's social support network using an ecological approach encourages them to venture out of their home more often, to seek additional services such as pharmacological and/or psychosocial interventions, or to enjoy the companionship of others. In this regard, these community-based groups have primary and secondary prevention potential.

References

Cooper, M., & Lesser, J. (2005). *Clinical social work practice: An integrated approach* (2nd ed.). New York: Pearson Education.

Cusicanqui, M., & Salmon, R. (2004). Seniors, small fry, and song: A group work libretto of an international singing group. In R. Salmon, & R. Graziano (Eds.), *Group work and aging: Issues in practice, research, and education* (pp. 189–210). Binghamton, NY: Haworth Press. Co-published simultaneously in *Journal of Gerontological Social Work, 44*, 189–210.

Fredriksen-Goldsen, K. I., Bonifas, R. P., & Hooyman, N. R. (2006). Multigenerational practice: An innovative infusion approach. *Journal of Social Work Education, 42*, 25–36.

Ghose, S. S., Williams, L. S., & Swindle, R. W. (2005). Depression and other mental health diagnoses after stroke increase inpatient and outpatient medical utilization three years poststroke. *Medical Care, 43*, 1259–1264.

Hatchett, B. F., Holmes, K., & Ryan, E. (2002). Attitudes of a predominantly Hispanic college sample towards older adults. *Journal of Gerontological Social Work, 37*(2), 45–59.

Hermoso, J., Rosen, A. L., Overly, L., & Tompkins, C. J. (2006). Increasing aging and advocacy competency: The intergenerational advocacy pilot project. *Journal of Gerontological Social Work, 48*, 179–192.

Ingersoll-Dayton, B., & Amdt, B. (1990). Uses of the genogram with the elderly and their families. *Journal of Gerontological Social Work, 15*(1/2), 105–136.

Roodin, P. (2005). Intergenerational perspectives in social work, social science, and the helping professions. *Journal of Intergenerational Relationships, 3*(1/2), 139–148.

Slaght, E., & Stampley, C. (2006). Promoting intergenerational practice. *Journal of Intergenerational Relationships, 4*(2), 73–86.

Vandsberger, E., & Wakefield, M. (2005). Service learning with rural older adults: Effects on students' career perspectives in gerontology. *Journal of Intergenerational Relationships, 3*(4), 83–97.

Wenzel, M., Pinquart, S., & Rensen, S. (2000). Changes in attitudes among children and elderly adults in intergenerational group work. *Educational Gerontology, 26*, 523–540.

Wilson, L. B., & Simson, S. (1991). The role of social work in intergenerational programming. *Journal of Gerontological Social Work, 16*(1/2), 87–95.

Wrenn, R. M., Merdinger, J., Parry, J. K., & Miller, D. (1991). The elderly and the young: A cooperative endeavor. *Journal of Gerontological Social Work, 17*(1/2), 93–103.

End-of-Life Care

Daniel Liechty

Group work is an effective method of helping in end-of-life care—and is particularly congruent with basic social work philosophy and education—and social workers have taken active, pioneering roles employing group work in the care of dying people and their families (Goelitz, 2004). As the issues most commonly experienced in end-of-life care and bereavement reflect normative life processes, both experience and research demonstrate that key therapeutic needs particular to this part of life are best addressed in a group setting (Steiner, 2005). The most important of these needs are now discussed.

The American ethos expects especially men, but also women, to "suffer in silence." Many find it difficult to overcome this cultural message that they should socially withdraw in times of vulnerability. Group work provides a *socially supportive* alternative to this withdrawal.

People in tragic circumstances report the benefits of recognizing that others face equally difficult situations, and yet life goes on. This helps people to cope despite current tragedies. This *normalization* of illness or other tragic circumstances is one of the most important recurring results in therapeutic group work.

Terminal illness, loss and death directly contradict the optimistic cultural values of eternal youth, vitality, beauty, health and success. Thus, people who are terminally ill or recently bereaved are vulnerable to social *stigmatization*, which may be maintained through their own internalized sense of stigma and shame. Therapeutic group work undermines this internal sense of stigma by providing an environment in which others share in similar circumstances. Behaviors of internalized stigma (e.g., a sense that there is a major part of one's life that ought not to be mentioned in the company of others) begin to dissolve.

The most enduring aspect of the family unit across history and cultures is that it is in the family that human beings get their primary emotional needs met. The group often functions as a *supportive substitute* or extensional family for those whose own families are separated by distance or death.

People in end-of-life care need emotional, psychological and spiritual support, but also express a strong desire to be supportive for others. Many professionals have noticed the therapeutic value of a person in need helping others. Helping others takes attention off of one's own problems, puts one's creativity to work and creates an empathic connection to others. Group participation naturally fosters this *mutuality of giving and receiving support*.

Groups contain a wider and deeper pool of experience and knowledge about available community resources than that of individuals. The *pooled knowledge and experience* contained within the group is also a valuable asset to the professional group leader, as it relieves the leader of the pressure to assume all the responsibility for maintaining completely up-to-date and exhaustive knowledge about resources in the local community (Gwyther et al., 2005).

Shared experience creates *shared perspectives*. Although professional education and practice experience may narrow the gap in perspective between social workers and their clients, group work brings clients with shared experiences together directly.

Especially for end-of-life groups centered on particular illnesses or diagnoses, there is always a valuable *psychoeducational* component in the group work. Learning about the illness itself, its nature, normal course of progress, psychological, mental and social consequences, and so on, is an important element in successful coping. This component is greatly enhanced in a group setting, as group members bring their own experiences, and inquiries, based on those experiences, to the group interaction.

There is growing recognition in the helping professions that humans are *spiritual* beings as well as social beings. Our sense of spirituality will also have a strongly communal quality. Many people report that there is a "group spirit," a sense of spiritual unity and blending available in a group setting that goes beyond the psychosocial element (Levin, 2001). This experience of spiritual unity and blending can be very beneficial across the psychological, social, spiritual and even physical spectrum, an experience most obviously available within a group work structure.

As terminal illness progresses, an increasing amount of the care takes place in the home (Waldrop, 2006). Patients and caregivers frequently comment on how "small" their world becomes. Participation in a group is one avenue by which a person's world is kept from shrinking faster than it otherwise might. It offers a powerful motivating force for continuing to "*get out of the house*" long after other places to go have lost their appeal. Likewise, for those who have spent weeks and months as primary caregivers, participation in a bereavement group often functions as the doorway back into a normal social life, with people who have some understanding of what they have been through as caregivers for a terminally ill spouse, family member or friend.

Effective group work in end-of-life care is most often attached to a medical setting, such as a hospital home care/hospice department, but is also found in nonmedical settings, such as general counseling facilities and in the facilities of organizations devoted to the research and education focused on specific diseases. Although the differences are mostly minor, it is worth noting that in medical settings, the group work is generally considered "auxiliary" to the medical handling of case, so that focus may be expected, for example, on using the group work to reinforce medical compliance, and perhaps also to be contoured by the guidelines of third-party payers; whereas in non-medical settings, the group work is more likely to be considered a service in its own right. Emerging technologies also are creating new settings for group work, such as phone-tree and online settings, which are in experimental stages of development and evaluation.

Group work is generally organized around four levels of functioning. The first level, task facilitation, organizes group activities around the accomplishment of particular tasks. The second level, psychoeducation, focuses on the presentation and discussion of information. The third level, counseling, begins to focus on feelings and emotions, and is aimed at increased psychological and social functioning through social support and increased awareness and personal insight. The fourth level, group psychotherapy, has goals similar to counseling (increased psychological and social functioning) but is more likely to include depth-exploration of emotional and psychological issues, and is more likely to utilize psychiatric diagnosis and categories of psychopathology in its course.

Professional ethical and legal issues attached to group work include specifically obtaining informed consent from group members for participation, along with clear prior communication on the expectations and limitations of confidentially within the group (Csikai, 2004). As in all areas of professional practice, the National Association of Social Workers and other codes of professional ethics expect avoidance of dual relationships, and achievement and maintenance of practice competency. A major issue for those working in end-of-life care in relation to practice competency is being very clear in one's own mind about competency limits. Specifically, one needs to be very careful to not dispense medical advice, but to refer all medical questions to the appropriate medical professionals.

References

Csikai, E. (2004). Social workers' participation in the resolution of ethical dilemmas in hospice care. *Health and Social Work, 29*(1), 67–76.

Goelitz, A. (2004). Using the end of groups as an intervention in end-of-life care. *Journal of Gerontological Social Work, 44,* 211–221.

Gwyther, L., Altilio, T., Blacker, S., Christ, G., Csikai, E. L., Hooyman, N., et al. (2005). Social work competencies in palliative and end-of-life care. *Journal of Social Work in End-of-Life and Palliative Care, 1*(1), 89–122.

Levin, J. S. (2001). *God, faith and health: Exploring the spirituality–healing connection.* New York. John Wiley.

Steiner, C. S. (2005). Grief support groups are used by few—are need's being met? *Journal of Social Work in End-of-Life and Palliative Care, 2*(1), 29–53.

Waldrop, D. P. (2006). Caregiving systems at the end of life. *Families in Society, 87*(3), 427–437.

Group Work and Community Context

Coalitions

Donna McIntosh and Margo Hirsch

Social workers, such as our own Jane Addams, appreciate both that one person can make a difference and also that there is power in numbers. Working with others may be for mutual aid, be focused on a single agenda, and can be time limited. Groups can be mobilized for passage of a key bill, serve as vehicles for systems change in a community, or elevate an issue to a social problem. Collaboratives, networks, and coalitions are all terms we utilize for different forms of these social action groups.

While some groups exist only until an issue is resolved, others evolve into well-established social action organizations. One familiar organizational model is the pyramid structure with members at the local, state, and national levels who are linked by name and mission. The National Association of Social Workers (NASW) is one such highly recognized social action group based on this model.

Another pyramid membership organization is the Empire State Coalition of Youth and Family Services (ESC), founded in 1974 as a loosely formed network of youth workers. It has evolved over time. Now, it is a well-established non-profit organization with 75 organizational and individual members who annually serve more than 15,000 runaway and homeless youth throughout New York State (Empire State Coalition, 2007). The ESC is membership linked nationally to The National Network for Youth (National Network for Youth, 2007). The evolution of this organization is discussed here, to illustrate the process.

What makes coalition membership networks, such as NASW and the ESC, sustainable? Gamson (1975) found that social action groups or movements found to be most successful in achieving goals were single issue with a strong organization structure. More recently, and drawing from Gamson's research, Mizrahi and Rosenthal (2001) present a conceptual framework for successful coalition building.

The first component of Mizrahi and Rosenthal's framework (2001) is internal and external conditions from inception to continuation of a coalition. ESC's membership has a historical commitment to the youth empowerment model of runaway and homeless youth services, which is manifested in the Coalition's mission statement and activities, and sustained the group during those periods when it existed solely on the efforts of its volunteers. A core group of the membership are "old timers," having been part of the service system and Coalition members almost from the beginning. From the onset, the early members of the Coalition were successful in writing the later enacted state runaway and homeless youth act. Over time, the Coalition has been able to draw membership from the new generation of youth workers and managers. ESC's staff and membership enjoy a credible reputation with funding, legislative, and regulatory officials. Finally, an important aspect of the Coalition is that while it is formed as a traditional organization with a board of directors, executive director, and staff, there is a "friendship" culture that is carried over from the early days. Friendship was a political instrument vital to the grassroots success of the settlement movement as workers joined forces with those in need (Schwartz, 2005). Organizations have not always found "friendships" among workers to be productive. But within coalition networks, even today, the friendship culture may well be a necessary component of sustainability.

The second component for successful coalition building is commitment to the common good (Mizrahi & Rosenthal, 2001). For ESC staff and members, commitment to the common good is manifested through advocacy and in the development of new program and service models adopted statewide and nationally. Such efforts recognize the Coalition's authority and expertise in training, and technical assistance.

The third element of successful coalition building according to Mizrahi and Rosenthal (2001) is contributions including resources, power, and ideology. ESC has a strong ideological commitment to the youth empowerment model that has been passed from generation to generation of youth workers. The Coalition has demonstrated diversity of resources with expertise in training, technical assistance, Web and technology development, and outreach to other coalitions and advocacy groups. The strong links forged with other advocacy groups increases the likelihood of success through greater power in numbers to achieve transformation, social change, and conflict resolution (Dessel, Rogge, & Garlington, 2006). Securing resources for staffing and operational expense for coalitions is challenging, given that opportunities are restricted by refraining from competition with member organizations, funders who prefer direct service or capital campaigns, and lobbying and advocacy legal limitations (key functions of coalitions). Power is also achieved through longevity and reputation of the staff and member leadership. However, at times of resource scarcity, coalescing the membership is challenged by limited travel monies and funding threats to membership organizations.

The final component of the conceptual framework is competence, generally focused on the leadership of a coalition (Mizrahi & Rosenthal, 2001). A major strength of ESC's professional development has been the respected longevity of leadership by the executive director. The executive director and core membership are well known and respected by county, state, and national officials. A measure of a coalition's leadership success is the invitations received from officials to participate in task forces and other forums for input and guidance.

Mizrahi and Rosenthal (2001) found achieving goals and gaining recognition from the social change target most importantly defined success. Another way to define this achievement of success is gaining legitimacy (Gamson, 1975). For coalitions whose origins began as time-limited but who are now full-fledged social movement organizations, with a network of membership at all levels of society with long records of achieving social change, this is legitimacy gained. ESC appears to have all of these elements developed within its organizational structure. As with other membership groups, the challenges of ensuring inclusion of a statewide membership at the table for coalition work, coupled with funding and lobbying restrictions, has challenged the Coalition's strength and sustainability. As with all coalitions and other social action groups that can continue to adapt to a changing landscape, a coalition's strength lies in a strong identity and mission back by the mobility, talents, and commitment of its membership and staff.

References

Dessel, A., Rogge, M., & Garlington, S. (2006). Using intergroup dialogue to promote social justice and change. *Social Work, 51*(4), 303–315.

Empire State Coalition of Youth and Family Services. Retrieved November 5, 2007 from http://www.empirestatecoalition.org

Gamson, W. (1975). *The strategy of social protest*. Homewood, IL: Dorsey Press.

Mizrahi, T., & Rosenthal, B. (2001). Complexities of coalition building: Leaders' success, strategies, struggles, and solutions. *Social Work, 46*(1), 63–78.

National Network for Youth. Retrieved November 5, 2007 from http://www.nn4youth.org/

Schwartz, W. (2005). The group work tradition and social work practice. *Social Work with Groups, 28*(3/4), 69–89.

Community Change

Mark Chupp

The early history of group work included community change as an integral component: "From its beginnings, group work practice and theory has been rooted in social reform, social responsibility, democratic ideals, and social action as well as social relatedness and human attachment" (Lee, 1991, p. 3, quoted in Finn, Jacobson, & Campana, 2004). As social work moved toward professionalization, however, group work largely shifted to an emphasis on a therapeutic, person-changing focus, while the more political strategies of knowledge development, community building, and social change receded to what is commonly referred to today as task group work (Finn, Jacobson, & Campana, 2004).

Historically, community group work surged in response to the myriad of social problems associated with industrialization. Saul Alinsky in the 1940s honed the use of organized groups as a vehicle for community change, leaving a legacy of community organizing that continues to the present (Rubin & Rubin, 2008). Today, neighborhoods and communities continue to organize themselves through task groups, which serve as the primary vehicle for community change. Block clubs, tenants, rights groups, issue committees, advocacy groups, and task forces all bring individuals together around a shared interest or goal. Often those who might have seen their situations as private troubles are brought together to identify relevant broader structural or public problems that can be addressed collectively. These task groups can function independently or with the support or sponsorship of a community-based organization, other nongovernmental organizations or public entity. In addition, community-based organizations create formal committees and boards that serve as task groups to define and implement organizational goals that further community change.

Community task groups may follow a specific approach to change or a blended approach. Rothman (1996) developed a well-known framework with three modes of community intervention: locality development, social planning/policy, and social action. The social action mode, commonly thought of as community organizing, relies extensively on task groups to affect change. Locality development promotes physical, economic, and social improvements through projects and programs that might or might not involve a task group of residents and other stakeholders to guide or advise the process. Social planning seeks to improve services, which might not involve an organized task group as professional agents drive the process, asking for input and feedback from unorganized residents. Rothman further articulated hybrid approaches that interweave elements from all three modes, any of which could employ task groups to some degree.

Many forms of social action with groups have been characterized as radical approaches in that they recognize the humanity and equality of all people (Gil, 1998) and as a result, initiate a structural analysis as a foundation for action that will lead to the necessary structural changes (Reisch, 2005). Feminist organizing (Gutiérrez & Lewis, 1998) and approaches using empowerment theory (Reisch, Wenocur, & Sherman, 1981) hold consciousness-raising among groups as an essential part of the process to bring about structural change. A number of these community change strategies have international roots, including action research (also know as community-based participatory research), popular education, and popular theater. Action research brings together external agents, often professional staff, to work in partnership with community members who together "combine their perspectives, resources, skills, and ideas to create solutions to community problems" (Schulz, Israel, & Lantz, 2004, p. 311). Popular education mobilizes groups for collective action through a consciousness-raising process of dialogue and reflection about the relationships of current conditions to historic, political, and economic contexts (Freire, 1970). Popular theater builds on the popular education foundation and emerged from Augusto Boal (1985) and his forum theater and theater of the oppressed. This methodology engages the group in analyzing a phenomenon and developing collective action, as the audience moves beyond interpreting a script to improvise acting out alternative scenarios, as spectators become actors or "spect-actors."

Regardless of approach, people come together to form a task group around a shared purpose, such as a specific issue, structural or institutional change, a shared goal, mutual need, or to improve relationships. The intended purpose might lend itself to one approach over another and to specific methods. An issue committee, for example, will typically utilize a community organizing or advocacy approach. Radical approaches all involve an educational or consciousness-raising step to critically analyze a situation according to a particular theoretical orientation. Internally, a task group might also include mutual aid or support to its members along with the primary community change goal.

Regardless of the approach, the structure of community task groups falls along several continua. The group can be formal or informal and have a set duration or be ongoing. Groups can have a fixed membership, open enrollment, or no membership status at all. Some task groups, such as a youth club, might be staff driven while others are entirely self-directed by its members.

Task groups for community change have a number of primary functions: exchanging information, sharing feelings, helping members get involved, developing facts and information relevant to the focus of the group, making effective decisions, solving problems, and monitoring and evaluating decisions or programs (Toseland & Rivas, 1995).

The role of the community social worker in task groups centers on capacity building, group functioning and productivity. Rather than a leadership role, the community worker promotes leadership development in the group and fosters self-directed and managed groups. In general, the worker ideally seeks to reach a level where the group is able to function on its own. As a task group begins, the community practitioner assists the group in contracting to reach agreement on why the group exists, for how long, the expectations of members, the group structure, ground rules, and the roles of staff and leaders (Ephross & Vassil, 2005).

Johnson and Johnson (2003) identify key characteristics of effective groups: mutual commitment to clearly operational goals, two-way communication, mutual leadership, appropriate decision making procedures, shared power, the ability to constructively challenge each other, ability to effectively resolve problems, mechanisms for mutual accountability, and the ability to engage the skills and expertise of group members. While some situations might require more unilateral decision making by a leader, effective groups generally draw on democratic processes and decision making to insure full voice for all members. The community social worker operates from a value base (equality, participation, justice) to promote inclusion and participatory decision making. This work can include coaching leaders, moderating disputes among leaders or between a leader and the group, and raising awareness of these values with members. At times, the worker might shift to become an animator (in popular education) or agitator in the group—a catalyst to get members to think critically, spark consciousness, encourage risk taking, or disrupt an unhealthy dynamic within the group (Finn et al., 2004).

References

Boal, A. (1985). *The theater of the oppressed.* New York: Theater Communications Group.

Ephross, P. H., & Vassil, T. V. (2005). *Groups that work: Structure and process* (2nd ed.). New York: Columbia University Press.

Finn, J. L., Jacobson, M., & Campana, J. D. (2004). Participatory research, popular education, and popular theater: Contributions to group work. In C. D. Garvin, L. M. Gutiérrez, & M. J. Galinsky (Eds.), *Handbook of social work with groups* (pp. 326–343). New York: Guilford Press.

Freire, P. (1970). *Pedagogy of the oppressed* (M. B. Ramos, Trans.). New York: Seabury Press.

Gil, D. (1998). *Confronting injustice and oppression: Concepts and strategies for social workers.* New York: Columbia University Press.

Gutiérrez, L., & Lewis, E. (1998). A feminist perspective on organizing with women of color. In F. Rivera, & J. Erlich (Eds.), *Community organizing in a diverse society* (3rd ed., pp. 97–116). Needham Heights, MA: Allyn & Bacon.

Johnson, D. W., & Johnson, F. P (2003). *Joining together: Group theory and group skills* (7th ed.). Englewood Cliffs, NJ: Prentice-Hall.

Lee, J. A. B. (1991). Foreword. In M. Weil, K. Chan, & D. Southerland (Eds.), *Theory and practice in social group work: Creative connections* (pp. 1–3). Binghamton, NY: Haworth Press.

Reisch, M. (2005). Radical community organizing. In M. Weil (Ed.), *The handbook of community practice* (pp. 287–304). Thousand Oaks, CA: Sage.

Reisch, M., Wenocur, S., & Sherman, W. (1981). Empowerment, conscientization and animation as core social work skills. *Social Development Issues, 5,* 108–120.

Rothman, J. (1996). The interweaving of community intervention approaches. *Journal of Community Practice, 3*(3), 69–99.

Rubin, H. J., & Rubin, I. S. (2007). *Community organizing and development* (4th ed.). Boston: Pearson.

Schultz, A. J., Israel, B. A., & Lantz, P. (2004). Assessing and strengthening characteristics of effective groups in community-based participatory research partnerships. In C. D. Garvin, L. M. Gutiérrez, & M. J. Galinsky (Eds.), *Handbook of social work with groups* (pp. 309–325). New York: Guilford Press.

Toseland, R., & Rivas, R. B. (1995). *An introduction to group work practice* (2nd ed.). Boston: Allyn & Bacon.

Rural Regions

Michael Kim Zapf

Most of the literature on social work with groups assumes an urban context where the worker and group participants do not know each other prior to the beginning of the group and do not encounter each other outside of scheduled group sessions. These assumptions do not hold in rural regions where group work presents specific challenges that have largely been neglected in the mainstream urban-based literature.

Throughout the developing literature on rural social work, issues of visibility and confidentiality have been highlighted as major challenges to conventional group work principles and practices (Ginter, 2005). Urban assumptions of non-contact outside of the group do not fit well with the community-embedded practice of rural social workers and their clients (Simon, 1999). These issues of visibility and confidentiality influence activities throughout the group work process in rural regions.

A social worker attempting to form a group in a rural area will likely have to alter conventional recruitment processes. In an urban center, the social worker will probably approach or invite potential members individually; a group member does not know the identity of the other members prior to the first session. Such an approach may not be fair in a rural area. A group member should not be surprised at the first session to discover Uncle Harry is also there, or their mechanic, or a parent of their child's best friend, or their employer. Each potential member of a rural group has the right to know who else will be there (and an opportunity to refuse participation), although this could take several rounds for the worker before composition is finalized.

Scheduling of groups in rural areas must take into account important seasonal and local social rhythms of the community (harvest periods, game patterns, fish migration cycles). Single-industry resource towns can pose special scheduling problems with the long hours and shift work required of residents. Regular celebrations or special events in rural regions (sports tournaments, harvest festivals, rodeos, etc.) can interfere with availability of group members, as can unexpected but significant communal events such as severe weather, natural disasters, or funerals.

Once the group is running, the existence of the group and the identity of participants will likely be known throughout the rural community. Members may well be visible traveling to, entering, and leaving the host facility. Community residents will recognize neighbors' trucks and cars in the parking lot during group time. Similar to the group members, the rural group worker also experiences the transparency of a fishbowl lifestyle where his or her actions outside of group will be visible to group members and the entire community. The social worker leading a rural group for convicted impaired drivers had better not retreat to the bar after group then drive home (everyone will be counting drinks). Group members and the larger community monitor the worker for integrity and behavior consistent with the purposes of the group.

A crucial consideration for any rural group will be how to handle contacts outside of the group. Group members and the worker can be expected to come into regular contact and interaction with each other in their various roles in the rural community. Protocols for such contact must be anticipated and discussed in the first session. Specific instances of community contact may be de-briefed in later sessions—a process which can take up a good bit of time.

Confidentiality concerns in rural groups extend beyond the immediate members of the group. Members sharing personal issues are likely to discuss partners, children, friends, co-workers, employers, etc., who may well be known to other group members. There is a responsibility to protect the rights of these third parties in group discussion. Conventional solutions such as changing names to disguise identity may not be adequate in rural settings where everyone knows whom you are talking about anyway.

Many agencies have a standard policy for social workers of not accepting gifts from clients because accepting a gift from a group member could open the door for dual relationships and potential misunderstandings. In a rural area, however, gifts (food, crafts, services) are often offered as a way of restoring balance. The worker may be a resident member of the rural community engaged with group members in relationships before the group starts and after it ends. Acceptance of a gift can represent a commitment to the larger goal of balance in the community, recognition that everyone has something valuable to offer. Of course, there are limits to be negotiated in the local context, but a blanket refusal of all gifts could distance the worker unnecessarily from the community.

Food can be an important component of any event in a rural community, and the group is no exception. An urban group might have a small budget for coffee and possibly treats, but any thought of a more elaborate meal provided by members could be considered inappropriate, counterproductive, and a waste of valuable time. In a rural setting, however, the social worker might do well to allocate some group time for food (and a schedule of responsibilities) because the offerings may arrive even if not solicited.

By the time food is shared and concerns around out-of-group contact have been addressed, there may be little time left in any given session of a rural treatment group for work on the declared purpose. One might wonder if treatment groups are even practical for rural social workers. The literature identifies group work as the least used modality of rural generalist practitioners (Gumpert & Saltman, 1998). Of those rural social workers who use groups, most are involved with existing community concern groups or natural groups rather than formed treatment groups. Rural practice is community-oriented and community-embedded, directed at community development or change. There is clear direction in the literature for rural social workers to work with groups already in existence rather than forming new groups (Collier, 2006; Templeman & Mitchell, 2004). Developing partnerships with existing groups (such as interagency committees, recreation groups, congregations, school or adult education classes, etc.) or connecting with the local "Hardly Worth Mentioning Groups" (Banks, 2004) allows the rural social worker to avoid many common concerns around formation and scheduling. Collaborative partnerships in rural regions also recognize existing community strengths and decrease the worker's status as expert or leader, a development more in keeping with rural notions of balance and mutuality.

The social worker who considers using group work in a rural area that includes a Native American population will likely encounter a strong local tradition of using circles (healing circles, sharing circles, learning circles) for both individual and community growth. Native American circles have their own protocols and philosophies which can be quite different from the assumptions of mainstream social work with groups. In a conventional group, the social worker attempts to create the necessary conditions of trust and sharing that allow a process of mutual aid to emerge in the middle phase of overall group development. Many Native American traditions, on the other hand, assume a positive flow of energy or spirit that gives direction to the circle from the outset (and before). Circle participants have only to connect with this pre-existing direction or flow rather than creating it anew each time through a worker's skills. Levels of sharing, intimacy, and commitment can be observed in the first minutes of a circle that might not be expected until later sessions of a conventional social work group. Rather than attempting to organize or run healing circles, the non-Native rural social worker would do well to participate and share in circles when invited, to learn of this approach and its power. The rural social worker must also realize that Native

American members recruited to a conventional group may have very different expectations of the process and potential outcomes.

References

Banks, K. (2004). "Hardly worth mentioning groups" and the informal community. *Rural Social Work, 9*(1), 34–41.

Collier, K. (2006). *Social work with rural peoples* (3rd ed.). Vancouver, Canada: New Star.

Ginter, C. (2005). Client confidentiality, anonymity, facilitator credibility, and contamination in rural family violence self-help groups. In K. Brownlee, & J. R. Graham (Eds.), *Violence in the family: Social work readings and research from northern and rural Canada* (pp. 90–104). Toronto: Canadian Scholars' Press.

Gumpert, J., & Saltman, J. E. (1998). Social group work practice in rural areas: The practitioners speak. *Social Work with Groups, 21*(3), 19–31.

Simon, R. I. (1999). Maintaining treatment boundaries in small communities and rural areas. *Psychiatric Services, 50*(1), 11.

Templeman, S. B., & Mitchell, L. (2004). Utilizing an asset-building framework to improve policies for rural communities. In T. L. Scales, & C. L. Streeter (Eds.), *Rural social work: Building and sustaining community assets* (pp. 196–205). Belmont, CA: Thomson Brooks/Cole.

Social Action

Jennie Fleming

Social action is an approach that predominately, but not exclusively, uses group-work. It is informed by and has some overlap with self-directed groupwork (Mullender & Ward, 1991), as it uses self-directed groupwork as an element; however, it is a distinct form of practice. Social action is a specific philosophy and theory for social change, that has its theoretical roots in the work of Paolo Freire (1970) and is also influenced by the disability movement (Oliver, 1992), black activists (Hooks, 1992), and the women's movement (Dominelli & McCleod, 1989; Evans, 1994). The social action approach was also strongly influenced by development theory, which is based on the premise that change can happen, but only if the groups concerned own it and are involved in creating the changes they want (Hope & Timmell, 1999).

The social action approach is made up of two essential and inseparable elements—the principles and the process. A key element of social action is the recognition of the power of groupwork—that people working collectively can be powerful. Another is that social action workers are not leaders but facilitators. The social action approach requires a change in the traditional role of the professional worker from that of the expert giving advice, leading and directing, to working in partnership: listening, posing questions, facilitating a process, supporting action and encouraging reflection. Their job is to enable groups to make decisions for themselves and take ownership of whatever outcome ensues.

Social action is thus not about professionals providing services or solutions but rather, about helping groups of people find their own solutions and become agents of change for themselves. Four main points distinguish social action from other mainstream community development or youth work approaches: (1) it recognizes that all people have the capacity to create social change and should be given that opportunity; (2) professionals work in partnership with group members; (3) the agenda is handed over to the community group, including youth groups; and (4) recognizes the need to explore with group members the origins of oppression, discrimination and disadvantage experienced by them, either individually or collectively. The approach stresses raising awareness of the causes and consequences of actions, fostering opportunities for new action, and learning about ways to change one's environment, and adds an emphasis on collective action to bring about social transformation.

Thus, social action emerged as a value-based group practice with a focus on social justice and rights. It concentrates on changing unequal power relations, between community groups and decision-makers and service providers within a framework of democratic accountability. Lombard (1991, p. 91) writes that social action is about working with less privileged groups in the community to make "greater demands on society at large for more resources and to demand treatment which is in agreement with justice". She goes on to write, "practitioners strive, therefore, to effect the redistribution of power, resources and decision making in the community" (Lombard, 1991, p. 92). Social action workers provide the framework for groups to consider their problems, issues and concerns. Participants provide the content, using their skills, knowledge and expertise. Group members create the knowledge and understanding, through active participation: describing, suggesting, analysing, deciding, experiencing and reflecting (Fleming & Ward, 1999). An example of social action in operation with a youth group is of young people identifying their relationship with local police as problematic and setting up a meeting with senior officers, which led to a renegotiation of the way in which their estate was policed.

Social action has been constantly developed reflectively, and in partnership between practitioners, service users and academics in the course of developing, carrying out and evaluating interventions, training, and action research (Harrison & Ward, 1999). However, at the heart of all social action is attention to group dynamics and groupwork processes, but self-consciously grounded in values and principles through which all aspects of practice should be filtered (Ward, 2000).

Social action has been used in many different settings in countries across the globe. It is truly an international practice that can be tried and adapted for many different settings. While the context may change, the values, principles and methods remain constant. These however, are not static or set in stone. They evolve, change and are built on every time a social action group meets. What is not negotiable, however, are the cornerstones of the approach.

Whilst using self-directed group work to inform the social action process, the social action approach has also advanced self-directed group work in a range of disciplines, for example training, research and education. Examples would include groupwork using the social action approach being used as the basis for a training methodology (Fleming, 2004), and as the basis for training for community workers and community activists in Peru. Social action has been used to inform transformational change in children's services in Russia and Ukraine (Fleming, 2000) and the development of more student led learning in the United States through a partnership with the National Writing Project (Berdan et al., 2006). Social action has also been used to develop community cohesion and enhance the understanding within communities as to what social capital means to them (Boeck & Fleming, 2002). One particular project explored if social capital can be built within communities; this involved working with a range of local community groups and service providers to help them understand the concept of social capital, its relevance to them and their communities and how they could see if their activities have any impact on social capital. Social action research has also developed as a distinct research methodology, an example of such work being the partnership between social action researchers and foster carers to undertake a research project about birth parent contact in foster carers' homes (Fleming, 2005; Fleming & Ward, 1999).

References

Berdan, K., Boulton, I., Eidman-Aadahl, E., Fleming, J., Gardner, L., Rogers, I. et al. (Eds.). (2006). *Writing for a change: Boosting literacy and learning through social action.* San Francisco: Jossey-Bass.

Boeck, T., & Fleming, J. (2002). *Social capital and the Nottingham social action research project.* Nottingham Social Action Research Project, Nottingham City Primary Care Trust, Nottingham, UK.

Dominelli, L., & McLeod, E. (1989). *Feminist social work.* London: Butterworth.

Evans, M. (Ed.). (1994). *The woman question.* London: Sage.

Fleming, J. (2000). Action research for the development of children's services in Ukraine. In H. Kemshall, & M. Littlechild (Eds.), *User involvement and participation in social care: Research informing practice* (pp. 65–81). London: Jessica Kingsley.

Fleming, J. (2004). The beginnings of a social action group. *Groupwork, 14*(2), 24–41.

Fleming, J. (2005). Foster carers undertake research into birth family contact—using the social action research approach. In L. Lowes, & I. Hulatt (Eds), *The involvement of service users in health and social care research* (Ch. 6). London: Routledge.

Fleming, J., & Ward, D. (1999). Research as empowerment: The social action approach. In W. Shera, & L. Wells (Eds.), *Empowerment practice: Developing richer conceptual foundations* (pp. 370–389). Toronto: Canadian Scholars' Press.

Freire, P. (1970). *Pedagogy of the oppressed.* New York: Seabury Press.

Harrison, M., & Ward, D. (1999). Values as context: Groupwork and social action. *Groupwork, 11*(3), 88–103.

hooks, b. (1992). *Ain't I a woman: Black women and feminism.* London: Pluto Press.

Hope, A., & Timmel, S. (1999). *Training for transformation* (Rev. ed., vols. 1–4). London: Intermediate.

Lombard, A. (1991). *Community work and community development.* Pretoria, South Africa: HAUM-Tertiary.

Mullender, A., & Ward, D. (1991). *Self-directed group work.* London: Whiting and Birch.

Oliver, M. (1990). *The politics of disablement.* Basingstoke, UK: Macmillan.

Ward, D. (2000). Totem not token: Groupwork as a vehicle for user participation. In H. Kemshall, & R. Littlechild (Eds.). *User involvement and participation in social care: Research informing practice* (pp. 45–64). London: Jessica Kingsley.

Social Capital

Paul Abels and Sonia Leib Abels

Social capital refers to the sum and substance of connections and networks a social unit has that can promote and empower its existence. It fosters an approach to practice that focuses on ways of developing and increasing the connections of persons, groups, communities, and institutions, in order to enhance their social, economic, and political resources. Helping individuals and groups develop, expand their social capital, and build connections to improve personal and civic welfare, is a natural outgrowth of social group work's historical development and an emphasis on mutual aid, in its standards (Association for the Advancement of Social Work with Groups, 1999, pp. 2–3) and in practice.

Supporters hold that the basics in building social capital lie in working to establish networks (Abels & Abels, 1981, p. 147), norms of interaction, reciprocity and trust, along with information (Northen, 1988, p. 67) that enable persons and institutions to connect more effectively in pursuit of shared objectives. The importance of these connections was brought into current focus by the publication of Robert Putnam's (2000) *Bowling Alone*, in which he signifies there is a disintegration of social connections in the United States. Evidence indicates that the depth of one's connections is related to life's opportunities, health, and survival, and has relevance for democratic decision making. Broader, stronger, and denser connections provide greater opportunities for positive outcomes, not only for individuals, but also for groups, institutions, society, and nations.

Social capital expands group work themes, of social support, integration, connections, economic well-being, civics, and mutual aid. It adds a bridging vision to mutual aid, which has generally focused on the *bonding* of members working toward goals in the group. That bridging vision extends the bonding connections externally. An example of extended connections was the bridging of a children's school adjustment group and a senior singing group (Cusicanqui & Slamon, 2004). International bridging is exemplified by the World Bank poverty programs, which view social capital as the institutions, relationships and norms that shape the quality and quantity of a society's social interactions: "Social capital is not just the sum of the institutions which underpin a society ... it is the glue that holds it together" (World Bank, 1999).

In the United States the social capital ideas emerged out of the progressive movement for political and civic reform the late 19th and early 20th centuries. This was reflected in part by the "Social Gospel," women's evolving civic initiatives (Spain, 2000), and the development of the settlement house and their "social goals" efforts (Papell & Rothman, 1962). The term "social capital" is credited to Lyda Juson Hanifan, an educational administrator who mobilized civic programs in rural school community centers, and identified it as "those tangible substances [that] count for most in the daily lives of people" (Hanifan, 1916, p. 130). Hanifan was concerned with the cultivation of good will, fellowship, sympathy, and social intercourse among those that make up a social unit. He embraced the idea that teaching social values was functional to emerging social institutions forming a democratic society.

Social capital's emphasis on the importance of extensive connections is reflected in the works of Jennings in education (1943) and Moreno's (1934) *Who Shall Survive* in psychology. Both stressed the significance of connections for growth and survival, often diagramming these connections. The sociograms were means of visualizing both persons' connections and isolation in the group. Such tools are frequently used to help members "see" their connections and build additional supportive connections. The worker also uses it as an assessment tool to help modify connection patterns. Workers also act to expand their own connections, and increase their pool of helping resources. Social capital practice encompasses persons and social units, expanding connections to and among institutions in ways that enhance the human condition, the institutions, and society. Workers as mediators may also help with problematic connections (Gitterman, 1991, p. 20).

Other studies also dealt with the importance of support networks and their importance for survival. Elliot Liebow's (1967) *Tally's Corner* noted that in the "street corner world," the construction of connections and the maintenance of personal relationships were of utmost importance to that culture. (Liebow in a personal conversation with the author expressed concern with the pernicious quality of criminal connections of some persons in his study.) Social capital became attractive to sociologists studying family and community, and the work of James Coleman (1988) increased interest on studying the subject.

The isolation of the aged is a major issue in social capital and social group work (Abels & Abels, 2004; McCallion & Toseland, 1995, p. 13). One study on residential aged care facilities suggested a strong relationship between the levels of social capital and the frequency and duration of visits by families and friends (Smeaton, Griffin, & Hampshire, 2003). During a Chicago heat wave, the lack of social capital led to the disproportionate death rate for aged persons with thin connections (Klinenberg, 2002). The lack of action by social welfare and other civic agencies aggravated the situation. Similar tragedies occurred during the heat wave in France in 2003, when 17,000 people died; the single largest group were aged with few connections if any (Tagliabue, 2003).

Ways of developing social capital vary from an infusing of World Bank funds to poor countries to *bettertogether*'s list of 150 items individuals and organizations can do in their communities (Bettertogether, 2000). Many programs call for skills and visions that social group workers can offer. These include their conceptualization, of and research on, mutual aid, their ability to make connections, to help persons develop trust and reciprocity, to generate the resources and connections with institutions that can support mutual goals, and their press toward community action and social reform. Such efforts will serve to expand persons' access to health services, economic well-being and a more civic society.

References

Abels, P., & Abels, S. (2004). *Extending social capital to the elderly: Connections that count.* Paper presented at the National Gerontological Conference, Council on Social Work Education, Anaheim, CA.

Abels, S., & Abels, P. (1981). Social group work's contextual purposes. *Social work with groups: Proceedings 1979 symposium* (pp. 146–170). Binghamton, NY: Haworth Press.

Association for the Advancement of Social Work with Groups. (1999). *Standards for social work practice with groups*. Akron, OH: Author.

Bettertogether. (2000). *150 ways to build social capital*. Retrieved June 20, 2006 from http://www.bettertogetherNH.org

Coleman, J. S. (1988). Social capital in the creation of human capital. *American Journal of Sociology, 94,* 95–120.

Cusicanqui, M., & Salmon, R. (2004). Seniors, small fry, and song: A group work libretto of an intergenerational singing group. In R. Salmon, & R. Graziano (Eds.), *Group work and aging: Issues in practice, research and education* (pp. 189–210). Binghamton, NY: Haworth Press.

Gitterman, A. (1991). *Handbook of social work practice with vulnerable populations*. New York: Columbia University Press.

Hanifan, L. J. (1916) The rural school community center. *Annals of the American Academy of Political Science, 67,* 130–138.

Jennings, H. H. (1943). *Leadership and isolation*. New York: Longmans Green.

Klinenberg, E. (2002). *Heat wave*. Chicago: University of Chicago Press.

Liebow, E. (1967). *Tally's corner*. Boston: Little, Brown.

McCallion, P., & Toseland, R. W. (1995). Supportive group interventions with caregivers of frail older adults. In M. Galinsky, & J. H. Schopler (Eds.), *Support groups: Current perspectives on theory and practice* (pp. 11–25). Binghamton, NY: Haworth Press.

Moreno, J. L. (1934). *Who shall survive? A new approach to the problem of human interrelations*. Washington, DC: Nervous and Mental Disease Publishing Co.

Northen, H. (1988). *Social work with groups*. New York: Columbia University Press.

Papell, C., & Rothman, B. (1962). Social group work models: Possession and heritage. *Journal of Education for Social Work, 2*(2), 66–77.

Putnam, R. (2000). *Bowling alone: The collapse and revival of American community*. New York: Simon and Schuster

Smeaton, T., Griffin, D., & Hampshire, A. (2003). Social capital in practice: Family and community connections—social capital in three residential aged care facilities. Retrieved June 16, 2008 from http://216239.51100/search?q+cache:qDUT...ocial+capital,+connections&hl=en&ie=UTF-8

Spain, D. (2000). *How women saved the city*. Minneapolis. University of Minnesota Press.

Tagliabue, J. (2003). Lack of air conditioning cited in France's death toll. *New York Times*, August 22, Section A, p. 3.

The World Bank. (1999). What is social capital? *Poverty Net*. Retrieved June 16, 2008 from http://www.worldbank.org/poverty/scaptal/whatsc.htm

Group Work and Organizational Context

Interdisciplinary Teams

Laura Bronstein and Julie S. Abramson

Interdisciplinary teams emerged in the 1940s and are currently employed in the majority of settings where social workers practice. Interdisciplinary teams call on the specialized knowledge of different groups of professionals as they work collaboratively with clients and families in meeting their goals. The term "team" was originally derived from Old English and first used to refer to "a group of animals harnessed together to draw some vehicle" (Dingwall, 1980, p.135). Various labels are used to describe teams of professionals, including, multidisciplinary, transdisciplinary, interprofessional, and interdisciplinary. Current descriptions of teams include clients and families as core team members along with the professionals serving them.

A model for interdisciplinary teamwork among social workers and other professionals describes the following as components of this kind of collaboration: interdependence, newly created professional activities, flexibility, collective ownership of goals, and reflection on process. This model includes the following as potential obstacles and their inverse, as supports for successful teamwork: structural characteristics (time and space for teamwork, administrative support, skilled team leadership, institutional value on diversity and equality); professional role (security in one's role, shared professional language and technologies, training for teamwork, dual affiliation with profession and team); personal characteristics (mutual respect, liking one's team mates, issues of color, culture and gender); and, prior history with teamwork (Bronstein, 2002, 2003).

Because the team is a group, group intervention principles can provide the foundation for addressing group process to promote effective teams. Social workers are in an excellent position to facilitate team process since their group work training provides much of the knowledge and skills necessary for competent teamwork. To draw on these skills successfully, social workers need to relinquish the false dichotomy between the skills they apply with clients and colleagues. Group-work-based intervention strategies and skills that team members and team leaders can draw on to facilitate team functioning include: (1) *monitoring and assessing team process*—the capacity to think simultaneously about treatment and team issues so as to see when the team process is supporting or impeding client-centered goals; (2) *contracting*—discussion at time of team formation of team goals, approaches to achieve these as well as identification of team leadership and roles and the impact of external forces (i.e., budget, policy, etc.); it is also important to re-contract with the team when a new staff member, client or family member joins the team; (3) *creating a climate of copenness*—*trust and group cohesion*—leadership strategies that facilitate a positive climate among team members including promotion of mutual aid processes, trust, and respect; (4) *dealing with conflict*—strategies that acknowledge the conflict and then explore the reasoning behind differing opinions; and (5) *developing positive, client-centered norms*—avoidance of blaming is critical at all stages of teamwork (Abramson & Bronstein, 2004).

The capacity to arrive at consensus in decision making is an underlying premise of teamwork; therefore, it is essential to understand the profound impact of the varied professional socialization processes through which each profession inducts its trainees to its professional world view (Specht, 1985). Social workers can prepare and guide clients/families to better understand different professional orientations and roles, while assisting them to communicate those aspects of their own culture and socialization that need to be taken into account in decision making. Additionally, social workers' ability to clearly articulate their own roles is critical (Abramson, 1993).

A number of areas can present ethical concerns for social workers in teams. Issues of confidentiality are embedded in the very nature of teamwork and can create difficulties when there are differing views of what is confidential. The ways that team members conduct themselves on the team can also raise ethical questions. Alliances among subgroups, hierarchical or status issues, unethical or incompetent behavior, and the integration of clients and families can all impact team decision making (Abramson & Bronstein, 2008).

It is important to recognize the challenges of fully including clients and families as team members, especially in light of their time-limited involvement, their perceived power-deficit, and "difference in perspective and training" from professionals. Even professionals have been found to feel "less than" when they see themselves as of lower status than collaborators or only part-time team members. A major factor affecting group processes is the degree of homogeneity amongst members. Whereas differences in racial composition of groups have been looked at, it has not been examined in interdisciplinary teams where racial difference between clients/families of color and white professionals is a common occurrence.

Emerging and critical trends in teamwork include greater inclusion of clients and families in varying ways, increasing research, and a more expansive definition of collaboration. Two major initiatives that include clients and families in teams are family group conferencing (FGC) and wrap-around services. FGC emerged from New Zealand, where it is now a legislated child welfare practice whose structure supports families at the center of the interdisciplinary team's work (Connolly, 2006; Pennell & Anderson, 2005). Its practice has been expanding internationally in child welfare, hospitals, and rehabilitation centers. Wrap-around services focus on coordination of all service providers involved in a client's care and these have also been evolving internationally (Kessler & Ackerson, 2004; Ogles et al., 2006). Both practices include interdisciplinary team members, families/clients at the center of care, and an emphasis on pre-planning to assure that all voices are heard in the meetings. Both FGC and wrap-around services involve one or more meetings with families, clients and the interdisciplinary team of professionals, with specific contracts and follow-up plans.

More research on the work of interdisciplinary teams needs to be done and explicitly tied to client outcomes. While there is much clinical wisdom and many case studies that guide this work, we need to increase efforts to develop evidence-based models to define and guide best practices. If this does not occur, this labor-intensive mechanism of service delivery may not have a future. Even teams without research capacities can use an existing team assessment tool that can be correlated with client outcomes as part of a formal team evaluation process (Abramson & Bronstein, in press).

Interdisciplinary teamwork is only one "type" of collaboration; it is not exercised in a void and is best achieved when interlocking with a number of other "types" of collaboration. These other forms of collaboration require many of the same skills necessary for interdisciplinary teamwork (Payne, 2000). Lawson, Bronstein, McCallion, and Ryan (2004) categorize these collaborative types as intra-organizational, inter-organizational or inter-agency, and community-based, among others; together they create an important synergy to support the work of interdisciplinary teams today and in the future (Abramson & Bronstein, 2008).

References

Abramson, J. S. (1993). Orienting social work employees in interdisciplinary settings: Shaping professional and organizational perspectives. *Social Work, 38*(2), 152–157.

Abramson, J. S., & Bronstein, L. R. (2004). Group process dynamics and skills in interdisciplinary teamwork. In C. Garvin, M. Galinsky, & L. Gutiérrez (Eds.), *Handbook of social work with groups* (pp. 384–399). New York: Guilford Press.

Abramson, J. S. & Bronstein, L. R. (2008). Teams. In T. Mizrahi, & L. Davis (Eds.), *The encyclopedia of social work* (20th ed., vol. 4, pp.199–20). New York: Oxford University Press.

Bronstein, L. R. (2002). Index of interdisciplinary collaboration. *Social Work Research, 26*(2), 113–126.

Bronstein, L. R. (2003). A model for interdisciplinary collaboration. *Social Work, 48*(3), 297–306.

Connolly, M. (2006). Fifteen years of Family Group Conferencing: Coordinators talk about their experiences in Aotearoa, New Zealand. *The British Journal of Social Work, 36*(4), 523–540.

Dingwall, R. (1980). Problems of teamwork in primary care. In S. Lonsdale, A. Webb, A., & T. L. Briggs (Eds.), *Teamwork in the personal and social services and health care* (pp. 111–137). London: Personal Social Services Council.

Kessler, M. L., & Ackerson, B. J. (2004). Wraparound services: An effective intervention for families impacted by severe mental illness. *Journal of Family Social Work, 8*(4), 29–45.

Lawson, H., Bronstein, L. R., McCallion, P., & Ryan, D. (2004). *Building coalitions and collaborations: A resource guide for the 21st century*. Albany, NY: New York State Office for Aging.

Ogles, B. M., Carlston, D., Hatfield, D., Melendez, G., Dowell, K., & Fields, S. A. (2006). The role of fidelity and feedback in the wraparound approach. *Journal of Child and Family Studies, 15*(1), 115–129.

Payne, M. (2000). *Teamwork in multiprofessional care*. Chicago: Lyceum Books.

Pennell, J., & Anderson, G. (Eds.). (2005). *Widening the circle: The practice and evaluation of family group conferencing with children, youths, and their families*. Washington, DC: NASW Press.

Specht, H. (1985). The interpersonal interactions of professionals. *Social Work, 30*(3), 225–230.

Involuntary Clients (Change Processes)

Michael Chovanec

Involuntary clients are present in a wide range of both voluntary and court-ordered groups, such as domestic abuse groups, adolescent school groups and groups within outreach programs in mental health. Yet group workers are provided few guidelines for engaging the involuntary client within the group.

Recent guidelines for involuntary clients have been applied to the developmental stages of group process (Rooney & Chovanec, 2004) and developed into training exercises for group work students (Chovanec, in press). The "stages of change" framework examines an individual's change process from engagement through behavioral change (Norcross, Beutler, & Clarkin, 1998; Prochaska, Norcross, & DiClemente, 1994). The framework suggests that one goes through a series of five stages with each stage linked to different interventions. Originally grounded in research on how chemical dependency clients stopped their drinking behaviors, the framework has been applied to a variety of other addictive behaviors, including smoking and weight loss. In *precontemplation*, group members do not identify a problem while others in their environment do. In *contemplation*, they begin to recognize they have a problem but are ambivalent about change. In *preparation*, they are beginning to make small efforts to change their behavior with these efforts becoming more consistent in the *action* stage. Finally in the *maintenance* stage, efforts are made to maintain the changed behavior.

The major goal of the facilitator within involuntary groups is to assist involuntary group members in transitioning to voluntary participants in the group process. This is done by supporting group members through the stages of change. Combining individual stages of change with stages of group development allows us to be more attentive to the individual change process within groups. The stages of change process runs sufficiently parallel to group development (see Figure 2).

Including stages of change allows us to identify group interventions that work best for individual group members depending upon their particular stage of group development. As illustrated in the diagram, in closed groups one can expect a smaller range of individual stages represented at each group stage of development, i.e. mostly pre-contemplators and contemplators in the beginning stage of group development. With open-ended groups there is a much wider range of individual stages represented with typically a cohort of group members moving through the group developmental stages (Schopler & Galinsky, 2005).

Pregroup-----Beginning---------------------------------Middle-------------------End

Precontemplation/Contemplation------Preparation/Action------Maintenance

Figure 2   Stages of change model parallel to group developmental stages closed group (Kurland and Salmon, 1998, group model) (closed group).

The challenge for the facilitator of involuntary groups is attending to the individual change process while also simultaneously attending to the stages of group development. The *Pre-group planning* stage is critical for involuntary groups since decisions made in this stage will impact whether clients remain in group or not. First decisions need to be made about the group structure and rules. Which rules are negotiable and which are not? Clear group structure and increased choices for members can reduce reactance and roadblocks to engagement (Rooney, 1992). Anticipating the concerns of the population served can assist the facilitator in engaging involuntary clients. A "tuning in" exercise originally developed to anticipate client concerns and fears in contracting with voluntary groups (Schwartz, 1976; Shulman, 2006), can be used to develop an opening statement in an orientation session. Facilitators provide basic information and join with potential group members by addressing questions upon entering the group. Orientation has been found to reduce attrition in domestic violence groups (Brekke, 1989; Tolman & Bhosley, 1987).

In the *Beginning stage* for closed-ended groups, the facilitator can expect mostly precontemplators with others further along in the change process (O'Hare, 1996). Involuntary group members present varying levels of resistance at this stage. For example, members may not respond to questions, complain about the "system" that got them there, or carry on off-topic side-conversations. The focus of intervention is on support, joining, and inclusion. A group opening statement similar to that used in orientation can be used to address questions and concerns. A group member's constrained "choice" of attending the group can be validated. Negotiable and non-negotiable group rules are clarified. Education on the problem behavior group members are alleged to possess can be presented without directly challenging group members. Contemplators can be assisted in examining the pros and cons of changing their behavior.

In open-ended groups, members farther along in the change process can assist the facilitator in the orientation process and model successful change. Group veterans discussing their change efforts assists newer group members to examine their own issues and provides guidelines on how they too might change. Also a direct challenge to new members can be effective if presented by credible veterans who have been challenged by similar problems and have been precontemplators and contemplators in the past.

The *Middle stage* of the group process is most similar to the middle stages of traditional voluntary groupwork. In both closed and open-ended groups, collections of group members are in the action stage; problems are being recognized and efforts are made to address them. Mutual aid is key in assisting group members in the change process (Gitterman, 2004). In this stage, group activities, such as individual tasks and role plays that address identified problems, can be helpful. In open-ended groups, veterans can be asked to guide individual presentations of the tasks, with facilitators overseeing the process.

Finally in the *Ending stage*, similar to voluntary groups, the focus is on assisting group members to maintain the changes they have made, as the group examines triggers to relapse. Group members brainstorm situations that will challenge them outside of group and provide ways to address them. Supports outside of the group are examined and encouraged. In open-ended groups leadership skills can be acknowledged and used to challenge members earlier in the process. Clear and specific ending criteria are useful in both open-ended and closed-ended groups, e.g., attending a specific number of sessions and completing a set number of tasks. This reduces group members' reactance when first entering the group and helps them to examine their own progress over time. For the facilitator, it makes it easier in giving feedback to group members regarding their progress and in providing progress reports to outside sources that request information.

One limitation of utilizing the individual stage model in conjunction with the group developmental stage models is its complexity. The combination of both individual and group level models makes it difficult to articulate, and more research examining group process of involuntary groups over time, is needed. However, using a group developmental model that incorporates the stage of change in working with involuntary groups provides a number of advantages for the group facilitator. The facilitator is more likely to anticipate initial resistance to change within the group setting and successfully engage involuntary group members in the group process. Power struggles early in group treatment are less likely to develop, and members are more likely to use the group process to develop mutual aid opportunities during the middle group stages. Finally, the facilitator is more likely to attend to the risk of relapse and to focus on group efforts to maintain individual changes.

References

Brekke, J. (1989). The use of orientation groups for hard-to-reach clients: Model, method and evaluation. *Social Work with Groups, 12*(2), 75–88.

Chovanec, M. (in press). Innovations applied to the classroom for involuntary groups: Implications for social work education. *Journal of Teaching in Social Work.*

Gitterman, A. (2004). The Mutual Aid Model. In C. D. Garvin, L. M. Gutiérrez, & M. J. Galinsky (Eds.), *Handbook of social work with groups* (pp. 93–110). New York: Guilford Press.

Kurland, R., & Salmon, R. (1998). *Teaching a methods course in social work with groups.* Alexandria, VA: Council on Social Work Education.

Norcross, J. C., Beutler, L. E., & Clarkin, J. F. (1998). Prescriptive eclectic psychotherapy. In R. A. Dorfman (Ed.), *Paradigms of clinical social work* (vol. 2, pp. 289–314). New York: Brunner/Mazel.

O'Hare, T. (1996). Court-ordered versus voluntary clients: Problem differences and readiness for change. *Social Work, 41*(4), 417–422.

Prochaska, J., Norcross, J., & DiClemente, C. (1994). *Changing for good.* New York: Avon Books.

Rooney, R. H. (1992). *Strategies for work with involuntary clients.* New York: Columbia University Press.

Rooney, R. H., & Chovanec, M. (2004). Social work with involuntary groups. In C. D. Garvin, M. J. Galinsky, & L. M. Gutiérrez (Eds.), *Handbook of social work with groups* (pp. 212–226). New York: Guilford Publications.

Schopler, J. H., & Galinsky, M. J. (2005). Meeting practice needs: Conceptualizing the open-ended group. *Social work with Groups, 28,* 49–68.

Schwartz, W. (1976). Between client and system: The mediating function. In R. R. Roberts, & H. Northen (Eds.), *Theories of social work with groups* (pp. 186–188). New York: Columbia University Press.

Shulman, L. (2006). *The skills of helping individuals, families, groups, and communities* (5th ed.). Belmont. CA: Thompson Brooks/Cole.

Tolman, R. M., & Bhosley, G. (1989). A comparison of two types of pregroup preparation for men who batter. *Journal of Social Service Research, 13*(2), 33–43.

Involuntary Clients (Engagement Processes)

Kay Goler Levin

Our theories of engaging clients in groups are predicated on work with voluntary clients. However, traditional ways of engaging clients are not effective with involuntary clients. Today, more and more clients are involuntary. They may be mandated for counseling by the courts, sent for therapy by schools, or directed to services from the inpatient mental health system.

An involuntary client is defined as "one who is forced to seek, or feels pressure to accept contact with a helping professional," and is further divided into two other categories, mandated clients and nonvoluntary clients. "Mandated clients must work with a practitioner because of a legal mandate or court order . . . [a] Nonvoluntary client is one who has contact with a helping professional through pressure from agencies, referral sources, other persons, family members, and/or outside events" (Rooney, 1992, p. 6). Initially group members may seem angry and argumentative, pushing boundaries and the group leader as well. For many of our vulnerable clients, anger is often the only way they have been able to feel visible in a system that has alternately ignored them or attempted to control their behavior.

Integrating these pertinent individual relational theories—*affect attunement* (Stern, 1985), *intersubjective space* (Stolorow & Atwood, 1983), *the holding environment*, (Winnicott, 1965), and *the zone of proximal development* (Vygotsky, 1978)—in conjunction with group development theories (Bion, 1961; Garland, Jones, & Kolodny, 1965; Schiller, 1997), and the group concept of mutual aid (Gitterman, 2004; Shulman, 1986; Steinberg, 1997) results in an innovative individual/group conceptual model that can guide theory and practice. Some group-related concepts can be regarded as foundational to our understanding of group engagement with involuntary clients. These include: anger and engagement within groups (Gans, 1989; Gans & Alanso, 1998), and the concept of reactance (Brehm & Brehm, 1981). They are especially useful when integrated with more commonly accepted theories of group development (Bion, 1961; Garland et al., 1965; Hartford, 1971; Schiller, 1997; Yalom, 1995), group development with involuntary clients (Behroozi, 1992; Billow, 2003; Cowger, 1979; Gans, 1989; Garvin, 1997; Markus & Abernethy, 2001; Pam & Kemker, 1993; Robbins, 2003), and mutual aid (Gitterman, 2004; Shulman, 1986; Steinberg, 1997). Because there are few theoretical models in the social work literature available to guide proactive work with involuntary groups (Behroozi, 1992; Rooney, 1992; Rooney & Chovanec, 2004), the integrated use of group theory with individual relational theories can provide a model to help us understand the initial process necessary for involuntary group members to engage (Levin, 2006).

Macgowan suggests that a group member is not fully engaged until there is minimal evidence of engagement in all seven of the following dimensions:

"(1) evidence of attendance; (2) verbal contribution, and/or participation in group activities; (3) support for the work of the leader; (4) interaction with members; (5) adoption of the mutual contract; (6) work on own problems; and (7) helping members in their work on their problems" (Macgowan, 1997, pp. 23–24).

Stolorow and Atwood's (1983) idea of *intersubjective space* is another way to look at the development of the group culture, as group members have the opportunity to observe, and learn from, each dyadic interaction. That *intersubjective space* expands and a culture of acceptance develops within it. "Relationships develop in the spaces in between the interactions." When one can conceptualize the relationship which develops at first between the group leader and group member as driven by *affect attunement* (Stern, 1985), it is easier to deal with and include angry group members. *Affect attunement* directs the group leader to assess the group member's affect and relate to it. Specifically, this helps the angry group member to eventually feel heard, accepted, and valued. This leads to the first practice guideline: Expect the group members to challenge authority, to see how far they can go and what reaction their actions and anger will elicit from the group leader. We should see these as reactance behaviors and understand the challenge as a sign of health (Brehm & Brehm, 1981), and realize that we must provide the initial boundaries.

Within that *intersubjective space*, the group members simultaneously experience a situation from their own individual lens, expectations, and experiences, as well as from their common experience within the group. Luria (1981) speaks of the universal "meaning" that people have of situations or experiences, and the individual "sense" that they bring to the "same" experience. What is unique to social group work and group psychotherapy is this process. Opportunities are provided within the shared group experience for each group member to learn from each other's perceptions and observations. This experience is, at once, the same and yet different. That *intersubjective space* expands and a culture of acceptance develops within it. Within involuntary groups, the practice guideline that emerges is that "the leader must initially provide the cement for the group and community as-a-whole, by dint of commitment to each person, making all members feel that it matters whether or not they are present" (Pam & Kemker, 1993, p. 432).

As other members watch the interaction of the member–leader dyad, a *"holding environment"* is created (Winnicott, 1965). Winnicott discussed the concepts of a *"holding environment"* and a *"good enough mother"* to help us understand the needs of the mother–infant dyad and what was minimally required for the positive development of the infant. Both the mother and child influence each other's development through their interactions. Winnicott's concepts can be applied to a well-functioning group, as the structure is parallel. The *"good enough mothering"* provided by the group therapist is what is necessary for the growth and development of the involuntary group. The *"holding environment"* that is developed, fosters the developing culture and norms of the group, and both members and leader influence each other. Other group members observe these initial interactions between the leader and group member. These observations result in the development of group norms based on the acceptance of anger and concern for the individual group member. This leads to the second practice guideline: Leaders should understand how important their initial acceptance of involuntary clients is, and how necessary to the developing group process. The group member must feel accepted, "anger and all" in order to engage. Group members recognize that "things are different here" (Levin, 2006).

A third individual-oriented theory applicable to group engagement is Vygotsky's (1978) "*zone of proximal development.*" Applied to involuntary groups, this is a way of explaining how interpersonal learning, growth, and change occurs within the group. Vygotsky (1978) envisioned: "learning taking place within a "*zone of proximal development.* . . . what a child can do with assistance from a more capable peer, or through adult guidance today, she will be able to do for herself tomorrow." The creation of an anger-accepting environment observed by all members of the group, in effect, works within a *zone of proximal development* where engagement in the group begins and grows into mutual aid. The process within the group of having one's anger accepted, listened to and validated, allows the group member to internalize the anger differently, and to then see themselves in a different light. This leads to the third practice guideline: The group leader works within the *zone of proximal development* between angry and isolated people who, when they feel listened to, respected, and capable of helping others, begin to see the group as "theirs" (Levin, 2006).

References

Behroozi, C. S. (1992). A model for social work with involuntary applicants in groups. In J. Garland (Ed.), *Group work reaching out: People, places and power* (pp. 223–238). Binghamton, NY: Haworth Press.

Billow, R. M. (2003). Rebellion in group. *International Journal of Group Psychotherapy, 53*(3), 331–351.

Bion, W. R. (1961). *Experiences in groups*. London: Tavistock.

Brehm, S., & Brehm, J. (1981). *Psychological reactance: A theory of freedom and control*. New York: Academic Press.

Cowger, C. D. (1979). Conflict and conflict management in working with groups. *Social Work with Groups, 2*(4), 309–320.

Gans, J. S. (1989). Hostility in group psychotherapy. *International Journal of Group Psychotherapy, 39*(4), 499–516.

Gans, J. S., & Alanso, A. (1998). Difficult patients: Their construction in group therapy. *International Journal of Group Psychotherapy, 48*(3), 311–326.

Garland J. A., Jones, H. E., & Kolodny, R. L. (1965). A model for stages of development in social work groups. In S. Bernstein (Ed.), *Explorations in group work* (pp. 17–71). Boston: Boston University of Social Work.

Garvin, C. D. (1997). Working with oppressed people in groups. *Contemporary group work* (3rd ed.). Needham Heights, MA: Simon & Schuster.

Gitterman, A. (2004). The Mutual Aid Model, In C. D. Garvin, L. M. Gutiérrez, & M. J. Galinsky (Eds.), *Handbook of social work with groups* (pp. 93–110). New York: Guilford Press.

Hartford, M. E. (1971). *Groups in social work: Application of small group theory and research to social work practice*. New York: Columbia University Press.

Levin, K. G. (2006). Involuntary clients are different: Strategies for engagement using individual relational theories in synergy with group development theories. *Groupwork, 16*(2), 61–84.

Luria, A. R. (1981). *Language and cognition*. New York: John Wiley.

Macgowan, M. J. (2003). Increasing engagement in groups: A measurement based approach. *Social Work with Groups, 26*(1), 5–28.

Markus, H. E., & Abernethy, A. D. (2001). Joining with the resistance: Addressing reluctance to engage in group therapy training. *International Journal of Group Psychotherapy, 51*(2), 191–204.

Pam, A., & Kemker, S. (1993). The captive group: Guidelines for group therapists in the inpatient setting. *International Journal of Group Psychotherapy, 43*(4), 419–438.

Robbins, R. N. (2003). Developing cohesion in court-mandated group treatment of male spouse abusers. *International Journal of Group Psychotherapy, 53*(3), 261–284.

Rooney, R. H. (1992). *Strategies for work with involuntary clients*. New York: Columbia University Press.

Rooney, R. H., & Chovanec, M. (2004). Involuntary groups. In C. D. Garvin, L. M. Gutierrez, & M. J. Galinsky (Eds.), *Handbook of social work with groups* (pp. 212–226). New York: Guilford Press.

Schiller, L. Y. (1997). Rethinking stages of development in women's groups: Implications for practice. *Social Work with Groups, 20*(3), 3–19.

Shulman, L. (1986). The dynamic of mutual aid. In A. Gitterman, & L. Shulman (Eds.), *The legacy of William Schwartz: Group practice as shared interaction* (pp. 51–60). Binghamton, NY: Haworth Press.

Steinberg, D. M. (1997). *The mutual-aid approach to working with groups. Helping people help each other.* Northvale, NJ: Aaronson.

Stern, D. N. (1985). *The interpersonal world of the infant.* New York: Basic Books.

Stolorow, R. D., & Atwood, G. E. (1983). *Contexts of being: The intersubjective foundations of psychological life.* Hillsdale, NJ: Analytic Press.

Vygotsky, L. S. (1978). *Mind in society: The development of higher psychological—processes.* Cambridge, MA: Harvard University Press.

Winnicott, D. W. (1965). *The maturational processes and the facilitating environment: Studies in the theory of emotional development.* Madison: WI, International Universities Press.

Yalom, I. D. (1995). *The theory and practice of group psychotherapy* (4th ed.). New York: Basic Books.

Vicarious Traumatization

Shantih E. Clemans

Workers in the trauma field are vulnerable to experiencing vicarious traumatization (VT), a phenomenon that characterizes the emotional, psychological, and spiritual consequences of secondary exposure to violence and abuse (Bride, 2007; McCann & Pearlman, 1991). A single session VT group is one step toward fostering a workforce competent in self-care. Combined with individual supervision, a VT group is an efficient method of introducing VT and providing mutual aid opportunities for workers. In such a group, workers are able to exchange feelings with others in similar jobs, thus creating connectedness and reducing isolation and hopelessness. A VT group is a practical forum for workers to recognize, in themselves and each other, symptoms such as numbness, disturbed sleep, or feelings of vulnerability.

This group requires a worker with a strong skill repertoire. Even in a single session group, a worker must deftly guide the group through its developmental phases. An atmosphere of confidentiality and safety must be quickly established. For true group work to happen, a worker also needs to consciously model and foster the give and take that is the hallmark of mutual aid (Kurland & Salmon, 1999).

Social group work is a time-tested, powerful approach to helping people heal from trauma (Knight, 2006). True to the parallel process, workers, like the clients they serve, also benefit from groups. Especially useful in educating workers about VT and in providing a forum of safety, connection, and skill building, the VT group model includes these segments: (1) Beginning; (2) Specific effects of VT; (3) Responding to VT; and (4) Ending and Transition.

A core goal of any mutual aid group is the creation of a safe, confidential and trusting atmosphere (Northen & Kurland, 2001). The rule, "what is said in group, stays in group," applies. The session may begin with the group worker making an opening statement (Shulman, 1971):

Welcome. We are here together because trauma work is both rewarding and emotionally challenging. Today, I will introduce you to VT and put a name to what you may already be experiencing. Your work can affect you in many different ways. I want us to talk together about common feelings and experiences. This is the beginning of a longer conversation.

In the beginning of any group, participants are unsure of whether they belong and are questioning how the group can actually help them (Glassman & Kates, 1990; Kurland & Salmon, 1999; Northen & Kurland, 2001). The beginning phase allows a group worker to refer to the group's purpose and provide hints to these wonderings:

- What is VT?
- What are the warning signs?
- Am I experiencing VT?
- How can I help myself and my colleagues?

Creative strategies can be employed to begin the exploration process. One idea is to have participants complete worksheets where they respond to prompts such as, "A specific way I am affected by VT is ...." Responses are then read aloud and a mutual exchange takes place. As the group progresses, the group worker provides a framework of common effects of VT (Clemans, 2004). A discussion ensues.

Worker: VT can affect you in three major ways: (1) feelings of vulnerability and fear, (2) difficulty trusting; and, (3) a changed worldview. Would anyone like to share an experience?

Ruth: I work in a domestic violence shelter and I can relate to what you just said about increased feelings of fear. I am always hyper-vigilant. I worry that I am in danger all of the time even though, rationally, I know I am not.

The mutual aid process unfolds as participants share their experiences and offers of help:

Meg: I know what you mean. I used to feel that way, but now I try to talk about my fears in supervision and leave it there. That has really helped.

Ruth: Well, I'd like to do that but I don't have an honest relationship with my supervisor.

Andre: Yeah, I have that problem too. But I found support from one of my co-workers. Is there someone else you feel safe with?

One important function of a group is the acquisition of new knowledge and skills (Northen & Kurland, 2001). A group worker presents VT response strategies in an easy to remember way: ABC: Awareness, Balance, and Connection (Saakvitne & Pearlman, 1996). The worker may use handouts or other exercises to help the participants develop a personalized self-care plan.

The ending of a group is a critical stage that cannot be overlooked (Berman-Rossi, 1992; Kosoff, 2003). Cognizant of numerous tasks to accomplish in a short period of time, a group worker needs to end in a purposeful way. As the group nears its conclusion, participants are asked to generate ideas as to how the work can continue. For example, they may decide to have a weekly peer group, a monthly speaker, or lobby to initiate an ongoing VT group.

Mutual aid groups are instrumental for trauma workers as they navigate the emotional consequences of their jobs. Even as a single session offering, VT groups hold the promise of normalizing feelings, reducing isolation, and providing a catalyst for future VT work.

There are several challenges in executing this model. Assessing the responsiveness of an agency is crucial. Although most agencies will welcome a "one-shot deal" VT group, some may see it as an intrusion on supervision. As trauma work becomes part of everyday social work practice, VT groups, run by social workers schooled in the group work method, need to be consistently offered on the agency level. VT groups also have a place for those in private practice.

References

Berman-Rossi, T. (1992). Empowering groups through stages of group development. *Social Work with Groups, 15*(2/3), 239–256.

Bride, B. E. (2007). Prevalence of secondary traumatic stress among social workers. *Social Work, 52*(1), 63–71.

Clemans, S. E. (2004). Life changing: The experience of rape crisis work. *Affilia: Journal of Women and Social Work, 19*(2), 146–159.

Glassman, U., & Kates, L. (1990). *Group work: A humanistic perspective.* Newbury Park, CA: Sage.

Knight, C. (2006). Groups for individuals with traumatic histories: Practice considerations for social workers. *Social Work, 51*(1), 20–30.

Kosoff, S. (2003). Single-session groups: Applications and areas of expertise. *Social Work with Groups, 26*(1), 29–45.

Kurland, R., & Salmon, R. (1999). *Teaching a methods course in social work with groups.* Alexandria, VA: Council on Social Work Education.

McCann, L., & Pearlman, L. A. (1991). Vicarious traumatization: The emotional costs of working with survivors. *Treating Abuse Today, 3*(5), 28–31.

Northen, H., & Kurland, R. (2001). *Social work with groups* (3rd ed.). New York: Columbia University Press.

Saakvitne, K. W., & Pearlman, L. A. (1996). *Transforming the pain: A workbook on vicarious traumatization.* New York: Norton.

Shulman, L. (1971). The dynamics of the first class. *Learning and Development, 3*(1), 1–8. Center for Learning and Development, McGill University.

Work Groups

Paul H. Ephross and Thomas V. Vassil

A review of much of the recent literature on social work with groups may lead to the view that the primary purpose of such work is to restore social function to people whose social function is impaired. Indeed, this is one of the foci of social work with groups. However, it is only one of them. Another important foci evolved from the organizational needs of the public and voluntary agencies that provided the services to clients. The working groups of these agencies deliver the services to the clients,

Recent scholarly works on groups have been written by university faculty in a communications department (Burtis & Turman, 2006) and faculty in programs in occupational therapy (Cole, 2005), The authors of this entry also have noted a variety of social trends that affect the importance of working groups.

In the study of leadership theory, Goffee and Jones (2002) refer to what they call "context theory." They note that they have "ransacked all the leadership theories to come up with four essential leadership qualities" (Goffee & Jones, 2002, pp. 63–70) for organizations of our time. They name these "sensing," "revealing weaknesses," "tough empathy," and "differentiation." The relevance of these ideas to the leadership activities of social workers in and with working groups seems to us both powerful and evident.

Early in the new century, three eminent applied social scientists discussed the changing definitions of the role of the "expert" (Bennis, Spreitzer, & Cummings, 2001). Observations by Bennis (Bennis et al., 2001, pp. 3–13), Lawler (p. 14) Stewart (p. 69) and Slater (p. 115) are beacons of light for social workers that fill professional roles for working groups. Slater, a renowned social scientist, commented:

> People don't need to be controlled and manipulated to commit themselves to a heartfelt vision, and being controlled and manipulated tends to destroy that commitment. Those trained to a mechanistic worldview often find it difficult to learn this. But, it becomes almost impossible if you've never learned it in relation to your own organization.
>
> (Bennis et al., 2001, p. 115)

But basic principles of working group function and process, based on broadly democratic social work goals, are being declared by management experts as principles of group and organizational operation. In our view, one cannot conceive of major organizational decisions without those decisions having been filtered, discussed, and processed by one, or more often several, small groups.

The world has caught up with the social work profession. Social work education teaches the principles of organization. The relationship between how a group is organized and operates, is now understood to influence not only members' feelings about, and investment in, the work-group, but also basic and important principles applicable to work groups no matter what the setting. It is ironic that management in some social work settings are looking to learn from the broader field of management, when that field sounds like social work theorists as they talk about human needs.

But what about specific techniques? Computerized methods are used in keeping track of resources, dealing with problems of planning and scheduling, and aiding a system of accountability for staff and how many units of work they have accomplished? What about hard-headed management techniques, adapted and adopted from the private sector?

Computers have certainly proven their use in various working groups concerned with research, accountability, measurement of client satisfaction, and community involvement, and many other measurement numbers. Computers can only measure what staff and working group members can conceptualize. Computerized management has its limitations and its talents, both set by the scope and vision of the human beings who comprise the staff. Relationships continue as the crucial stuff of group life, along with the social goals of social work: equality, mutual respect, groups that belong to their members, tolerance and relationships of mutual regard and shared purpose, and democracy at work.

The distribution of population in the United States is changing, and the life cycle has, it seems, added a generation within the lifetime of many Americans. It is commonplace to hear of people undertaking business ventures, assuming leadership responsibilities in communities, and continuing to work through the sixth and seventh decades of their lives. This extension provides challenges, but also opens new possibilities. There now exists a large body of experienced, qualified lay and professional leaders who have the time and the educational qualifications needed to form the planning and working groups, to advise management and to become part of it in some instances, and to form representative governance bodies and citizen's panels on many social welfare issues and in many social work organizations.

We believe that the finest days of participatory management lie ahead and this is the basic framework for professional practice with working groups.

References

Bennis, W. E., Spreitzer, G. M., & Cummings, T. C. (Eds.). (2001). *The future of leadership.* San Francisco: Jossey-Bass.

Burtis, J. O., & Turman, P. D. (2006). *Group communication pitfalls: Overcoming barriers to an effective group experience.* Thousand Oaks, CA: Sage.

Cole, M. B. (2006). *Group dynamics in occupational therapy* (3rd ed.). Thorofare, NY: Slack.

Goffee, R., & Jones, G. (2002). Why should anyone be led by you? *Harvard Business Review, 80*(September/October), 63–70.

Workplace Coaching

Gregory J. Tully

In recent years a group work practice area has emerged within the field of occupational social work. It involves group work practice with employees, managers, and executives who seek to improve their workplace performance and address their struggles related to personal issues, interpersonal relations, and systemic challenges in the work environment. Utilizing group work theory, strategies, and skills, mutual aid is fostered through discussion and feedback, resulting in the "coaching" of group members to improve both individual and team performance and consequently organizational performance.

Social work in the workplace, providing counseling and supportive services within the world of work, has long been an established field of practice for social work professionals. Kurzman and Akabas (1981) identified the importance of this area, stating:

> The myth that work and the rest of life exist in two separate worlds has been exposed for the denial it represents ... No longer are communities willing to accept the concept that the behavior of work institutions is economic, the behavior of communities social, and never the twain shall meet.
>
> (p. 52)

By the 1990s, occupational social work expanded as services and activities increased within occupational settings for employees and their families (Googins & Davidson, 1993; Ramanathan, 1992). The field of coaching, which has received ever increasing attention in the literature (Kampa-Kokesch & Anderson, 2001), first came into focus within organizational practice in the 1980s (Tobias, 1996), and has grown significantly in recent years (Grodski, 2002). The growth of social work involvement with coaching is evidenced by increases in social work conference presentations, articles in social work publications, and the number of states offering social work continuing education credits for coaching workshops (Caspi, 2005).

Large organizations across the world employ counseling professionals, including social workers, to provide group facilitation for workplace professionals seeking coaching for workplace-related needs. The needs of the group members are often similar and represent a variety of workplace issues. Many lack confidence as they have moved quickly "up the corporate ladder" and feel uncertain in their current role. Others have never remedied problematic communication skills or a personality style that is not flexible enough for the workplace setting. Another common need shared by group members results from their chronic unwillingness to fully evaluate career satisfaction and to examine stress that may have developed while trying to balance both work and home life. Finally, group members often need to address feelings resulting from workplace bias or discrimination related to diversity issues.

Over a period of days or weeks, group activities, group discussion, quantitative measures, and mutual feedback are all utilized by group leaders to coach group members in achieving goals related to individual, team, and workplace growth and satisfaction. Group members might examine personal issues by completing quantitative measures that evaluate personality style or workplace "type", and subsequently sharing outcomes with the group. Personal issues can also be addressed by utilizing autobiographical exercises that encourage group members to relate historical life experiences that might be impacting current behavior.

Interpersonal issues that group members experience in their relationships with bosses, colleagues, or from direct reports can be examined through both group discussion and quantitative measures. Interpersonal communication growth can be achieved by utilizing role plays that either improve communication skills or teach confrontational techniques useful in the workplace. Group members can address the larger systemic issues they experience in their organizations by participating in exercises that address motivational techniques useful within organizations or by engaging in discussions that explore workplace bias or discrimination related to gender, ethnicity, sexual orientation, religion, or other diversity areas.

Many of the common benefits that the practice of social work with groups provides, such as universality, a sense of hope, reality testing, altruism, acquisition of knowledge and skills, mutual support, and cohesiveness (Northen & Kurland, 2001), can be experienced by group members in these workplace coaching groups. For example, hope can be instilled as group members hear about the experience of a group member who in the past has successfully resolved a difficult workplace issue; feelings of universality may be achieved as a group member recognizes that a problem with a boss or a direct report is shared by other group members; reality testing can occur when group members challenge a member who feels his or her workplace issue is insurmountable: altruism might be evidenced when a more experienced workplace professional in the group shares workplace wisdom with a less experienced group member. Finally, mutual support, cohesiveness, and increases in knowledge and skills, are often achieved as members gradually assist one another, grow closer as a "whole" group, and learn from one another.

For social workers who coach workplace professionals in groups, certain universally accepted group work leadership techniques are of import. Of primary importance are the leadership techniques of encouraging and assisting group members with participation (Gitterman & Shulman, 2005; Kurland & Salmon, 1993; Steinberg, 2004), providing empathic, positive feedback to group members (Shulman, 1999), and recognizing the unique diversity of each member within the group (Gitterman, 1994; Shulman, 1999). For example, in workplace coaching groups, initially structuring coaching group content is effective, but being flexible and allowing the mutual workplace expertise in the group to emerge and flourish, with the group members contributing to the content, is important. In addition, providing empathic, positive feedback to group members on a consistent basis is important because many of the workplace professionals have experienced workplace feedback that is often critical and lacking in support. Finally, it is important for the group leader to consistently recognize the uniqueness of each group member because coaching groups are often composed of diverse individuals representing a variety of workplace environments.

As social work strives to fulfill the service needs presented by individuals in the new millennium, social workers skilled in group work will be increasingly called upon to address the needs of clients working in challenging, changing, and stressful environments (Gitterman, 2001). These include global organizational environments. As a result, group work coaching should increase in demand and gain even greater attention as an emerging field of social work practice for group workers.

References

Caspi, J. (2005). Coaching and social work: Challenges and concerns. *Social Work, 50*(4), 359–362.

Gitterman, A. (2001). *Handbook of social work practice with vulnerable and resilient populations.* New York: Columbia University Press.

Gitterman, A., & Shulman, L. (Eds.) (2005). *Mutual aid groups: Vulnerable and resilient plopulations and the life cycle* (3rd ed.). New York: Columbia University Press.

Googins, B., & Davidson, B. (1993). The organization as client: Broadening the concept of employee assistance programs. *Social Work, 38*(4), 477–484.

Grodski, L. (Ed.). (2002). *The new private practice: Therapist-coaches share stories, strategies, and advice.* New York: W.W. Norton.

Kampa-Kokesch, S., & Anderson, M. (2001). Executive coaching: A comprehensive review of the literature. *Consulting Psychology Journal: Practice and Research, 53*(4), 205–228.

Kurland, R., & Salmon R. (1993). Not just one of the gang: Group workers and their role as an authority. *Social Work with Groups, 16*(1/2), 153–169.

Kurzman, P., & Akabas, S. (1981). Industrial social work as an arena for practice. *Social Work, 26*(1), 52–60.

Northen, H., & Kurland, R. (2001). *Social work with groups.* New York: Columbia University Press.

Ramanathan, C. (1992). Employee personal stress and productivity: Implications for occupational social work. *NASW Journal,* 234–239.

Shulman, L. (1999). *The skills of helping individuals, families, groups, and communities.* Itasca, IL: F. E. Peacock.

Steinberg, D. (2004). *The mutual-aid approach to working with groups.* Binghamton, NY: Haworth Press.

Tobias, L. L. (1996). Coaching executives. *Consulting Psychology Journal: Practice and Research, 48*(2), 87–95.

Group Work Leadership

Co-Leadership

Kathryn S. Collins and Marceline M. Lazzari

Co-leadership occurs when two or more persons act as mutual decision-makers, contribute to the knowledge base, share power, assume responsibility for the outcome and product of the group, and facilitate the workings of a group. Hierarchal leaders view decision making as a top-down process and believe subordinates must carry out the wishes from the chain of command without question. Co-leadership differs from this model by acknowledging co-workers as co-creators of the strategic process; thereby, the accomplishments of the whole group are valued over the success of one individual (Pearce & Conger, 2003; Troiano, 1999). Further, research has shown that complex projects and tasks requiring great amounts of creativity are well suited for co-leadership (Pearce, 2004), and through co-leadership, the group may move more easily toward a shared leadership model (Pearce & Conger, 2003). Co-leadership represents a relational process that can lead to an ideal of shared leadership among all group members. All persons, whether or not in formal leadership positions, have the capacity to assume leadership roles (Schein, 2006).

In social work practice, co-leadership is not a new concept. Since the early 1950s, the benefits of shared leadership in the facilitation of groups, as well as individual and family counseling, have been researched, reviewed, and discussed (Middleman, 1980; Nosko, 2002; Solomon, Loeffer, & Frank, 1953). For example, social work group co-leaders benefit from combining insights about intricate group dynamics and keeping two sets of eyes on the situation, rather than one. Further, group members benefit from viewing healthy relationship negotiation between the group leaders (Vannicelli, 1992).

Social work should delve deeper into the implementation of co-leadership for roles within agencies, organizations, and institutional groups, including higher education. Such groups could include member and staff groups, as well as those at the administrative and executive levels. Other professions, such as nursing and medicine, have found the benefits of joining interdisciplinary strengths and creating shared decision making that enhance patient care and administrative/staff productivity (Steinert, Goebel, & Rieger, 2006), through co-leadership models in the health and mental health milieus. In the past two decades, there has been over $5 trillion worth of mergers among business and industries. Heenan and Bennis (1999) identified companies, such as AT&T, Microsoft, Intel, Viacom/CBS, and Charles Schwab, that have been operating with some form of co-leadership at their executive levels. Likewise, the complex challenges facing the social work profession require a range of administrative options. Co-leadership can be a vehicle to promote shared leadership and, most importantly, shared responsibility to work toward viable and successful solutions. Expecting one leader to solve problems by him or herself simply does not work.

There may be barriers to co-leadership of groups within agencies, organizations, and institutions (Galinsky & Schopler, 1980; Starak, 1981). Specifically, Seers, Keller, and Wilkerson (2003) identified the major factors in the barriers of shared leadership, and with modification social work can apply these to co-leadership approaches. These factors include: group members not "buying into" the idea, status/power differentials between co-leaders, one leader emerges from the two, co-leaders do not share a mutual commitment, and/or there is status seeking, no shared leadership theories, and little diversity in co-leaders and/or among group members.

It is important for co-leaders to encompass unique characteristics, which include the following:

1. Co-leaders maintain equal credibility, motivation, and commitment. Co-leadership should not be chosen simply because one leader does not want to work alone or want to do all of the work. Co-leaders merge their abilities and strengths from different areas, thereby bringing unique division of responsibilities by understanding the talents and gifts each person brings to the leadership roles. Furthermore, co-leaders have the ability to delegate and generate collective governance among stakeholders, whether clients or colleagues.
2. Co-leaders uphold a shared vision of the role and the mission of the group they are leading. Often, the vision and mission are mutually agreed upon by staff and the administrative leadership, in order to facilitate meeting future goals and objectives and to create a common history of the group as a whole.
3. Co-leaders know how to solve conflicts constructively, and use integrity and analytical skills to enrich creative innovations and solutions of the group members. Problem-solving and strong interaction skills accelerate diversity, creativity, and complex empowerment approaches within the group. Leadership expert, Ronald Heifetz from Harvard's Kennedy School of Government, holds that authoritarian leaders do not solve problems because they do not mobilize people to develop practical solutions (as cited in Richman, 1988).
4. Co-leaders maintain a sense of humor and they know how to use it. Filipowicz (2003) offers that leaders can use humor to enhance communication in interpersonally difficult situations, relieve stress, and in helping to uncover group dynamics and processes. According to Filipowicz, research suggests, "humor conveys information, generates affect, and draws attention."

(p. 30).

Social work educators are in unique positions to influence the emerging generation of future leaders. By paying attention to the nature of classroom structures, relationships, and assignments, one can create opportunities to both model and challenge students to assume co-leadership roles. Such approaches require vision, risk-taking, power sharing, and trust in the potential of students to assume responsibility not only for their own learning but for the success of the entire class. Careful attention must be paid to mutual respect, mutual decision making, support of one another, adaptation, common values and goals, collective and individual identity, cooperation, respect for different views, and effective conflict resolution.

Additionally, choosing curriculum that includes a discussion of the pros and cons of co-leadership models in facilitating treatment groups, as well as staff, member, and administrative groups, provides students with the opportunity to apply critical thinking skills across group contexts. Co-leadership is not in and of itself good or bad, but rather an opportunity to interact in ways that may be more collaborative and reflective of social work values. Some experts in group work prefer individual leadership over co-leadership, due primarily to the additional time and effort required to be an effective model and to negotiating the intricacies of co-leadership relationships (Ephross, 2005). Co-leadership requires a complex array of skills and a commitment to sharing power and responsibility (Starak, 1981).

Social work administrators likewise have opportunities to distribute formal power in ways that promote co-leadership and shared responsibility. Operating from a power-sharing approach is not easy as current hierarchical structures present resistance to such models. However, the benefits may far outweigh the risks and provide a solution to the leadership crisis that currently plagues organizations, institutions, government structures, and corporate America. It is possible to sustain co-leadership models when participants commit to and maintain hope in the potential of shared power and responsibility among all stakeholders to address the complexities facing us as a profession in a society plagued by the misuse of power.

References

Ephross, P. H. (2005). Social work with groups: Practice principles. In G. L. Greiff, & P. H. Ephross (Eds.), *Group work with populations at risk* (2nd ed., pp. 1–12). New York: Oxford University Press.

Filipowicz, A. (2003). Humor as a leadership tool. *Leadership, 13*(1), 30.

Galinsky, M. J., & Schopler, J. H. (1980). Structuring co-leadership in social work training. *Social Work with Groups, 3*(4), 51–63.

Heenan, P., & Bennis, W. (1999). *Co-leaders: The power of great partnerships.* New York: Wiley.

Middleman, R. R. (1980). Co-leadership and solo-leadership in education for social work with groups. *Social Work with Groups, 3*(4), 39–50.

Nosko, A. (2002). Adventures in co-leadership in social group work practice. *Social Work with Groups, 25*(1/2), 173–180.

Pearce, C. L. (2004). The future of leadership: Combining vertical and shared leadership to transform knowledge work. *Academy of Management Executive, 18*(1), 47–57.

Pearce, C. L., & Conger, J. A. (Eds.). (2003). *Shared leadership: Reframing the hows and whys of leadership.* Thousand Oaks, CA: Sage.

Richman, T. (1988). Leadership expert Ronald Heifetz. *Inc. Magazine.* Retrieved August 7, 2007 from http://www.inc.com/magazine/19881001/5990.html

Schein, E. H. (2006). Leadership competencies: A provocative new look. In F. Hesselbein, & M. Goldsmith (Eds.), *The leader of the future 2: Visions, strategies, and practices for the new era* (pp. 59–70). San Francisco: Jossey-Bass.

Seers, A., Keller, T., & Wilkerson, J. M. (2003). Can team members share leadership? Foundations in research and theory. In C. L. Pearce, & J. A. Conger (Eds.), *Shared leadership: Reframing the hows and whys of leadership* (pp. 77–102). Thousand Oaks, CA: Sage.

Solomon, A., Loeffer, F. J., & Frank, G. H. (1953). An analysis of co-therapist interaction in group psychotherapy. *International Journal of Group Psychotherapy, 3*, 171–180.

Starak, Y. (1981). Co-leadership: A new look at sharing group work. *Social Work with Groups, 4*(3/4), 145–157.

Steinert T., Goebel, R., & Rieger W. (2006). A nurse–physician co-leadership model in psychiatric hospitals: Results of a survey among leading staff members in three sites. *International Journal of Mental Health Nursing, 15*(4), 251–257.

Troiano, P. (1999). Sharing the throne. *Management Review, 88*, 39–43.

Vannicelli, M. (1992). *Removing the roadblocks: Group psychotherapy with substance abusers and family members.* New York: Guilford Press.

Co-Working

Mark Doel

Co-working refers to the presence of two group facilitators who, together, take responsibility for leading the group. "Solo-led" groups are those with a single facilitator, and those with more than two facilitators are sometimes referred to as "multiple-led." Other kinds of group are those, which are "self-led," with no professional groupwork facilitator.

There have been few systematic studies of the prevalence of co-working, but it seems to be much more widespread in the United Kingdom than in the United States. Of the 1,463 groups in Caddick's (1993) probation survey in England and Wales, 87% were co-led or multiple-led; coincidentally, exactly the same percentage as the co-worked groups in Doel and Sawdon's (1999) groupwork project in northern England. On the other hand, the *Handbook of Social Work with Groups* (Garvin, Gutiérrez, & Galinsky, 2004), largely American in perspective, has neither co-working nor co-leading in the subject index.

Perhaps the economics of co-leadership help to explain its prevalence or relative absence; two or more practitioners are more costly than one. Where these costs are already being met, such as the large public social work departments in the United Kingdom, it is perhaps easier to hide them; where there is a more direct economic relationship, the doubled cost might be prohibitive.

Co-working can be seen as a way of managing high-risk groups, such as offenders groups. In some agencies, we can speculate that the prevalence of co- or multiple-led groups reflects health and safety policies. Multiple-led groups also offer the agency flexibility, with a team of three or four workers providing two facilitators at any one session of the group, so the demands on workers' time are shared and cover is available if a worker is absent. Multiple leaderships are more likely to occur in multi-professional settings such as Youth Offending teams (Doel, 2006). Although staff development can be one of the benefits of co-working (see below) there is little evidence to suggest that agencies use co-working as an explicit strategy to promote professional development.

Co-working has certain intrinsic benefits. In Doel and Sawdon's (1999) group-work project, the percentage of solo-work groups in the failed sample (36%) is almost three times the percentage of solo-work groups in the successful sample (13%). We have some evidence, then, that co-working can help to sustain the group, or certainly the plans for a group, by sharing tasks and responsibilities. Brown (1994) captures the inherent advantages:

> Most of the potential benefits for group members arise from having two workers with distinctive characteristics who, in combination, can offer the group and individual member more than either would be able to alone.
>
> (p. 78)

"Co-working is the embodiment of certain strands of feminist philosophy" (Butler & Wintram, 1991, p. 39), in which support can develop into mutual courage, for example, in leading new, risky group exercises. Two workers can "lead with four eyes," with one groupworker focusing on the group as whole, whilst the other attends to individuals within the group.

Co-workers offer an experience of diversity for group members, perhaps with a mixed gender or mixed race leadership, which in turn can provide a good role model for the members. Taking turns to introduce different topics or themes in each session means a welcome change in voice, style and approach and more variety in the group.

Working together has been noted as the only occasion in the working week in which a practitioner directly observes the practice of a colleague, and has his or her own practice observed, too (portfolios of groupwork practice in Doel, 2006). These groupworkers found this to be a supportive activity, which contributed to their professional development, perhaps even more so than one-to-one supervision from a manager (Doel, 2006). Usually, they felt that being watched improved their practice (they would prepare more conscientiously and feel more responsibility for the joint working) rather than making them inhibited or self-conscious. In some cases, where one worker was a more experienced groupworker, it was a chance to mentor the novice groupworker.

Co-working also has certain intrinsic problems. Since co-workers should spend time preparing for, and de-briefing from, groups to avoid confusion and disagreement over roles, it can be a timely process (Brown, 1994). Although involving most of a team in a multiple-led group can broaden the support for the group, it can also make it difficult to maintain continuity and cohesion.

Co-working can lead to competitive behaviour. Is my co-worker more popular in the group, does he or she lead in directions that I do not think benefit the group, and is he or she too dominant, too passive? In response to the question, what were your feelings and thoughts before the first session of the group? One co-worker "wrote of her concerns about her own competence, especially in front of her co-worker, perhaps heightened by the fact that the co-worker was from a different professional group" (Doel, 2006). If co-workers are focusing on their own relationship rather than the group process, the group is likely to suffer. An obvious point that needs to be stated: the quality of the co-working relationship will affect the quality of members' experience in the group. It has the potential, therefore, to serve as a poor role model as well as a positive one.

Good preparation and debriefing, open communication and access to shared consultation with an independent and experienced groupworker are all likely to ensure that group members benefit from a group that is facilitated by more than one groupworker.

References

Brown, A. (1994). *Groupwork*. Aldershot, UK: Ashgate.

Butler, S., & Wintram, C. (1991). *Feminist groupwork*. London: Sage.

Caddick, B. (1993). A survey of groupwork in the Probation Service in England and Wales. In A. Brown, & B. Caddick (Eds.), *Groupwork with offenders*. London: Whiting and Birch.

Doel, M. (2006). *Using groupwork*. London: Routledge.

Doel, M., & Sawdon, C. (1999). *The essential groupworker*. London: Jessica Kingsley.

Garvin, C. D., Gutiérrez, L. M., & Galinsky, M. (Eds.). (2004). *Handbook of social work with groups*. New York: Guilford Press.

Leadership

Steven Rose

Leadership of social work groups bears a direct relationship to leadership in general. Groups and leadership represent microcosms of society. Group type affects group leadership. In task groups, for example, leadership tends to be more directive than in other type of groups. The leader is responsible for the goal-centered, productive activities of the group (Toseland & Rivas, 2005). The leader structures and organizes the group in such a way for it to efficiently and effectively conduct its work. Leadership varies in individual change-oriented and problem solving groups according to members' needs as well as practice models. With the leader's assistance, the group evolves a culture of mutual aid, facilitating problem solving and social, emotional, and/or cognitive-behavioral change.

Many social work groups contain structured leadership roles, as in role-playing activities, thereby enhancing leadership development among members within the group (Rose, 1989). Co-leadership of groups involves persons exercising leadership with the group, as well as with one another; senior, experienced group leaders mentor junior, novice leaders. This pattern of supervision and education is common within group services.

Membership is the other side of the coin. An effective leader is able to see the group from the same perspective as that of the members, and thus empathy and role-taking ability are crucial aspects of effective group leadership. Other important characteristics include the ability to support members and to have their support and confidence too. The leader must be familiar with the path that the group will be taking in order to lead them down it. Group leaders are ethically, culturally, racially, and gender sensitive (Reed, 1985).

By virtue of training and disposition, much leadership style in social work groups has traditionally emphasized the social–emotional dimension. However, increasingly, with the advent of task-centered and cognitive models of group work practice, with the latter's emphasis on the importance of situational leadership, there has been a shift towards task-oriented leadership styles.

Social psychology and political science are sources of leadership theory that are applicable to social work groups. The most widely known, classic theory of group leadership style is that of laissez-faire, democratic, and autocratic leadership (Lewin, Lippitt, & White, 1939). The laissez-faire style is sometimes considered to be a non-leadership style, since it represents a passive, inactive style. The democratic style of leadership is intermediate in structure and direction. The autocratic style of leadership is aggressive in nature. Each style tends to result in predictable emotions and actions by group members. Members of social work groups often prefer and are most satisfied with a democratic style of leadership, as it empowers them to participate and have input to the direction and process of the group, while simultaneously validating the legitimacy of the leader. The laissez-style and autocratic styles tend to result in frustration and aggression among members.

A prevalent view of group leadership is that it resides in the formal leader of the group. In this view, the formal leader provides the group with its identity, essence, and personality. Another view, perceives group leadership to be distributed throughout the entire group. As a distributed function of the group, leadership comprises three dimensions: (1) the persons who enact the role of leading the whole group, whether or not they are formally designated as leaders; (2) the persons who enact the leadership role within sub-groups; and (3) all the persons in the group assuming leadership roles. In self-help groups, for example, the role of the leaders is the same as that of the members. In fact, self-help groups may rotate leadership duties and responsibilities among the membership, rather than have a separate, formal leadership.

References

Lewin, K., Lippitt, R., & White, R. (1939). Patterns of aggressive behavior in experimentally created "social climates." *Journal of Social Psychology, 10*, 271–299.

Reed, B. G. (1985). Gender issues in training group leaders. In M. Sundel, P. Glasser, R. Sarri, & R. Vinter (Eds.), *Individual change through small groups* (2nd ed., pp. 310–323). New York: Free Press.

Rose, S. R. (1989). *Working with adults in groups: A multi-method approach.* San Francisco: Jossey-Bass.

Toseland, R. W., & Rivas, R. F. (2005). *An introduction to group work practice* (5th ed.). Boston: Allyn & Bacon.

Mentoring

Cheryl D. Lee and Eliette Montiel

Mentoring is typically described as a one-on-one relationship between a mentor, who shares experiences and provides guidance, and a mentee, who is relatively new to the chosen field of work or education (Buell, 2004; Dubois, Holloway, Valentine, & Cooper, 2002; Girves, Zepeda, & Gwathmey, 2005; Scisney-Matlock & Matlock, 2001). Interactive group mentoring is an alternative to the traditional, two-person, mentoring relationship. Group mentoring programs place an experienced organization veteran with a group of less-experienced prodigies. Members exchange ideas, analyze issues, receive feedback, and obtain guidance as a group. In the process, they bond as a group (Buell, 2004). Participants bring knowledge and experience to the group and increase their knowledge and comfort, essentially functioning as co-facilitators (Sands & Solomon, 2003). Mentoring has been shown to be effective by increasing graduation rates, insuring employee success, reducing stress, and raising self-esteem (Cole, 2007; Girves et al., 2005; Scisney-Matlock & Matlock, 2001).

Group mentoring reflects the tripartite historical roots of social group work—the settlement, the progressive education, and recreation movements of the early 20th century (Ephross, 2005; Gitterman & Shulman, 2005). Jane Addams (1910, 1930) and other settlement workers were mentors to immigrants who wanted assistance with education, work, and family matters. An increasing number of people who seek mentoring are also from oppressed populations lower-socioeconomic status. They desire empowerment to navigate and change professional and educational systems. These types of organizations provide formal mentoring programs to help their employees/students.

The progressive education movement recognized the power of peer groups to foster democratic participation and cooperative learning (Dewey, 1916). It was not only the all-knowing teacher that provided information in a classroom, but students, and especially, adult learners brought valuable experiences, to share. Similarly, the mentor has wisdom, but the mentee arrives with knowledge, experiences, and strengths that can benefit the group. The recreation movement emphasized that people would grow from participating together in enjoyable activities (Ephross, 2005). Mentoring groups benefit from outings, conferences, and celebrations.

In a recent study, Horace (2004) demonstrated the value of group mentoring as a way to provide guidance, support, and resources for nine older adolescents faced with deciding what to do with their lives after high school. The inner-city youth received average grades and had been overlooked by guidance counselors. They became involved in an agency that provided a mentoring group during the school year and at summer camp. The youth obtained information about applying to college and discussed fears, hopes, and feelings with each other and a worker. In another study, Girves et al. (2005) demonstrated that alternative mentoring, done in collaborative groups, improved retention and success of women college students who were encouraged to enter the historically underrepresented fields of science and engineering. Based upon their findings, they concluded that universities need to provide an infrastructure that supports mentoring, in order for these types of programs to be successful.

Life Model theory, which asserts that people encounter stresses during life transitions, while experiencing hostile environments, and/or when interpersonal maladaptive processes exist (Gitterman & Germain, 2008; Gitterman & Shulman, 2005), applies to group mentoring. Mentees often emanate from oppressed groups and seek empowerment to negotiate and change systems (Breton, 2006; Freire, 1993). Mutual aid theory provides a conceptual framework (Gitterman & Shulman, 2005; Schwartz, 1986). The group worker mediates and lends a vision of hope; group members need and hold each other accountable; a contract is negotiated; resources are shared; dialectical and authentic communication transpires; the all in the same boat phenomena reassures, and, a strengths perspective is paramount.

Skills utilized in group mentoring reflect social work group practice (Toseland & Rivas, 2005). The group worker plans, recruits, explains the purpose, and initiates a contract with members (Kurland & Salmon, 1999). Listening is an important skill (Ephross, 2005). The worker comments about similar and different themes, and summarizes, reaching for input (Gitterman & Shulman, 2005). The worker encourages sharing of information. Commitment on the part of the group worker is critical to the success of the group.

Oppressed people want their mentors to respect their cultural values (Scisney-Matlock & Matlock, 2001). Mentees will be sensitive and distance themselves if mentors have biases or stereotypes about them. They may have difficulty adapting to a school or work situation related to their differences. A meta-analysis of 55 studies found that matching ethnicity or gender of the mentor did not influence academic success but that the quality of the relationship had bearing (Dubois et al., 2002).

A group of nine at-risk college students met for 2 years as a result of a formal mentoring program to increase graduation rates of first-generation university students. The mentor/author, Lee, recruited mentees from an entry level social work class. They were advised that the purpose was to help them succeed at the university. The group met every two weeks for an hour session before their evening classes. This was both a homogenous (all women and mostly social work majors) and a heterogeneous group (a variety of ethnic cultures, single and married students, parents and non-parents, and a person with physical disabilities, etc.). In addition to the regular meetings, the group planned social events such as backyard barbecues. Members brought family members to the events, promoting group cohesion and understanding of their families/culture.

In the middle phase of this group, sessions related to passing courses and applying for graduate schools. Also members discussed personal concerns. The mentor attended to participants and their participation; common themes were highlighted, and members lent support. The group coalesced. One of the mentees exclaimed: "No one in my classes is friendly toward me, but I finally feel I've made good friends with the social work students in here."

There was also a social action component to the group. Members presented the group's work at the Association for the Advancement of Social Work with Groups symposium. They wrote the proposal, created the presentation, practiced, and evaluated. They were empowered and verbalized this feeling by stating: "We could show that we were not just measly students." The students graduated in spite of incredible obstacles—care giving for family members, financial hardships and illness. Several are enrolled in graduate social work programs.

Group mentoring is a promising method of creating a productive and humane work force. Organizations should consider group instead of one-on-one mentoring in order to serve more people without sacrificing quality. Group mentoring has the advantage of mutual aid. For continued progress, mentoring in groups needs to be documented, researched, and evaluated.

References

Addams, J. (1910). *Twenty years at Hull House*. New York: Macmillan.

Addams, J. (1930). *The second twenty years at Hull House*. New York: Macmillan.

Breton, M. (2006). An empowerment perspective. In C. Garvin, L. Gutiérrez, & M. Galinsky (Eds.), *Handbook of social work with groups* (2nd ed., pp. 58–75). New York: Guilford Press.

Buell, C. (2004). Models of mentoring in communication. *Communication Education, 53*(1), 56–73.

Cole, D. (2007). Do interracial interactions matter? An examination of student–faculty contact and intellectual self-concept. *The Journal of Higher Education, 78*(3), 249–281.

Dewey, J. (1916). *Democracy and education*. New York: Macmillan.

Dubois, D. L., Holloway, B., Valentine, J. C., & Cooper, H. (2002). Effectiveness of mentoring programs for youth: A meta-analytic review. *American Journal of Community Psychology, 30*(2), 157–197.

Ephross, P. H. (2005). Social work with groups: Practice principles. In G. Grief, & P. Ephross (Eds.). *Group work with populations at risk* (2nd ed., pp. 1–12). New York: Oxford University Press.

Freire, P. (1993). *Pedagogy of the oppressed*. New York: Continuum. (Original work published 1970.)

Girves, J. E., Zepeda, Y., & Gwathmey, J. K. (2005). Mentoring in a post-affirmative action world. *Journal of Social Issues, 61*(3), 449–479.

Gitterman, A., & Germain, C. B. (2008). *The Life Model of social work practice: Advances in theory and practice* (3rd ed.). New York: Columbia University Press.

Gitterman, A., & Shulman, L. (Eds.). (2005). *Mutual aid groups, vulnerable and resilient populations, and the life cycle* (3rd ed.). New York: Columbia University Press.

Horace, C. (2004). One group's journey from camp to college. *Social Work with Groups, 27*(4), 31–50.

Kurland, R., & Salmon, R. (1999). *Teaching a methods course in social work with groups*. Alexandria, VA: Council on Social Work Education.

Sands, R. G., & Solomon, R. (2003). Developing educational groups in social work practice. *Social Work with Groups, 26*(2), 5–21.

Schwartz, W. (1986). The group work tradition and social work practice. In A. Gitterman, & L. Shulman (Eds.). *The legacy of William Schwartz: Group practice as shared interaction* (pp. 7–27). Binghamton, NY: Haworth Press.

Scisney-Matlock, M., & Matlock, J. (2001). Promoting understanding of diversity through mentoring undergraduate students. *New Directions for Teaching and Learning, 85*, 75–84.

Toseland, R., & Rivas, R. F. (2005). *An introduction to group work practice* (5th ed.). Boston: Allyn & Bacon.

Group Work and Technology

Online Support

Andrés Arias Astray and Ana Barrón López de Roda

Broadly defined, online support groups (OSGs) consist of a collection of people who share the same or similar circumstances or conditions joining together voluntarily *via computer-based technology* for the purpose of offering and receiving mutual support, sharing personal experiences, gathering information, pooling resources, and finding new ways of coping. In a more restrictive sense, and in order to distinguish them from online self-help groups, which are controlled by the members themselves, the term refers only to professionally run group strategies based on the protected effect of social support (Henry, 1997). Computer-based, cyber, electronic, email, Internet, network, technology-based, virtual, and Web-based are some of the other expressions used that are interchangeable with the term online to name this kind of group strategy in which members are physically separated and connected only by technology.

At present, thousands of self-help and OSGs exist on the Internet to deal with a large number of social care and health issues (Eysenbach, Powell, Englesakis, Rizo, & Stern, 2004; Schopler, Abell, & Galinsky, 1997; Winzelberg, 1997). Many traditional face to face (f2f) support groups have established OSGs (Alexander, Peterson, & Hollingshead, 2003; Braithwaite, Waldron, & Finn, 1999), and social workers have started to use them not only as facilitators, but also as benefactors, in order to improve their professional activity and coping skills (Meier, 1997).

OSGs require access to a computer connected to the Internet via modem. Four primary forms of OSGs have been described in the literature (Toseland & Rivas, 2005): chat rooms, bulletin boards, email, and mailing list servers. Chat rooms consist in virtual space, available during specific periods of time, where participants can communicate interactively with each other, sending and receiving messages in real time. In contrast, bulletin boards are online messages centres, open 24 hours a day, where at any time participants can leave messages and expect to read responses to messages that themselves or other individuals have left. Using email, participants can send and receive messages to particular individuals of their group. Finally, mailing list servers are programs that allow participants to send and receive messages to or from an entire list of subscribers as they occur or are scheduled. Consequently, depending on the networking format, OSGs can exist as synchronous groups (e.g., chat rooms), where members exchange messages in real time, or as asynchronous groups, where participants are not connected at the same time but can post messages to which other individuals can respond at any time (e.g., bulletin boards). Also, they can be text-based, when communication is limited to alphanumeric data, or Web-based, when the written messages can be enriched with audio and video data, and links to other Web sites (Meier, 2004).

Although similar in philosophy and intervention techniques, OSGs show evident advantages when compared with face-to-face groups (Braithwaite et al., 1999; Finn, 1995, 1999; Finn & Lavitt, 1994; Schopler et al., 1997; Weinberg, Schmale, Uken, & Wessell, 1995; White & Dorman, 2001; Winzelberg, 1997). First, they benefit from the absence of geographical, temporal, and size group restrictions. When communication is asynchronous, members potentially have access to support 24 hours a day, 7 days a week. Furthermore, some individuals might find it more convenient to participate in OSGs from their own home or office than in person: those who live a great distance from services, have demanding work hours, do not have convenient means of transportation, or suffer rare conditions, chronic illness or disabilities. Second, participants with interpersonal or communication difficulties may also find that sharing information in written form in a safer way to take part in a group. Third, since OSGs provide opportunities for large numbers of members to participate, they also increase variety and diversity of support. Fourth, anonymous participation, free from physical or social status cues, reduces salience of irrelevant personal differences, offers privacy, and potentially facilitates disclosure, especially in groups dealing with stigmatized or "taboo" issues. Fifth, when OSGs are open, non-members can benefit by learning about the participants' perspectives when they "lurk" (i.e., read messages but not participate) in an OSG without disturbing the group process. This can be the case with future group support leaders during their training. Finally, cost of services can be reduced when users already have the necessary computer equipment, because fewer resources are required to set up and moderate a group.

However, OSGs also feature some disadvantages (Finn & Lavitt, 1994; Meier, 2004; Winzelberg et al., 2003; Walstrom, 2000). These include, among others, that participants must have access and know how to use computers and the Internet, and that they should be able to communicate effectively in written form. Potential limitations also comprise the risk of increased isolation, misinformation, confidentiality violation, and destructive or hostile interactions among members.

Although research is nascent, OSGs have already been shown to contain therapeutic elements and some of the benefits observed in face-to-face groups (Barrera, Glasgow, McKay, Boles, & Feil, 2002; Finn, 1995; Weinberg, Uken, Schmale, & Adamek, 1995; Winzelberg et al., 2003). However, it is acknowledge that more systematic and controlled studies are needed in order to provide robust evidence of their potential therapeutic effects (Eysenbach et al., 2004).

References

Alexander, S. C., Peterson, J. L., & Hollingshead, A. B. (2003). Help is at your keyboard: Support groups on the Internet. In F. Lawrence (Ed.), *Group communication in context: Studies in bona fide groups* (pp. 309–334). Mahwah, NJ: Lawrence Erlbaum.

Barrera, M., Glasgow, R. E., McKay, H. G., Boles, S. M., & Feil, E. G. (2002). Do Internet-based support interventions change perceptions of social support? An experimental trial of approaches for supporting diabetes self-management. *American Journal of Community Psychology, 30*(5), 637–654.

Braithwaite, D. O., Waldron, V. R., & Finn, J. (1999) Communication of social support in computer-mediated groups for people with disabilities. *Heath Communication, 11*(2), 123–151.

Eysenbach, G., Powell, J., Englesakis, M., Rizo, C., & Stern, A. (2004). Health related virtual communities and electronic support groups: Systematic review of the effects of online peer to peer interactions. *British Medical Journal, 328*, 1166–1171.

Finn, J. (1995). Computer-based self-help groups: A new resource to supplement support groups. *Social Work with Groups. Special issue: Support groups: Current perspectives on theory and practice, 18*(1), 109–117.

Finn, J. (1999). An exploration of helping processes in an online self-help group focusing on issues of disability. *Health and Social Work, 24*(3), 220–231.

Finn, J., & Lavitt, M. (1994). Computer-based self-help groups for sexual abuse survivors. *Social Work with Groups, 17*(1/2), 21–46.

Henry, N. I. (1997). Getting acquainted with support and self-help groups on the Internet. *Health Care on the Internet, 1*(2), 27–32.

Kurtz, L. F. (2004). Support and self-help groups. In C. D. Garvin, L. M. Gutiérrez, & M. J. Galinsky (Eds.). *Handbook of social work with groups* (pp. 139–159). New York: Guildford Press.

Meier, A. (1997). Inventing new models of social support groups: A feasibility study of an online stress management support group for social workers. *Social Work with Groups, 20*(4), 35–53.

Meier, A. (2004). Technology mediated groups. In C. D. Garvin, L. M. Gutiérrez, & M. J. Galinsky (Eds.). *Handbook of social work with groups* (pp. 479–503). New York: Guildford Press.

Schopler, J. H., Abell, M. D., & Galinsky, M. J. (1997). *Social Work, 43*(3), 254–266.

Toseland, R. W., & Rivas, F. R. (2005). *An Introduction to group work practice* (5th ed.). Boston: Pearson Education.

Walstrom, M. K. (2000). "You know, who's the thinnest?": Combating surveillance and creating safety in coping with eating disorders online. *CyberPsychology & Behavior, 3*(5), 761–783.

Weinberg, N., Schmale, J. D., Uken, J., & Wessell, K. (1995). Computer-mediated support groups. *Social Work with Groups, 17*(4), 43–54.

Weinberg, N., Uken, J. S., Schmale, J., & Adamek, M. (1995). Therapeutic factors: Their presence in a computer-mediated support group. *Social Work with Groups, 18*(4), 57–69.

White, M., & Dorman, S. M. (2001). Receiving social support on line: Implications for health education. *Health Education Research, 16*(6), 693–707.

Winzelberg, A. J. (1997). The analysis of an electronic support group for individuals with eating disorders. *Computers in Human Behavior, 13*(3), 393–407.

Winzelberg, A. J., Apers, G. W., Roberts, H., Koopman, C., Adams, R. E., Ernst, H., Dev, P., & Taylor, C. B. (2003). Evaluation of an Internet support group for woman with primary breast cancer. *Cancer, 97*(5), 1164–1173.

Online Groups

Brian E. Perron and Thomas J. Powell

Online groups are a way of using the Internet to bring people together with a common purpose, including the provision of self-help, social support, and psychoeducation. Depending on their format, they may be referred to as electronic groups, listservs, forums, and mail groups. Online groups can be standalone support options for people, or they can be a supplement to face-to-face groups or professional services (Kurtz & White, 2007). Many Web sites allow anybody to join an existing group or start a new one. The proliferation of these groups is likely to continue. They are available 24/7 and can be a boon for people with mobility problems, rare disorders, or without access to face-to-face groups or professional services. Besides motivation, the only requirements to participating are regular Internet access, and basic computer and Internet navigation skills.

The patterns of communication within online groups are the same as those used in face-to-face self-help groups (Beder, 2005; Finn, 1999; Perron, 2002; Salem, Bogat, & Reid, 1997). Online groups produce similar positive effects as their face-to-face counterparts, as participants can capitalize on the experience of people coping successfully with a variety of problems (Eysenbach, Powell, Englesakis, Rizo, & Stern, 2004; Humphreys, 2004; Murray, Burns, See Tai, Lai, & Nazareth, 2005; Powell, Yeaton, Hill, & Silk, 2001). It should be noted that the vast range of health and behavioral problems addressed in online groups make it difficult to systematically compare the experience and outcomes of their participants. Systematic comparisons are further complicated by the wide variety of online group formats and participation. Thus, significant gaps in the knowledge regarding the effectiveness of online groups remain.

As previously described, online groups have many appeals and show promise for offering a wide range of support for a variety of issues. However, there are potential pitfalls with online groups that also need to be recognized. For example, they have a potential for malice that is different from that associated with face-to-face groups. Some professional organizations, such as the Depression and Bipolar Support Alliance (2007), have disbanded the use of online groups due to *trolls*—that is, persons posting intentionally controversial or malevolent messages. Legal liability is another serious issue of concern for organizations offering online groups.

From an individual standpoint, online groups may be a way for some people to resist participating in a more intensive face-to-face group. Since online group participants may be living in different communities, states, or countries, they may not have familiarity of local resources that might be available in face-to-face groups. Online groups may also be inaccessible to persons with certain disabilities, such as significant hand tremors, and those on the wrong side of the digital divide (Lieberman et al., 2005).

The challenges posed by online groups for social workers are substantial. In their own groups, social workers use concepts to intervene in the group to advance individual and group goals. With online groups they can help their clients understand what is going on but they cannot directly intervene. The consequences of this difference may be understood by reference to group cohesion, or the lack thereof, in online groups, which, typically, have members joining and dropping out on a regular basis. This impedes cohesion, and heightens the risk that a solid group identity stage will not be reached (Shulman, 2005). In such circumstances social workers must help their clients understand how online groups differ from face-to-face groups, and especially from those that are professionally led. Other concepts such as member roles can also be useful to social workers with clients in online groups. Such groups are different from those facilitated by social workers where it is possible to address and indeed inhibit the development of a variety of roles such as the provocateur, the scapegoat, or the monopolizer (Hepworth, Rooney, Rooney, Storm-Certifried, & Larsen, 2006). However, in an online group the social worker is limited to helping the client understand the phenomena and interpret it in a constructive non-demoralizing way. This is not entirely a disadvantage with the online group since the social worker does not have to be concerned about the possible tension between group and individual goals. In the online context the social worker can be solely oriented to helping the client attain his or her individual goals.

Given the proliferation and widespread use of online groups, social workers and other human service professionals should be aware of the potential positive and negative effects of online groups on their individual clients. From a practical standpoint, social workers might consider asking clients if they are currently participating in online groups, while recognizing that many might fear disapproval. If clients are online group participants, social workers could provide additional information on participating effectively and raising awareness of safety issues. Knowledge on these vast topic areas can be obtained from other resources, such as the *Self-Help Magazine*. Social workers might benefit from knowing the client's perspective on whether the online group enhances or detracts from the professional service. If clients have not had any exposure to self-help groups, they might be asked whether they think it might be useful to get the perspective of those who have had successful experience with similar issues.

The availability and accessibility of online groups continues to grow. With new software and hardware developments, it is impossible to know how they will be used and in what format. However, at present, the possibilities for integrating online groups with professional services seem endless. Social workers and research face a daunting task of trying to understand their effectiveness. It is a task that will become more pressing with a clientele that grows up in the information age.

References

Beder, J. (2005). Cybersolace: Technology built on emotion. *Social Work, 50*(4), 355–358.

Depression and Bipolar Support Alliance. (2007). *DBSA live chat changing format.* Retrieved September 2, 2007 from http://www.dbsalliance.org/site/PageServer?pagename=support_chat

Eysenbach, G., Powell, J., Englesakis, M., Rizo, C., & Stern, A. (2004). Health related virtual communities and electronic support groups: Systematic review of the effects of online peer to peer interactions. *British Medical Journal, 328*(7449), 1166–1170.

Finn, J. (1999). An exploration of helping processes in an online self-help group focusing on issues of disability. *Health and Social Work, 24*(3), 220–231.

Hepworth, D. H., Rooney, R. H., Rooney, G. D., Strom-Gottfried, K., & Larsen, J. H. (2006). Intervening in social work groups. *Direct social work practice: Theory and skills,* (7th ed., pp. 495–520). Belimont, CA: Thomson Brooks/Cole.

Humphreys, K. (2004). *Circles of recovery: Self-help organizations for addictions.* New York: Cambridge University Press.

Kurtz, E., & White, W. (2007). *Telephone- and internet-based recovery support services*. Chicago: Great Lakes Addiction Technology Transfer Center.

Lieberman, M. A., Winzelberg, A., Golant, M., Wakahiro, M., DiMinno, M., Aminoff, M., & Christine, C. (2005). Online support groups for Parkinson's patients: A pilot study of effectiveness. *Social Work in Health Care, 42*(2), 2–23.

Murray, E., Burns, J., See Tai, S., Lai, R., & Nazareth, I. (2005). Interactive health communication applications for people with chronic disease. *Cochrane Database of Systematic Reviews, 4*, 1–70.

Perron, B. (2002). Online support for caregivers of people with a mental illness. *Psychiatric Rehabilitation Journal, 26*(1), 70–77.

Powell, T. J., Yeaton, W., Hill, E. M., & Silk, K. R. (2001). Predictors of psychosocial outcomes for patients with mood disorders: The effects of self-help group participation. *Psychiatric Rehabilitation Journal, 25*(1), 3–11.

Salem, D. A., Bogat, G. A., & Reid, C. (1997). Mutual help goes on-line. *Journal of Community Psychology, 25*, 189–207.

Shulman, L. (2005). Group work method. In A. Gitterman, & L. Shulman (Eds.), *Mutual aid Groups, vulnerable populations, and the life cycle* (3rd ed., pp. 38–72). New York: Columbia University Press.

Telephone Groups

Ronald W. Toseland

Telephone groups are a relatively new modality for social group work practice. Advances in telephone technology during the 1980s and 1990s made it possible to have group meetings on the telephone with a number of participants. Teleconferencing or the conference call was first written about in a book by Kelleher and Cross (1990). Used widely in business and industry, through the pioneering efforts of some individuals during the 1990s, telephone groups have gradually begun to be used in the social services primarily to support chronically ill and disabled persons and their family caregivers. (Schopler, Abell, & Galinsky, 1998; Schopler, Galinsky, & Abell, 1997).

There are a number of advantages to the use of telephone groups as compared to face-to-face meetings. Telephone groups provide access to the homebound, those who cannnot leave the person for whom they are caring, those who lack transportation, live in rural areas, or who want to avoid the time it takes to get to a face-to-face meetings. Telephone groups are also especially attractive for those with rare chronic illnesses, where there may not be enough members to form a face-to-face support group within a reasonable distance of a meeting place. Another advantage of telephone groups is that they appeal to those who are shy, or uncomfortable in engaging in face-to-face meetings (Galinsky, Schopler, & Abell, 1997; Glueckauf & Loomis, 2003).

It has been reported that members of telephone groups experience greater group identification and have more social influence on one another than in face-to-face groups (Galinsky, Schopler, & Abell, 1997; McKenna & Green, 2002). Because there are no visual cues, members tend to focus on their common situations and problems without the distraction of non-verbal appearance and observable behavior (Toseland & Rivas, 2009). There is less influence of status hierarchies, because the main focus of members is on the issues which brought them to the group, rather than their personal appearance and other non-verbal cues, such as race or ethnicity. Because members' identities are not revealed to the extent they are in face-to-face groups, telephone groups can increase confidentiality for those with problems that may be perceived as stigmatizing.

There are a number of issues that the group worker needs to consider when leading telephone groups. Because of the lack of visual cues, the worker should be more active in several ways. First, it is important for members to state their first name before they speak until members get to know each others' voices. The leader often needs to model this behavior and remind members to state their names before they speak.

Second, the worker should take a more active role in the interaction processes that occur among members. Because there are no visual cues, two or more members may initiate conversation, or respond to each other, at the same time. Workers can help by clarifying who is speaking and by sorting out who will speak in what order. Because members sometimes forget to identify themselves when speaking, the worker can help by asking speakers to identify themselves, or by asking members if they know who is speaking. Also, there can be hesitation or a pause before responding, because members are not sure if someone else is planning to respond. The worker can help by inviting members to respond, especially those who may have brought up similar issues or expressed similar emotional reactions in earlier group sessions. Group go-rounds can also be used more frequently to make sure that everyone has a chance to participate.

Third, because members cannnot see each other, it is important for the worker to clarify members' reactions to other members' disclosures, and the impact of members' disclosures on each other. The lack of visual cues makes it especially important to help members communicate without misunderstandings. The worker may have to be more active in prompting members to clarify statements that may not be clear to all members, and seeking out members' reactions to what others have said.

There are two important limitations to the use of telephone groups that should be considered. One of the main limitations of the use of telephone technology is the cost of providing the service. The costs associated with a teleconference meeting vary by the provider used, and the location of the group members who are being served. In 2006, the cost of using a commercial provider to set up a meeting for eight participants living in a five county region within one state was over $100 for a one-hour session. There are two ways to reduce these costs. One way is to use a voice-over internet provider. Various voice-over internet protocol services are available and they vary in cost and quality but can bring the cost of a meeting down considerably. For example, in 2007, the provider Skype can link up to nine outside callers through a computer-initiated voice-over Internet protocol (VOIP) at very low cost. The call must be initiated by the group worker with a personal computer, using VOIP technology and a relatively low cost headset.

The group members receiving the call can receive it via computer or regular telephone equipment. Those that choose to receive the call via computer must have a properly configured computer, a headset and a free Skype membership. It is also possible to buy the telephone equipment needed to make conference calls and this may be an option for some social service agencies that are planning to use teleconferencing services frequently.

Another limitation of the use of telephone groups is obtaining reimbursement for services. Although some states reimburse for telephone services under their Medicaid program, it is not clear at this time how many states have opted to do so. There is a trend toward capitated services for some client populations. If telephone services can be associated with reduced costs because of reduced travel time by providers, telephone groups may be seen as a cost-effective alternative to individual casework or face-to-face groups. Research is needed on this emerging service to make the case that telephone groups should be reimbursable.

Although telephone groups have not, for the most part, been rigorously evaluated, recent reviews about the effectiveness of telephone groups are positive (Glueckauf & Ketterson, 2004; Toseland & Rivas, 2009; Toseland, Naccarato, & Wray, 2007). Most of the studies have been based on case reports or small non-randomized intervention studies. One rigorously controlled study comparing telephone groups for spouse and adult children caregivers found that they were more effective for adult children caregivers than for spouses (Smith & Toseland, 2006). Other recent rigorously controlled studies indicate that telephone groups plus care management was more effective than usual care for reducing depression among outpatients (Ludman, Simon, Tutty, & Von-Korff, 2007) and that they had some benefit for female caregivers of persons with dementia (Winter & Gitlin, 2007). Still, a review for this encyclopedia entry revealed that there are relatively few studies of telephone groups in the literature between 2000 and 2007. Therefore, more studies are needed of the effectiveness of this modality.

References

Galinsky, M., Schoplen, M., & Abell, M. (1997). Connecting group members through telephone and computer groups. *Health and Social Work, 22*(3), 181.

Glueckauf, R., & Ketterson, T. (2004). Telehealth interventions for individuals with chronic illness: Research review and implications for practice. *Professional Psychology: Research and Practice, 35*, 615–627.

Glueckauf, R., & Loomis, J. (2003). Alzheimer's caregiver support online: Lessons learned, initial findings and future directions. *NeuroRehabilitation, 18*, 135–146.

Kelleher, K., & Cross, T. (1990). *Teleconferencing: Linking people together electronically.* Norman, OK: University of Oklahoma Press.

Ludman, E., Simon, G., Tutty, S., & Von-Korff, M. (2007). A randomized trial of telephone psychotherapy and pharmacotherapy for depression. *Journal of Consulting and Clinical Psychology, 75*(2), 257–266.

McKenna, K., & Green, A. (2002). Virtual group dynamics. *Group Dynamics, 5*(1), 116–127.

Schopler, J., Abell, M., & Galinsky, M. (1998). Technology-based groups: A review and conceptual framework for practice. *Social Work, 43*(3), 254–267.

Schopler, J., Galinsky, M., & Abell, M. (1997). Creating community through telephone and computer groups: Theoretical and practice perspectives. *Social Work with Groups, 20*(4), 19–34.

Smith, T., & Toseland, R. (2006). The evaluation of a telephone caregiver support group intervention. *The Gerontologist, 46*(5), 620–630.

Toseland, R., Naccarato, T., & Wray, L. (2007). Telephone groups for older persons and family caregivers: Key implementation and process issues. *Clinical Gerontologist, 31*(1), 59–76.

Toseland, R., & Rivas, R. (2009). *An introduction to group work practice* (6th ed.). Needham Heights, MA: Allyn & Bacon.

Winter, L., & Gittlin, L. (2007). Evaluation of a telephone-based support group intervention for female caregivers of community-dwelling individuals with dementia. *American Journal of Alzheimer's Disease and Other Disorders, 21*(6), 391–397.

Index